Writing Margins

ᛓ *The Textual Construction of Gender*

in Heian and Kamakura Japan

Harvard East Asian Monographs, 201

Writing Margins

ೞ *The Textual Construction of Gender in Heian and Kamakura Japan*

Terry Kawashima

Published by the Harvard University Asia Center
and distributed by Harvard University Press
Cambridge (Massachusetts) and London, 2001

Printed in the United States of America

The Harvard University Asia Center publishes a monograph series and, in coordination with the Fair-
bank Center for East Asian Research, the Korea Institute, the Reischauer Institute of Japanese Studies,
and other faculties and institutes, administers research projects designed to further scholarly understanding of China, Japan, Vietnam, Korea, and other Asian countries. The Center also sponsors projects
addressing multidisciplinary and regional issues in Asia.

Library of Congress Cataloging-in-Publication Data

Kawashima, Terry.
    Writing margins : the textual construction of gender in Heian and Kamakura Japan /
Terry Kawashima.
        p. cm. -- (Harvard East Asian monographs ; 201)
    Includes bibliographical references and index.
    ISBN 0-674-00516-3 (cloth : alk. paper)
       1. Japanese literature--Heian period, 794–1185--History and criticism. 2. Japanese
literature--To 1600--History and criticism. 3. Marginality, Social, in literature. 4. Ono,
Komachi, 9th cent. 5. Murasaki Shikibu, b. 978? Genji Monogatari. 6. Hashihime. I.
Title. II. Series.

PL 726.2.K366 2001
895.6'090014--dc21   00-054119

Index by the author

    ⊙   Printed on acid-free paper

Last figure below indicates year of this printing
11 10 09 08 07 06 05 04 03 02 01

to my parents

Acknowledgments

My interest in the issue of "marginalized women" in premodern Japan can be attributed to a number of factors. One factor might be my family background. My father was born into a relatively unusual family circumstance; it was perhaps this positionality that led him to become interested in the study of texts by similarly "marginal" peoples during his college years. There was a copy of *Ryōjin hishō* in my house for as long as I can recall. My mother's side of the family, a more "ordinary" lineage of middle-class background, always stressed reading as the most worthwhile activity; they succeeded in piquing my interest in premodern Japanese literature by providing me with a children's anthology of the "classics" (which, interestingly, did not contain *Ryōjin hishō*). I spent my childhood in Nagoya, which, in a Tokyo-centric world, was (and still is) frequently considered a classic example of unsophisticated urban sprawl; this experience may also have been a factor in my interest in "the margin." Finally, my formative years in the United States as an "Asian female" gave me plenty of opportunities to reflect upon the complex issues of gender and ethnic/racial positionality. I therefore owe this book to a number of inspirational sources.

I express my deepest gratitude to my dissertation advisors, Edwin A. Cranston and H. Richard Okada, who patiently and painstakingly read my drafts and provided me with invaluable suggestions and input. I also thank Hino Tatsuo at Kyoto University, who kindly advised me during my stay there, and Nakamae Masashi of Kyoto Women's University, who generously shared his knowledge of Buddhist *setsuwa*. I am grateful to my former colleagues at the University of Minnesota, especially Sarah Pradt, who saw to it that my first year of teaching and manuscript revision was as painless as possible under the circumstances, and Ann Waltner, who has been a constant source of encouragement. David Branner, who was at Minnesota during the 1997–98 academic year, provided me with vital fonts (vowels with macrons). Friederike von Schwerin-High kindly helped me with translations of German-language scholarship pertaining to topics covered in this book. I am grateful for the support of my colleagues at Wesleyan University, particularly those in the Department of Asian Languages and Literatures and the East Asian Studies Program. I also wish to thank Tomiko Yoda, who organized a panel at the Association for Asian Studies 1998 annual meeting in which I presented a portion of my third chapter; the feedback from the panelists was very helpful. Brian Ruppert, whose interest in women and Buddhism overlaps with mine, has been a good friend with whom I have been able to exchange ideas about gender and religion. I thank Stephen Teiser for sharing his knowledge of Buddhist scriptures. Last but certainly not least, I am greatly indebted to my editor, John Ziemer, who has been a vital and generous source of information and advice since the beginning of the manuscript process; he greatly facilitated the successful completion of this project, and I remain very grateful.

I owe acknowledgments to several organizations that granted me the financial assistance necessary for the writing of this book: The Japan Foundation, which supplied much-needed funding for my research in Japan through its Doctoral Fellowship program, and the Office of the Vice President for Research and the Dean of the Graduate School of the University of Minnesota, which provided the Grant-in-Aid of Research, Artistry, and Scholarship, the Faculty Summer Research Fellowship, and the McKnight Summer Fellowship, all of which enabled me to complete this book.

I began this preface with my family, and I will end by mentioning them again here: many thanks to my mother, Sue Atsuko Kawashima, my father, Toshikuni Kawashima, my maternal grandmother, Mitsuko Nagahama, and my late maternal grandfather, Kishirō Nagahama, all of whom supported me unwaveringly throughout my scholarly career. I also express sincere thanks to all of the members of my family-in-law: Alison, Roger, Jessie, and Dan. Finally, nothing would have been possible without the constant encouragement and support of my spouse, Alex Des Forges.

T.K.

Contents

Part III: Hashihime

Reference Matter

Writing Margins
ଓ *The Textual Construction of Gender*
in Heian and Kamakura Japan

Introduction

What is a "margin"? How does one come to conceive of something or someone as "marginal"? In texts from the mid-Heian to the early Kamakura periods (tenth through thirteenth centuries) in Japan, certain figures appear, at first glance, to be "marginal," or removed from the "centers" of power. The question is: Why do we see these figures in this way? I suggest we adopt a two-part approach to this question. First, we must examine the details of the marginalizing discourse found in these texts. Who is portraying whom as "marginal"? For what reason? Is the discourse consistent? The investigation of the textual effects generated in this era is the first task at hand. Second, we must locate our present-day readings of these texts within the context of both Japanese and European-language scholarship. Twentieth-century scholars of mid-Heian to early Kamakura Japanese literature tend to assume that certain groups or figures represented in texts occupied a fixed position in society, at the "margin." Different scholars have used varying terms to refer to the position of these figures, including but not limited to "bottom layer" and "outcast." Although the terms may differ, the phenomena to which they refer are constant; these scholars have created "marginality" as an identifiable quality. "Marginality," in their understanding, points to the existence of certain groups or characteristics at the fringes of a social system. This placement is justified by those in power, referred to as the "center," through the labeling of these groups or characteristics as undesirable or unwanted. Is this understanding a helpful tool in studying "marginal" figures, or does it, in fact, inscribe certain modern-day biases and misconceptions about these figures into the texts studied?[1]

This book seeks to reconsider the definition of the margin and marginality, as well as the underlying assumptions about the center/margin power structure, through the examination of a selected group of texts from the late tenth to the early thirteenth centuries. Specifically, I look at cases in which gender plays a prominent role in the process of marginalization. Instead of conceiving of the entire category of women as (essentially) marginal, I focus on specific figures or groups of women who have usually been considered marginal in previous scholarship: women entertainers/prostitutes, an impoverished old woman, and a female bridge deity who turns into a demon. Scholars have generally approached these cases with the assumption that the marginality of certain female types or figures was to be taken for granted; they have then read the texts in an attempt to reinforce this preconception. In rethinking such biased readings, several questions come to mind. For what reasons is the marginality of particular women assumed, and are such reasons valid? In the past, the margin has usually been treated as a stagnant, pre-existing state of being that is occupied at different times by different groups. But does the margin consist of a series of slots to be filled? Who or what occupies the center? Is it possible to hear the voices of those who supposedly occupy the margin, and is the margin always a passive victim of oppression?

In the chapters to follow, I address these questions in trying first to formulate new readings of specific texts in order to de-essentialize the marginality of the female figures and, second, to propose new theories about the margin, marginality, and marginalization that are inspired by but proceed beyond past conceptualizations. In re-examining these supposedly marginal figures, I explore the ways in which certain aspects attributed to the state of being a woman came to be constructed as marginal in this period. In discussing this production of marginality, I focus on *how* that marginal state itself is constructed; there is a need to examine specific cases in which marginalization takes place in order to problematize the notion that the marginal condition is universal, monolithic, and uniform throughout time.

---

1. I have placed quotation marks around the words "margin," "marginal," and "center" in this opening paragraph to highlight my understanding of "marginality" as an ascribed status, not an "objective reality." Although I forgo the use of quotation marks around these words in the remainder of this book (except for instances of extra emphasis), the contingency of these terms should be assumed throughout.

What is achieved by focusing on marginality? There are a number of possible answers. First, I define the margin not as a synonym for "something insignificant" but as an unstable and negotiable result of textual effects generated by authors and compilers who display desires to promote certain ideas and practices at the expense of the targets of marginalization. In other words, studying the phenomenon of marginalization is not an investigation of an obscure and independent unit of society called the margin but an exploration of the very workings of the relationship between textual representation and claims to power. Second, a discussion of female figures and types who have been previously considered marginal reveals the stereotypes and assumptions of twentieth-century scholars; this revelation shows the extent to which any academic scholarship, including this present study, must be understood in its context. Furthermore, a fair number of the texts that I have selected have not been studied extensively, especially in non-Japanese-language scholarship. There is a need to transform the marginal status of these texts in certain academic circles; to dismiss the study of these texts as peripheral would be to obey the currently established canon blindly.

I begin by outlining some theories of the margin to illustrate recent concerns and debates over this concept and by attempting to forge a paradigm that, in a dialectic manner, pushes these theories further.

THE MARGIN, MARGINALITY, MARGINALIZATION:
THEORIES AND RECONSIDERATIONS

The general question of the relationship between the center and the margin has been discussed at some length already, especially by theorists of literature, anthropology, the colonial/postcolonial subject, and gender. Many scholars see the works of Jacques Derrida as the beginning of a new understanding of the margin. In the essays collected in *Of Grammatology* and *Margins of Philosophy*, Derrida concentrates, as a strategy of reading, on aspects previously considered marginal to various texts. This approach has been interpreted as a "double grafting" in which "on one hand, the marginal graft works . . . to reverse a hierarchy, to show that what had previously been thought marginal is in fact central. But on the other hand, that reversal . . . does not lead simply to the identification of a new center, but to a subversion of the distinctions between essential and inessential."[2] The deconstruction of

---

2. Culler, *On Deconstruction*, p. 140; see also pp. 215–16.

the binary opposition is crucial to the de-essentializing of the center and margin in that it shows they are products of cultural negotiations; however, the process through which such negotiations are produced has not been adequately discussed. In other words, the problematic aspects of the end results of marginalization have been addressed, yet there is still a need to examine the act itself in order to grasp how and why specific instances of marginalization occur.

Scholars with postcolonial concerns begin with the deconstructive premise and continue to grapple with the issue of center and margin. Perhaps the most prominent is Gayatri Chakravorty Spivak, who uses the concept of the margin in a number of strategic ways. It is, for one, a site from which one can reveal the workings of power in a postcolonial world; she asserts that the term "marginality" is a catachresis which shows that "cultural commitment" to the term operates through "negotiable agendas"[3]—that is, we need to note who is labeling whom the margin. Spivak also wrestles with the question of the identity of the margin and proposes that it is a shifting one generated by the marginalizing agency. Moreover, the naming of the margin by the center and the attention the center pays to the margin frequently mask a "repression" and can result in tokenism.[4] She warns, for example, that the center often makes claims regarding the authenticity of the margin's inhabitants: "When a cultural identity is thrust upon one because the center wants an identifiable margin, claims for marginality assure validation from the center."[5] Spivak presses the issue further by asking, in the context of colonial production, "Can the subaltern speak?" She answers in the negative and concludes: "What I find useful is the sustained and developing work on the *mechanics* of the constitution of the Other; we can use it to much greater analytic and interventionist advantage than invocation of the *authenticity* of the Other."[6] Spivak presents crucial insights into the understanding of marginality: the identities of the margin and the incorporation (whether through valorization or ostracization) of the marginalized into the discourse of the center are constructions of the latter, and it is our continual task to try to expose these constructions.

---

3. Spivak, *Outside in the Teaching Machine*, p. 65.
4. Spivak, *In Other Worlds*, p. 107.
5. Spivak, *Outside in the Teaching Machine*, p. 55.
6. Spivak, "Can the Subaltern Speak?" p. 294.

Spivak asserts elsewhere, however, that the "marginal in the narrow sense is the victims of the best-known history of centralization: the emergence of the straight white christian man of property as the ethical universal," and "when in search of absolute justifications, remember that the margin as such is wholly other."[7] Although these statements can be regarded as motivated pronouncements implemented in order to critique the oppressive mechanisms of, for instance, colonizing powers, there remains a sense that the characteristics of the categories of people who are placed in the margin are knowable and constant—this sense, again, generated strategically so that Spivak can illustrate the disparities of power in the colonial and postcolonial worlds.[8] I expand on this observation below; for now, I point out only that within the useful paradigm of the shifting identity of the margin, Spivak permits the emergence, albeit temporarily and consciously for particular purposes, of a picture of the margin as a pre-existing space occupied by steady and readily recognizable members (such as "the colonized"). This representation of the margin enables a strong and effective critique of nineteenth- and twentieth-century colonialism/neocolonialism; its "application" to texts from mid-Heian to early Kamakura Japan, however, gives rise to several problematic points, since in the latter case, the marginality of certain groups or figures itself remains highly questionable.

Other critics who deal with questions of postcoloniality include Homi Bhabha, who has explored the possibilities of minority discourse. In one of his works, he focuses on internal margins, such as the place of migrants within a discourse of modernity and national identity. He, like other postcolonial critics, opposes the pluralistic picture of harmonious diversity and remains optimistic about the margin as a potential site for disrupting and displacing totalizing narratives, in this case narratives of nationhood:

The boundary that secures the cohesive limits of the Western nation may imperceptibly turn into a contentious internal liminality providing a place from which to speak both of, and as, the minority, the exilic, the marginal and the emergent.

and,

[Minority discourse] contests genealogies of "origin" that lead to claims for cultural supremacy and historical priority. Minority discourse acknowledges the status of

---

7. Spivak, "Theory in the Margin," pp. 157–59.

8. Spivak (ibid., p. 159) notes that the "marginal" in the *general* sense is "no more and no less than a formula for doing things."

national culture—and the people—as contentious, performative space of perplexity of the living in the midst of the pedagogical representations of the fullness of life.[9]

In this way, he problematizes the idea of the monolithic national culture; again, however, in his enthusiasm for the possibilities of intervention that he sees as inherent in "minority discourse," the identities of the "minority" and the "margin" remain curiously opaque and prefigured. On the other hand, Bhabha does focus on temporality and performative time as crucial features of cultural narrative in showing that the construction of nationhood is always-in-progress and that not all participants of a nation function or articulate themselves in the same temporality as the majority. The idea that the dominant worldview of a culture is necessarily repeatedly and perpetually generated in order to sustain itself suggests the extent to which exertions of power are dynamic actions, not static givens.

Another example is Diana Fuss, who investigates the intersection of psychoanalysis and studies of colonialism to show how each can assist the other in revealing the political significance of a process called "identification," the "internalization of the other," which is "itself an imperial process, a form of violent appropriation in which the Other is deposed and assimilated into the lordly domain of Self."[10] Fuss, like Bhabha and Spivak, deals keenly and sensitively with the different configurations of images of and interactions between colonizer and the colonized, and yet, as I discuss below, such binary distinctions are ultimately problematic when critics neglect their own role in the construction of the margin.

A different configuration of the center/margin is offered by Jonathan Crewe, who likewise begins with the assumption that deconstruction has already collapsed the center-margin binary. He proposes an alternative that he calls "the logic of the middle ground," a place "between" described in roundabout fashion as a "buffer zone," "negotiating table," "realm of mediation" (among others), in which "the self is always in the process of performative renegotiation."[11] Crewe thus attempts to respatialize the binary by reconceptualizing the center as the middle ground in which an unstable, nonintegral subject constantly negotiates its positionality. This understanding offers one possible route out of the center-margin dichotomy and refocuses

---

9. Bhabha, *The Location of Culture*, pp. 149, 157.

10. Fuss, *Identification Papers*, pp. 4, 145.

11. Crewe, "Defining Marginality?" pp. 126–28.

our attention on the center, which is no longer a stable or monolithic collective. However, the "middle ground," conceived spatially, is a simplistic insertion of a third element into the binary, and the new relationship between the three poles remains unclear. Is there only a middle ground from which centrality or marginality is suggested, or do subjects shift in and out of the three demarcated spaces? If the latter, then how are such movements informed, governed, motivated?

Another view of the question of center and margin can be found in the field of anthropology. Yamaguchi Masao, for example, has approached the relationship between the margin and the center from a perspective informed by structuralism. In his many writings, he refers to theories of the margin proposed by Edward Shils, Victor Turner, and Michel de Certeau and asserts that the margin is a polysemic, liminal space that is produced by a center by necessity, since without identifying certain elements in society as the excluded other, the identity of the community (= center) cannot be formulated. In other words, not being the margin is the essential step in the creation of the center's identity; the exclusion of particular concepts or characteristics is not an incidental or accidental social phenomenon but the very foundation of a society as such. In addition, the excluded are often things that the remaining center then fears the most, such as menstrual blood (= women); this fear reveals that the excluded elements are believed to hold a certain amount of power.[12]

In many ways, this paradigm is useful in considering the relationships of power that exist in the act of marginalization. Yamaguchi illustrates the extent to which marginalized groups are made marginal for socially constructed reasons; his theories empower the excluded by revealing that the inhabitants of the margin are not ostracized because they are inherently undesirable, immoral, or otherwise base. This perspective liberates groups that have suffered from a discourse which naturalizes their marginality; his assertions therefore have the potential to play a significant role on the political front (such as issues concerning the *buraku* community, for example). On the other hand, Yamaguchi's theory suggests that the only agent with the ability to act is the center, no matter what the circumstances; marginalization is a one-way street in which victims are formed according to the center's needs.

---

12. See four works by Yamaguchi Masao: *Bunka to ryōgisei; Chi no enkinhō; Bunka jinruigaku no shikaku;* and *Tennōsei no bunka jinruigaku.* Yamaguchi's theories about the "powers of the weak" are strongly influenced by Victor Turner's works.

Although these victims occupy a liminal space in which they are permitted to play important and powerful roles at given moments, such as during certain rituals, they are forced to remain in the marginal, liminal space in an unchanging, timeless state of (structuralist) limbo. The center as agency also remains too monolithic; the subtle possibilities raised by the question "Who is performing the marginalization?" are erased, as the picture of the unstoppable and united marginalizing machine called the center emerges.

More recently, Anna Lowenhaupt Tsing has offered further perspectives on the issue of marginality in the field of anthropology.

Margins here are not a geographical, descriptive location. Nor do I refer to margins as the sites of deviance from social norms. Instead, I use the term to indicate an analytic placement that makes evident both the constraining, oppressive quality of cultural exclusion and the creative potential of rearticulating, enlivening, and rearranging the very social categories that peripheralize a group's existence. Margins, in this use, are sites from which we see the instability of social categories. . . . My interest is in the zones of unpredictability at the edges of discursive stability, where contradictory discourses overlap, or where discrepant kinds of meaning-making converge; these are what I call *margins*.[13]

Imagining from the point of view of the margin, therefore, permits insight into the workings of the center, and historical specificity is key in understanding particular marginal configurations. In her works, Tsing is interested primarily in how a particular marginalized group "engage[s] [its] marginality by protesting, reinterpreting, and embellishing [its] exclusion," but she is too confident that "an out-of-the-way place is, by definition, a place where the instability of political meaning is easy to see. The authority of national policies is displaced through distance and the necessity of reenactment at the margins."[14] Her assertion that we should approach the margin as a constructed identity, however, is a useful starting point in that it de-essentializes the category and allows a group to counter its marginality through a dialogue with the marginalizing discourse; the latter move is an alternative to the more monolithic, stagnant view of the margin offered by Yamaguchi.

Many of the scholars cited above are deeply concerned with the issue of gender in relation to the question of marginality. Indeed, there is a lively

---

13. Tsing, "From the Margins," p. 279.
14. Tsing, *In the Realm of the Diamond Queen*, pp. 5, 27.

debate over questions about identity, power, and marginality as they intersect with the concept of gender. One tendency has been to equate the margin with woman in an attempt to bring attention to woman's disempowerment and marginalization; this universalization of the category "woman" has been re-examined in recent years, for example, in Toril Moi's critiques of Julia Kristeva's theories. Kristeva has been interested in marginality as a subversive position both linguistically and socially, and Moi points out that although the equation of femininity with marginality with subversion permits an anti-essentialist view of the "feminine," the equation erases differences within the margin, such as women and working class.[15] Similarly, Tsing argues that psychoanalytic feminist theory has "formulated one globally and historically homogeneous kind of 'woman' . . . female marginalization is parallel in its form to the marginalization of the colonized, the nonwhite, the poor. This is a formulation in which the intersection of gender with class, race, or national status remains invisible."[16]

Judith Butler has directed our attention to the constructedness of "sex" as well as "gender" by showing that the seemingly prediscursive quality of sex is, in fact, an effect produced by gender; she argues that

the institution of a compulsory and naturalized heterosexuality requires and regulates gender as a binary relation in which the masculine term is differentiated from a feminine term. . . . Gender proves to be performative—that is, constituting the identity it is purported to be. In this sense, gender is always a doing, though not a doing by a subject who might be said to preexist the deed. . . . There is no gender identity behind the expressions of gender; that identity is performatively constituted by the very 'expressions' that are said to be its results.[17]

Butler's insistence on the performative nature of gender can help us greatly in thinking about the margin; just as the female/male gender binary is always in the process of constructing itself, and there is no such thing as a predis-

---

15. See the chapter "Marginality and Subversion: Julia Kristeva" in Moi, Sexual/Textual Politics.

16. Tsing, In the Realm of the Diamond Queen, pp. 17–18. Tsing also notes that although some feminists have proposed that female marginality must be studied in relation to the specific conditions of women's lives (such as being a "minority," etc.), Trinh Min-ha, among others, has pointed out that attention to "cultural difference" can potentially slip into exploitative and discriminatory discourse (see the chapter "Difference: A Special Third World Women Issue" in Trinh, Woman, Native, Other).

17. Butler, Gender Trouble, pp. 22–23, 25.

cursive gender identity, the center/margin binary can also be conceived as a performative construction of identity in which there are no pre-existing categories—the categories are constantly produced and re-produced through the expressions of marginalization. This paradigm reveals, again, the extent to which identities are always constructed products. Butler's assertion that notions of gender "support masculine hegemony and heterosexist power" leaves questions, however, about the homogeneity of this dominant power and the possibilities for displacement within the very discourses that seem to support such power.

CB

Several problematic points remain unresolved in theoretical discourses on the margin. One issue is the naming of the marginal position: in talking about the margin, theorists are frequently confident and in agreement that they are able to identify characteristics that define certain groups as marginal. The colonized, for example, appear to be always *a priori* marginal, as do minorities, migrants, and the poor; even though these categories themselves are recognized as discursive constructions, their status as the marginal is presumed to be self-apparent. The colonization of a vast part of the world in the past few centuries, the suppression of minority interests, and the ostracization of the poor in a large number of countries are undeniable; however, in the case of Heian and Kamakura Japan, the limited number of surviving documents as well as the conflicting opinions expressed in them suggest that, under some circumstances, claims that a group possessed prefigured, essential marginality should be approached with suspicion. In the case studies in the chapters to follow, I hope to contribute to the thinning of the opacity of the term "the margin" in this way. In addition, the assertion that the colonized peoples are by definition marginal must be differentiated from the views held by some scholars of Japanese literature who unquestioningly assume that certain categories of people in tenth- to thirteenth-century Japan were marginal. The former is often an intentional use of marginality as a concept so that contemporary oppressive structures can be delineated and exposed; the latter, as I hope to show, is a misreading of earlier texts that reproduces oppressive structures and extends their reach.

A second problem is the remaining tendency to insist on some variation of the center-margin binary, even though the constructedness of each position has been raised as an issue. As in the case above, the retention of this system can be read as a strategic device that allows certain postcolonial critics to critique particular hegemonic discourses by calling attention to the centrality of such discourses and the urgency of paying attention to the margins. In the absence of that particular postcolonial goal, however—when, in fact, the hegemonic quality of the marginalizing discourse of the center itself is in question—the primacy of the binary configuration poses a problem.

Third, some of the critics cited above are concerned primarily with the subject position of the marginal; in other words, they focus on how the margin can speak back to the center. In the case of the texts examined in the following chapters, except for the very mediated example of the lyrics section of *Ryōjin hishō* (Secret handbook of dust on the beams; mid- to late twelfth century), the marginalized are not permitted to speak back. In other words, the overwhelming majority of these texts are representations *of* marginalized figures, not representations *by* these groups. Given this situation, then, the answer to Spivak's question "Can the subaltern speak?" is quite clear; not only can the subaltern not speak even when their fragmented voices exist, as in the case of the colonial experience, but the marginalized of late tenth- to early thirteenth-century Japan truly cannot speak, since their silence is now forever guaranteed by the oblivion created by the accumulation of "history" on the side of the dominant (even though the identity of the dominant is not at all constant through time).[18] Unfortunate though this may be, what we are left with are textual attempts to inscribe certain targets as marginal; the focus on the *process* of marginalization, instead of the reactions and interactions of the marginalized, will prove most useful in examining the texts at hand. The focus on the possessors of speech capable of marginalization may at first seem like a return to an analysis that portrays the discourse of the powerful as incontestable.[19] What I am suggesting here, however, is not that the silencing of the margin

---

18. By this statement, I mean that the myth that the "voices of the marginalized" can be heard (transparently) in the texts must be re-examined, since such "voices" are always mediated through the process of compilation and editing, which is most often performed by the elite. It is important, of course, to consider to what extent any "voice" can be heard "through" any text, after decades of critical problematization of the integral subject/author. For the purposes of this discussion, I maintain that those who try to situate themselves at the "center" are more positionally capable of impregnating texts with their motivations, regardless of whether the resulting textual effects produced by this act are consistent with such motivations.

19. Bhabha's assertion, mentioned earlier in this chapter, that we need to examine the ways in which the "powerful" (e.g., the so-called first-world nations) already contain internal disruptions, is one example of the ways in which the powerful is *not* incontestable.

forbids any resistance against the marginalizing logic or slippage in it, but that texts display a range of representational possibilities of the same figures for different reasons and that marginalizing texts themselves often already contain contradictory and conflicting discourses that throw into question the very centrality of their position in the first place.

What vision of the center-margin configuration, then, might help us move away from a seemingly uncrackable binary opposition that forever reproduces the relationship through its very invocation? I begin with the perspective offered by past theorists that the margin is a construction and develop this claim further by shifting the focus to the ways in which this construction is produced. Perhaps it is more useful to think that the static categories "center" and "margin" do not exist as such. In other words, these two opposed, abstract, and metaphorical spaces are not themselves the most significant components in marginality. Only the process, marginalization, exists; this process acts on specific targets at particular textual moments and thereby creates a temporary position of superiority for the speaker/marginalizer in a manner reminiscent of the structuralist-inspired explanation offered by Yamaguchi but in a much more limited arena. Marginalization is thus a *specific* act; no textual instance of marginalization proves the existence of a timeless or universal center and margin. The binary categories are the *effects* produced by the process and are useful only in delineating the unstable relative positions that are discursively placed by the texts for particular reasons. In this paradigm, then, there is no single center surrounded by a single margin; instead, different and fleeting instances of marginalizer/marginalized relationships appear and reappear in a dynamic fashion.

Each single moment of marginalization, textual or otherwise, has an effect only when the representation is charged with sufficient social energy—that is, circulated and reproduced (orally or in writing) in a social context. Marginalization can be said to produce temporary and motivated representations of the "more central" and the "more marginal," and when enough representations of one or the other are amassed, they can have an effect in arenas beyond the particular instances of marginalization. This understanding of the production of the marginal resembles Butler's view of gender when she claims that "gender is the repeated stylization of the body, a set of repeated acts within a highly rigid regulatory frame that congeal over time to produce the appearance of substance, of a natural sort of being,"[20] but in the

20. Butler, *Gender Trouble*, p. 33.

cases of marginalization in mid-Heian to early Kamakura Japan, the "regulatory frame" is not as rigid as that which she proposes.

Furthermore, if we regard the speaker/marginalizer as attaining a more central position through marginalization (as opposed to a speaker who already occupies a position at the center before making the marginalizing textual utterance), the idea that a center acts on a margin becomes more nuanced. Rather than talking about the appropriation of the margin, we might find it more useful, under certain circumstances, to regard the act of appropriation as a part of the process of marginalization, since the margin does not exist outside the process. My focus on marginalization as an act as opposed to the margin as an object may be analogous to Catherine Bell's views on "ritualization." She questions the category of "ritual" as theoretical construct and focuses on the process of "ritualization" as a "strategic way of acting" in a social context, as opposed to the fetishized object called "ritual."[21] I emphasize the importance of concentrating on the act of marginalization because the examples that I have chosen for this book necessitate a rethinking of the "center/margin" binary; any assertion that the figures examined in the following chapters are essentially marginal is tied to the question of gender. In these instances, gender is not an incidental issue but a crucial factor in the process of marginalization that I will outline; ideas about and representations of specific kinds of women are constructed as marginal, and this act is performed by the very ascription of characteristics associated with women as marginalizing. To claim that the feminine margin already exists prior to the texts is to buy into the arguments of the texts blindly. Marginalization is a strategic and dynamic act that benefits from the obstruction of its motivated and constructed origins; in other words, since the marginalizer attempts to portray the target group or individual figure as *inherently* marginal, the constructedness of the resulting marginality is difficult to assess at first glance. However, the violence of the marginalization of certain female figures as well as the erasure of these women's "voices"[22] in the canon of Japanese literature

---

21. See Bell, *Ritual Theory, Ritual Practice*, particularly the Introduction.

22. Here, I refer not to the possibility of transparent readings of "women's voices" from this period but to the fact that a less-mediated text by the female figures whom I study in this book does not exist (despite the presence of canonical texts written by women in the Heian period); e.g., *Ryōjin hishō* was compiled by a male retired emperor and is not a collection of songs compiled by the women performers themselves, and *Kokinshū* includes a large number of poems attributed to women but was compiled by a number of aristocratic men.

from this period has already been performed; we must not add to this violence by allying ourselves unthinkingly with the marginalizing discourse.

But the possibilities for counter-marginalizing utterances continue to exist within the process of marginalization itself. Since each marginalizing textual moment is performative in that the center and margin are temporarily generated by a speaker whose positionality is not fixed, marginalization does not guarantee that a stable center consistently or successfully victimizes the margin. Such textual moments are governed by a number of different—and sometimes conflicting—interests and result in effects that can be contradictory; for example, when the Buddhist distaste for death and impurity contributes to the marginalization of dead women's representations and yet is implicated in the simultaneous appearance of quasi-necrophiliac desires. Approaching marginalization as a dynamic process suggests that the disparate positions of power created by the specific instances of marginalization are not at all monolithic or stable over time.

Finally, in using the term "motivated," I do not intend to invoke the figure of the Author/Self who exists prior to and outside a text and whose "intentions" represent the "true" reading of a text; rather, my aim is to turn our attention to close textual and intertextual readings that suggest why marginalizing discourses occur in specific passages. Such readings range from an analysis of explicit declarative statements by an author about why a tale collection was compiled to considerations of more subtle textual effects. For example, I understand "attitudes" as something produced through the reading process, as opposed to something that belongs inherently to an author. Being attentive to such "effects," admittedly, can be a minefield, since such an approach problematizes scholarly authority and points to its contingency; however, the recognition that marginalizing processes are motivated is crucial if we were to attempt to unravel the center-margin dichotomy.

The most urgent tasks in studying marginalization are to recognize (1) that different historical moments have varying configurations of conditions that produce and are produced by this process, (2) that marginalization involves struggles and negotiations in which different people or groups of people marginalize certain groups or characteristics for various reasons, (3) that it does not generate omnipresent effects in that not all groups in a society may recognize a particular marginalizing process, and (4) that it can create paradoxical results of temporary empowerment. The fluidity of the marginalizing processes enables conflicting claims concerning a particular group to coexist synchronically and diachronically. Only by examining these claims and their contexts can one begin to explore the whole configuration of marginalization in a specific historical period.

THE TIMES OF THE TEXTS:
SOME BROAD TRENDS

Most of the texts that I have chosen in order to explore the process of marginalization were produced between the mid-Heian and early Kamakura periods—roughly the late tenth to the early thirteenth centuries. Scholars have repeatedly characterized this era as turbulent: it encompasses the height of aristocratic power represented by the success of a particular branch of the Fujiwara family, the waning of this power and the increase in the political strength of retired emperors, and the subsequent rise of the warrior class as the ruling elite. The transition is marked by a series of civil disturbances in the twelfth century, culminating in the famous Genpei wars, which began in 1180 and whose repercussions were not settled until 1189. Since this book is concerned primarily with issues pertaining to certain female figures, I focus here on the views of scholars who have dealt specifically with women's history.

The characterization of this era as turbulent is at least partially endorsed by historians of women, who tend to regard the period as one in which women, particularly upper-class women, became less visible in the "public" sphere and suffered from increasingly oppressive conditions because of the consolidation of male-privileging ideology, which appeared as a consequence of the establishment of the family system (ie) headed by a male. Evidence such as the decrease in instances of direct and equal inheritance by women after the eleventh century, the change from uxorilocal to virilocal marriage, the simultaneous emphasis on the supposed impurity of women's bodies and biological functions and the apparent focus on motherhood as a supporting mechanism for the propagation of family lineages, and the exclusion of women from sacred spaces supports this view.[23] Needless to say, this overall scheme remains a contestable generalization; it does not hold consistently across the various social classes, examples of powerful women like

---

23. For discussions of these examples, see Minegishi, *Chūsei wo kangaeru*; Joseishi sōgō kenkyūkai, *Nihon josei seikatsushi*; idem, *Nihon josei shi*, 1 and 2; and Tabata, *Nihon chūsei no josei*. For more general discussions, see Sōgō joseishi kenkyūkai, *Nihon josei no rekishi: sei, ai, kazoku*; and idem, *Nihon josei no rekishi: bunka to shisō*.

Bifukumon'in,[24] Hōjō Masako,[25] and Tomoe[26] that counter the discourse of the declining position of women in society do exist (although the significance of their constructed images of power can certainly be debated), there are conflicting interpretations of the details of women's inheritance and property rights,[27] and transgressions of regulations and ideals remained possible.

Although a thorough re-examination of this view is beyond the scope of this book, I wish to note two points in particular. First, for the most part the various texts that I examine in detail here reveal an overall intensification of attempts to disempower certain aspects of constructed femininity as time progressed. For example, the figure of the renowned *waka* poet Ono no Komachi (active mid-ninth century) becomes the target of increasing marginalization, and the demonic version of Hashihime, a female bridge deity, is later pacified. Second, it is important to keep in mind that this broad trend remains a generalization. As I will show, the marginalizing process is not simply a uniform and incontestable force acting on the female figures but is often a conflicted act that is not necessarily universally recognized; at any one moment, different textual claims can assert varying degrees of marginalization and even empowerment. The examples that I study add further nuances to the accepted paradigm, which holds that women in general suffered increasing oppression. Each of the chapters to follow discusses in more detail the "historical" circumstances specific to an individual case.

---

24. Bifukumon'in (1117–60) was the consort of Emperor Toba and mother of Emperor Konoe, said to be one of the key players in the Hogen disturbance (1156), and a crucial supporter of Taira no Kiyomori. Other examples of influential women in the imperial household include Taikenmon'in (1101–45), another consort of Emperor Toba and mother of emperors Sutoku (who may actually have been the son of Toba's father, Emperor Shirakawa) and Goshirakawa; and Goshirakawa's consort Tango no Tsubone (d. 1216), a backer of Emperor Gotoba and a manipulator of court politics.

25. Hōjō Masako (1157–1225) was the wife of the shogun Minamoto no Yoritomo. After Yoritomo's death in 1199, she took the tonsure and became known unofficially as *ama shōgun* ("the nun shogun"); she had great influence over shogunal successions and politics in general.

26. Tomoe (n.d.) was the concubine of Minamoto no Yoshinaka (a.k.a. Kiso Yoshinaka, 1154–84) and was said to have been a courageous warrior whose martial skills surpassed those of men.

27. For a detailed discussion of women's inheritance and property in the late Heian to Kamakura periods, see Nomura Ikuyo, "Ōken no naka no josei," as well as other chapters in Minegishi, *Chūsei wo kangaeru*; and Gomi Fumihiko, "Josei shoryō to ie," in Joseishi sōgō kenkyūkai, *Nihon josei shi 2*.

I have also chosen to focus on this period because the scholars who have examined the status of marginalized women, especially recent scholars who question women's unchanging marginality, have devoted much of their attention to the Medieval period (roughly very late twelfth century to the end of the sixteenth century). Attention to pre-Medieval conditions has been relatively sparse. This book aims to investigate further what came before the Medieval period, and how processes of marginalization that began in the Heian period were later continued and/or transformed. This study does not delve into the marginalization of the figures that I have chosen in the rest of the Medieval period and beyond, but, suffice it to say, changes in the representation of these figures continued after the early Kamakura period.

Buddhist texts, ideological formations, and practices appear repeatedly in my analysis of textual production throughout this book. Quite often, specific marginalizing views of women and their characteristics are rooted in one or another Buddhist perspective or agenda. Recent feminist critiques of "Buddhism" in the period under investigation stress the increasingly male-privileging, female-disempowering aspects of the various schools of thought during this time, especially those that focus on the concept of *jōdo*, the Pure Land,[28] and the centrality of the Lotus Sutra within the Tendai school of thought, important because of the text's famous "Devadatta" chapter, which includes the concept of the Five Obstructions.[29] For example, both Ōgoshi Aiko and Minamoto Junko argue that gender is a central question in any discussion of Buddhism; more specifically, they point out such phallocentric maneuvers as the naturalization of the sinfulness of sexuality (and therefore of women who induce sexual desire in men); the marginalizing discourse of the "dragon girl," which permits women's attainment of Buddhahood only through women's recognition of their own obstructed and inferior positionality within the Buddhist worldview; and the rhetoric of *kū*, or emptiness, which appears to be an empowering concept for women since it obliterates the difference between men and women and yet ultimately allows the survival of the (male-dominant) status quo by rendering everything illusory so that any effort at social change becomes futile.[30] They also argue that, for the

---

28. Ōgoshi and Minamoto, *Kaitai suru bukkyō*, p. 107.

29. The Five Obstructions are the five incarnations women are said to be unable to achieve: Brahmā, Indra, Māra, cakravarti-rāja, and Buddha.

30. Ōgoshi et al., *Seisabetsu suru bukkyō*, pp. 12–13, 30–32; see also Ōgoshi and Minamoto, *Kaitai suru bukkyō*, p. 73. They also critique the Pure Land paradigm as propagated by both

most part, Buddhist-inspired thinking in Japan increasingly stressed women's sinfulness during and after the Heian period,[31] which is consistent with the view that women are impure (*fujō*), a concept I discuss in detail in Chapter 4.

Minamoto and Ōgoshi's analyses call attention to the urgent need for feminist inquiries into Buddhism, especially within Japanese scholarship. They do, however, tend to present Buddhism as a strong and universal force whose oppressive powers were totalizing, and their arguments are occasionally ahistorical. A fruitful approach in examining gender and Buddhism would be to keep Minamoto and Ōgoshi's criticisms in mind while questioning how and why specific attributes associated with women were prone to marginalization by certain texts that laid claim to Buddhist inspiration and asking whether "oppressive" moves were completely successful within the framework of Buddhism.

Another scholar who has attended to the problem of women and Buddhism in the Heian and Medieval periods is Taira Masayuki, who has critiqued previous approaches to women and *ōjō*, or rebirth in the Pure Land, including a well-known study by Kasahara Kazuo. Whereas previous scholars whose understanding of Buddhism in Japan hinges on the Pure Land school of thought focused too heavily on the "newness" of seemingly pro-woman ideas articulated by both Hōnen and Shinran (1133–1212 and 1173–1262, respectively; founders of Pure Land schools in Japan) around the turn of the thirteenth century, Taira argues that an examination of earlier centuries is necessary for a full understanding of the issue. He asserts that, throughout the Heian period, differing views on women's *ōjō* existed, but there was a general increase in discriminatory views of women in many Buddhist schools as the era progressed and ideas about impurity and taboo became popular. He points out that such views began to appear around the mid-ninth century and continued virtually unchanged even in Hōnen's and

---

Hōnen and Shinran during the period under discussion. Although some scholars have claimed that Hōnen's and Shinran's views empowered women, Minamoto (ibid., p. 140) insists that, in fact, they were highly oppressive. As for the Pure Land rhetoric of "everyone will be saved, even the lowest of the low," that very phrase succeeds in positioning certain people as "the lowest of the low" even as it hides this manipulating move by emphasizing that they, too, will be saved; in other words, the religious rhetoric constructs social stratification (ibid., p. 92). In the case of women, their sinfulness (*tsumi-bukasa*) was emphasized in order to show that Pure Land belief would save even the most sinful (ibid., p. 96).

31. Ōgoshi and Minamoto, *Kaitai suru bukkyō*, p. 81.

Shinran's thought. This rhetoric of the obstructions confronting women and their sinfulness was crucial in establishing that Buddhism, which could save even such people, was compassionate.[32] Many other scholars have dealt with such issues; one of whom is Nishiguchi Junko, whose contributions I mention in Chapter 4. Taira's explanations are broadly in keeping with the general historical trends outlined above; like Minamoto and Ōgoshi, he insists on the prevalence of discourse that oppressed women in this period as well as the increasing nature of this oppression. Again, I begin with these observations and re-examine them through the examples to follow.

This is not to say, however, that Buddhist ideologies and practices are the sole or consistent cause of gender marginalization in the works discussed in this book or even that Buddhist-informed individuals are uniform in their views or actions. To portray "Buddhism" as a timeless, homogeneous, and unchanging oppressor of women would be to miss the intricate ways in which different configurations of specific Buddhist discourses empower or marginalize ascribed gender characteristics.[33] It would also be to ignore other rhetorics of "sinfulness" that came to even include the very class in control of the central government; seemingly disempowering discourses were employed strategically in an effort to produce desired results, such as the continued and/or increased patronage of certain Buddhist schools by those in power.[34] The marginalization of female entertainers, old beggars, and demons should be understood within this context of particular interests as well as effects, intended or not. In other words, while keeping in mind the broad tendencies suggested by the scholars whose views I have outlined above, my intention is not to present Buddhism as a monolithic philosophical system

---

32. Taira, *Nihon chūsei no shakai to bukkyō*; particularly sect. 4, "Josei to bukkyō."

33. For example, the "Devadatta" chapter in the Lotus Sutra, which contains the controversial passage about the dragon girl becoming a buddha—a popular trope that appears repeatedly in Heian literature—was not at all an important focus in Buddhist discourse during the Nara period (710–84); in fact, before the Nara period, versions of the Lotus Sutra may have been missing this chapter altogether (see Yoshida, "Ryūnyo no jōbutsu," p. 58; and Ōgoshi and Minamoto, *Kaitai suru bukkyō*, pp. 61, 64). Such shifts in emphasis indicate the extent to which discourses are advanced, negated, and otherwise manipulated at specific historical points based on different motives.

34. Brown, "'Even Sinners Like Us.'" Brown notes the ways in which the *jishū* school of thought of Pure Land Buddhism described the *bushi* military class as being "sinful" because of their occupation—killing people; this discourse made this ruling class likely candidates for patronizing a school of thought preaching that even the most sinful would be saved.

or practice but to examine specific instances in which certain texts promoting particular Buddhist-related interests, such as the propagation of the chanting of the *nenbutsu* (the invocation of the buddha Amitābha), come to marginalize particular groups of women or individual female figures in the mid- to late Heian period. The readings to follow are not intended to be simple reinforcements of the historical and/or Buddhist schemes that attempt to describe changes in the position of women. Rather, they aspire to show the extent to which contradictions and ambiguities existed within the processes of marginalization.

೮೪

This book is divided into three parts, each of which focuses on a different female figure or type. In each of these examples, gender and marginality interact in ways that shed new light on both the processes of marginalization and the construction of gender during the mid-Heian to the early Kamakura period; each chapter takes issue with particular scholars who locate a specific figure or group as essentially marginal.

Part I is intended to illustrate the extent to which previous assumptions about the margin and its inhabitants need to be reconsidered. It investigates the figures of the *asobi* (also called *asobime*) and the *kugutsu*, women entertainers who frequently practiced prostitution as well. My overall point is that the "marginal asobi/kugutsu" is a double-layered construction: first, specific attempts at marginalizing these women were performed in the tenth to thirteenth centuries, and second, these figures are presented as *a priori* marginal by twentieth-century scholars. Chapter 1 questions scholarly debates in which the lifestyles and practices of women entertainers are "described" via textual "evidence." I instead propose that such representations are fluid sites for both marginalization and empowerment depending on a text's discursive aims and even on its unintended effects; it is necessary to analyze when and how marginalizing processes occurred in Heian and Kamakura texts, as well as to problematize modern scholarship that neglects this process. Specifically, I examine two generic categories—Chinese-style prose/poetry and *setsuwa* "tale" literature—that present varying portrayals of women entertainers depending on their literary and allusionistic concerns and religious motivations. I conclude with a brief examination of textual examples referring to women entertainers that are credited to women authors in order to illustrate the point that marginalizing discourses are not omnipresent and that they cannot be attributed to essentialist assumptions about gender solidarity. The figures of the asobi and the kugutsu emerge as strate-gically and unevenly marginalized textual constructions.

In Chapter 2, I first investigate a case of late Heian marginalization by fo-cusing on a particular collection of songs that these women sang called *Ryōjin hishō*, compiled by the retired emperor Goshirakawa (r. 1155–58). I trace the ways in which this powerful male compiler simultaneously elevated and deni-grated women entertainers in his work. I argue that this phenomenon is a re-sult of Goshirakawa's desire to establish song-singing as a legitimate path to attaining rebirth into the Pure Land (ōjō) and to declare himself the only authentic authority on the orthodox lineage of song-singers. The first motive led him to privilege women entertainers, who "possessed" the songs profes-sionally, and the second to marginalize them in an attempt to co-opt their art form as his monopoly. I then turn to two particular songs in *Ryōjin hishō* that many scholars have interpreted as admissions by women entertainers of their own "sinful" status. I unravel these arguments and show that these scholars are literally putting words into the mouths of late Heian women entertainers, thereby revealing the extent to which the construction called the "marginal asobi/kugutsu" is part of a modern-day scholastic project. Overall, my point in Part I is that in all texts women entertainers are socially situated through an interested effort; their positionality in a certain text represents more a rhetori-cal strategy than a "reflection" of social "reality."

Part II examines another marginalizing process at work. Shortly after her death, the famous mid-ninth century poet Ono no Komachi acquired a reputation as an amorous woman. In subsequent years, she came to be por-trayed in various stories as a wandering, impoverished old woman or a pile of bones lamenting her existence in a poem. I argue in Chapter 3 that the nar-ratives that marginalize Komachi's figure through a strategic use of the dis-course of female aging sought to negate the characteristics that empowered her sexually and culturally: her physical beauty and literary reputation within the capital. Gendered critiques, mobilized through the invocation of extreme poverty and physical degeneration in the representations of old women, were employed for different reasons. In the examples I explore, one is religious: Komachi is adduced as an example of undesirable endings that result from factors ranging from her family's overambitiousness to her own arrogance and abundant sexuality. The other is social: she is cited as a figure who embodies characteristics "unsuitable" for a military-class wife. The most significant aspect of the marginalization of Komachi through the discourse of female aging, however, is the great impact of these representations on the understanding of her figure among those who possessed literary power in the generations after Komachi's time; such understandings led compilers and commentators to shape Komachi's literary oeuvre. In other words, poems were attributed and unattributed to her based on the judgments of editors who assessed the poems as fitting or not fitting her image. Such is the capacity for literary molding that marginalizing processes possess; the very question of female agency is rendered problematic by the discursive forces that are revealed to have constructed Komachi's figure.

Chapter 4 continues the investigation of Ono no Komachi as a discursively constructed figure by focusing on textual examples that cast her as a dead woman, specifically a lone skull in a field, who recites poetry in order to draw attention to her discomfort. Just as the discourse of female aging was aimed specifically at combating women's sexuality through the rhetoric of inevitable material and physical loss, the rhetoric of female death was imbued with Pure Land notions of impurity and decay and thereby made into an object of loathing. Through this discourse, Komachi's figure was marginalized; furthermore, in the representations I examine, she is shown as losing her connection to the sources of her cultural capital: her physical residence within the boundary of the capital and her full command over her poetic repertoire. The texts that represent Komachi as a skull therefore signify a double-pronged attack on her figure: not only does she become a helpless object to be manipulated, either by a male protagonist, author, or monk who can contemplate the supposedly abhorrent nature of feminine flesh and the meaninglessness of sexual desire, but also her capacity for literary creation in its full potential is truncated and eventually stolen from her altogether. There is an attempt to disengage Komachi's physical being—her flesh, the source of her beauty—from her literary talents; this division diminishes considerably the effects of these powers as a combined unit and thereby allows the marginalizing objectification of both her (lack of) physicality and her (lack of) authorial powers of agency. Such maneuvers, however, were neither uniformly consistent nor entirely successful; I note instances in which the "undesirable" returns as a paradoxically desirable object. Gendered marginalization, again, proves to be a highly uneven process.

Part III contains the fifth and final chapter, which addresses more explicitly the possibilities for conflict and contradiction within the marginalizing process itself. I focus on the figure of Hashihime, a female bridge deity who in the Heian period is represented as a pining woman longing for her lover. In later texts, however, she becomes a woman possessed with jealousy who turns herself into a powerful demon by entering a river. I argue that these representations are intimately related to the practice of polygyny; she is aestheticized as an ideal lover but is also feared as a potentially disruptive threat to this system of female-male relationships. The process by which this relatively benign figure came to be constructed as a fearful demon is closely associated with jealousy, a quality often linked with the feminine in this period. Hashihime's transformation shows not only that her marginalization is fluid over time but also that the marginalized being can be ascribed powers that threaten the well-being of the marginalizers. This threat, in turn, can provoke further responses of marginalization.

By examining the ways in which marginalizing discourses target female figures, I do not mean to suggest that no such counterpart existed for male figures. Famous examples such as Yamato Takeru (n.d., quasi-mythical), the imperial prince sent away on difficult military missions by his father, and Sugawara no Michizane (845–903), the scholar/official–turned–exile–turned–vengeful spirit, immediately come to mind as marginalized male figures; male itinerant performers and the problematic category of *hinin* (literally, "not human"—the so-called "outcasts" both male and female) add to the list and beg for further analysis. This book focuses on female marginalization partly as a means to focus my study more sharply, but partly as a way to highlight the ways in which female figures tended to be systematically targeted by marginalizing discourses because they were identified *as women*, unlike male figures, whose marginalization was not contingent on their "maleness."

I end this Introduction with a brief explanation of my approach to translation. I have tried to follow the Japanese texts as closely as I can, instead of omitting details for the sake of "smooth readability" in English. I have organized *waka* translations into two-line (*kami no ku* and *shimo no ku*) divisions. Imperfect as these solutions may be, it is my hope that the translations contribute positively to the body of premodern Japanese texts in English.

Part I
Women Entertainers

1   *Fragmented Margins:*
The Asobi and Kugutsu

Women entertainers of the pre-Edo era, especially the Heian and Kamakura periods, have traditionally received little scholarly attention compared with that given their post-1600 counterparts. This lack of attention is due partly to the scarcity of textual evidence and partly to the largely monolithic approach of modern scholars, who tend to view women entertainers as inherently "sinful" and uniformly ostracized. This chapter reconsiders such assumptions by examining two contrasting broad generic categories that depict these women, Chinese-style prose and poetry and setsuwa (tale literature). I hope to reveal the extent to which such representations are textually constructed through layers of allusions, rewritings, and declarations of intent. In other words, the figure of the "woman entertainer" is neither a transparent reflection of some "reality" nor a montage of random qualities; rather, it is a mosaic of different and often-conflicting characteristics projected by various authors for reasons of their own. The marginality of these women entertainers, argued tirelessly by twentieth-century scholars both Japanese and Euro-American, emerges not as a static and unambiguous attribute but as a diverse collection of textual attempts to position these women literally, historically, socially, and religiously.

This chapter focuses on two groups of women entertainers especially active during the mid-Heian to early Kamakura periods: the asobi and the kugutsu. The composite image of the asobi that can be gathered from the texts of this period is that they spend most of their time on boats, which they row to approach travelers and perform their songs and dances, that some of them are proprietors of inns, that each group has a leader, the *chōja*, and that they engage in prostitution. Kugutsu women, on the other hand, are portrayed as members of a migrant group, in which the men practice hunting and perform and the women sing and lure customers for prostitution.[1] Both the asobi and the kugutsu were specialists in a genre of song called *imayō*. Imayō, which means "in the modern style," refers both to the broader category of songs in fashion and to a narrower group of songs belonging to the specific genre with this name. "Modern style" referred to this genre's differences from previous *kayō* (song) categories such as *saibara, fūzoku,* and *rōei*.[2] Imayō songs were sung mainly by professional women entertainers and by the aristocrats who patronized them.

The asobi and the kugutsu have received considerable attention in Japanese *minzokugaku* (folk studies), especially in the past two decades. Nakayama Tarō was one of the first scholars in the twentieth century to conduct a large-scale study of the history of prostitution in Japan. He examined the status and practices of prostitutes and concluded that especially in pre-Edo times the position of prostitutes was not always considered lowly and that they had originally been *miko*, or women who served native deities.[3] The controversial scholar Yanagita Kunio also speculated that the asobi originated in the miko.[4] The next wave of scholarship appeared in the 1960s, when Takikawa Masajirō wrote a series of books on the asobi and the kugutsu. These works contributed not only to the widening of interest in these groups of women but also to the popularizing of the unfortunate views that prostitution was unquestionably "sinful" in pre-Edo Japan, that the asobi and kugutsu were socially ostracized throughout these times, and that the "lewd" practices of these women stemmed from a non-Japanese source.[5]

In the 1980s, various scholars critiqued Takikawa's discriminatory theo-

---

1. The two groups were sometimes conflated, as we shall see below in this chapter. Two other groups of women were associated with entertainment and prostitution in the mid-Heian to early Kamakura periods: the *miko*, whose formal functions were to serve as shrine workers and to perform divinations in trances, and the *shirabyōshi*, who were most distinctively characterized by their dancing style and cross-dressing costume.

2. Geinōshi kenkyūkai, *Nihon geinōshi*, 2: 112.

3. See Nakayama, *Baishō sanzen-nen shi*.

4. See, e.g., Yanagita, *Teihon Yanagita Kunio shū*, 8: 355–56.

5. See Takikawa, *Ukareme, asobi, kugutsume*; and idem, *Yūjo no rekishi*.

ries and sought to re-examine the status and practices of women entertainers, and proposed a range of theories, particularly about their origins. One of the most prominent of these scholars, Amino Yoshihiko, questioned the assumption that the asobi and kugutsu were lower-class people who were only occasionally permitted to interact with the upper class. He proposed instead that the asobi originated in the *jokan*, or women who served at court; he reconciled his claim with Nakayama's theory that the asobi originated in the miko by arguing that the jokan similarly possessed sacred qualities because of their service in the divine imperial household. He speculated that some jokan who excelled in the performing arts came to form a professional family line that developed into the asobi.[6] Gotō Norihiko also suggested that the origins of the asobi, kugutsu, and *shirabyōshi* were intimately tied to professional women entertainers at court.[7] On the other hand, Gorai Shigeru traced the origins of the asobi to the *asobibe*, who may have performed pacifying rituals at imperial funerals in the pre-Heian periods.[8] Toyonaga Satomi examined the position of the chōja and concluded that there were established and competing groups of asobi, each led by a chōja who had administrative control. She emphasized the importance of differentiating among various groups of the asobi/kugutsu, who were divided according to both geographical location and social class.[9] In addition, other scholars such as Saeki Junko,[10] Ōwa Iwao,[11] and Michael Stein[12] have written works

---

6. Amino, "Yūjo to hinin/kawaramono." Fukutō Sanae ("Ukareme kara asobi e") takes a similar stance in asserting that women who served at court, who also performed songs and dances at official banquets in the period of the *Man'yōshū* (completed 759?), can be considered the first women entertainers, who later professionalized themselves in practicing just performance.

7. See Gotō, "Asobi to chōtei, kizoku."

8. See Gorai, "Chūsei josei no shūkyōsei to seikatsu." The exact nature and role of the asobibe remains unclear and has been much debated; see, e.g., Takagawa, "Asobibe denshō kō."

9. Toyonaga, "Chūsei ni okeru asobi no chōja ni tsuite."

10. See Saeki Junko, *Yūjo no bunkashi*. This work attempts to situate the asobi as women of the "sacred sex" in that they possessed sacred powers through their sexuality. Saeki seeks to read texts in which the asobi appear against theories promoted by past (male) scholars such as Takikawa. Although I find the work empowering for women, it suffers from instances of ahistorical textual analyses and uncontextualized comparisons of literatures from different parts of the world. A similar tendency can be found in Suzuka, "Yūjo gensō."

11. Ōwa, *Yūjo to tennō*.

12. Stein, *Japans Kurtisanen*.

focusing exclusively on women entertainers, and collections of scholarship on women's history also include chapters on these women.[13]

These works focus on the issue of the social position of the asobi in pre-Edo Japan and tend to utilize textual productions as pieces of "historical evidence," often as "proof" that a particular practice or attitude existed or did not exist. Scholars have cited many passages from extant works to substantiate their claims of the marginal status of the asobi during these eras. Although this practice has some validity, treatment of the text as a transparent source of "facts" ignores the constructed aspect of these writings—that is, this approach takes documents at face value without considering their context, such as the literary tradition to which they belong, their generic characteristics, authorship, and stated aims. In other words, recent scholarship critiquing the "marginal" status of women entertainers to the contrary, a more thorough examination of the texts themselves—what they promote and for what reason—is still in order, so that we can situate their discourses within contexts that directly affect the interpretations of these utterances. Such an examination also reveals conflicting discourses within the texts themselves; these texts are not necessarily monolithic in opinion. This chapter moves away from the view that texts are unmotivated, "neutral" products that reveal a "truth" about the time in which they were written and considers them instead as works that generated their own views about "truth" for specific purposes.

CHINESE-STYLE WRITINGS:
TEXTUAL ECHOES AND STRATA OF ALLUSIONS

Male aristocrats of the Heian wrote a number of texts using Chinese characters and Chinese-style grammar that are cited in modern scholarship on women entertainers. Before using these writings as "historical documents," however, we must ask several questions about them. To what extent do these texts look back to sources in the Chinese and Japanese literary traditions, for example, in terms of phrasing and imagery? Are the literary devices found in them "faithful" representations of the lived reality of asobi and kugutsu or do they owe more to previously established tropes, images, and

---

13. See, e.g., "Chūsei no 'asobi,'" in Sōgō joseishi kenkyūkai, *Nihon josei no rekishi: sei, ai, kazoku,* pp. 78–86.

phrases? What are the complexities and contradictions that structure these representations?

Prose "Essays"

The two mid-Heian sources cited most often as descriptions of women entertainers are *Yūjo no ki* (An account of the *yūjo* [sinified reading of *asobi*]) and *Kairaishi no ki* (An account of puppeteers) by Ōe no Masafusa (1041–1111). These short "essay-style" (*zuihitsu*) passages in *kanbun*, or Chinese-style writing, were probably composed late in Masafusa's life. They are important by virtue of being two of the few pieces of writing that focus exclusively on the asobi and the kugutsu and have therefore been cited repeatedly by modern scholars as evidence of the practices of these peoples. A close examination of these texts is necessary in order to situate the discursive figurations of women entertainers in Masafusa's works.

The beginning of *Yūjo no ki* (for a translation, see the Appendix, pp. 295–97) is full of movement, as the narrative told from a traveler's viewpoint unfolds. We encounter various named locations, such as Kaya, Eguchi, and Kanzaki, all famous for asobi women. Only after the presentation of the place-names do we encounter a description of the women:

The singing women form groups; poling small boats, they reach the ships and offer bedroom companionship. Their voices halt the clouds in the valley, and their melodies linger in the waterside breeze. There is no one who passes by who does not forget all about one's home. . . . It may be that under heaven this is the most amusing place.[14]

After this "ethnographic" description, the attention shifts to the personal names of asobi and traces the founder of each location ("Eguchi was started by Kannon"), thereby genealogizing and individually identifying the famous women. The narrator then vouches for their wide-ranging appeal, from "high court nobles at the top to commoners at the bottom," and notes that some "become wives or concubines and are cherished until their death." Their particular habit of worshipping the *hyakudayū* (deities of crossroads and sexual unions, also known as *dōsojin*) is mentioned, and the focus moves once again to the telling of instances in which high-ranking men patronized certain asobi. Finally, the narrative returns to an explanation of locations and

---

14. Yamagishi et al., *Kodai seiji shakai shisō*, p. 154.

the types of patrons each place is likely to attract and presents a detailed account of the way the women divide the material compensations for their services.

Kairaishi no ki (for a translation, see Appendix, pp. 297–98) is a less fragmented essay that emphasizes the supposedly nomadic qualities of the kugutsu. The opening passage states that "the kugutsu have no established places to live and have no houses to protect." The narrator calls their tent a "yurt" (*kyūro*; Chinese reading: *qionglu*) and likens their lifestyle to "the customs of the Northern Barbarians" (*hokuteki*; Chinese reading: *beidi*). After discussing the men, who hunt on horseback and perform acrobatic acts and magical tricks, he introduces the women:

The women put on "sad-face" makeup, do the "bent-at-the-hip" walk, and smile the "toothache-smile"; donning vermilion and wearing white powder, they sing songs and provide licentious pleasures and thus seek to charm.

After an inventory of the sumptuous rewards the kugutsu women receive as payment, the narrator explains:

They do not plow even one *se* of rice fields, nor do they pick even one branch of mulberry. In this manner they do not subject themselves to prefectural officials, none of them is a regular dweller, and they are naturally equivalent to "drifters." They do not recognize even the royalty at the top, nor do they fear provincial governors. They take not having any taxes and levies as their lifetime enjoyment.[15]

There is then a mention of their worship of *hyakugami*, which is presumably related to the asobi's hyakudayū. Place-names, ratings of each location, and the naming of famous kugutsu emerge as important concerns here too; the passage ends with a lengthy list of the song types that they are known to sing and with the statement: "[These singers] are indeed exceptional under the heavens. Who can possibly not feel compassion toward them?"

At first glance, it may be tempting to conclude that the "descriptions" of the lives of the asobi and kugutsu accurately reflect the customs and practices of these women (and men, in the case of the kugutsu), in almost a "guidebook" style. However, it has been recently suggested that Masafusa, a middle-ranking aristocrat, was attracted by the supposed "freedoms" of the asobi and the kugutsu and that he chose to emphasize and exaggerate these

---

15. Ibid., p. 158.

because he viewed them as intriguingly exotic.[16] Below, I take this hint further by examining these passages in more detail; instead of assuming that Masafusa was "recording data accurately" and that he acted as a transparent medium in communicating the situations that he observed, I contextualize his work as a textual construction of a particular time, place, and author who was working within a specific generic and literary heritage.

First, it is crucial to note that a number of passages that seem at first to be Masafusa's direct observations of the daily lives of the asobi and kugutsu in fact are references to a work written at least fifty years earlier by another scholar of the Ōe family, Ōe no Mochitoki (also read Yukitoki) (955–1010).[17] Masafusa noted at the very end of *Yūjo no ki* that Mochitoki had also written about these women and tried to distinguish himself from his predecessor by claiming that he was augmenting Mochitoki's text by writing about other aspects of their lives. However, the relationship between these two texts is not as simple as an "older historical record" and a "new addendum." A closer look at this earlier text, which clearly influenced Masafusa's writings significantly, reveals that his pieces about the asobi and kugutsu cannot be understood entirely in terms of their claim to be objective records of contemporary practices.

Yūjo wo miru (On seeing the *yūjo*), a preface to a poem or poems by Mochitoki, is included in volume nine of the *Honchō monzui* (The essence of writings in our country), a fourteen-volume collection of 432 poems and writings in the Chinese style from between 810 and 1037, compiled by Fujiwara no Akihira (989–1066),[18] and modeled after *Wen xuan* (Selection of refined literature).[19]

Yūjo wo miru

In the third month of the second year,[20] Governor of Iyo province and Supernumerary Provisional Captain of the Left Division of the Bureau of Horses Minamoto no Kanesuke[21] went to the Southern Sea Circuit in the spring and stayed at Kayō

---

16. Amino, "Yūjo tachi no kyozō to jitsuzō," pp. 4–70.

17. Fukazawa, *Chūsei shinwa no rentanjutsu*, p. 111. Fukazawa points out that the passage concerning the husbands and parents of asobi women is repeated in Ōe no Masafusa's *Kairaishi no ki*.

18. Also the author of *Shin sarugakuki*, discussed below.

19. *Wen xuan*: a Chinese anthology of poetry and prose from the early sixth century (Liang dynasty).

20. The second year of Chōtoku (996).

21. Minamoto no Kanesuke (?–1002) was a courtier of the fourth rank.

on the way. Kayō is sandwiched between the three provinces of Yamashiro, Kawachi, and Settsu and is one of the most vital ports in the realm. From the west, from the east, from the south, from the north, among those who come and go there is not one who does not take this route.

The life there is such that those who advertise and sell the charms of women, both old and young, have banded together; their villages line the river. They tie their boats at the front of the gate and wait for customers on the river. Those who are young wear rouge and powder, and they sing and make merry and thus seduce the hearts of people; those who are old bear umbrellas or pole the boat and consider these their tasks. As for those who have husbands, [their husbands] blame them when their licentious activities are few, and as for those who have parents, [their parents] only hope that [their children] are lucky in gaining patronage. It is not a matter of human feelings, but this is the custom. Perhaps they are named so because they wander about, so their names are based on actuality.

Ah, the jade-green curtains and the crimson bedroom—even though their etiquette is different from the rules of conduct of marriage, being atop the waves inside a boat brings the same joy—the rendezvous of a lifetime. Every time I see these things when I pass along this road, there has not yet been a time when I do not sigh deeply. I say, why don't you use the heart that favors the ways of love and draw nearer to the path that favors virtue?[22]

Several passages are strikingly similar to those in Masafusa's *Yūjo no ki* and *Kairaishi no ki*. For example, the opening description of the roads of the travelers in *Yūjo no ki* closely resembles that of the earlier work. Also, the portrayal of the husbands and parents of kugutsu women who entertain travelers and the appearance and activities of these women (rouge, powder, singing, and "merrymaking") in *Kairaishi no ki* is very similar to the corresponding passages in *Yūjo wo miru*. It is as if Masafusa composed two separate pieces based loosely on this single work by Mochitoki. Such similarities suggest two things: first, Masafusa was keenly aware of the established discursive tradition of writing about this subject; although this factor does not preclude his own contributions to this tradition, its presence cannot be ignored in considering Masafusa's works. Second, the categories of asobi and kugutsu were not necessarily clear-cut in Mochitoki's time, since descriptions of practices defined later as peculiar to one group appear as characteristics of both groups in his work. Masafusa's creation of two separate documents implies that the distinction between the two groups came to be

---

22. Ōsone et al., *Honchō monzui*, pp. 60–61.

emphasized only relatively late, with particular attributes assigned to each. This tendency may have stemmed from the desire of the ruling class to organize and classify people over whom they had less direct control due to their wandering status, as well as from a romanticization and exoticization of women entertainers as a whole.

Mochitoki's work in turn draws heavily on Chinese philosophical, historical, and literary texts. For example, the phrase "from the west, from the east, from the south, from the north" is found in *Shijing* (Book of odes),[23] and the references to both makeup powder and the bearing of an umbrella come from passages in *Shiji* (Records of the Grand Historian).[24] The jade-green curtains are found in a *fu* poem by the fifth-century poet Xie Tiao (among others),[25] and the crimson bedroom is in a piece of regulated verse by the Tang poet Wang Yin[26] as well as various other poems from the Tang period and earlier. The exact phrase "to sigh deeply" can be found in *Chuci* (Songs of Chu),[27] and the last sentence, "Why don't you use the heart that favors the ways of love and draw nearer to the path that favors virtue?" is an allusion to the *Analects*, in which Confucius states "I have not yet seen a person who favors virtue to the same extent that he favors the ways of love."[28] Such sources situate this piece in its context; we cannot assume that all the descriptions given here were intended to be or were in fact received by contemporary readers as "factual records" of the life of an asobi.

Aside from *Yūjo wo miru*, Ōe no Masafusa's description of the kugutsu was also directly influenced by images from Chinese historical texts. The passages describing the activities of the kugutsu as *kyūba wo wakimae* (using horses and bows), their dwellings as *kyūro sencho* (tent with felt curtains), their wanderings as *mizukusa wo oite mote ishi* (chasing the water grass), and their customs as *hokuteki no narai ni nitari* (resemble the customs of Northern Barbarians) closely resemble the depiction of Xiongnu, a horse-riding people based in what is now Mongolia, in *Hanshu* (History of the Former Han

---

23. See the poem "Wen wang yousheng," in the Daya section of *Shijing*.

24. For "makeup" (*zhifen*), see "Ningxing liezhuan"; for umbrella (*teng*), see "Pingyuan jun / Yu qing liezhuan," both in *Shiji*.

25. See the poem "Ni Song 'Yu Fengfu'" by Xie Tiao (A.D 464–99) in *Xie Xuancheng ji*, pp. 7–8.

26. See the poem "Houting yuan" by Wang Yin (n.d.). in *Quan Tangshi*, pp. 1470–71.

27. See first line, verse 4, of "Lisao" in *Chuci*.

28. See the chapter "Zihan" in the *Analects* (*Lunyu*). All references above are noted in both Ōsone et al., *Honchō monzui*, pp. 60–61; and in Kakimura, *Honchō monzui chūshaku*, pp. 194–96.

dynasty). The phrases describing the erotic appearances and gestures of the kugutsu, such as *teishō* (sad-face makeup), *setsuyōho* (bent-at-the-hip walk), and *kushishō* (toothache-smile) can be found in *Hou Hanshu* (History of the Latter Han dynasty).[29] Ironically, it seems that in order to domesticate and therefore understand the phenomenon of these wandering peoples, Masafusa had to resort to what he considered to be Chinese "equivalents." The use of such equivalents is consistent with the genre in which he was writing; this move in turn simultaneously made the kugutsu more foreign in quality.

It has also been pointed out that Masafusa's works can be placed in a tradition of works such as *Shin sarugakuki* (A new account of *sarugaku*), which I discuss next, which were aristocratic accounts of commoners' occupations. It is likely that a member of the nobility writing for audiences of the same class would be motivated to exaggerate and focus on "exotic" details that could make the work more appealing to its readers.[30] Furthermore, Masafusa's motivation in writing these two pieces (and others like *Rakuyō dengakuki* [An account of *dengaku* in the capital] and *Kobiki* [An account of fox trickery]) may have been to imitate the Chinese tradition of unofficial "strange tales," which functioned as a display of the virtuosic range of a writer of official records. Masafusa, the author of more "mainstream" works such as *Zoku honchō ōjōden* (More biographies of those from our country who have achieved rebirth in the Pure Land), could have been trying to show off the full spectrum of his writing talents by engaging in the portrayal of these "strange" peoples.[31] The descriptions in *Yūjo no ki* and *Kairaishi no ki*, therefore, should not be taken at face value.

The differences between Masafusa's two works and their influences, however, are important as well. For example, unlike *Yūjo wo miru*, *Yūjo no ki* and *Kairaishi no ki* list the names of established asobi women and kugutsu groups; this situates these texts in a specific context. The presence of these specificities is perhaps what has led some scholars to accept these two works unquestioningly as statements of historical "fact." One reading of these texts, then, is to regard them as a mixture of concrete lists and stereotyped portrayals. The lists provide a lineage and organization to these groups instead of leaving them as amorphous, unnamed, and thus uncontrollable masses of people. In other words, the portrayals of these groups made use of words

---

29. Fukazawa, *Chūsei shinwa no rentanjutsu*, pp. 110, 120.
30. Amino, "Chūsei no tabibito tachi," pp. 162–63.
31. Ohara, *Bunjin kizoku no keifu*, pp. 179–82.

and images that were either standard at the time in case of the asobi or considered to be the Chinese equivalents in the case of the kugutsu; the genealogizing and ranking of women entertainers who are cited by name may have served as displays of authority and/or as handbooks for potential clients who sought knowledge about those whom they would patronize.

As for the overall attitudes that result from the textual effects in these three works, the middle passage of *Yūjo wo miru* presents the practices of these people relatively non-judgmentally; it concedes that the encouragement of prostitution by the husbands and parents of the asobi was unusual, but notes merely that this was their custom. In the last passage, Mochitoki enters a reverie about the wonders of being on an asobi's boat but ends with a reference to the *Analects*. There are conflicting messages of longing for pleasure and Confucian values, and the piece ultimately ends with a criticism of the "ways of love." Despite this disapproving note, Mochitoki does not touch on the "morality" of asobi women; in fact, the most openly critical phrase, "it is not a matter of human feeling," applies to the women's families.[32]

Yūjo no ki presents an even less critical view of the life of an asobi. Masafusa focused on their singing skills and noted that some asobi were patronized generously by people of high rank. The kugutsu, both men and women, who appear in *Kairaishi no ki* are portrayed as fearless and independent of control by a higher authority. In describing the prostitution of the women and their families' view of this profession, Masafusa simply said: "Their parents and husbands truly do not [admonish them]"; this remark is not followed by any statement like Mochitoki's "it is not a matter of human feeling." Such lack of moral judgment gives this text an objective flavor, which certainly has contributed to its characterization as an eyewitness record by twentieth-century scholars.

In comparing the attitudes expressed by Mochitoki and Masafusa in these pieces, we find that chronology is not necessarily consistent with the change in attitude often asserted by many scholars who study women entertainers. It is commonly assumed that women entertainers were respected and occupied a fairly high position in society before the Heian period, but that this situation steadily changed for the worse over the years. However, the earlier *Yūjo wo*

---

32. The phrase can be interpreted not only as "the women involve themselves in relationships devoid of love" but also as "such attitudes go against the expectations of usual human feeling," which imparts a critical tone.

miru seems less enthusiastic about the asobi than Masafusa's two works; this suggests not that the "decline" in their status was irreversible, continuous, and teleological, but that each textual moment represented a specific instance of marginalization or empowerment, and these moments do not necessarily constitute a seamless narrative of "degeneration."

Scholars writing on women entertainers in the mid-Heian period also frequently cite a passage in *Shin sarugakuki*, composed by Fujiwara no Akihira toward the end of his life. The passage begins with the presentation of a sarugaku performance and commentaries about the art and then focuses on a particular family in the audience and lists the various personalities and occupations of the family members, of which there are 29 in all. The portrayals of the characters are often quite extreme; each is either a model of perfection or utterly despicable. Ōe no Masafusa is thought to have been influenced by Akihira's work in his writing of *Yūjo no ki* and *Kairaishi ki*.[33]

In this series of family portraits, the sixteenth daughter is introduced as an asobi:

The sixteenth daughter is the chōja [leader] of the night-working *ukareme* [an older term for asobi], the love-favoring one downriver in Eguchi. What she is used to is the task of entertaining on the river [boat], and what is talked about is her irreverent manners at the bottom of the slope. During the day she bears a big umbrella and allows her body to those high and low. At night she beats the rim of the boat and gives her heart to the customers coming and going. Now, her abundantly-sexual conduct and trying-to-gain-favor, her skills at supine postures and "nurturing the wind," her virtues of "harp-strings and barley-teeth,"[34] and her uses of "flying dragons and tiger steps"[35]—there are none that she does not employ. Not only that, but her voice is like the kalaviṅka bird, and her form is like that of a heavenly maiden. Even the songs of Miyaki and Kokarasu and the voices of Yakushi and Naruto[36] lag far behind. Compared to hers, they are not even worth considering. Therefore, who would not be cast under her spell? What kind of person would not be smitten? Ah, while she is still young, she may pass her days selling herself, but after her colors fade, how will she spend the rest of her life?[37]

---

33. See, e.g., Nihon koten bungaku daijiten henshū iinkai, *Nihon koten bungaku daijiten*, 6: 114.

34. Euphemisms for the types of reactions of the female genitalia, as seen in *Ishinhō*.

35. Two of the Nine Sexual Techniques described in *Ishinhō*.

36. Miyaki, Kokarasu, Yakushi, and Naruto are names of famous asobi.

37. Shigematsu, *Shin sarugakuki / Unshū shōsoku*, pp. 47–48.

This passage, like Ōe no Masafusa's works, is explicitly influenced by texts composed earlier in the Heian period. The four special sexual techniques described in four-character compounds can be found in the first Japanese text on the practice of medicine, *Ishinhō* (Crucial medical methods), by Tanba no Yasuyori (ca. 984). It is a compilation of medical texts from the Sui and Tang dynasties in China.[38] Again, we see an author taking Chinese terminology and applying it to a supposedly "Japanese" phenomenon; rather than interpreting this passage as a faithful recording of the practices of asobi women during Akihira's time, then, we may treat it as one representation— by an aristocratic author—that contributed to the construction of this very category, "asobi."

This passage might seem at first to be an unflattering portrayal of the asobi because of the last sentence, which casts an ominous shadow on her future. However, other passages in *Shin sarugakuki*, particularly those about women, express judgments very sharply and use extreme words to denounce or praise the subject's character and/or appearance; there is little neutral ground in the portrayals of the family members. This section, which not only lacks ruthlessly condemnatory vocabulary but also contains positive assessments of the woman's abilities and looks, should be taken as a relatively complimentary portrayal. In fact, since the other family members praised by Akihira are celebrated as absolute masters in their chosen fields, the description of the sixteenth daughter can be regarded as a similar commendation of her adeptness at her occupation. Her skills, which range from luring customers to sexual techniques, are listed without moral judgment. She is especially praised for her talent in singing songs and is named as the one with the most beautiful voice in her profession.

Shin sarugakuki's attitude toward women's sexuality is an interesting issue. Fukutō Sanae points out that "wanton" women are depicted as "evil," as seen in the cases of the first wife, who cannot abandon the thought of sex even in old age, and the thirteenth daughter, who "does not choose high or low [rank] in her lewd behavior."[39] The condemnation of explicit displays of sexual desire by women can be established; however, these two cases present women who are not professionals at the art of sexuality. In fact, these criticisms can be contrasted sharply with the depiction of the sixteenth daughter,

---

38. Fukutō, *Heian chō no onna to otoko*, p. 74.
39. Ibid., pp. 82, 87.

who is an asobi by profession. Akihira's text, then, seems to make a special exception in the case of the asobi: adeptness at sexual techniques is more of a virtue, since it makes the asobi more skilled as a professional. This text suggests that although women's sexuality may have been marginalized overall, such oppression was not always applicable to the asobi, whose relationship to sexuality occupied a special position. Clearly, the asobi were not always ostracized for their sexuality.

Kanshi

Another genre of Heian writing also utilized both Chinese orthography and grammar. A number of *kanshi*, or Chinese-style poems, focus on the asobi or the kugutsu. As in the prose examples cited above, in poetry both the asobi and the kugutsu were represented discursively through the use of multi-layered allusions and conventional terminology. I first examine a series of poems about the kugutsu that borrow extensively from the pre-existing vocabulary used to portray women entertainers. I then note that kanshi also display another aesthetic: they are notable for the absence of the figures of these women themselves in the texts—in other words, the trope of women entertainers in this genre becomes a sort of "empty margin."

A series of Chinese-style poems (for translations, see the Appendix, pp. 298–301) about the kugutsu appears in the ten-volume collection *Honchō mudaishi* (Irregularly titled poetry of our country; probably 1162–64), compiled about a decade or so before *Ryōjin hishō* by an unknown compiler, possibly Fujiwara no Tadamichi (1097–1164). Most of the poems in this anthology are seven-character *lüshi* (regulated verse).[40] In this series of poems, the same images recur: the traveler, the inn, the cold moon, the autumn wind, the wandering life, the prostitution of kugutsu women, their makeup and appearance, and the singing of songs. Many of these images are found in the kanbun works by Ōe no Masafusa and Ōe no Mochitoki discussed in the previous section, which suggests that these tropes circulated widely in this period. For example, the reference to dust on the beams, which is the essence of the title *Ryōjin hishō* (see Chapter 2), appears in these poems as well as other works including Masafusa's. The image was apparently associated with songs sung for entertainment, especially by the kugutsu women. A reference

---

40. Zoku gunsho ruijū kanseikai, *Gunsho kaidai*, 5: 9–10.

to the Xiongnu connects one poem with *Kairaishi no ki*, which uses the words "Northern Barbarians"—a term that includes the group of people known as Xiongnu. This association seems to have produced an even heavier emphasis on the wandering life of the kugutsu than that found in the prose works examined above; textual examples from the Heian period countering this romanticized view of the nomadic life suggest that this trope was highly allusionistic and literary in its origins.[41] Both the evocation of "tents" and clear allusions such as "they don't pick mulberries for a living, they don't produce from the land"[42] closely echo Masafusa's works and imply that there was a dynamic yet limited set of literary devices used to portray the kugutsu, especially the women. In addition, certain images such as "moth-brows" are found repeatedly in Chinese poetry from the Tang period and earlier. Other evidence of borrowed images includes the "looking-out-for-husband rock" in the poem by Fujiwara no Atsumitsu (1063–1144); this image appears in a poem by the Tang poet Helan Sui (Helan Jinming, fl. mid-eighth century) about a female entertainer that is included in *Wakan rōeishū* (Japanese and Chinese poems to sing; ca. 1012; see below).[43]

As in the passage in the *Shin sarugakuki* on the sixteenth daughter, there is particular attention paid to the approach of old age for kugutsu women (and possibly also men, to some extent) in these poems; passages such as "in her twilight years, she tends the wormwood-roof hut in [his] absence / customers en route and travelers on their way avert their eyes in pity from afar; / this is indeed due to hair that is white and a face empty and wrinkled"; "they are deeply resentful that old age has come upon their voices and looks"; "what will they do after their years spent in these tents? / their beautiful

---

41. See, e.g., *Konjaku monogatari* (compiled by [an] unidentified compiler[s] between 1110 and 1120), Chapter 28, Story 27, tells of a kugutsu man who is hired to become an assistant to a provincial governor. Although the narrative pokes fun at his kugutsu origins, the man continues to hold his position even after his former occupation become known. This story therefore represents a counter-narrative to the seemingly monolithic discourse of the "nomadic kugutsu."

42. The passage in Masafusa's *Kairaishi no ki* is: "they do not plow even one *se* of rice fields, nor do they pick even one branch of mulberry."

43. For a detailed discussion of the impact of Chinese poetry (particularly the work of Bo Juyi) on Japanese kanshi, see Smits, "Reading the New Ballads." He asserts that Japanese poets chose to downplay the highly political aspects of Chinese poems that take the "social fringe" as their topic and instead turned them into "exotic subject matter"; the kugutsu poem series can be understood as one such attempt (see ibid., pp. 177–79).

appearances will change and depart, wounding their hearts."[44] I argue in later chapters that the discourse of aging was employed as a powerful means to mitigate the potentially threatening capacities of abundant female sexuality; here, I simply note that these ominous phrases feed off the earlier work by Akihira, not to mention such influential Tang poets as Li Bai (701–62; see, e.g., his *Changgan xing*) and Bo Juyi (772–846; e.g., *Pipa xing*; see Chapter 3).

This series of poems, then, should be situated in a genealogy of texts that continually allude to and borrow from previous texts while generating some new tropes, as in the case of the kanbun examples discussed earlier. There are certain differences between the two genres, however. In kanshi, the focus is less on the kugutsu group overall (as described in Masafusa's *Kairaishi no ki*) than on kugutsu women in particular. Masafusa's own poem in this series can serve to illustrate this point; "The Kugutsu Magogimi" is entirely about a specific kugutsu woman. In comparison to kanbun writings, pity and concern for the kugutsu in old age is amplified in these poems to the extent that it becomes a major theme. Overall, however, it is apparent that the portrayals of the asobi and the kugutsu found in kanbun and kanshi texts heavily refract Chinese constructions of women entertainers and do not necessarily "reflect" the conditions of women entertainers in Heian Japan.

Other sets of kanshi contain many of these same tropes yet also represent (or do not represent) women entertainers in a different manner. The first example is found in *Wakan rōeishū*, a two-volume collection of 588 kanshi by both Chinese and Japanese poets and 216 waka poems; both categories were set to music and intended to be sung accompanied by instruments. It was compiled by Fujiwara no Kintō (966–1041) around 1012, but most of the poems date from an earlier period. The anthology contains a section titled "Yūjo," which contains three kanshi about the asobi:

719   Across the autumn waters, the sash jewel of the yūjo has
          yet to ring
        The cold clouds well up above the "looking-out-for-husband"
          mountain in vain.

                                                              —Helan Sui

720   The jade-green curtains in the crimson bedroom
        although it strays from the [marriage] rites and regulations

---

44. Toyoshima, *Gunsho ruijū* 9, pp. 15–16; and Homma, *Honchō mudaishi zenchūyaku*, vol. 1.

in a boat above the waves
the happy meeting of a lifetime is no different from this.

—Igen[45]

721   [She] plays the Japanese harp languidly, looking down on the
      moon reflected upon the waters
  Pushing high the Chinese oar [she] enters into the mist above
      the waters.

—Jun[46]

The first poem, by Helan Sui, brings together the image of the yūjo and the legend of the chaste wife who turned into stone while waiting for her husband's return; the "looking-out-for-husband" rock/mountain became a motif in poems about women entertainers. It is found in kanshi by Japanese poets discussed above, even though its use tends to be ironic and not necessarily morally judgmental. Number 720 is a poetic summary by Ōe no Mochitoki taken from his *Yūjo wo miru*. The work, which exhibits an ambivalent attitude toward the yūjo, is here crystallized into the only passage that is explicitly enthusiastic about the asobi and their practices. If Mochitoki himself chose to transform this passage into a poem, then his view of the asobi cannot be said to be particularly condemnatory.

What is of interest here is that in all three poems emphasize the asobi's absence from the scene—that is, the figure of the asobi either does not materialize or quickly fades from view. In the first poem, the sound of her sash jewel has yet to ring, which means that she has not yet entered the scene; in the second poem, the asobi's presence is alluded to by her surroundings, the "jade-green curtains and the crimson bedroom," but there is no description of a particular woman. In the last poem, the asobi disappears rapidly into the veil of the misty waters.

This absence of the figure of the asobi is continued further in *Shinsen rōeishū* (New selections of poems to sing), a later example of a two-volume collection of poems for singing styled after *Wakan rōeishū*. It was compiled by Fujiwara no Mototoshi (d. 1142), probably during the reign of Emperor Toba (1107–23). Among its 746 selections are four kanshi poems in its "Yūjo" section:

---

45. Ōe no Mochitoki. For notes to this poem, see *Yūjo wo miru*, above, from which these lines are extracted.

46. Minamoto no Shitagō (911–983).

1   In the south, the north, the east, the west, they do not fix a place to live
the wind and water are their hometown, their boats are their homes.

—"Yenshang fu" by Bo Juyi

2   Upon the eastern boat, upon the western boat, it is silent without
    a word spoken
only looking at the river's heart, the autumn moon is white.

—"Pipa yin" by Bo Juyi

3   Their houses sandwich the river from the south and north shores
their minds mingle with the high and low, the boats that come and go.

—"Yūjo no shi" by Igen

4   The cassia flowers in the autumn are white, the clouds over the quiet land
the reed leaves in the spring are green, the water is cold under the heavens.

—"Yūjo no shi" by Igen

The choice of these poems by the editor of *Shinsen rōeishū* suggests that at this later date, the images associated with the asobi had become even more oblique and focus no longer on the figure of a woman but on the materials that suggest her presence: the boat and the river. The word yūjo does not appear in any of the poems, and the only reference to the wandering lifestyle appears in the first poem by Bo Juyi. The second poem by Bo Juyi presents boats that hint at the presence of the yūjo, yet since other images in this poem are common in many Tang poems that are not associated with the yūjo, the connection becomes rather vague. There is a similar tendency in the two poems by Igen (Ōe no Mochitoki); the first refers specifically to the yūjo's lifestyle of entertaining people of various social classes on boats, but the second lacks any such images except for "water." The emphasis on the absence of the actual figure of the woman entertainer in poems, seen in the earlier *Wakan rōeishū*, is continued and taken a step further in this collection. This trend may indicate that the image of the asobi had dissipated and become so vague that it was no longer identifiable, singular, and concrete, or that conversely, it had become so fixed that remote allusions were sufficient to allow people to conjure up a specific image.

Such tropes for women entertainers were not limited to kanshi, however; the imagery spilled over generic boundaries and produced a web of consequences. Waka poems associated with the asobi were influenced by the conventions developing in kanshi. The "Yūjo" section of *Wakan rōeishū* contains one waka poem whose author is not specifically identified as an asobi but is nevertheless associated with the asobi through its very inclusion in this section:

722　*shiranami no　　yosuru nagisa ni　　yo wo sugusu*
　　　　ama no ko nareba　　yado mo sadamezu
　　　At the beach　　where white waves wash ashore　　I spend my nights/life
　　　since I am the child of fisher folk　　my lodging is not fixed.

—A fisher's poem

This waka, despite its classification, does not mention the terms asobi or yūjo; rather, it refers to fisher folk. I propose that the association between a fisherwoman and the asobi/kugutsu trope is that the asobi were reputed to live by the water and the kugutsu were represented as not having a fixed place of residence. It seems, then, that the existence of these elements in a poem was a major reason for including this poem in the "Yūjo" section and that these characteristics were among those most obviously associated with these women.

Such strong ties among the imagery of boats as residence, the floating lifestyle, and women entertainers produced a network of fascinating associations. One prime example can be found in *Shinsen rōeishū*, which contains the following waka poem in its "Yūjo" section:

668　*kokoro kara　　ukitaru fune ni　　norisomete*
　　　　hitohi mo nami ni　　nurenu hi zo naki
　　　Of my own free will　　I have boarded　　a sad floating boat;
　　　since I boarded it first there is not a single day　　that I am not
　　　drenched by the waves.

—Komachi

It is interesting that a poem attributed to the famous poet Ono no Komachi (active mid-ninth century) was included in this section.[47] I address the relationship between Komachi and sexuality in more detail in Chapter 3. Here I mention only that by the time of the compilation of this collection, Komachi's reputation as an *irogonomi* (one who favors the ways of love) was becoming established; thus it is likely that the jump from her constructed figure to women whose profession was to favor love was not a significant leap. As for the poem itself, as seen in the case of kanshi poems in *Shinsen rōeishū*, it seems that images which came to be associated with the asobi, here the

---

47. This poem appears in the imperial anthology *Gosenshū* (ca. 950s).

boat and the waves, were the main reason for the inclusion of this poem in the "Yūjo" section. Both this example and the previous one from *Wakan rōei-shū* show that the tropes of the asobi as formulated in the realm of poetry had developed to the point where the presence of someone not directly named as an asobi but who shared some characteristics with them could create a strong relationship between the poem and the asobi. The developments I have traced in poetry, mainly kanshi, indicate not only that literary allusions and generic conventions played significant roles in the formation of tropes concerning women entertainers but also that the tropes themselves became increasingly diffuse and highly associative in character.

Kanbun "Records": Conflicting Views

A third genre, documents commonly classified as "historical records" and "diaries," was also written in the kanbun style. These texts usually consist of passages headed by the reign year, the month, and the day followed by an account of events on that particular date. The accounts are characterized by their unadorned, pithy style and are useful for examining how the asobi and kugutsu are treated in both official and private records, so that we may compare these treatments with those in more elaborate accounts such as *Yūjo no ki*. Unlike the latter, which is a consciously literary work that revels in its allusions to past texts, the former tend to lack such references and are more concerned with the details of specific events. This is, of course, not a claim that such "records" somehow describe an "objective reality" more accurately than do works such as *Shin sarugakuki*; the usefulness of the comparison lies in its revelation of conflicts and inconsistencies in the representations of women entertainers and the consequent illumination of the unevenness of the discourse. Certain details found in these records are consistent with the portrayals cited above, such as the liaisons between at least a select stratum of asobi women and aristocrats and the often-plentiful rewards these women received as payment for their performances.[48] There are, however, notable

---

48. There are numerous examples of such passages; one example is found in *Fusō ryakki*, a 30-volume work attributed to the priest Kōen (?–1169; he was a master of Hōnen) completed sometime between 1094 and 1107. It is a history from the reign of the mythical first emperor, Jimmu, to 1094, during Emperor Horikawa's reign. The entry dated the third year of Jian (1023), the twenty-ninth day of the tenth month, reads: "While we headed for Eguchi, the traveling women entertainers came floating down on their boats and offered songs. Moved by the advertisement of their talent, it was ordered that 100 *koku* of Sanuki rice be given to them"

contradictions between these records and the prose works mentioned earlier; the differences help illustrate the extent to which textual representations of women entertainers may be determined by the genres of writing in which they appear.

Chūyūki (Diary of the Nakamikado Minister of the Right), Fujiwara no Munetada's (1062–1141) diary covering the years 1087 to 1138, records that on the sixth day of the fourth month of the second year of Eikyū (1114), a group of kugutsu filed an official complaint with the *kebi'ishi* (guards/police) ministry that an official had injured one of them and plundered a horse and some cotton. This official was fired and jailed as a result of this complaint.[49] This entry suggests that the kugutsu had enough power not only to bring suit but also to win it and that they sometimes worked within the bureaucratic system to obtain their goals. Such a statement contradicts descriptions of the romanticized and Sinicized vision of the kugutsu's "free-floating" status in society presented in *Kairaishi no ki* and *Honchō mudaishi*; it suggests that those texts must be read as products of allusionistic layers and literary conventions. Also, a well-known passage in *Azuma kagami* (Mirror of the east) indicates that on the tenth day of the fifth month of the fourth year of

---

(Mosume, *Shinchū kogaku sōsho*, 6: 364). This passage shows that the asobi were rewarded for their performance with goods such as rice, and rather plentifully in this case. That they were paid well for their performances is evident from other records as well, including the passage in Minamoto no Morotoki's (1077–1136) *Chōshūki* (records events between 1111 and 1136) dated the second year of Gen'ei (1119), the ninth month. On the third day, Morotoki describes the frolicking between asobi women and courtiers on boats well into the night. The names of asobi and their patrons are given, and there is a sense that the services and talents of these women were received with enthusiasm. The entry for the sixth day contains the following passage: "On the sixth day, we left Kanzaki, and at Takahama we summoned six asobi and gave them rewards for their performances. We granted the chōja Kinju three robes and a single-layer robe, to Kumano, Eguchi, and Iyo, we granted three robes, and to Hiwa (of Eguchi) and Wazuru [we granted] each one robe. Aside from these the governor of Iyo gave rice and such" (Kawamata, *Shiryō taisei*, pp. 160–61). These passages again indicate that courtiers were routinely entertained by the asobi, who advertised their own skills and delivered performances. This resulted in the asobi's reception of customary rewards such as clothes and rice from their patrons.

49. Amino, "Chūsei no tabibito tachi," p. 176. Amino also mentions that a group of kugutsu took a *zasshō* (an administrator of *shōen* estate finances) to court in 1249 and won the case, which shows that they were not just free-floating outcasts; at least some of them not only managed inns but also practiced farming and were able to work within the governmental system to gain a victory when their rights were violated (see Amino, "Asobi tachi no kyozō to jitsuzō," p. 71).

Kenkyū (1193), Minamoto no Yoritomo (1147–1199) appointed Satomi Yoshinari (n.d.) as the *bettō* to oversee the affairs of the asobi; this record has been cited as evidence that the asobi had official ties with the government, which recognized them as professionals.[50] This passage dates from a somewhat later period than the writings of Masafusa and his predecessors; however, since the impact of the latter remain strong in present-day scholarship on women entertainers, it is important to keep in mind the ambiguity of the trope of the asobi as amorphous groups of river wanderers.

Another example that contests the representation of women entertainers in both kanbun essays and kanshi can be found in *Ryōjin hishō kudenshū* (Collection of oral transmissions concerning *Secret Handbook of Dust on the Beams*; ca. 1169–85). Although this is not a kanbun text, I discuss it here since it contains a passage that directly challenges the depiction of these women in the Chinese-style works I have already examined. As noted above, the ominous fates of both the asobi and kugutsu in their later years are repeatedly invoked in kanbun and kanshi works. *Shin sarugakuki* poses the rhetorical question: "Ah, while she is still young, she may pass her days selling herself, but after her colors fade, how will she spend the rest of her life?" Poems in *Honchō mudaishi* titled "Kugutsu" contain passages such as "customers en route and travelers on their way avert their eyes in pity from afar, / this is indeed due to hair that is white and a face empty and wrinkled." In striking contrast, *Ryōjin hishō kudenshū* tells of the relationship between Minamoto no Kiyotsune (n.d.), the maternal grandfather of the traveling monk-poet Saigyō (1118–90), and a famed imayō song-master named Mei. The passage states that he had so lost interest in her as a lover that her eyelashes touching his back made him shudder, but because he valued her remarkable singing skills, he still lived with her and cared for her until her death, even after she had become a nun.[51] Mei's story provides an answer to Akihira's question above: after her "colors fade" and she ceases to possess sexual capital, it is still possible for a woman entertainer to spend the rest of her life with her patron who takes care of her needs until her last days—provided that her singing skills are outstanding. Although this story is called a rare case no longer seen in the era of *Ryōjin hishō*, it illustrates the power that could be exerted by a singer in retaining her ties with her patron, so that she can continue to live a

50. Ibid., p. 182.
51. Kobayashi Yoshinori et al., *Ryōjin hishō, Kanginshū, Kyōgen kayō*, p. 162.

secure life. A little later in the same work, Kiyotsune lectures a disciple, Otomae, when she complained about the constant singing in her training:

Why do you despise songs so much? When you are young, you can be like this, but when you grow old and there is no one to pay attention to you, since [songs] are things that never disappear from the world, there may be some upper-class nobles who favor songs who, when they have doubts about the way a song is sung, may come calling on you, saying, "Such-and-such person might know." Only if [you] know the art of song can [you] have such things happen [to you after you grow old].[52]

Fortunate old age is indeed what Otomae found when the retired emperor Goshirakawa summoned her to become his teacher; their relationship is discussed in much greater detail in Chapter 2.

The crucial point is that the trope of the desolate, abandoned woman entertainer found in kanbun and kanshi works presents only one side of the discourse about these women. The predictions concerning these women's waning fortunes are based on a single aspect of their livelihood: their sexuality; in making pronouncements about the futures of these women, the authors of these texts ignore the other equally vital part of the asobi's and kugutsu's occupations—their singing. These two skills should be considered as intricately linked and strategically invoked powers possessed by women entertainers—one is not subordinate to the other, and an entertainer could utilize both skills in varying degrees at different stages in her life in order to secure a living. *Ryōjin hishō kudenshū* thus permits us to see clearly not only the emphasis on the sexuality of women entertainers in Chinese-style essays and poems but also the overall constructedness of these figures. *Kudenshū*, however, is in turn a highly motivated text that presents women entertainers in a particular light, as we shall soon see.

THE ASOBI IN SETSUWA: TWO CONTRASTING VIEWS

The ideas that women are sinful beings and that women's sexuality is sinful appear often in Japanese Buddhist-inspired literature of the late Heian to the early Kamakura periods. In the case of the asobi in particular, I noted above that scholars have tended to assume that their sinfulness was a given, due to their explicit association with sexuality. I now re-examine this

---

52. Ibid., p. 163.

assumption by turning first to a group of setsuwa stories that contradict the "sinful" portrayal of asobi. In these texts, an asobi is shown to have direct access to the divine through her performance of an imayō song. Although these texts empower these women by noting their association with the divine, the works also exhibit the complexities of such empowerment, for the extreme privileging of women's sexuality can also be read as a projection of male desires to co-opt the asobi and their powers into the Buddhist realm. I then focus on textual examples from the same era that explicitly present the asobi as sinful beings for different reasons. A declaration of "sinfulness," however, is not a universal or "objective" description; rather, these works indicate that the use of the concept of sin in the context of women's sexuality can be a strategic move by an author to promote or denounce certain Buddhist paradigms and that "sinfulness" was neither an inherent nor an essential quality of sexuality. In other words, I question the proposition that the sin of women's sexuality, and therefore the sinfulness of the asobi women, was a monolithic and universal tenet in late Heian society and instead suggest that women's sexuality was presented as a sin at specific moments for specific purposes.

An important concept in the marginalization of women entertainers is that of "sinfulness"; expressions of denigration repeatedly describe them as particularly "deep in sin," as we will see in some of the examples below. Here this term is not used in the Christian sense of "sin" but as the translation of the term *tsumi*, which emerged as a significant concept in Buddhism, especially among the discourses of the Pure Land. This term has many definitions: crime, evil, acts that violate human norms, things that good people criticize, transgressions of the regulations set by a king, acts such as killing living things and telling lies, the harming of a lay person by a practicing monk/nun, the punishment for evil deeds, and suffering. Overall, it describes deeds criticized by most groups that claim to follow the Buddha.[53] Tsumi, like marginality, which it helps to define, is a construction born out of a particular matrix of ideologies and refers to actions or ways of existence condemned by them. Again, who is condemning whom to support what kinds of thinking is important here; tsumi is a malleable and changeable concept, not a universal, pre-existing condition. As I hope to show, "sinfulness" was ascribed to the asobi/kugutsu for motivated reasons at specific

---

53. Nakamura Hajime, *Bukkyōgo daijiten*, pp. 450–51, 973.

times, and it was by no means an essential definition of these women in the historical period under examination.

The essential quality of the asobi's "sinfulness" is already suspect from one of the earliest mentions of the asobi, frequently cited by scholars who study these women. The text is *Wamyō ruijushō* (A lexicon of Japanese readings of words), a dictionary compiled by Minamoto no Shitagō (911–83) around 931–38, which contains an entry on the asobi. The oldest edition containing this entry dates from sometime in the Kamakura period (the Shinpukuji edition); it lists different aliases and categories within or related to the asobi profession.[54] The entry distinguishes between the asobi, who "wander about" during the day, and the *yahochi*, who practice "lewd activities" at night. The passage could be construed as a reference to the distinction between "day shifts" and "night shifts," but since the word "wander" is not as explicit as "lewd," this distinction might suggest that the asobi were associated broadly with the state of wandering and not just with sexual deeds, as were the yahochi. Why, then, were the asobi called "sinful"—even to the extent that their represented figures in texts implicate themselves as being "sinful"? I explore possible answers to this question below.

The Chōja at Kanzaki as the Incarnation of Bodhisattva Fugen

In two setsuwa stories, Shōkū *shōnin* (holy person) desires to worship a "living bodhisattva" and goes to see the chōja (leader) of an asobi group in Kanzaki, who reveals herself to be the incarnation of the bodhisattva Fugen (Samantabhadra). These stories are significant for their topic, the asobi as a deity, their relative lack of negative views of the asobi's social status, and the portrayal of the asobi's ability to achieve ōjō (rebirth after death in the Pure Land) through the singing of imayō songs. These narratives portray the asobi as a powerful and active agent in the invocation of the divine. The two stories present the same plot in contrasting ways, and I argue that the differences stem from the context of each work.

The first example is from *Kojidan* (A discussion of past matters), a six-volume setsuwa collection compiled by Minamoto no Akikane (d. 1215) around 1212–15. The work contains many passages selected from previous

---

54. Kyōto daigaku, Bungakubu, Kokugogaku kokubungaku kenkyūjo, *Shohon shūsei Wamyō ruijushō (honbun hen)*, p. 539.

setsuwa collections and is characterized by a lack of commentaries by the author. Chapter 3, Story 95, tells the following tale:

The shōnin at Shosha (Shōkū) prayed that he might behold a living bodhisattva. A dream oracle said, "If you desire to behold a living bodhisattva, go see the leader of the asobi at Kanzaki." And thus, overjoyed, he went to Kanzaki. When he came upon the house of the leader, the current crowd had gathered and were in the middle of a rowdy banquet. The leader sat at the side, holding the *tsuzumi* drum, and beat the first phrase of the *ranbyōshi* dance. The lyrics went, "At the Mitarai shores in Murozumi along the Suō sea / the winds do not blow, but little waves rise." At this moment, the shōnin materialized strange thoughts, and as he slept and put his hands together in prayer, this asobi leader appeared in the form of Fugen. Riding a six-tusked white elephant, shining forth a light from between her brows, [she] cast light upon people both monk and lay. [She] said in an indescribably wondrous voice, "In the great ocean of Truth and the Undefiled, even though the winds of the Five Dusts and Six Desires do not blow, there is not a moment when the waves of various relations and True Suchness do not rise." At this time, the shōnin worshipped and showed respect, and wiped away tears of emotion. When he opened his eyes, [she] returned to the form of a woman, playing "Murozumi Along the Suō Sea." When he closed his eyes, [she] appeared again in the shape of the bodhisattva and performed the dharma text. After paying respects like this several times, the shōnin left for home in tears. At this time, this leader suddenly arose from her seat and came chasing after the shōnin through an alley. She instructed him, saying, "Do not speak about this to anyone." After saying this, she died immediately. At this time, the sky was filled with an extraordinary fragrance, it is said. Since the leader suddenly died, the banquet's spirits fell, it is said.[55]

The chōja in this story not only achieves ōjō after finishing her imayō performance, but in the closed eyes of Shōkū, she appears in the form of Fugen, or the bodhisattva Samantabhadra. The song that the leader sings plays a crucial role in her transformation into a bodhisattva in the eyes of Shōkū. The imayō lyrics induce a trance-like state in Shōkū, and the lyrics, which echo the Buddhist prayer, themselves also undergo transformation into a Buddhist chant. What is crucial in this example is the role of the imayō song—here clearly, because of its meter, not a waka poem made into a song; it is presented prominently and unambiguously. There is no effort to hide the significance of the imayō here as the catalyst of both the asobi's transformation and Shōkū's sacred vision.

---

55. Kobayashi Yasuharu, *Kojidan*, 1: 303–4.

Why is the power of imayō represented so clearly here? A clue might be found in figure of Shōkū (910?–1007). He is well known for his association with the poet Izumi Shikibu (977?–1036?), who is said to have addressed her famous poem "kuraki yori . . . " to him; interestingly enough, this poem appears in the Muro asobi's story in *Hosshinshū*, which is discussed in the next section of this chapter. This suggests that a number of stories about the asobi form an interconnected web. Although officially Shōkū is identified as a monk of the Tendai sect since he is believed to have been a disciple of Ryōgen (912–85), he is also reputed to have been a *hijiri*, a "holy man" wandering ascetic, who was based on Mt. Shosha in Harima province. He appears in various setsuwa stories that note his unconventional ways, including volume 12 of *Konjaku monogatari* (Tales of times now past) and the middle volume of *Honchō hokke genki* (Accounts of auspicious signs of the Lotus Sutra in our country); he is often portrayed as an eccentric figure. The significance of his presence in the *Kojidan* story is the relatively unorthodox nature of his practice; since he was not a promoter of the nenbutsu, for example, he had no particular stake in denying the asobi's powers of imayō ōjō and replacing it with another path to ōjō. In other words, Shōkū's practices are not presented as being in conflict with imayō ōjō, whereas the chanting of the nenbutsu was often positioned as being in direct opposition to it, as we will see below.

This passage is also marked by the lack of judgmental comments by the narrator concerning the fact that an asobi is an incarnation of the bodhisattva Fugen; the story is told matter-of-factly, without overt descriptions of the moral character of any of the figures that appear. In fact, when the dream oracle tells Shōkū to go see the asobi leader, his reaction is simply described as happiness, not surprise. Even when the leader changes into Samantabhadra, the tone of the narration remains constant. This narrative, then, is characterized by the non-condemnatory presentation of the powers of imayō and of the sacred quality of the chōja.

Shōkū's story, however, later underwent transformations. One example is found in *Jikkinshō* (Ten lessons explained; ca. 1252; for a translation, see the Appendix, pp. 301–2), a three-volume collection of setsuwa stories compiled by an unknown individual who served the Hōjō regime and took the tonsure later in life. The introduction declares the text's intentions as a piece of didactic literature aimed at youngsters, mainly of the newly risen ruling *bushi* (military) class, and indicates that the author compiled the work while passing the days as a recluse in the eastern mountains. *Jikkinshō* contains two stories about the asobi; one about the ōjō of an asobi named Toneguro, which is discussed in depth in the next chapter, and one about the encounter between Shōkū and the asobi leader (Chapter 3, Story 15) who is the incarnation of Fugen.

One immediately recognizable difference between this version of the story and the one in *Kojidan* is its length. The narration of the plot up to the death of the chōja is relatively similar although more detailed, but whereas the *Kojidan* version ends at the point of her expiration, *Jikkinshō*'s version continues with two distinct additions. The first is the narrator's commentary concerning the whole incident:

Since this woman, the leader, was the kind to favor the ways of love, who would have known that she was the incarnation of the bodhisattva? This example shows that the compassionate vow of the buddhas and bodhisattvas [is such that] they use *upāya* (expedient means) to teach sentient beings, and they take various forms to instruct; these forms are not base.

The second addition, which immediately follows the comment above, chronicles the interactions of the monks Shōkū, Eshin, and Danna:

This shōnin (Shōkū) is a person of no learning. When the Junior Archbishop Eshin [= Genshin] and Archbishop Danna [= Gaku'un] came over to discuss the dharma text, to their question "Can the person who attains enlightenment alone reach the place of the Buddha?" he answered, "To reach or not to reach, this does not matter; it is profitless [to ask]." When they said, "Only by debating the dharma gate shall the eyes of wisdom open. We came because we thought that would not be possible in this kind of countryside." He answered, "This dharma gate was opened by Fugen, who came here." At this time, Eshin could not halt the thoughts to follow him in reverence and worship, so he prayed and said to Danna, "Recite words of praise for this hijiri."

> "The colors of my body are like the Golden Mountain
> orderly and majestic, it is indescribable.
> It is as if amidst pure lapis-lazuli
> the true golden image appears,"

so he recited and worshipped.[56]

This narrative is also found in *Kojidan*, but in a separate story (Chapter 3, Story 24). The story in the *Jikkinshō*, then, is a combination, augmentation, and variation of two *Kojidan* stories.

---

56. Izumi, *Jikkinshō*, pp. 59–60; Kawamura, *Jikkinshō zenchūyaku*, pp. 189–94.

Even though the basic elements of the story in the first half, such as the chōja's appearance as Fugen, her performance of an imayō song that precipitates Shōkū's vision, and her ōjō, are similar to those found in *Kojidan*, there are several important differences. For example, *Jikkinshō's* story about Shōkū and the chōja contains clear expressions of moral judgment by the narrator concerning the status of the asobi. They appear in two places: Shōkū's surprise after the dream oracle, and the passage immediately following the death of the chōja cited above that begins "since this woman, the leader, was the kind to favor the ways of love." Whereas in *Kojidan*, Shōkū is described as being "overjoyed" at his dream oracle and apparently goes to visit the chōja at Kanzaki without any reservations, the Shōkū of *Jikkinshō* wakes up from the dream and considers it "strange." These comments suggest that it is unusual to be told that an asobi could be a living bodhisattva. The narrator's comments following the achievement of ōjō by the chōja, as indicated by the extraordinary fragrance after her death, are not found in *Kojidan* and are crucial in illuminating the critical views of the narrator: this incident was truly unexpected and unusual, and those who favor the ways of love are far from being likely candidates for incarnations of a bodhisattva. Such pronouncements might be rooted in the compiler's declared practice of chanting the nenbutsu.

As for the attachment of the story about Shōkū and Eshin at the end, it can be read as an attempt to illustrate the remarkable yet eccentric nature of Shōkū: he stays in the countryside and is visited by Fugen. The portrayal of him as a far-from-everyday, unusual figure reinforces the extraordinary aspect of the whole story; it implies that only such a special person can encounter or recognize such a rare occurrence.[57] This emphasizes the exceptional character of the chōja's being an incarnation of Fugen and the fact of her ōjō. By firmly positioning this incident in the realm of the extraordinary, this narrative relegates the asobi's associations with the divine to the level of a miraculous accident; it negates the possibility that an asobi could have regular interactions with the sacred or that imayō performances by asobi could consistently produce ōjō.

---

57. It is not clear whether the people attending the banquet are able to see the figure of Fugen; although the passage states that the light from between its eyebrows shone on everyone, the chōja appears as Fugen only when Shōkū's eyes are closed. The same situation exists in *Kojidan's* version, but the emphasis upon the "extraordinary" is not nearly as prominent in that story compared to *Jikkinshō's* version.

It is, however, important to note that despite these marginalizing tendencies, we do not find a stable, monolithic discourse of marginalization, one that completely delegitimizes the asobi's religious powers. Why might *Jikkinshō* have taken an approach in which the asobi are, on the one hand, frowned upon as women who "favor the ways of love," yet, on the other hand, raised as a worthy example of remarkable instances of ōjō? One answer to this question can be found in the textual claims of the collection as a whole. *Jikkinshō* presents the aesthetics and pastimes of the Heian court as a model for which one should strive, but it is also striking in its methodical portrayal of such skills as a means to advance one's political, social, and religious standing. The text states that talents in the literary and performing arts can help one attain one's goals and reap rewards, even if one is of lowly status such as the asobi and the kugutsu; such people who are adept at the art of singing or waka have been patronized by the upper class, and their poems have been included in imperial anthologies (Chapter 10, Story 50). In general, excelling at the arts is a convenient way to distinguish oneself from one's peers so that one is able to catch the attention of those in power: "Even those who are pleasing in appearance and are of high rank, if they stand next to a lowly but talented person, the former's rank and appearance will become insignificant"[58] (Chapter 10, Introduction).

Within this framework, the (supposed) cultural legacies of the Heian court become something that a young man should cultivate for his own advancement; this opportunistic attitude may have been appropriate during the turbulent period following the Jōkyū disturbance (1221).[59] The possibility of attaining prominence in one public arena or another suits the concerns of the text's audience, the military class; if there was a sense that they had power but not "culture" or hereditary "rank," the claim that "culture" could be learned and that one's talents could overpower "rank" legitimized the ruling position of the military class within society: "The bushi must be the leaders during times in which disarray must be brought to order; thus their status is equal to that of literary scholars."[60] What better way to illustrate the potential for fluid social, political, and religious mobility based solely on the powers of one's talents than by citing an asobi who possesses both performative skills and religious power? The *Jikkinshō* case illustrates how the

---

58. Asami, *Jikkinshō*, p. 386.

59. Geddes, *A Partial Translation and Study of the "Jikkinshō,"* p. 86.

60. Asami, *Jikkinshō*, p. 446.

interests of the male bushi class can intersect with the empowerment of women entertainers; the motivations behind marginalization and legitimization are complex and sometimes unexpected.

Overall, these stories about the asobi chōja at Kanzaki and Shōkū's encounter with her illustrate two significant trends in the portrayal of the asobi women in literature. First, as noted above, neither attempts to replace the crucial role of imayō singing in attaining ōjō. Second, these stories reveal that the motivations of the compiler have a significant influence on how the story is told and give the stories different flavors. The compiler of *Kojidan* made no declaration of didactic intentions or overt ties to Pure Land Buddhism, such as having taken the tonsure or chanting the nenbutsu. In other words, even though the collection is interested in Buddhist practices in general, it does not exhibit a devotion to nenbutsu in particular; this factor is likely to have contributed to *Kojidan*'s non-judgmental presentation of events. On the other hand, although *Jikkinshō*'s narrative marginalizes the asobi at one level, the collection's constant interest in promoting "talent" and "ability" as key factors in upward mobility tempers the marginalization process and affirms the empowering portrayal of the woman entertainer as a powerful religious icon.

The Asobi at Muro

The mid-Heian to the early Kamakura periods also saw the appearance of a cluster of stories in which an asobi at a place called Muro either renounces her lifestyle or expresses remorse about her existence even though she eventually attains ōjō. These stories commend the asobi for her decision to stop practicing her occupation, and their overall tone is didactic—even such a "sinful" person as an asobi is able to attain ōjō if she devotes herself to *particular* Buddhist practices. I emphasize "particular" here, since it is the key to unraveling the representations of the supposedly "sinful" asobi: on closer inspection, these narratives emerge as attempts to render the asobi's vehicle for enlightenment as an ineffective medium for communicating with the divine, while simultaneously offering alternative, apparently more powerful modes for achieving the same goal, such as the chanting of the nenbutsu.[61] As men-

---

61. Abe Yasurō ("Seizoku no tawamure to shite no geinō," p. 185) has suggested that texts about Hōnen dating from the early fourteenth century were designed to promote nenbutsu at the expense of the asobi and their profession, both sexual and artistic; the current discussion

tioned above, the act of song-singing was understood as being a vital part of the asobi's profession and was often regarded as a direct method for achieving rebirth in the Pure Land. By dismissing this power of song and portraying the women who perform such songs as "sinful" beings who require the assistance of others to secure a positive place in the Buddhist realm, these stories attempt to dismantle the effectiveness of song-singing and assert the superiority of other practices that were—or were hoping to establish themselves as—more mainstream.

The depiction of the asobi as "sinful" beings who must rely on Buddhist practices other than the one they perform professionally and regularly in order to attain ōjō challenged and tried to negate the group of texts discussed above in which the asobi is able to evoke the sacred by singing imayō songs. One could argue that those who had an interest in promoting other specific Buddhist practices had a stake in downplaying, if not destroying, the image of the asobi powerful enough to attain ōjō simply through singing imayō songs, since such direct access to ōjō posed a challenge to both established and nascent Buddhist orders and their supporters. Scholars have argued that the asobi had a prominent role in religious activities; in this light, the denial of their powers within the Buddhist context could be extended to the denial of their religious powers overall. For example, Toyonaga Satomi suggests that the asobi chōja may have been responsible for the maintenance of local deities, especially the hyakudayū; there seems to have been intricate power relationship between these women and local individuals and eminent families.[62] It has also been suggested that the asobi originated from miko,[63] but this theory remains mostly speculative in that it relies on somewhat tenuous connections between depictions and comments in pre- and early Heian sources (such as Ame no Uzume's dance in the *Kojiki* [A chronicle of past matters]) and those in later texts. What is significant here is that the Buddhist discourses of marginalization did discredit such possibilities for women entertainers. The "marginalized" and "sinful" asobi found in the texts to follow, then, are not "proof" of a static "feminine margin"; rather, they are charged figures embroiled in battles among competing Buddhist practices.

---

attests to the extent and complexity of the conflict between nenbutsu, Pure Land discourse, and the asobi in earlier centuries.

62. Toyonaga, "Chūsei ni okeru asobi no chōja ni tsuite," pp. 408, 421.

63. See Nakayama, *Baishō sanzen-nen shi*; and Gorai, "Chūsei jōsei no shūkyōsei to seikatsu."

Kamo no Chōmei's (1155?–1216) *Hosshinshū* (An anthology for awakening the desire for the Buddhist path) is thought to have been compiled in the late twelfth century, slightly later than *Ryōjin hishō*; it includes a narrative about an asobi from a place called Muro. The following passage is found in Chapter 6, Story 10:

The matter of an asobi of the inn at Muro singing a lewd song and tying the Buddhist knot of relation with the shōnin (holy person).

In the Middle [Past], there was a person called Shōshō hijiri.[64] On the night that he happened to be staying at a place called Muro in Harima province, as the moon was shining bright and beautiful, the asobi began to sing songs one after another as they came and went. [He] looked on, thinking "how moving and pitiable!" when a certain asobi aboard a boat came rowing over toward the hijiri's boat. The [hijiri's] oarsman reprimanded, "How dare you, this is a monk's boat; have you lost your mind?" Saying, "I see that [it is a monk's boat]; how could I have overlooked something like that?" [the asobi] beat her tsuzumi drum and sang this song two or three times:

> *kuraki yori   kuraki michi nizo   irinubeki*
> *haruka ni terase   yama no ha no tsuki*
> From the darkness   into a path of darkness   I must enter;
> shine all the way afar   moon at the mountain's edge.

She said, "That I am of such deep sins is due to deeds in my past life. It seems that this world is going to end as a dream. Please be certain to save [me]. Even though this is a small token, I wish to tie a Buddhist knot of relation with you," then rowed away. Afterwards, [the hijiri] said to other people, "It was so [sadly] moving, I could not help the tears falling."[65]

At first glance, this narrative is strongly characterized by expressions of criticism and disdain concerning the asobi; these occur at three levels: the narrator (in the title), the oarsman in the story, and the asobi herself. However, although this passage appears superficially to represent a straightforward marginalization of the asobi, a detailed examination reveals certain nuances that resist a simple reading. The criticisms are strategically voiced in an attempt to render one method of religious salvation superior to another.

First, the passage is ambivalent. The oarsman's hostile reaction to the approach of the asobi's boat stems from the fact that his passenger is a Buddhist monk. His angry words therefore may owe less to her social position in

---

64. Minamoto no Tokinobu, active around 1013.
65. Miki, *Hōjōki/Hosshinshū*, pp. 280–81.

general than to the belief that monks were not supposed to patronize prostitutes. This interpretation is reinforced by an example from *Kojidan*, in which a lay person who used to patronize a particular asobi is embarrassed by her presence after he takes the tonsure (Chapter 2, Story 6). Second, throughout *Hosshinshū* women as a category, not just the asobi, are portrayed as beings deep in sin.[66] Since the words "deep in sin" in this story are found elsewhere in the collection, it cannot be assumed that this criticism is aimed only at the asobi and her profession in particular. Finally, the extant editions of the *Hosshinshū* date from the Edo period, and the variations among the editions suggest that many changes were made in the text since the time of Chōmei.[67] This is especially important when considering that "lewd song," the most obvious moral judgment about the asobi and their art, appears in the title of the story. Evidence elsewhere in this work suggests that the title of the story may have been added at a later date.[68] The title is not necessarily a reliable indicator of Chōmei's or his contemporaries' views. These issues suggest that the attitudes of the author and/or speaker concerning the asobi should not be taken completely at face value.

The clearly critical elements of the text are strategically presented. This story depicts an asobi in the act of singing a song, presumably an imayō, which she explains as an offering to the monk so that she may tie a Buddhist knot of relation. The motion of song-singing, then, is presented as a mere element in a sacred transaction: for the "payment" of performance-as-capital, she receives, in exchange, the services of a (male) monk who will "save" her and therefore act as a broker in placing her in a better light within the Buddhist matrix. Song-singing is here tamed from an act that communicates directly with the sacred (as we will see in Chapter 2) to an offering to a human agent with access to sacrality. This textual maneuver becomes especially poignant in view of the stories described above in which an asobi evokes the sacred and attains ōjō through the singing of imayō songs. In those stories,

---

66. See, e.g., Chapter 5, Story 2, "Koreie and His Consort's Attainment of Ōjō in Sudden Death," and Chapter 5, Story 3, "The Story of a Mother Who Became Jealous of Her Daughter . . . ," and Chapter 6, Story 13, "The Story of Jōtōmon'in's Lady-in-Waiting Who Lived Deep in the Mountains . . . ."

67. Miki, *Hōjōki/Hosshinshū*, pp. 416–17.

68. The title of Chapter 5, Story 2, names the protagonist as "Koreie," even though in the body of the story itself he is only identified as "some sort of *ben* (controller), I have heard, but I have forgotten his name." This suggests, as indicated by the annotator, that the title was added at a later time by another person (Miki, *Hōjōki/Hosshinshū*, pp. 204–6).

imayō is a vehicle that permits an asobi to attain ōjō without the aid of any-one else, but in *Hosshinshū* the asobi needs assistance in achieving salvation.

The identity of the male protagonist, Shōshō, is also significant in con-sidering the reasons behind the asobi's gesture of portrayed subservience. He was born Minamoto no Tokinobu and had attained the rank of Minor Captain before taking the tonsure; he was active around 1013 as a Tendai monk and established Shōrin-in in Ōhara. The crucial detail of his religious piety is that he was known as a practitioner of *shōmyō*, the ritual singing of Buddhist texts such as sutras and dhāraṇī.[69] He represented, then, a perfor-mative Buddhist practice that was different from, if not in competition with, the performative ōjō-inducing art of imayō that was embodied by the asobi. By presenting a story in which an asobi, possessor of imayō, expresses defer-ence and yields to the powers of Shōshō, who is associated with Tendai and shōmyō, Chōmei's collection argues for the superiority of the latter, more established, male mode of performative Buddhism over the less orthodox, female mode of religious performance and ōjō. The relative dating of *Hosshinshū* and *Ryōjin hishō* (particularly the *Kudenshū* section) reveals an in-teresting picture: *Ryōjin hishō* presumably preceded Chōmei's work, and as we will see in the next chapter, the compiler Goshirakawa was a practitioner of shōmyō but ultimately declared imayō singing a wondrous and rightful method for achieving ōjō. In other words, even though Goshirakawa did not compare the two oral performance forms directly, the fact that the culmina-tion of his lifelong devotion to performing arts and Buddhist practices is a collection of imayō songs and a treatise on them, not shōmyō, suggests that he championed imayō as a special and effective method for enlightenment. If Chōmei sought to counter Goshirakawa's privileging of imayō in order to promote Tendai and Pure Land discourses, then a story in which asobi and their imayō songs play second fiddle to the powers of an established male monk was a convenient means for achieving his goal.

The song the asobi sings is a famous waka poem, said to have been com-posed by Izumi Shikibu, a prominent and prolific female poet who served at court and gained a reputation as a woman of many affairs. This poem is in-cluded in volume 20 of the waka anthology *Shūishū* (An anthology of waka gleanings; compiled 1005), and Chōmei was clearly aware of it, for he in-cludes a discussion of this poem in his work of waka criticism, *Mumyōshō*

---

69. Sōgō bukkyō daijiten henshū iinkai, *Sōgō bukkyō daijiten*, 1: 762.

(Nameless notes).[70] In a debate over the poetic merits and faults of Izumi Shikibu and Akazome Emon (ca. 960s–1040s), another famous woman poet, he argued that Izumi Shikibu was a talented poet but that her less-than-positive reputation makes her pale in comparison to Akazome Emon as a person; he then cited a passage from *Murasaki Shikibu nikki* (Murasaki Shikibu diary) that describes Izumi Shikibu's personality.[71] The reason for the appearance of this particular poem/song here may be twofold. First, the introductory passage to this poem in *Shūishū* indicates that Izumi Shikibu addressed this poem to the monk Shōkū, the protagonist of the asobi-as-Fugen narratives. Like the asobi in the *Hosshinshū* story, she is said to have been seeking to tie a knot of Buddhist relation with him. Second, by this time, Izumi Shikibu had gained a reputation as a person with deep "sins" who was nevertheless able to achieve ōjō. This attribute may have aligned her with the asobi women in the mind of Chōmei. These characteristics associated with this poem had been or were in the process of being established by the late twelfth century. For example, *Mumyō zōshi* (Nameless writings; around 1198–1202?), a critique of *monogatari* narratives by the Daughter of Fujiwara no Shunzei (around 1170?–1252?), states that Izumi Shikibu had sent this poem to the monk Shōkū, who then gave her his *kesa* surplice in return; she sees this gift right before her death. The passage reads:

To the place of the hijiri at Mt. Shosha,

> *kuraki yori   kuraki michi nizo   irinubeki*
> *haruka ni terase   yama no ha no tsuki*
> From the darkness   into a path of darkness   I must enter;
> shine all the way afar   moon at the mountain's edge.

So she composed and sent it. [He] sent her no reply, but a kesa surplice instead. It was after seeing it that she died.

When I hear that it was due to this incident that Izumi Shikibu, a person who must have been deep in sin, was able to be saved in her next life [i.e., achieved ōjō], I feel envious beyond all things.[72]

The presence of this famous poem by Izumi Shikibu in this story, then, alludes to the supposed circumstances of the composition of this poem and to the attributes of the poet herself, which emphasize the dedicatory, help-

---

70. Miki, *Hōjōki/Hosshinshū*, p. 281n11.
71. Yanase, *Kamo no Chōmei zenshū*, pp. 74–80.
72. Kuwabara, *Mumyō zōshi*, p. 114.

seeking aspect of the asobi's song/poem, as well as her irogonomi (love-favoring) tendencies.

The figure of the asobi at Muro appears in different guises in later collections, and her abandonment of song-singing and resulting direct access to divinity becomes even more blatant in some works. One example is *Kankyo no tomo* (A friend in a recluse life; ca. 1222; for a translation, see the Appendix, pp. 303–4), attributed to the priest Keisei (1189–1268). This story concerns a repentant asobi's self-sacrifice. The Middle Counselor Kenki (Minamoto no Akimoto, 1000–1047) casts his favors on a certain asobi from Muro, but their affair comes to an end, and she returns to her family in Muro. She thereupon renounces her occupation and "purifies her mind and chants the nenbutsu prayer" to such an extent that she ignores her household duties and her family begins to decline. The impoverished woman has no means to carry out the proper Buddhist rituals and offerings after her mother's death; in order to secure funds, she resorts to her former profession by selling her services to a man who happens to be a low-ranking retainer of her former patron. Afterwards, she immediately performs the requisite services and becomes a nun. The Middle Counselor hears of the matter and sheds tears.[73]

The text is obviously didactic in tone and forthrightly and literally marginalizes the asobi as a category by describing them as leading a "peripheral existence." The details of the representations in this particular story, however, are crucial in analyzing how and why such marginalization occurs. First, the passage focuses on a particular type of Buddhist practice as an exemplary mode of conduct: the "reformed" asobi chants the nenbutsu, and the fact that she became a nun and "secured a quiet place and followed Buddhist practices strictly" is clearly foregrounded. These two aspects—the chanting of the nenbutsu and becoming a nun—contradict the portrayals in other texts of the capabilities of the asobi. The women in those tales perform imayō songs (not the nenbutsu) and can evoke the divine and attain enlightenment in their very bodies (without having to become nuns). In *Kankyo no tomo*, the privileging of the nenbutsu and nunhood is plainly established at the expense of the asobi's ability to achieve ōjō by practicing her profession. Second, the narrator spends a significant amount of time marveling that such a woman renounced this world. This act of piety, however, is credited

---

73. Koizumi et al., *Hōbutsushū, Kankyo no tomo, Hirasan kojin reitaku*, pp. 419–21.

not to the asobi's own potential for goodness but to the influence of the Middle Counselor: the last passage suggests that he had begun to express a waning of his interest in her precisely in order to bring forth "the color of enlightenment to a person who otherwise would never have awakened." In this manner, the asobi not only is barred from unassisted communication with the divine while still in her secular manifestation but also is represented as incapable of generating her own desire to renounce the world in the manner endorsed by the narrator. Through these maneuvers, the woman entertainer is virtually stripped of the powers of agency: she becomes merely a passive receiver of assistance and influence.

The main elements of the story are the filial asobi, the remarkableness of her developing *hosshin* (the desire to follow the Buddhist path) when many women succumb to resentful attachment, and the power of the Middle Counselor to bring about this miracle. This story speaks from a clear stance concerning the asobi: they are sinful, and their activity is regrettable, but they may be commended if they stop engaging in their sinful activities and develop hosshin. Yet when we consider *Kankyo no tomo* in its entirety, we can again find other possible reasons for such statements as well as hidden ambivalences. The collection was intended as a didactic text for women, and women's activities in general are criticized throughout the text. The asobi, then, are by no means the only targets of moral judgment. Furthermore, the narrator states that the asobi in the story had refused to resume her old profession once she returned from the capital and concentrated on her Buddhist practices, and the fact that she entertained and probably engaged in prostitution with the retainer of the Middle Counselor is presented as a filial duty undertaken to obtain enough money to complete the proper Buddhist rituals after the death of her mother. Even the Middle Counselor is deeply moved on hearing this story. Even though the text denounces the profession of asobi, such activities may be permitted under certain circumstances, such as to fulfill a filial obligation and religious duty.

A later text that presents the trope of the asobi at Muro can be found in the setsuwa collection *Senjūshō*, which was compiled ca. 1250–70, by an unknown person (although it is often attributed to Saigyō). Story 3 in Chapter 3 (for a translation, see the Appendix, pp. 304–5) is similar to the *Kankyo no tomo* narrative: Middle Counselor Akimoto had ceased his relations with an asobi, she renounces her life to become a nun, she eventually achieves ōjō because of her association with that "extraordinary person," and the Middle

Counselor enables her enlightenment. The details differ significantly, however. Her mother does not appear, and consequently there is no story of filial
piety. The asobi does not conduct business with the Middle Counselor's retainer; on seeing him, she simply cuts off her hair and sends a waka poem
along with it. Her former lover sees the poem and is moved to tears. The
narrator is quite explicit about her devotion to the nenbutsu: "This nun did
nothing but chant the nenbutsu prayer night and day, and finally she attained the ōjō she had sought." In this example, there is a double attempt to
eradicate the association between asobi and imayō songs: the emphasis on
the oral performance of the nenbutsu minimizes other such religious vehi-
cles (such as the singing of imayō), and the insistence that the asobi wrote a
waka poem to give to the Middle Counselor through his retainer (that is, instead of performing it orally, as she did in the *Hosshinshū* text) takes the
power of oral performance away from her altogether. Orality is a crucial aspect of the asobi's practice of performing arts, as I will show in the next
chapter; negating this association can be interpreted as a final nullification of
their religious prowess.

These narratives concerning the asobi at Muro marginalize the asobi by
attributing sinfulness to them, minimize their inherent powers to attain ōjō,
and manipulate their figures in order to support the causes the texts promote, namely, Tendai and Pure Land Buddhist discourses and the practice
of nenbutsu. The view that the asobi were "sinful" continued and became
amplified in later periods, as seen, for example, in the noh play *Eguchi* (attributed to Kan'ami, 1332–84), in which the spirit of an asobi from Eguchi expresses remorse over her own sinfulness not only as a woman but particularly as an asobi.[74] Nevertheless, the texts exhibit uncertainty over the exact
reasons why an asobi could achieve ōjō. This ambiguity shows that their relationship with ōjō was debatable and unfixed, especially in light of the existence of stories of an asobi's achieving ōjō through imayō. The stories of

---

74. Specifically:

zaigō fukaki mi to umare   koto ni tameshi sukunaki kawatake no nagare no onna to naru
     saki no yo no mukui made   omoiyaru koso kanashikere.

born as one who is deep in sin [= a woman]   especially, that I have become
among them the rare woman of the floating bamboo [= an asobi];
     even to the karmic retribution from past lives   my thoughts reach, this is
     indeed so sad.

from *Eguchi*, in Koyama et al., *Yōkyokushū*, 1: 268.

"sinful" asobi represent only one of the many conflicting representations of the asobi in literature.[75]

CB

I have chosen a handful of textual examples that represent the asobi and kugutsu in order to highlight the heterogeneous, genre-bound, and motivated qualities of discourses about these women. Those texts that utilize Chinese-style writing, both prose and poetry, often construct representations of women entertainers based on layers of specific allusions traceable to Chinese literary sources. The varying fashions with which texts that do not exhibit such qualities depict the women suggest that the "marginal" asobi and kugutsu are a monolithic assumption. Setsuwa stories either marginalize or empower the asobi depending on the underlying religious or secular discourse they seek to advocate. There are, of course, numerous other instances in which women entertainers are mentioned, and I will end with brief discussions of selected works attributed to female authors in order to compare their depictions to those of their male counterparts examined above.

Yamato monogatari (Tales of Yamato; completed around 951, edited to the present state around 1000; for a translation, see the Appendix, p. 306) is a series of short vignettes centered around the composition of particular waka poems in courtly settings. Its author is not known but is speculated to have been a woman serving at court. Two of these stories present a woman entertainer's interaction with a retired emperor. In Section 145, an ukareme (another term for asobi) named Shiro is summoned by Emperor Uda (867–931) and succeeds in fulfilling his command that she compose a waka poem about a particular situation; the narrator states: "So she composed; [the emperor] was very much impressed and gave her rewards."[76] Section 146 also focuses on an asobi:

The Teiji emperor went to the villa at Torikai. As usual, there was a "play" [of music]. "Among the ukareme around here who are here in large numbers, is there one whose voice is charming and artistic?" [he] asked, and the ukareme answered, "One

---

75. For example, another noh play called Murogimi, attributed to Zeami (1363–1443?) or a member of his circle, is mainly a celebratory work, in which the kami (deity) at Muro appears to dance, lured by the singing and music of Murogimi, an asobi, and her company.

76. Katagiri et al., Taketori monogatari, Ise monogatari, Yamato monogatari, Heichū monogatari, p. 365.

called the daughter of Ōe no Tamabuchi is here in a rare appearance," so they said; thus [he] looked over and saw that her appearance seemed neat, and feeling moved, he had her draw nearer. He had her questioned, "Is this true?" and so on, and in this process had everyone compose a poem on the topic Torikai [bird-keeping/keeper]. He said to the ukareme, "Tamabuchi was quite adept at things, and composed poetry very well, for example. Depending on how well you can handle this topic, Torikai, I shall recognize you as his child," so he said. She agreed to this challenge, and immediately she composed:

> asamidori   kaiaru haru ni   ainureba
>   kasumi naranedo   tachinoborikeri
> in the pale-green shade   a worthy spring   I have found;
>   thus although I am not even haze   I have been able to rise.

At this time the emperor expressed his words of deep praise and shed tears. Since others were fairly drunk, they were even more prone to tears. The emperor granted her an *uchiki* robe and a divided skirt. "All high-ranking courtiers, princes, and low-ranking courtiers, those of you who do not remove a layer of your robes to give to this [woman], leave your seat immediately!" he said, thus in seated order those both high and low in rank all gave her [a layer of their robes]; she could not drape all of them across her shoulders, so she piled them up in two rooms. It went like this, and when [the emperor] was about to depart, there was one called Shichirōgimi of the Southern Palace, and since the emperor had heard that he had built a house near the place where this ukareme was living, he ordered him to look after her. "Pass on to the retired emperor the things that this [woman] requests. The things that the retired emperor gives will be passed on through Shichirōgimi. In all matters, make sure she does not see any suffering," he said, so [Shichirōgimi] always called on her and looked after her.[77]

These two passages illustrate the figure of the ukareme as perceived by the female author/compiler of this monogatari. Several aspects of the depiction are notable. First, the ukareme in both narratives express their recognition that their social status is far below those of the emperor and aristocrats. Second, despite this, the ukareme in story 146 is stated to be the daughter of Ōe no Tamabuchi, a provincial governor of Hyūga (or Tanba, according to some editions), whose great-uncle was the famous poet Ariwara no Narihira (825–80). The emperor is skeptical at first of her claimed origins, which must be proved through her skills at waka composition. Third, the adeptness of the ukareme women in both tales at composing waka poems is

77. Ibid., pp. 366–67.

greatly emphasized, and no mention is made of imayō. Fourth, they are rewarded abundantly for their skills. The emperor in story 146 orders an aristocrat to look after the woman entertainer for the rest of her life; this treatment could stem from her status as Tamabuchi's daughter, for which she deserved special attention, yet the story does establish that a fairly high-ranking official's daughter could be an ukareme. Overall, then, the position of the woman entertainer as seen in *Yamato monogatari* is clearly lower than that of courtiers, yet these women can be of aristocratic lineage, and some are highly commended for their poetic skills. Moreover, neither narrative makes critical comments about the nature of the woman entertainer's profession, or mentions "sinfulness." This passage shows that the ukareme can be associated solely with waka poetry without marginalization: in the Muro narratives, waka were ascribed to the asobi in order to erase the religious threat of imayō, but in *Yamato monogatari*, Tamabuchi's daughter uses her skills in waka composition to secure her livelihood.

A mid-Heian diary, *Sarashina nikki* (Sarashina diary), which was written by the Daughter of Sugawara no Takasue (1008–after 1059), also mentions the narrator's encounters with asobi women and their performances in two separate passages. The first describes her memory of a meeting with three asobi women in her childhood travels:

At the place called Mount Ashigara, a frightening dark path continued for four to five days. Even when I finally reached the foot of the mountain, I could not see the sky too well, and it was just so dense with foliage that I found it quite frightening. When I was staying at an inn at the foot of the mountain, the moonless night was so dark and one could lose the way in the blackness; but from somewhere three asobi women appeared. One was about fifty years old, the other about twenty, and the third around fourteen or fifteen. [People] put an umbrella in front of the inn and had them sit there. The men lit torches to look, and the women said that they were granddaughters of an asobi named Kohata of long ago. Their hair was quite long, their bangs hung down just right over their foreheads, and they were pale and neat in appearance; people were impressed and said things like "they could become servants at court just as they are now." The asobi's voices were incomparable, and they sang songs splendidly as their clear voices rang up into the sky. People were so moved and called them to come nearer and reveled in amusement, when the women, hearing someone say "the asobi in the Western provinces surely cannot sing as well," charmingly sang, "compared to the asobi at Naniwa . . . [we are much less skilled]." Since their appearance was so neat, and their voices comparable to none, people found it difficult to part with them and sobbed as the women departed to go into that terrifying mountain. It is no wonder, then, that my young mind found it a pity to have to leave this inn.[78]

The second passage is brief and describes an incident in her adult life:

Because of a certain turn of events, I went down to Izumi around autumn, and the scenery on the way from the place called Yodo was so amusing that it cannot be described sufficiently. On the night that I stayed at a place called Takahama, it was very dark as the night progressed, when I heard the sound of an oar. According to the questions and answers exchanged, it seemed that asobi women had come. People were excited by this and had that boat dock. In the light of distant torches, the sleeves of their single-layer robes long, they hid their [faces] with fans and sang songs; I found it so moving.[79]

In both passages, the narrator focuses on the beauty of the appearance and the voices of the asobi women and expresses no negative or condemnatory views about their profession. The first passage, which describes the astonishment of the audience that the three asobi looked suitable enough to become servants at court, implies that at least to this unidentified audience, the social status of the asobi was not exceedingly high in general; however, this implication cannot be read to suggest that the asobi were "sinful" beings, for court service was exceptional for most non-aristocratic people. The narrator instead repeatedly emphasizes the incomparable quality of their singing, the enthusiasm with which audiences received these women, that she was very moved by their performances, and the fact that they maneuver adeptly in darkness, which ordinary people find frightening. The narrator does not refer to the asobi's prostitution at all, in contrast to works edited or written mostly by men. This example clearly shows that examining works written only by men provides a limited portrait of the figure of the asobi, especially since prostitution is tied so intimately to the question of the relationship between the sexes. *Sarashina nikki* thus establishes that for this author, a woman, the most important characteristic of an asobi was her musical performance.

Another oft-cited passage in which an asobi appears is in *Eiga monogatari* (A tale of flowering fortunes), a "historical monogatari" written around 1027 to 1092 by one or more unidentified author(s), Akazome Emon possibly

---

78. Fujioka et al., *Izumi Shikibu nikki, Murasaki Shikibu nikki, Sarashina nikki, Sanuki no Suke no nikki*, pp. 291–92 (passage 5).

79. Ibid., p. 354 (passage 30).

being one of them. If she indeed wrote this text, then the passages below are other examples of a woman writing about the asobi. Chapter 31, Section 23, states:

. . . When [the emperor's entourage] was going downriver, they came upon a place called Eguchi, and asobi women competed with each other in coming to service, some with the moon drawn on their umbrellas and some with mother-of-pearl inlay and flecked gold. Their singing voices and the voice of the waves washing ashore onto the reeds—Eguchi, it seemed as if it were beyond description.[80]

Chapter 38, Section 23 has the following passage:

Between seven and nine o'clock in the morning, boats were cast out to go downriver, when two boats of the asobi at Eguchi came up. [The emperor] gave them rewards but did not give them the clothes he was wearing.[81]

These passages, like the ones in *Sarashina nikki*, illustrate that aristocratic encounters with the asobi were treated as fairly commonplace events, and the descriptions focus on their mercantile zeal, splendid singing voices, and reception of rewards. In none of the examples credited to female authors (at least potentially) do we find the particular stock phrases and terms so consistently present in men's writing, especially in Chinese; there is a distinct absence of speculations about the asobi's fate after she ages, descriptions of her advanced sexual techniques, and the "jade-green curtains" and "crimson bedrooms" found repeatedly in Chinese literary texts of the Six Dynasties and Tang periods.

This is not, however, to claim that there was necessarily a "sisterhood" among women writers and entertainers that resulted in the sympathetic portrayal of the latter by the former or to promote a gendered essentialism in which female writers, by definition, write texts that subvert "patriarchy" and works written by men. Instances of marginalization do occur in narratives by women, and the crucial task here is not to condemn such occurrences as "betrayals" against one's own kind, but to situate the marginalizing process so that its motives and effects are clarified. A famous passage critiquing the asobi can be found in *Genji monogatari* (The tale of Genji; ca. a few years after 1000), by Murasaki Shikibu. In the "Miotsukushi" chapter, Genji encounters a group of asobi women during a visit to the Sumiyoshi shrine:

---

80. Matsumura, *Eiga monogatari zenchūshaku*, 6: 236–40.
81. Ibid., 7: 263–65.

On [his] way home to the capital, [Genji] enjoyed leisurely outings, but his mind still lingered over [the matter of Akashi no Ue]. A group of asobi had gathered, and despite their aristocratic nature [the men] were young and curious, and it seems they fixed their eyes upon the women. However, [Genji] thought, "Well, how would it be really? Whether or not something is interesting or moving all depends upon the partner. Even in an irregular relationship, if there were anything fickle about the partner, it would not be worth putting one's heart into it." He felt it distasteful that [the asobi] were getting carried away putting on their charms.[82]

As in *Yamato monogatari*, *Sarashina nikki*, and *Eiga monogatari*, there is no mention of the "sinfulness" of the women's profession. However, Genji's attitude toward these women is not exactly enthusiastic; he finds their manners "distasteful," and his comment "even in an irregular relationship" sets apart a relationship with an asobi as one that would not be rewarding. He thereby presents himself as different from the merely ordinary men who find the women desirable.

This passage, like the others, must be read within the framework of the entire text in order to understand its significance. Although it can be argued that among a certain group of aristocrats during this period it was considered distasteful to enter into a relationship with an asobi, it does not necessarily follow that this was because the asobi were marginalized in the same way as they were in some of the setsuwa stories discussed above. In other words, these women are not singled out for their "sinfulness" in this work. For example, in the "rainy night" discussion in the Hahakigi chapter, young aristocratic men maintain that courting a woman in the lower classes (below the *zuryō* rank) is undesirable. One could frown on a relationship between an aristocrat and an asobi in a similar way without bringing in elements of their "sinful" sexuality, which is not even mentioned in the passage above. In fact, what is criticized is the quality of fickleness in relationships in general, not "sin." The issue of faithful attention to a lover is important in this particular context, since at this point Genji is concerned with his promises to Akashi no Ue. In other words, the passage attempts to distinguish Genji from common men as one who values (at least in his thoughts) lasting commitment; a liaison with an asobi is an example of unsatisfying and fleeting relationships. This passage, then, is another example in which contextualization reveals the significance of the statements made about asobi women.

---

82. Ishida Jōji et al., *Genji monogatari*, 3: 37–38. See also Abe Akio et al., *Genji monogatari*, 2: 297–98.

Given the diversity and complexity of the texts that mention women entertainers, the asobi and kugutsu in particular, it would be difficult to maintain that they occupied an undisputed and immovable position as a marginalized people. In fact, explicit expressions of condemnation based on their sexuality are limited to specific works in particular genres. Moreover, each of the genres that expresses negative opinions about the asobi/kugutsu marginalizes them in different ways. For example, the kanbun/kanshi works express pity toward these women for their lifestyle through the employment of allusionistic devices, whereas setsuwa stories motivated by specific modes of Buddhist discourse focus on the asobi's supposed sinfulness and helplessness within the framework of ōjō in order to delegitimize imayō as a powerful religious vehicle and to promote the nenbutsu. Furthermore, works written by or attributed to women tend to lack morally critical comments about the asobi and show the extent to which such women could be socially high-ranking and extremely talented as well as materially comfortable, and *Genji* shows that "female authorship" does not easily equate with a sense of gender solidarity. These examples illustrate that marginalizing processes are interested, diverse, and inconsistent; "marginality" is an inconsistent result of motivated attempts by certain groups to exclude others from access to sources of power. The figures of the asobi and kugutsu are neither "representations" of a prediscursive "true" state of these women nor simply the random creations of each author.

2　Manipulating Margins:
'Ryōjin hishō' and Goshirakawa

In the preceding chapter, I argued that the figure of the marginalized asobi
and kugutsu is a complex and motivated web of textual constructions. In order to undo assumptions about the nature of the margin, I continue this vein
of investigation in this chapter by examining two further instances of marginalizing processes. First, I turn to a twelfth-century collection of asobi and
kugutsu's songs compiled by a retired emperor who was deeply committed
to the practice of this art form. Of the many questions we might ask about
this text, those important for the present discussion are: Are the representations of women entertainers transparent depictions of "historical reality"?
What motivated the retired emperor to compile this work, and how did
these motivations structure his depiction of asobi and kugutsu? As I will
show, several paradoxical discourses in the collection simultaneously privilege and marginalize women entertainers. How do these conflicting portrayals work to position both the compiler and the professional performers of
the songs? And how are these positions related to questions of gender, sexuality, and religiosity?

　In the second half of the chapter, I discuss examples of twentieth-century
understandings of late Heian women entertainers in order to illustrate how
contemporary scholarship can contribute yet another layer to the marginalizing process. I focus on two particular songs in the collection whose interpretations have repeatedly stirred controversy. By noting the ways in which
such interpretations are colored by assumptions about the figures of women
entertainers, I hope to show the contributions and complicity of recent

scholarship in the construction of these women as "marginalized" beings. Marginalizing processes do not simply "end" at the time the original texts are written; each subsequent interpretation of those texts makes claims that accumulate and result in further marginalizing effects.

Ryōjin hishō was originally a twenty-volume collection of imayō songs popular in twelfth-century Japan and commentaries about their practice. It was compiled by Goshirakawa (1127-92), who was emperor from 1155 to 1158 and held power as a retired emperor from 1158 to his death. He took the tonsure in 1170 and was guided in his Buddhist studies by a Shingon monk. His *insei*, the de facto rule by a retired emperor, was interrupted from 1179 to 1181 by the Genpei war. The exact dates of compilation of the first ten volumes of *Ryōjin hishō*, which contain the song lyrics, are not known, but the second set of ten volumes, titled *Ryōjin hishō kudenshū*, is known to have been compiled between 1169 and 1185;[1] thus, it is likely that the lyrics were anthologized during this general time period as well. *Kudenshū* describes Goshirakawa's views, his criticism of the techniques of others, and his practice of the art of imayō, to which he was extremely dedicated. The entire work was believed to have been lost from the time of its mention in *Tsurezuregusa* (Essays in idleness; around 1330) until the rediscovery of a fragment of Chapter 1 and all of Chapter 2 in the lyrics section and Chapter 10 of *Kudenshū* in Meiji 44 (1911) by Wada Eison. A year later, a reproduction was published and received enthusiastically by both scholars and poets. In all, 566 songs, as well as a substantial prose chapter on imayō and its practice, survive to this day.

In twentieth-century scholarship, *Ryōjin hishō* is frequently used as a favorite source for the "manners and customs" of people who lived in the late Heian period. In Chapter 1, I have discussed the problems of such a stance. Recent historical and minzoku studies on the position of women entertainers, despite a frequent lack of nuanced approaches to "textual evidence," have pointed out the variety of viewpoints on these women and show that the asobi and kugutsu were not consistently "marginal" figures in society. In contrast to such findings, scholars of literature specializing in *Ryōjin hishō*, such as Watanabe Shōgo and Baba Mitsuko, have continued to interpret its songs without paying much attention to scholarship challenging the "mar-

---

1. The exact date of the completion of *Kudenshū* is a matter of debate; see Baba Mitsuko, "*Ryōjin hishō* seiritsu kō," among others.

ginal asobi" paradigm.[2] They still tend to perceive women entertainers as *a priori* "marginal" figures aware of their ostracized and "sinful" existence. Too often in the past, *Ryōjin hishō* has been unquestioningly treated as a "reflection" of the times, a collection of "common people's voices" by both Japanese scholars and the few Western scholars who have studied it.[3] The fact that

---

2. See, e.g., Konishi, *"Ryōjin hishō" kō*; Watanabe Shōgo, *"Ryōjin hishō" no fūzoku to bungei* (on p. 42, for example, Watanabe tries to portray the asobi in a "positive" light by conceding that "although they had feelings of shame, they had freedom . . . even when they behaved as asobi, [others felt] pity but did not look down upon them too frequently." Clearly, the author assumes that "shame" and "pity" were inherent in the lives of the asobi. See also note 11 to this chapter); Shinma and Shida, *Kayō*, vol. 2; Baba Mitsuko, *Imayō no kokoro to kotoba*; and idem, *Hashiru onna* (for a detailed discussion of Baba's views, see the second part of this chapter). In English-language scholarship, Michele Marra continues the line of "the asobi as 'defiled' beings" argument in his article "The Buddhist Mythmaking of Defilement," pp. 49–65, by arguing that Buddhist discourse in Medieval Japan "transform[ed] the courtesan into a Buddha-to-be (bodhisattva) [which] led to a restorationist act of order in which the danger of defiled margins was silenced and erased" (p. 51). Marra assumes some sort of a pre-existing "defiled margin" in other, non-Buddhist religions such as shamanism, Shinto, or Daoism (none of which he cites specifically with examples). As I will try to show in this chapter, to the contrary Buddhism seems to have been one of the crucial arenas of the marginalization of the asobi/kugutsu. Marra also reads the Shōkū stories discussed in the first chapter from this perspective and treats the versions of this trope as a singular product rather than as different manifestations of a similar plotline. Such assumptions and the unification of different narrative "versions" seem to play dangerous roles in the interpretation of the positionality of women entertainers. The assumption of the asobi's "peripheral status" is also seen in Yung-Hee Kim Kwon's article "The Female Entertainment Tradition in Medieval Japan." She states that the asobi's status in the twelfth century represents a "downfall" compared to their former position as the asobibe at imperial funeral services and that they "experienced a drastic dislocation both in their status and function and found themselves at the periphery of their society"; their loss was recovered through their artistic skills, which permitted them again to associate with the imperial court. This rise-and-fall scheme, popular among Japanese and European scholars as well (one example of the latter is Michael Stein's *Japans Kurtisanen*, which sees the asobi as part of an unbroken line of "courtesans" leading up to the present-day *geisha*), treats the question of the positionality of the asobi as a monolithic object subjected to uniform waves of social change rather than as a constantly contested and diverse ground.

3. There are numerous examples of this; for instance, the description *shomin kayōshū* (common people's *kayō* song collection) used by Niunoya Tetsuichi ("Chūsei teki geinō no kankyō," p. 47). Yung-hee Kim [Kwon] (*Songs to Make the Dust Dance*, p. xiii) states that the songs "are popular songs of anonymous people—the unofficial voices from an age long past." Although later (ibid., p xvi) she does allow for the possibility that the "poet/singer . . . assume[d] the surrogate voices of many classes," she does not directly address the problem of the mediation by a retired emperor and what that implies.

Ryōjin hishō was compiled by a retired emperor suggests that such an unmediated transmission is unlikely. I will try to show in this chapter that *Ryōjin hishō* in fact is a complex site of the doing and undoing of power through motivated textual constructions. In fact, the "marginal asobi/kugutsu" is a double construction: first created in the mid-to late Heian period, and then re-created and elaborated by twentieth-century scholars.

THE POLITICS OF
ORALITY, LINEAGE, AND REBIRTH

The conflicting discourses that exist in *Ryōjin hishō* and *Ryōjin hishō kudenshū* serve both to privilege and to denigrate the women entertainers who professionally practiced and maintained a lineage of imayō. In examining these discourses, I explore the positionality of these women in late Heian society and how the marginalizing process constructs and unconstructs these women's "marginality" as well as the speaker/marginalizer's "centrality" in strategic ways. I discuss the contrast between the marginalizing tendencies of the *Kudenshū* and the notable absence of marginalization in the song lyrics section and argue that this paradoxical configuration is a result of Goshirakawa's religious aspirations. More specifically, I show that he had to empower the asobi and their art in order to establish the genre as one worthy to pursue and anthologize for the attainment of Buddhist rebirth in the Pure Land, but in order to guarantee his monopoly of this art (and therefore this method of achieving desirable rebirth), he also used Buddhist-influenced rhetoric to express disdain for them. I also address the characteristics of the text as a written product that attempts to legitimize an oral art form, and relate the politics of orality and literacy to the question of marginalization.

"Orality" and "literacy" can be regarded as elements in a problematic dichotomy entangled in hierarchical discourses of cultural teleology; scholars such as Brian V. Street, in his critique of Walter J. Ong and Jack Goody, have illustrated the constructed and contingent aspects of these categories.[4] I

---

4. The issue of the definitions of the categories "oral" and "written" has been discussed in European language scholarship for some time. Well-known scholars such as Jack Goody and Walter J. Ong have drawn clear distinctions between these two modes of communication by assigning certain characteristics to each medium, with specific implications about the people who use them. For example, Ong states in *Orality and Literacy* that "without writing, human

invoke the dichotomy here not as an attempt to resurrect it unproblematically but to suggest that the specific examples of Ryōjin hishō and Kudenshū
contribute further to such critiques: both of these works clearly reveal the
"oral" and the "written" to be motivated textual constructions. Both the oral
and the written modes existed in the various textual genres of Heian Japan;
here, I am interested in how Ryōjin hishō and Kudenshū consciously and strategically draw a distinction between vocal performance and writing and

---

consciousness cannot achieve its fuller potentials . . . orality needs to produce and is destined
to produce writing" (pp. 14–15) and that writing as a storehouse for knowledge "freed the
mind for more original, more abstract thought" (p. 24). These statements, among many others throughout his book, suggest that Ong views "orality" and "literacy" as essential categories
with timeless, unchanging properties caught in a teleological movement of "progress" from the
primal oral to the advanced written, even though he concedes that both categories often coexist in a society and that the written is not necessarily superior to the oral in that qualities of
the latter are unfortunately lost in the former: "Orality is not despicable. It can produce creations beyond the reach of literates" (ibid., p. 175). Ong also indicates his agreement with Jack
Goody, who associates the development of logic and the abstract with the embrace of writing
by a culture (Street, Literacy in Theory and Practice, p. 5). Both scholars claim that whereas literacy made it possible for cultures to "develop abstract thought" and to preserve unchanging
traditions through the transmission of written texts, oral cultures remain fickle, "primitive,"
and able to grasp only the immediately concrete.

Recently, there have been re-examinations of such assumptions about "orality" and "literacy." Brian Street (Literacy in Theory and Practice, p. 61) critiques these views by pointing out
that not only are these two categories impossible to separate neatly from each other in cultures where they coexist, but that the qualities ascribed to each category (rationality, logic,
etc., versus mysticism and magic) often interact in ways that promote or play off of each
other, invalidating a strict teleological model. Most important, Goody's portrayal of literacy as
"a neutral technology" hides the fact that "it is a socially constructed form whose 'influence'
depends on how it was shaped in the first place. This shaping depends on political and ideological formations" (Street, Literacy in Theory and Practice, p. 65) and that notions of teleological development and the "primitiveness" of the oral stem from imperialistic attitudes that treat
the cultural conditions of colonized countries, often presented as "oral" cultures, as "primitive"
and "underdeveloped." Ruth Finnegan (Literacy and Orality: Studies in the Technology of Communication, "Introduction") similarly challenges assumptions about "oral" communities and
"revolutions" brought about by literacy and critiques the approach that views writing as an
empirical, consistent "technology" with agency that acts on its passive recipient, "culture."
Again, as in the case of marginality itself, it seems more important to explore the ways in
which orality and literacy are promoted, denigrated, and manipulated according to the interests of particular people at specific times than to make pronouncements about the essential
nature unique to each form and inseparable from it. Ryōjin hishō is a particularly suitable text
to explore this issue, in that it is a written text about an oral art form.

privilege and promote the former through the use of the latter in order to achieve a particular Buddhist goal.

Specifically, my argument unfolds in three separate steps. First, the provisional privileging of the oral that appears throughout both *Ryōjin hishō* and *Kudenshū* can be explained in two ways: one, that it was an attempt by professional practitioners of an art form that was primarily based on oral performance to promote themselves and their craft through the singing of songs, and two, that such a positioning of the oral was necessary in order to institute imayō ōjō, or the attainment of ōjō through the performance of imayō, as an authorized, effective, and preferred method of attaining ōjō. Second, after placing the oral art of imayō upon a coveted pedestal, Goshirakawa manipulated his ties with specific imayō "masters" in order to create a position of authority for himself; in trying to establish his own orthodoxy, he placed his teacher's lineage in a position of power. Third, the authority granted imayō could come only from its reproduction in written form, and the compiler Goshirakawa ultimately appropriated imayō from the women who practiced them both by turning their oral art form into a written product and by marginalizing these women as unfit to continue the "correct lineage" of the imayō tradition.

Privileging Oral Performance

In many ways, *Ryōjin hishō* is a text about orality; imayō is a performative art form in which the voice plays the most important role. *Ryōjin hishō* itself, however, is a written text that talks about its own inadequacies as a written text about an oral genre yet establishes the legitimacy of the genre through its very nature as a written text. The politics of orality and literacy become evident when we consider who possessed the powers of the voice and/or the brush, but the text does not simply privilege one over the other, for reasons that I shall explore below. The privileging of the oral that appears throughout both *Ryōjin hishō* and *Kudenshū* was necessary in order to institute imayō ōjō as an authorized method of attaining rebirth into the Pure Land. In relation to the issue of marginalization and the position of women entertainers of the era of *Ryōjin hishō*, orality and literacy are issues that affected the ways in which the construction of their position fluctuated within a single text. The asobi's and the kugutsu's close ties to oral art forms are established repeatedly and prominently not only in *Kudenshū* but also in other texts in various genres during this period that emphasize their singing. Shifts in the attitude toward orality (through the mode of writing), then, could affect the depiction of their very existence in a text, since a crucial part of their profession involved oral performance.

One of the distinguishing characteristics of the singing of imayō songs compared to other musical arts popular among aristocratic circles in the late Heian period is that whereas the latter involved either a soloist or an ensemble playing musical instruments, the focus of imayō was almost exclusively on the human voice. Imayō singing was accompanied only by a tsuzumi drum or the rhythmic tapping of a fan.[5] This starkly minimalistic approach permitted the voice to stand almost alone. The voice possessed important religious attributes in the time of Ryōjin hishō. For example, the renegade characteristic of the act of raising one's voice for chanting or reciting has been noted by Amino Yoshihiko, who states that despite frequent notices seen in temple and shrine compounds throughout the Ancient to Medieval periods that prohibit loud acts, including the loud chanting of sutras and banquets, there are many examples of such behavior, including tales in Konjaku monogatari of both a monk and a nun chanting sutras loudly in spite of the rules, resulting in an expulsion in the former case and the attainment of ōjō in the latter.[6] Goshirakawa himself studied shōmyō with the monk Kakan, who was in turn a disciple of the Tendai monk Ryōnin (1073–1132), who had established the shōmyō tradition in the Tendai school and developed a neume-type notation.[7] The concept that singing or melodic chanting of Buddhist-related passages could serve as devotional practice was being established during the late Heian period as the shōmyō dō (the "way" of shōmyō),[8] and Goshirakawa must have been familiar with the religious potential of the role of the voice in Buddhist practice. What is important here, however, is that Goshirakawa ultimately privileged imayō over shōmyō, as we will see below, even if the latter had prepared the grounds for his appreciation of the oral religious arts. This preference contrasts sharply with the example raised in Chapter 1 in which imayō is subordinated to shōmyō in the story about the monk Shōshō in Hosshinshū.

The asobi and kugutsu, professional practitioners of imayō, participated in religious displays of the voice. It has been proposed that imayō songs (the

---

5. Sugano, "Goshirakawain no imayō," pp. 55–57.
6. Amino, "Mizube no nigiwai," pp. 194–96.
7. Enoki, Nihon bukkyō bungaku to kayō, p. 78.
8. Ōsone et al., Man'yō/kayō, p. 366.

hōmon no uta, or songs about the dharma text, in particular) developed out of *hokke hakkō* ceremonies offered as prayers for the dead during which the Lotus Sutra was recited[9] and that the asobi and kugutsu participated in these rituals. Passages in *Kudenshū* concerning offerings of flowers in the fifth and ninth months refer to rituals in which the Lotus Sutra was recited and these groups of women sang.[10] These women, then, were also officially involved in religious ceremonies in which their oral role played a large part.

Ryōjin hishō itself is full of different sounds, most prominently the sound of religious incantations. The term "koe" appears frequently in the songs of *Ryōjin hishō*, and an examination of these usages shows that the term is deeply rooted in religious functions. "Koe" is used a total of sixteen times in the extant chapters of this collection. In thirteen of these instances, the term appears by itself, to signify sounds in nature, percussion, or the chanting of religious incantations. In songs that describe the human production of koe, it almost always occurs in the context of chanting a sutra. In addition, as a compound form, koe describes the chirping of a plover (song 16), the sound of a tsuzumi drum struck as an offering (song 562), and the voice of the dragon girl presumably preaching the dharma (song 231). Again, the only sentient agent that generates koe is a female divine figure preaching the Buddhist law. Furthermore, *Ryōjin hishō kudenshū* illustrates the importance that Goshirakawa placed upon the art/skill of the voice, or *koewaza*. There are numerous occasions in which other terms related to oral interaction appear in *Ryōjin hishō* as well. Terms such as "iu" (to say), "kiku" (to hear, listen to), "toku" (to preach), "tonau" (to chant), and "yomu" (to recite) are used over a hundred times. Many of these instances are found in songs directly associated with the practice of Buddhism, such as the hōmon no uta.

In contrast, terms associated with written works or the act of writing appear only a handful of times throughout the songs in *Ryōjin hishō*. "Kaku," "to write," is used only four times (songs 139, 239, 346, and 461), of which two uses are in phrases that include reciting as well (songs 139 and 461). Two directly describe the writing of sutras (songs 139 and 239), whereas the religious elements in the other two are present but less actively devotional. The

---

9. For a detailed discussion of hokke hakkō and imayō, see Takagi, *Heian jidai hokke bukkyōshi kenkyū*.

10. Niunoya, "Chūsei teki geinō no kankyō," p. 14. Niunoya maintains that ceremonies focusing specifically on the Devadatta chapter, which presents the story of the dragon girl's achievement of enlightenment, became particularly popular around the time of Goshirakawa.

brush, or "fude," appears three times: once in a song that also includes the term "kaku" (song 239), once to praise a fine-quality, wealth-inducing brush (song 478), and once in a "list" song about various *tori* (a pun on "birds" and "to take"), in which the term "one who takes up the brush" appears (song 357). There is only one reference to a written *kana* character, in a list song about things that are perfectly straight (song 435). The term "hōmon" (dharma text) is used twice, but in both instances it is followed by the action "to preach," or "toku" (songs 50 and 174); this implies that hōmon's primary role in these songs was not as written product but as object to be recited. Lastly, in a similar maneuver, a song praising the written letters of the Lotus Sutra ends by focusing on its oral performance:

288　*moji goto ni　　johon dai ichi yori　　jugaku mugaku "sarainiko" ni itaru*
　　　made　　yomu hito kiku mono mina hotoke
　　　Each and every letter　　from the first of the preface chapter　　　　to
　　　"those who have received teachings and those without all bowed and
　　　left,"　　those who recite [this sutra] and those who listen are all buddhas

Two points about these examples are noteworthy. First, of the songs that refer to the act of writing, only one mentions the writing of sutras as a devotional practice (song 139) for people in general, and two focus on animals as the agents who perform these acts (a deer in song 239, a plover in song 346). Compared to the instances in which the term "koe" appears, the association of the act of writing with Buddhist religious practice is not as strong as the tie between Buddhist practice and the human voice. This observation is reinforced by the fact that two of the ten songs referring to writing are list songs that focus exclusively on wordplay, not on religious devotion. This relative detachment of writing from religious practice is significant when one considers that the copying of sutras as offerings to Buddhist deities and institutions was a common and important activity among aristocratic circles at the time. The strong emphasis on the religiously oral in *Ryōjin hishō's* songs becomes even more striking in this context. Second, half the songs that mention writing also contain references to recitation, and this draws attention away from writing alone. The fact that the act of writing is often paired with an oral element, whereas oral actions are presented on their own suggests the supplementary position of writing.

Furthermore, it was not enough to simply perform oral religious productions; the marking of expertise and skill in oral performance as desirable is clearly evident in some songs. For example, the one song that explicitly praises a particular vocal technique, *kowabiki* ("the drawing out of the voice," as in a long-held note; song 231), is the one mentioned above in which the dragon girl is the singer. Whether this figure is the one that appears in the Lotus Sutra is not established, yet it seems likely, since the dragon girl appears repeatedly in this context in *Ryōjin hishō*. If she is indeed the same as the dragon girl in the Devadatta chapter of the Lotus Sutra, then the emphasis on her beautiful singing technique is interesting in that no such attribute is mentioned in the sutra. This song, then, can be read as a promotion of the oral through its association of the singer with the dragon girl, a female figure in a canonical Buddhist text who achieves enlightenment despite her womanhood; this link is founded on the commonality of their skill in the vocal arts. When the singer is an asobi or a kugutsu, the connection between her and the dragon girl implies that the singer, who is capable of singing wonderfully, just like the dragon girl, is capable of miraculous deeds. Another example of the stress on talent in practicing an oral art form is song 443, which lists those who can read the sutra "splendidly." Among them are a person from Eguchi and two from Yodo, all of whom may be asobi since these locations were famous centers of asobi. If these figures are indeed asobi, then the song suggests that they were not only skilled performers of imayō songs but also skilled and entertaining reciters of sutras. Since many imayō songs, especially those classified as hōmon no uta, deal directly with sutra passages and content, it is likely that these are famous sutra-reciting asobi.[11] In both of these examples what is emphasized is not only the art of oral performance but also the skillful and impressive ways in which the singer performs. In light of the various other songs in *Ryōjin hishō* that focus on the oral, the desire generated by these two songs to seek or attain expertise in singing places the professionals of this art in an admired and coveted position.

---

11. Watanabe Shōgo (Emoto and Watanabe, *Shomin bukkyō to koten bungei*, p. 27), commenting on these sutra-chanting asobi, avers that they could not possibly have understood the meaning of these sutras (since even aristocratic women could not read *mana* texts) and that they were merely mimicking the sounds of others chanting sutras. This kind of dismissal is representative of the attitude some scholars have taken toward the asobi: due to the asobi's supposedly "lowly" status, their performances were unsophisticated, amateurish gimmicks (ibid., p. 28), and they were too ignorant to understand the meaning of the sutras. I have tried to illustrate throughout this chapter why such assumptions need re-examination. The notion that some (e.g., male monks) "understand" a sutra as they recite it whereas others ("lowly" women entertainers) "merely" chant it is never substantiated.

Overall, then, the songs emphasize the significance and validity of oral displays of religious devotion while relegating the written display to a minor role that often requires supplementation by the oral. More important, the fact that the concept of the oral is promoted orally produces a double layer of reinforcement that served to assure that all who practiced this art form were indeed followers of an effective path. It especially empowered the professional practitioners of these songs, the asobi and the kugutsu, who benefited from the advertisement of their skills in this manner. By singing songs that promoted the very action of oral performance, they could secure their own positions as teachers and guides to this particular path of devotion.

If *Ryōjin hishō's* lyric sections privilege the oral, the *Kudenshū* section uses imayō to promote certain religious and political agendas of Goshirakawa through an emphasis on oral performance. In the preceding chapter, I suggest that Buddhist setsuwa stories marginalize the figure of the asobi as "sinful" in order to advance a particular Buddhist practice that may have been in competition with or threatened by imayō ōjō. *Kudenshū* similarly illustrates the way in which the oral performance that makes imayō ōjō possible can conflict with other Buddhist practices, in this case, a practice that also involves oral recitations. Consider, for example, a passage in which Goshirakawa sings imayō to comfort his teacher, Otomae, who has fallen ill:

> zōhō tenjite wa   yakushi no chikai zo tanomoshiki   ichido na wo
>   kiku hito wa   yorozu no yamai nashi to zo iu
> "In the wake of the Formal Law   the vows of the Medicine
>   Buddha are indeed dependable;   those who hear his name
>   just once—   all their ills will be cured, they say."

So I sang two or three times over for her to hear, which she appreciated more than sutras. Saying "Having received this [performance], perhaps my life has been prolonged," she rubbed her palms together and wept in joy. This I found moving, and I returned.[12]

The key phrase is "which she appreciated more than sutras"; here, listening to the singing of imayō is clearly valued more highly than the chanting of sutras. Otomae's profession may have led to her preference for imayō, and she may have been an exception in favoring them over sutras, but Goshirakawa's frequent reiteration of the powers of imayō ōjō throughout *Kudenshū*

---

12. Kobayashi Yoshinori et al., *Ryōjin hishō, Kanginshū, Kyōgen kayō*, p. 164.

suggests that by noting Otomae's hierarchy of preferences, he sought to secure the status of imayō singing in terms of its religious efficacy.

Furthermore, after Otomae's death, Goshirakawa himself performed
dedicatory rituals for the sake of her afterlife, such as the recitation of the
Amida and Lotus sutras. On the first anniversary of her death, however, after the recitation of the Lotus Sutra, he sang various imayō taught by Otomae, since "she had loved songs more than sutras," as prayers for her afterlife. He then described a dream of his consort, Tanba no tsubone, in which a
white-robed Otomae visits him singing imayō. In this dream, she expresses
great praise for his performance, and then says, "Since I have received this
[performance], my body feels at ease, and I am happy." After this, imayō
were sung on every anniversary of Otomae's death to ensure that she would
enjoy a happy afterlife.[13]

In this episode, the chanting of the sutras is replaced by the singing of
imayō, and the deceased attests to their efficacy by appearing in a dream and
expressing appreciation. This incident serves as another proof of the powers
of imayō singing and augments other *Kudenshū* stories of imayō ōjō by
showing that not only can one attain ōjō by singing imayō at the moment of
death, but also imayō can be employed as dedicatory performances to assure
a happy afterlife. That it is Tanba no tsubone who reportedly had this
dream is notable, since she is known to have been an asobi.[14]

Aside from the attainment of ōjō, other miraculous powers of imayō
singing noted in *Kudenshū* are its ability to gain its singer promotions in office and heal illnesses. The former is exemplified by the case of Minamoto
no Atsuie (1032–90), who is said to have been hired by the deity at Mount
Kimpu because of his impressive singing voice; the latter is suggested by the
many cases in which both men and women chase away their own or another
person's disease, for example, Mei, who heals Kiyotsune, and Michisue, who
sings himself to recovery.[15] The tradition of imayō healing can also be seen
in later works such as *Jikkinshō*, which contains a story about a man who
cured his wet nurse's illness by singing a "popular song."[16]

---

13. Ibid., pp. 164–65.

14. Also, if, as some scholars suggest, the asobi originated in shamanistic women (miko), it
would have been appropriate for Tanba no tsubone to have had a dream about Otomae's
spirit.

15. Kobayashi Yoshinori et al., *Ryōjin hishō, Kanginshū, Kyōgen kayō*, p. 179.

16. Kawamura, *Jikkinshō zenchūyaku*, p. 625.

Narratives that reinforce the superiority of imayō over other types of rit-ual performance in impressing divinities appear repeatedly in the second half of *Kudenshū*. These passages describe Goshirakawa's pilgrimages to various shrines and temples. In most instances, Goshirakawa only briefly mentions the recitation of sutras or the performance of some other art form such as *kagura* (performances of songs and dances dedicated to various kami); his focus is, rather, the dedicatory singing of imayō and signs of the deities' appreciation in response to the songs. Although other devotional rites are listed along with imayō, by highlighting imayō singing and the enthusi-astic reactions of divinities to it, Goshirakawa succeeds in depicting imayō singing as the most important and effective medium for expressing religious devotion.[17]

The conception of oral performances as occasion- and context-bound was also used strategically in order to elicit the full potential of imayō songs: differences in the lyrics of a song in its various performances could be con-sciously and purposefully created—that is, they were the result not of "acci-dental" memory loss during an oral transmission but of conscious intent. In the case of an imayō song, the anonymity of its composer permitted its lyrics to be changed to suit an occasion, a specific performative moment. The contexts of the songs are not given in the collection of lyrics, contrary to the practice common in poetry collections since the *Man'yōshū* (An anthology of ten thousand leaves/generations; ca. mid-eighth century). Although waka poetry came to be evoked, recontextualized, and dynamically shaped—even changed—by later poets and anthology compilers, from the very beginning imayō has been distinguished by its lack of situational context and its ex-pectation of perpetual recontextualization. Clearly, *Ryōjin hishō* was intended to be a collection of songs devoid of specific context precisely so that they could be sung on a number of different occasions. This fluidity magnifies the importance of the performer and oral performance—the crucial aspect of imayō practice was not the lyrics themselves preserved statically in writing but the ways in which the lyrics could be contextualized, interpreted, and

---

17. Baba Mitsuko ("Hachiman imayō jigentan") asserts that whereas the parts that quote Otomae and other women performers' views and opinions about imayō can be called the *imayō gatari* (discussions/tales of imayō) as traditionally practiced by these women, the sec-tions that tell of Goshirakawa's pilgrimages and the deities' appreciation of his performances represent his own, new imayō gatari and cast him as an heir to this tradition.

customized.[18] Variations in oral performance were born out of a conscious sense of appropriateness to the occasion of their production; this, in turn, magnified the powers of orality.

Battles over Lineages: Genealogy and Power

I now turn to a specific rhetorical maneuver within *Kudenshū* that, I will assert, is a strategic move by Goshirakawa to position himself as the sole inheritor of the authentic imayō heritage. A significant portion of this text is devoted to a dispute between Goshirakawa's teacher of imayō, Otomae, and a rival, Akomaru.[19] The controversy concerns the style in which certain songs are preformed, with each woman claiming the superiority of her own tradition. In claiming these lineages, the exactitude with which a singer can reproduce her deceased master's performance is crucial; convincing others of the accuracy of one's transmission was the way in which one acquired authority and power. Otomae is challenged by Akomaru, who claims that Otomae is not a practitioner of the truly authentic style of imayō for the following reasons: first, although Otomae positions herself as correctly transmitting the performance style of her master, Mei, Otomae is merely an adopted daughter of Mei and not her biological daughter; Akomaru therefore speculates that Mei did not treat Otomae as her real heir and failed to teach her everything about the art. Second, Akomaru notes that Otomae had left Mei's care and headed for the capital at a fairly young age, so her training must have been short and incomplete. Otomae hears of this slander and retorts by stating that she had always heard from other imayō masters that Akomaru's mother, Waka, was not a particularly authentic or gifted practitioner of imayō, suggesting that Akomaru could not be a great or legitimate performer if her mother, her master, was less than extraordinary. Otomae then suggests that Goshirakawa summon the singer Kodaishin, the daughter of (Ō)Daishin, cousin of Akomaru and a superior heir (according to Otomae) to the tradition of an earlier master of imayō, Shisan.

---

18. Itō Takahiro ("Imayō no ba ni okeru shutai no mondai") suggests that whereas waka stood for a "direct" and "heartfelt" communication between its original composer and the divine, imayō was a mediated practice in which the performer played the role of a shamanistic medium in the communication between the audience and the divine. Although his generalizations about waka are quite debatable, he does provide a possible analogy in highlighting the vital role of the performer in imayō singing.

19. See Kobayashi Yoshinori et al., *Ryōjin hishō, Kanginshū, Kyōgen kayō*, pp. 157–60.

So I [Goshirakawa] summoned [them]. Kodaishin, Akomaru of Sawa, Enzu, Tarekawa, and Akomaru's daughter were among those who gathered. At the spacious palace grounds of Hōju temple, there was an imayō performance. When [people] heard Kodaishin perform the ashigara, they said that it was not at all different from my [style]. [The style] did not resemble Akomaru's, but it was not different from this "capital-style ashigara"[20] of Otomae. . . . Those seated in the audience [were] Narichika, Sukekata, Chikanobu, Narifusa, Suetoki, the priest Renjō, Yoshimori, Hirotoki, Yasuyori, and Chikamori; Suetoki, seated at the lowest place, praised [the performance] enthusiastically and expressed his deep impressions and admiration over the fact that [Kodaishin's] singing style was not different from [Otomae's and Goshirakawa's]. . . . Akomaru became angry and hit Kodaishin hard on her back, saying "Why don't you sing the song that's supposed to be so good?" Everyone felt hatred [toward Akomaru]. . . . Otomae and her two daughters heard Kodaishin's song from inside the palace, and deeply moved, Otomae said, "I feel as if I am hearing the song sung by Mei long ago." After this, Kodaishin's reputation became even better.[21]

In this passage, there is a repeated and strong emphasis on the lack of difference among the singing styles of Kodaishin, Otomae, Mei, and Goshirakawa and their style's distinction from that of Akomaru, who is portrayed in a less than flattering manner. This quality of sameness is the crucial factor that establishes the rightful line of the imayō tradition as that of Otomae and Goshirakawa. In Kudenshū's lineage-building and authentication project, therefore, exactitude in oral transmission is the key element in promoting or discrediting various lineages of imayō practice; this suggests that the "oral," rather than being a self-evident category that is "less advanced" than the "written," can be better understood as a rhetorical device strategically employed by the compiler, and that this rhetoric is ultimately motivated by his desire to assert the legitimacy of his own artistic lineage. Also, Otomae's victory as an actual occurrence is established by having an eyewitness at the scene relate the confrontation; this pose of truthfulness was crucial in validating her authority.[22] This lineage is further enforced in a passage in which Otomae tells Goshirakawa that a certain style of singing, the furukawa, had been kept strictly secret between Mei and herself and not taught to even (Ō)Daishin and Kodaishin. The existence of this highly guarded secret

---

20. Akomaru had insulted Otomae's style in this fashion; see ibid., p. 158.
21. Ibid., pp. 158–60.
22. Baba Mitsuko, "'Imayō gatari' no hōhō to hyōgen," p. 64.

serves to set Otomae apart even from Kodaishin, a renowned and popular singer. In this case, then, it is the presence of difference that serves to distinguish and privilege Otomae as the single proper authority.

In turn, the portrayal of the competition among these women and the victory of the lineage begun by the imayō master Shisan and followed by Mei, Otomae's stepmother, ultimately functions to establish Goshirakawa as *the* most suitable person to compile the definitive collection of imayō in the form of *Ryōjin hishō*: the judgments of the singing styles of the disciples of past imayō masters are based on their likeness to Goshirakawa's style. His authority is reinforced by the statement that since Otomae had retired at a fairly early age, she had no other disciples who had received her teaching in full.[23] The text thus implies that Goshirakawa is her only true disciple. Goshirakawa then proceeds to focus on evaluations of the performances and skills of his disciples. He begins by stating that he had learned everything that Otomae had to teach him in ten-plus years and mastered her style with complete accuracy.

I wanted to teach someone about all the training and practice during these years and have later generations call it "that style," but that even though I have students I do not have any disciples who would continue this lineage is such a regrettable thing.[24]

The words "that style" are usually interpreted to mean "Goshirakawa's style"; by this point, he seems to have taken over the lineage of Mei and Otomae that he sought to establish firmly.

His lament that he lacks an heir simultaneously concentrates authority in his figure and validates *Ryōjin hishō* as the only repository of this rightful line. The title *Kudenshū* itself attests to that which this text seeks to be but cannot become. It is an "orally transmitted teaching," which is in fact written down. By its very medium of presentation, it fails to exist in its declared state; the written characters *kudenshū* betray its intention. The rhetoric, then, is that oral performance is superior to a written rendition of it; however, authentic oral performances will no longer be possible after Goshirakawa's time. Despite its inadequacies because of its written nature, *Kudenshū* is situated as the only repository of "true" imayō. Although the last, "addendum" section of *Kudenshū* states that he has found two students whose "styles do

---

23. Kobayashi Yoshinori et al., *Ryōjin hishō, Kanginshū, Kyōgen kayō*, p. 162.
24. Ibid., p. 165.

not differ too much from [his],"[25] he does not call them "disciples." In fact, he eradicates the possibility of an oral transmission of his "true" style by entrusting its preservation to a written medium. This maneuver ensures that he has no rivals to match him in his lifetime and even beyond, as he himself declares the inferiority of a written work that seeks to convey an oral art form.

The Ultimate Goal: Goshirakawa's Monopoly

In the end, those who co-opt the lineage from women entertainers such as Otomae and Mei are aristocratic men: the two people Goshirakawa named not as disciples but quasi-heirs who might do an adequate job of continuing the tradition are Minamoto no Suketoki (d. 1159) and Fujiwara no Moronaga (1138–92). Suketoki belonged to a family specializing in the *eikyoku* (vocal arts) tradition, and Moronaga was a well-known instrumentalist, especially on the *biwa* lute. No woman heir, aristocrat or asobi, is named. Baba Mitsuko has suggested that *Ryōjin hishō* represents an attempt to integrate these women and other "marginalized" figures such as cormorant fishers into the Buddhist paradigm of salvation[26] and that *Kudenshū* is a proclamation of Goshirakawa's superiority over other practitioners of imayō.[27] His act of co-optation, however, does not end here.

Goshirakawa further reinforces his privileged position by denigrating the asobi's status at the end of *Kudenshū*:

My body has passed over fifty years; everything seems like a dream, like an illusion. I have already passed the halfway point [of my life]. Now, I intend to cast aside everything and seek ōjō. Even if I were to sing imayō again, how can [I] not be welcomed on the lotus seat? This reason being that those like the asobi board boats and float upon the waves, dip oars into the flow, dress up in their robes, favor the ways of love, favor the love of people, and even when they sing songs, since they seek only to be heard as skilled, they have no other thoughts, they sink into sin and do not know to seek the shores of enlightenment. Even they can attain ōjō if the one thought arises in their hearts. The songs of the dharma text (hōmon no uta) do not deviate from the sacred teachings. Each scroll of the eight volumes of the Lotus Sutra emits light, and every character of the twenty-eight chapters is a golden Buddha. How can

---

25. Ibid., p. 180.
26. See Baba Mitsuko, *Hashiru onna*.
27. See Baba Mitsuko, "'Imayō gatari' no hōhō to hyōgen."

the literary deeds of the secular realm, actually the seeds of the vehicle to praise the Buddha, not become the "turning of the dharma wheel"?[28]

The vocabulary is typical of the Buddhist-inspired characterizations of the asobi seen in this chapter, as would be expected from a person who had taken the tonsure.

Goshirakawa's critical perception of the asobi in this passage, however, is curious in light of the fact that one of his consorts was Tanba no tsubone, an asobi from Eguchi whose father was Ki no Takasuke (n.d.), an official in charge of people who made their livelihood from rivers and oceans. She played an important role in choosing the successor of Emperor Antoku (r. 1180–85), Emperor Gotoba (1180–1239; r. 1183–98), through a dream oracle, and she also bore Goshirakawa a son who later became the sixty-third *zasu* (head monk) of the Tendai school.[29] Many asobi women enjoyed the favor of politically powerful figures, especially starting around the time of Goshirakawa.[30] Also, in Goshirakawa's lifetime, there are other notable examples of women entertainers who became consorts of prominent warriors or

---

28. I.e., preaching the dharma. Kobayashi Yoshinori et al., *Ryōjin hishō, Kanginshū, Kyōgen kayō*, pp. 179–80.

29. Gotō, "Asobi to chōtei, kizoku," pp. 4–80; Ōwa, *Yūjo to tennō*, p. 205. Their sources are *Gyokuyō* and *Tendai zasu ki*. Ōwa (pp. 215–17) claims that Goshirakawa perceived his life as two worlds, one the public/political, and the other, the religious/amorous/artistic; in the latter world, distinctions of social status and genealogy did not matter to him, and therefore he was able to marry an asobi and devote himself to the pursuit of imayō. He has trouble explaining the passage cited above, however, and states that "from the standpoint of the self-awareness of human-ness" (meaning at the "human" level, which supposedly does not discriminate, as opposed to a "social" level, which is aware of status and positionality), Goshirakawa was able to appreciate imayō and asobi, even though he harbored discriminatory thoughts about the status of the asobi. This kind of explanation, which resorts to the establishment of a universal humanity that can be neatly separated from the social, dismisses the conflicting discourses that existed in the construction of the text *Ryōjin hishō*.

30. Fukutō Sanae ("Ukareme kara asobi e") argues that recent findings that the establishment of the *ie* or the family system around this time diminished the importance of the origin and status of the mother and the absence of records of aristocratic women becoming asobi after the story in *Yamato monogatari* invalidate the claim that the asobi's social status was fairly high based on examples like Tanba no tsubone (Goshirakawa's consort). She asserts that since women in general were considered less important in society than before, only the offspring that a woman produced were important; thus it did not really matter who the mother was. Although I agree with Fukutō that it is difficult to establish that the asobi were unequivocally high-ranking, I view these factors as signs of ambivalence and fluidity in the status of the asobi.

bore their children; among a group called the *shirabyōshi*, a type of woman entertainer who performed songs and dances dressed in aristocratic menswear, there were cases such as Tokiwa, the mother of Minamoto no Yoshitsune (1159–89), and Shizuka, his lover. After Goshirakawa's reign, some well-known examples include Emperor Gotoba's consort Kamekiku, who is known to have been a major cause of the Jōkyū insurrection in 1221;[31] Akomaru, the mother of Nijō Sadasuke, the son of Fujiwara no Chikanobu (1137–97), one of Goshirakawa's close retainers; and the shirabyōshi Gojō Yasha, the consort of Tokudaiji Kintsugu (1175–1227) and mother of his son Sanemoto, who later reached the rank of *daijō daijin* (chancellor).[32] In fact, recorded instances in which women entertainers occupied significant positions as either consorts, lovers, or mothers of men in power begin to appear around Goshirakawa's time and increase in number during the Kamakura period. The social positions of these women as seen in texts, then, were potentially wide-ranging; although some texts criticized them for their supposed sinfulness, others depicted some of them as close to centers of power.

A later example that epitomizes the complicated relationship between the imperial household and women entertainers is the document *Imayō no ranshō* (The origins of imayo; n.d.; possibly mid- to late thirteenth century, although Baba Mitsuko claims that it could have been written as early as the time of *Ryōjin hishō*),[33] a lineage chart showing the transmission of the "proper" tradition of imayō. The chart claims that the locus of imayō orthodoxy was a daughter of Emperor Murakami (r. 946–67) called Miyahime, the original practitioner.[34] This document can be interpreted either as an indication that the asobi/kugutsu were considered to be rightful artistic descendants of an art form that originated in the imperial household, thereby implying that their status was quite high, or as a manifestation of appropriation in which the imperial structure claims as its own an oral art form performed by professional women entertainers. It may be a combination of both. A similar claim of imperial origin can be found in *Denpō-e ryūtsū* (Standard version of the illustrated biography of Hōnen; ca. 1237); according to this document, Emperor Kōkō (r. 884–87) sent his daughters to Muro,

---

31. Hosokawa, *Idatsu no nihon chūsei*, p. 151.

32. Toyonaga, "Chūsei ni okeru asobi no chōja ni tsuite" pp. 412–17.

33. Baba Mitsuko, *Imayō no kokoro to kotoba*, pp. 272–74.

34. See the chapter on this lineage chart in ibid., p. 272–311. See also Konishi, "Ryōjin hishō kō," pp. 610–14.

and the asobi descended from them; many later biographies of Hōnen, the founder of the Pure Land school, also list this event.[35]

One might argue that since the passage explicitly names only the asobi, not the kugutsu, as those who "sink into sin," Goshirakawa was marginalizing only a particular segment of women entertainers. As noted above, Goshirakawa's imayō teacher was an old kugutsu woman named Otomae, whom he revered as the only rightful practitioner of "true" imayō. Nowhere, however, does the Kudenshū compare the asobi and kugutsu or declare one superior to the other in terms of skill or lifestyle. The phrase "those like the asobi" also leaves ambiguous and open-ended the identity of the remaining practitioners of imayō; kugutsu could certainly be included in this category.

Goshirakawa clearly regarded imayō as a crucial vehicle for attaining ōjō, and the association between imayō and asobi was undeniable, as the passage itself suggests. The question still remains: Why did Goshirakawa denigrate the asobi at the end of Ryōjin hishō kudenshū, despite his intimate familial and professional ties with women entertainers and the striking extent to which he privileged their art, imayō? There are a number of possible explanations. Scholars tend to explain Goshirakawa's extreme interest in imayō and asobi women by resorting to a concept of "art" as a class- and ideology-blind arena that permits both "high and low" to interact.[36] This idealized vision ignores the fundamental issues of gender, occupation, and marginalization that are fused together in this passage. Another explanation cites the prevalent Buddhist discourse of the supremacy of the way of the Buddha, which chooses to save even the "lowest of the low."[37] As I have shown in the preceding pages, however, the assumption that all the asobi occupied such a social position needs to be re-examined.

A clue for finding an answer to this question can be found in this passage's placement in Kudenshū: it appears toward the very end of the text. As outlined in detail above, Goshirakawa devotes the entire work to establishing the miraculous powers of imayō and his position of orthodoxy within the "correct" lineage. In this process, he chips away at the authority of professional women entertainers even as he portrays them as powerful possessors of the art of imayō; with the only rightful transmitter of the heritage,

---

35. Gotō, "Asobi to chōtei, kizoku," pp. 4–79.

36. See works by Baba Mitsuko cited in the bibliography; Ōwa, Yūjo no tennō; and Yamada Shōzen, "Goshirakawa wa naze teihen no imayō ni tandeki shita ka," pp. 32–37.

37. Vollmer, Professionen und ihre "Wege" im mittelalterlichen Japan, pp. 126–28.

Otomae, dead, Goshirakawa succeeds in taking over the tradition and religious powers of these women. Ending this process by condemning the asobi's ways completes his appropriation, as he puts them, so to speak, in their place. In stating that the way in which these women practice imayō singing, that is, without "seeking the shores of enlightenment," is inferior to his own execution, he condemns these women for their supposed behavior and excludes them from the lofty sphere in which he has placed the art form. His insistence that these women "favor the ways of love" and "sink into sin" shows that these women and their sexuality were constructed as undesirable precisely for the purpose of marginalizing them in order to distinguish their "inferior" practice of imayō from Goshirakawa's own "superior" practice. This passage contrasts sharply with the song lyrics section of Ryōjin hishō, which is notable for its lack of critical comments concerning these women; again, this illustrates that gendered marginalization is neither accidental nor monolithic. Most important, Goshirakawa's monopoly signified his authority over imayō ōjō, which is ultimately what he sought to achieve.

What other reasons might a powerful retired emperor who had taken the tonsure have had for privileging song-singing and oral performance? One possible reading is that Goshirakawa's association with imayō can be read as an attempt to distinguish himself from other members of the imperial clan. For example, Gomi Fumihiko notes that Emperor Sutoku (r. 1123–41), Goshirakawa's older brother, was an avid supporter of waka poetry and supposedly criticized his younger brother as a man of "neither literary nor the martial arts" since imayō did not fit the first category. The bitterness between the brothers and their factions culminated in the Hōgen disturbance in 1156. Gomi also notes that Goshirakawa became familiar with imayō by frequenting the residence of his mother, Taikenmon'in, who is said to have disliked waka and preferred other arts such as imayō.[38] These observations suggest that imayō was considered to be an art form not traditionally patronized by male powerholders in the imperial household; Goshirakawa's patronage of this practice, therefore, appears to have been regarded as unusual and distinctive and was sometimes under attack. His authority over the imayō genre can thus be interpreted as a symbol of his uniqueness and possibly "renegade" quality, which added to his charisma.

---

38. Gomi, "Goshirakawa hō-ō no jitsuzō," pp. 10–11. For the passage concerning Sutoku's opinion of Goshirakawa, see Tochigi et al., Hōgen monogatari, Heiji monogatari, Jōkyūki, p. 14.

Even outside the imperial family, imayō may have served as Goshira-kawa's distinguishing characteristic. Pierre Bourdieu theorizes that members of the upper class seek to distinguish themselves from the upper-middle class by deliberately promoting culturally "distasteful" or "low-class" activities.[39] In an age in which a former emperor could be exiled or punished and engaged in war just as other aristocrats and members of the imperial household did, Goshirakawa's alliance with an untraditional art form helped set him apart from those below. When that art form came to be practiced by his circle of retainers, he had to trump them once again by creating a definitive work (Ryōjin hishō) in the genre and declaring himself to be the ultimate authority. In other words, he made imayō his trademark, and the performance of imayō sometimes served as a ritual display of his power. For example, Hyakurenshō (a history of the years 968–1259 by an unknown compiler, ca. early thirteenth century) states Goshirakawa celebrated the funeral of Taira no Kiyomori (1118–81), one of his prime political enemies, with a banquet of imayō singing.[40] His hosting of a performance of the art form that he had co-opted can be interpreted as marking his political prowess during a period of transition and turmoil through the use of a genre of performance that he claimed as his own.

In addition, that the practice of imayō was not merely an aesthetic, leisurely, apolitical activity becomes clear when we look at Goshirakawa's close circle of retainers. These retainers were mostly imayō practitioners, and they used their skills in this art form to gain more favor with him. Goshirakawa in turn responded to their efforts by providing opportunities for economic and social advancement.[41] Imayō can therefore be regarded as a vital political skill that directly affected a retainer's position in society. In this context, women entertainers were a commodity or tool manipulated and presented by an aristocrat in order to achieve a goal. An incident following Goshirakawa's death as seen in Jien's (1155–1225) Gukanshō (Selected humble opinions), however, illustrates that the exploitation of another's profession or position in society to advance one's own interests was a two-way street. The account states that one of Goshirakawa's close retainers, Minamoto no Nakakuni (fl. late twelfth–early thirteenth centuries), and Nakakuni's wife claimed that the spirit of Goshirakawa had repeatedly requested enshrine-

---

39. See chap. 1, "The Aristocracy of Culture," in Bourdieu, Distinction.
40. Motoki, "Goshirakawa-in to heishi," p. 75.
41. Shimizu, "Ryōjin hishō kudenshū kan jū e no renkan," p. 39.

ment and worship. Their efforts were unsuccessful, and they were punished by confinement at a temple. The support given the proposal by miko, dancers, and other performers has led the scholar Nishiguchi Junko to speculate that they wanted to establish a kind of "performing arts center."[42] Although their attempt was unsuccessful, Goshirakawa's retainers and performers were attempting to utilize and manipulate his figure and authority to achieve a goal of their own. Imayō, then, served to establish and reinforce Goshirakawa's power, especially over his retainers, but his power in turn could be used in an attempt to empower a group that practiced imayō. This delicate web of interrelationships cannot be described simply as the exploitation of the "periphery" by the "center."

Despite the strong intersecting forces of marginalization and empowerment visible in Ryōjin hishō's two sections, ambiguities remain. It has been suggested that the Kudenshū passage quoted above which seems to belittle the status and pursuits of the asobi nevertheless makes the asobi's attainment of ōjō critical to Goshirakawa's attainment of ōjō since he had made the former the necessary condition for the latter. In other words, if even the asobi can attain ōjō, surely he can attain it. However, if the asobi cannot attain ōjō, then his own success becomes less certain; he therefore had a stake in illustrating the instances in which asobi attained ōjō with ease.[43] The marginalization of the asobi in the final passage, then, is far from being a totalizing discourse. In addition, Goshirakawa's expression of devotion to Buddhist enlightenment and rebirth into the Pure Land should also be placed within the context of his religious concerns as a whole. Buddhism was not the sole object of his practice, and it is difficult to separate out "pure" Buddhist practices from others—a common characteristic of religious practice in general during this period. He made unusually frequent pilgrimages to Kumano, a center of native Japanese religious practices, and Ryōjin hishō itself contains many verses about specific shrines. In this light, Goshirakawa's privileging of imayō can be understood as a form of discursive insurance: he will attain ōjō, since he is practicing a large number of paths believed to induce the process. It is likely that all these factors contributed to Goshirakawa's complicated attitude toward the asobi.

I have tried to illustrate that in examining the relationship between Goshirakawa and women entertainers, we can see how discourses about oral

---

42. Hosokawa, Idatsu no nihon chūsei, pp. 15–18.
43. Shimozaki, "Ryōjin hishō ni miru nyonin ōjō," p. 35.

performance and genealogy were manipulated in order to ensure the retired emperor's religious salvation and that the trope of the "marginalized woman entertainer" was an effect produced in the course of this maneuver. The process of marginalization is a complex and motivated one: the initial elevation of the status of the asobi and the kugutsu occurred because of their intimate professional ties to the songs in whose patronage Goshirakawa had a great stake, and their marginalization took place because these women had to be separated from their songs in order to give Goshirakawa an artistic and religious monopoly. *Ryōjin hishō* is a display of the negotiations in the giving and receiving of authority that constitute the "margin" and the "center"; the distinction between these categories themselves is formed, erased, and reformed according to these negotiations.

"SINFUL WOMEN":
INTERPRETING THE ASOBI

I now turn to two songs from the lyrics section of *Ryōjin hishō* in order to examine interpretations by modern scholars who assume that women entertainers were "marginal" beings. The ways in which modern scholarship reads "marginality" into songs sung and possibly composed by women entertainers reveals its desire to construct interpreted "proofs" of what scholars already presume to be true; in this sense, the marginalization of professional female imayō singers of the late Heian period is a process that continues into the present day.

As we saw in the previous chapter, for a variety of reasons, "sinfulness" was used strategically in certain texts to attack the position and profession of women entertainers. As I will explore below, however, many modern scholars have unquestioningly fixed on the "sinful" nature of the asobi when interpreting the songs of *Ryōjin hishō*. We need to begin by understanding how the discourse of sin operates within the collection as a whole. The word I translate as "sin," *tsumi*, appears ten times in this work, four times as a single term,[44] all in songs in the hōmon no uta section. The term also appears in six compound forms; three times as *zaishō* (sinful obstruction),[45] twice as

---

44. Songs 56, 167, 171, and 236.
45. Songs 52, 171, and 202.

tsumibito (sinful person),[46] and once as zaigō (sinful deeds).[47] The first two compounds appear in the hōmon no uta section; tsumibito is found in the shiku no kamiuta (quatrain songs about deities) group but is clearly Buddhist in tone, referring to the Prajñā-pāramita and Lotus sutras. Interestingly enough, none of the songs with terms related to "sin" is specifically about the asobi or even women in general; "sin" appears almost always in decidedly Buddhist settings, and the subject is never specified, an omission that gives these songs a generally inclusive feeling in that everyone is sinful to some extent and must seek to escape this sin.[48]

Furthermore, it is crucial to note that the *song lyrics* of Ryōjin hishō do not contain words of the asobi's self-marginalization. This feature is especially striking in contrast to the explicit marginalization of women as a general category—not women entertainers in particular—in the songs. The following are some examples:

116   *nyonin itsutsu no sawari ari   muku no jōdo wa utokeredo*
        renge shi nigori ni hirakureba   ryūnyo mo hotoke ni narinikeri

---

46. Songs 198 and 423.

47. Song 283.

48. Compare songs about asobi women with songs about *ukai*, or cormorant fishers. These songs have been cited repeatedly by scholars such as Baba Mitsuko as an example of a group of people who were marginalized, supposedly like the asobi. The songs about cormorant fishers, however, contain explicit judgments about these people; similar judgments about the asobi cannot be found in this collection:

355   *ukai wa itooshi ya   mangō toshifuru kame koroshi   mata u no kubi wo*
        yui   genze wa kakutemo arinubeshi   goshō wagami wo ikani sen
    Cormorant fishers, I feel for them   killing turtles that live for ten thousand
    years   also tying the necks of cormorants—   in this world,
    it may be like this, but   in later lives what shall become of me?

440   *ukai wa kuyashikaru   nani shini isoide asariken   mangō toshifuru kame*
        koroshiken   genze wa kakutemo arinubeshi   gose wagami wo ikani senzuran
    Cormorant fishers are regrettable;   why did they rush so and fish   and kill
    turtles that pass ten-thousand kalpas*?   in this world, it may be like this,
    but   in later lives what shall perhaps become of me?

(*a unit of time that is almost immeasurably long; an eternity)

These songs identify the profession and the feeling of regret and remorse forthrightly, leaving little room for doubt as to the subject and sentiment expressed. They are remarkably different from the ambiguous songs 359 and 380 discussed below, which simply name aspects and objects associated with the asobi's profession without any sense of moral judgment.

For women there are Five Obstructions[49]   the untainted Pure Land may
be far away, but   as the lotus blooms out of the murky waters
even the dragon girl became a buddha.

117   *ōyosu nyonin hitotabi mo   kono hon zusuru koe kikeba*
    hachisu ni noboru chūya made   nyonin nagaku hanarenan
    Even the average woman, just once   if she hears this sutra chapter
    chanted   by midnight of the ascent to the lotus   forever she can
    escape her womanhood.[50]

These songs clearly state that women have obstructions (which men do not
have), that womanhood is like the murky waters of a pond, and that escap-
ing from womanhood is desirable. Nowhere in *Ryōjin hishō* is there a song
attributing similar hindrances or sinfulness to the asobi. There are songs
that speak of one's sinful character, and these have often been interpreted as
an admission of sin by the asobi themselves.[51] Unlike songs 116 and 177, however, these lyrics do not identify the speakers or overtly subject them to marginalization. Moreover, the universality of sinfulness is common in Buddhist
rhetoric, and songs about tsumi cannot simply be assigned to the asobi. Due
to the absence of contextualization in the presentation of the lyrics in *Ryōjin
hishō*, songs that may fit singers in various situations cannot be simply attributed to the asobi alone. To reiterate, the marginalization of women as an
entire group, then, is explicitly attempted in the two songs cited above; the
marginalization of the asobi as a category, by contrast, is not.

Hence, we must not begin reading the songs of *Ryōjin hishō* with pre-
sumptions about the perceptions or the portrayals of the asobi. In this section I will show that the songs of *Ryōjin hishō* play at best an ambiguous role
in commenting on the social position of the asobi as they regarded themselves and as others perceived them; in fact, compared to the presence of
forthright statements about the status of women in general and cormorant
fishers (another occupational group commonly believed to have been "outcast") in particular, there is a distinct *absence* of derogatory statements about
the asobi or any other group of women entertainers in the songs. I will illus-

---

49. The five incarnations women are said to be unable to achieve: Brahmā, Indra, Māra,
cakravarti-rāja, and Buddha. Scholars have pointed out that in Japan the term had come to
indicate hindrances inherent in women apart from this specific definition, as a general reference to women's sinful character (Ōgoshi and Minamoto, *Kaitai suru bukkyō*, pp. 75–76).

50. Kobayashi Yoshinori et al., *Ryōjin hishō, Kanginshū, Kyōgen kayō*, p. 37.

51. Ōwa, *Yūjo to tennō*, pp. 221–23.

trate this point by focusing on two songs that modern scholars of Ryōjin hishō have interpreted as the asobi's recognition of their "sinfulness" and their expression of remorse. These scholars assume that marginalization, once attempted, is complete, omnipresent, and unnegotiable; this has led them to construct the figure of the self-marginalizing asobi in this text. I argue instead that the songs of Ryōjin hishō do not inherently contain recognitions of the asobi's marginalized status—which was particularly fluid and unstable in the late Heian period—and reconsider this construction by examining the text in detail.

"Asobi wo sen to ya umareken": The Question of "Play"

359   asobi wo sen to ya umareken   tawabure sen to ya mumareken   asobu
          kodomo no koe kikeba   waga mi sae koso yurugarure
          Born [in this world] to play?   Born [in this world] to jest?
          When I hear playing children's voices,   my very body starts
          to tremble.[52]

The controversies over the interpretation of this song, unquestionably the best known of the songs in Ryōjin hishō, reveal clearly how the preconceived notions about the asobi affect interpretations, which in turn serve to reinforce the constructed images of the asobi. For example, Konishi Jin'ichi, one of the first scholars to examine Ryōjin hishō, interpreted the song as an expression of an asobi's remorse over her sinful deeds.[53] Iwanami's Nihon koten bungaku taikei, a standard set of the classics, has a similar interpretation: the "sinful asobi who come to be moved by the purity (of the children)."[54] Aileen Gatten, who translated one of Konishi's works into English and was undoubtedly affected by his views on the song, rendered it as

Are we born for lives of easy pleasure?
Are we on this earth to flirt and sport?
When I hear children's playful voices
My whole body shakes with remorse.

Konishi states that "the speaker is a courtesan, reflecting on her life."[55] The

---

52. Kobayashi Yoshinori et al., Ryōjin hishō, Kanginshū, Kyōgen kayō, p. 102.

53. Konishi, "Ryōjin hishō" kō, p. 468.

54. Morisue, "Ryōjin hishō no warabeuta," as noted in Yokoi, Chūsei minshū no seikatsu bunka, p. 93. Yokoi (p. 88) himself agrees with this interpretation.

55. Konishi, A History of Japanese Literature, 2: 399.

idea of remorse plays a central role for Konishi here, not because the original text contains the word "remorse"—it does not—but because he believes that the asobi, being prostitutes, must have regarded their profession as sinful and depraved. Views on prostitution that were not necessarily present during the era in which the song was composed have been read into this text, and they must be recognized as such.

A similar anachronism is pointed out by Imahori Taitsu in his discussion of a famous scene involving an asobi at the Muro inn in the *Hōnen shōnin gyōjō ezu* (Commemorative illustrations of Hōnen's life; ca. 1307–17), which is often used in debates about the asobi. This example illustrates the biased views of many scholars concerning the asobi's views of themselves. Imahori shows that scholars such as Kasahara Kazuo, Takikawa Masajirō, and Gorai Shigeru have drawn conclusions about the asobi in the late Heian era based on this scroll even though it dates from about one hundred years after the death of Hōnen in 1212 and therefore is a questionable source for the attitudes of Hōnen and others in his time.[56] Imahori also questions past interpretations of song 359, although he does not provide an alternative reading. He finds that during the Heian period, not only did the asobi not regard themselves as sinful, neither did society in general; only over the course of the early Kamakura period, between 1200 and 1300, was "sinfulness" gradually inserted into stories about the asobi.[57] He shows that in an earlier scroll depicting Hōnen's life (*Denpō-e*, ca. 1237), the story about the asobi's meeting with Hōnen is told without moral judgment, and the lecture by Hōnen in *Gyōjō ezu* on the sinfulness of being an asobi and laments about sin by the asobi themselves are absent; rather, the focus is on the fact that the asobi attained imayō ōjō at the time of her death.[58] The way in which the implications of *Gyōjō ezu* have been forced on texts of earlier periods clearly indicates how the positioning of the asobi has been manipulated by anachronistic approaches. Furthermore, in *Gyōjō ezu*, Hōnen is shown preaching the benefits of the nenbutsu: the asobi casts away her lifestyle to focus solely on the

---

56. Imahori, *Jingi shinkō no tenkai to bukkyō*, pp. 196–200. Gorai especially sees this scroll as a basis for reading remorse and a sinful conscience into song 359 of *Ryōjin hishō*. In addition, as scholars such as Amino Yoshihiko points out, Takikawa elsewhere makes sweeping racist and sexist arguments concerning the asobi; that his works are still consulted unproblematically as one of the major sources for the study of the asobi should be reconsidered.

57. Imahori, *Jingi shinkō no tenkai to bukkyō*, pp. 201, 212, 272.

58. Ibid., pp. 205–9.

chanting of the nenbutsu and finally achieves ōjō—a plotline that should sound familiar after the analyses in Chapter 1 of this book. This particular representation has been recently interpreted as a blatant attempt by the Pure Land school to popularize the nenbutsu at the expense of the asobi's moral position.[59]

Yet many recent scholars still share Konishi's interpretation,[60] including Baba Mitsuko, who has written prolifically on *Ryōjin hishō* and is interested in women and others who appear to be marginalized. She argues that song 359, among others (which I will address below), expresses "the guilty conscience of [those whose] profession is to 'play' and 'jest.'"[61] In a recent book, *Hashiru onna—uta no chūsei kara* (The woman who runs: from the Medieval world of popular songs)—she discusses her interpretation of this song in detail; since her views represent many of the biases of modern scholars concerning the asobi that I am trying to reveal, I will examine each of her arguments in detail.

One of Baba's central points is that the asobi, as well as other *shokunin* (people who were categorized according to their jobs that required special skills), were co-opted mainly by Buddhists into singing songs that lament their own position in society. She places song 359 in the same category as works such as *Futsū shōdōshū* (Standard anthology for preaching; ca. 1297) and *Senjūshō* (An anthology of selected texts); the former contains a kanshi poem in which an asobi laments her lifestyle, and the latter has a story about an asobi at Eguchi, who provides lodging for a night to the monk Saigyō and becomes a nun after talking with him remorsefully about the sinful life of an asobi.[62] Buddhist rhetoric did contribute greatly to the denigration of certain groups of people, including women in general and those who killed animals, but this reading of song 359 is questionable on two grounds. First, elsewhere in *Senjūshō*, male religious figures are shown struggling to reconcile the asobi's "sinful" activities with their achievement of ōjō.[63] *Senjūshō* as a whole, then, cannot be said to declare unambiguously that asobi are evil, sinful beings; the placing of words of remorse in the asobi's mouth in this particular

---

59. Abe Yasurō, "Seizoku no tawamure to shite no geinō," p. 185.

60. See, e.g., Ōwa, *Yūjo to tennō*, pp. 222–23, among others.

61. Baba Mitsuko, *Imayō no kokoro to kotoba*, p. 168; also see idem, "Uta to setsuwa," pp. 143–63.

62. Baba Mitsuko, *Hashiru onna*, pp. 184–205.

63. Yasuda et al., *Senjūshō*, 1: 119–21.

story must be considered in light of privileged alternatives raised in the attempts to explain how an asobi is able to attain ōjō, namely, by pointing out that she is now devoted to the practice of Buddhism as a nun. Second, both *Futsū shōdōshū* and *Senjūshō* date from considerably later and thus are not directly relevant in interpreting songs in *Ryōjin hishō*.

In *Hashiru onna*, Baba Mitsuko also cites one poem each from *Goshūishū* (The latter anthology of waka gleanings; ca. 1088) and *Sanboku kikashū* (An anthology of useless trees and strange poems), a personal poetry collection of Minamoto no Toshiyori (1055–1129) from around 1127, in order to establish that the verbs "asobu" and "tawaburu" refer both to the passage in the Lotus Sutra in which even child's play is considered a way to enlightenment and to the sexual and performative "play" of the asobi; she proposes that the latter was condemned by Buddhism.[64] The question of the terms "asobu" and "tawaburu" is an important one, and I explore the concept of "play" in detail later in this section. Below are the poems cited by Baba containing the verbs "asobu" and "tawaburu"; yet I submit that they do not necessarily present the activities described by these verbs as something to be lamented.

The *Goshūishū* poem and its introduction read as follows:

When the hijiri of Shosha was performing rituals for the tying of the knot of Buddhist relations, among the various people who sent him contributions, [toward one] perhaps he had reservations, and he did not take [her contribution] for a while, so [she] composed:

—asobi Miyaki

1197   *tsu no kuni no*   *naniwa no koto ka*   *nori naranu*
       asobi tawabure   *made to koso kike*
       What is not (Naniwa of Tsu province) the Law?
       Even playing and jesting [lead to ties with Buddhism], I hear.[65]

The pun on "asobi," the speaker's profession, and "asobi tawabure," the activities described in the Lotus Sutra, seems to be the main element of the poem. Even though the asobi may also be referring to her own profession, the poem does not inherently contain the moral judgments on the activity of asobi tawaburu that Baba is trying to find, especially since these same words are used in the Lotus Sutra to describe a child's actions that lead to enlightenment. Moreover, the *Goshūishū* poem is important for what it does not say,

---

64. Baba Mitsuko, *Hashiru onna*, pp. 196–98.
65. Kubota and Hirata, *Goshūi wakashū*, p. 389.

considering the supposed context in which it was composed. The introduction to the poem states that it is a poem by an asobi named Miyaki sent to the monk Shōkū, who refused to take donations from her for an unspecified reason, usually interpreted as the sinfulness of her profession. This assumption may not be valid in light of the stories about Shōkū examined in Chapter 1. In *Kojidan*, he seems to have no problems accepting an asobi leader as an incarnation of bodhisattva Fugen. However, if Shōkū did express disdain toward the asobi's profession, then Miyaki's reply is significant for its unapologetic tone and her clever play with words, which shows the illogical nature of Shōkū's refusal. As noted above, *Ryōjin hishō* also does not contain songs by or about the asobi that indicate a recognition of marginal status through expressions of remorse and lament.

Similarly, the *Sanboku kikashū* poem cited by Baba focuses on the pun on "asobi" (the profession) and "asobi tawaburu" (the words used in the Lotus Sutra):

820   *kashima e wa   asobi shi niya to   tsukinuran*
         tawabure ni temo   omoi kakenu wo
         "To Kashima   [he] has come to play"—   is this why they've
         drawn near?
         Even in jest   I wouldn't even think of it.[66]

The speaker, presumably Toshiyori, notes that asobi women's boats are approaching him; he speculates that they assume that he has come to the island of Kashima to "play," even though such activities are far from his mind since Toshiyori is mourning the death of his father. In other words, there is a sense of appropriateness—an activity that might be acceptable otherwise is considered unsuitable during times of mourning; the existence of detailed regulations for mourning and taboos surrounding a death in this era is well known. There is no condemnation of or contempt for the activity of asobi tawaburu per se. Toshiyori included five other poems related to the asobi in this collection, but none of these expresses a moral judgment on these women.[67]

Other usages of "asobu" and "tawaburu" together in waka suggest that they neither necessarily invoke the image of asobi women nor carry negative

---

66. Sekine and Furuya, *Sanboku kikashū*, pp. 23–24. Poem 821, which follows this example, states that Toshiyori considered having a young asobi, Shiro, stay the night, but because it was at an inappropriate time (*worifushi waroshi*), he sent her back.

67. See Ogawa, "Toshiyori to imayō," p. 17.

connotations. For example, the introductory passage of *Toshiyori zuinō* (Essential matters according to Toshiyori), a *kagaku* (waka studies) text by Minamoto no Toshiyori from around 1115, which Goshirakawa mentions in *Ryōjin hishō kudenshū* as a model for his own text, states: "The poems in the Yamato language, since they are the jestings and play (tawabure asobi) of our country Akitsusu, began in the times of the gods and have never been discontinuous to this day."[68] It has been pointed out that tawabure asobi here is a positive quality of waka poems, because Toshiyori viewed tawabure and asobi as national activities pursued by the gods; this contrasts with later kagaku works such as *Ōgishō* (Notes on arcane matters; ca. 1135–1144) and *Korai fūteishō* (Notes on the state [of poetry] since past times; ca. 1197–1201), which regard asobi and tawabure as frivolous and undesirable qualities in waka poems.[69] This usage, then, is a clear case in which these terms appear in a positive light.

A later example that hints at the non-marginalizing usage and interpretation of asobu and tawaburu even in the Kamakura period is a passage about the Sannō deity in *Yōtenki* (An account illuminating the heavens), a collection of setsuwa about the origin of the Hiyoshi Sannō deity from around 1242. A monk named Keizo comes to worship the August Deity of the Grand Shrine and encounters a group of noisy children. Keizo shoos them away in order to offer his worship, and that night the Sannō deity appears to him in a dream, chastises him for having chased the children off, and says: "I am actually no different from children in loving playing and jesting [*yūgi*—the same characters read 'asobu' and 'tawaburu']." The next day Keizo goes to join the children in their play and sings an imayō song found in *Ryōjin hishō* (song 411).[70] This story illustrates an instance in which children's playing and jesting are associated with a deity and an imayō song is sung as an offering to the deity, along with the display of play that includes children. These factors suggest that by this period, children playing and jesting had become a common image, possibly made popular by the song in *Ryōjin hishō*, but that the activity notably lacked any connection with asobi women or sinfulness—rather, it was understood as a positive religious activity.

Finally, even a seemingly condemnatory usage of the terms "asobi tawaburu" can be ambivalent. Story 33 in Chapter 17 of *Konjaku monogatari* tells

---

68. Hashimoto et al., *Karonshū*, p. 41.

69. Kufukihara, "Tawabure uta no jidai," pp. 44–45.

70. Sugano, "*Ryōjin hishō* zenshi," pp. 195–96.

of a young monk who spends too much of his time in asobi tawabure to the neglect of his Buddhist studies. A bodhisattva manifests itself as an attractive young woman who promises to become his wife and consummate their sexual union once he becomes a learned monk. He is so inspired by this prospect that he achieves scholarly heights, after which the woman disappears and the bodhisattva reveals the entire plan. The content of the monk's asobi tawabure is not outlined in detail, but there is a suggestion that it was related to sex, since the bodhisattva explains that the incarnation was a woman because of the monk's "inclination toward" women.[71] At first glance, the narrative might appear to be a general denunciation of asobi tawabure; however, upon further consideration, it becomes clear that such activities are thought to distract a *monk* from his studies but that even his interest in such activities could eventually lead him to become an august religious figure. The latter point especially resonates with the children's "playing and jesting"; in this case, it is a monk's "playing and jesting," or his desire to do so, that drives him to achieve knowledge and prominence within the Buddhist system.

Other interpretations of song 359 do not necessarily assume that it is an expression of the "sinfulness" of the asobi, yet still believe it to represent an asobi's "voice." In *Songs to Make the Dust Dance*, Yung-Hee Kim identifies the subject of the song as an asobi woman and translates it as:

> Was I born to play?
> Was I born to frolic?
> As I hear the children playing,
> even my old body starts to sway.

She proposes that the speaker is an old asobi who celebrates the magical aspect of performance, exemplified by children at play; "her life of flirtation and pursuit of love will end in time, but the delight she finds in songs and entertainment will continue to live on."[72] Kim does not make explicit assumptions about remorse and sin, yet she still privileges the "magic" of entertainment over the asobi's life of prostitution.[73] Kim and those who interpret the poem in a similar fashion assume that the asobi viewed "art" as

---

71. Mabuchi et al., *Konjaku monogatari shū*, 2: 420–33.

72. Kim, *Songs to Make the Dust Dance*, p. 133.

73. Her view is shared for the most part by Shinma Shin'ichi, another prominent *Ryōjin hishō* scholar, who interprets this song as the words of an asobi who cannot help responding to the singing of children and letting her body sway (Shinma and Shida, *Kayō*, pp. 87–89) and by Watanabe Shōgo in "*Ryōjin hishō*" *no fūzoku to bungei*, pp. 239–42.

somehow loftier, more lasting, and therefore more important than the "pursuit of love," when in fact it is not even clear that performance and prostitution were neatly separated as different activities. In the end, even in this interpretation, the notion that the song is somehow still related to asobi women remains inescapable. When we consider the counterarguments I outline above, it becomes clear that the automatic assumptions that song 359 is by an asobi or portrays an asobi and that it is condemnatory in tone are hasty readings fueled by the preconception that asobi considered themselves sinful beings and by the views of modern scholars about prostitution.

Let us now examine in detail the specific vocabulary of song 359. Baba has also argued that the verbs "asobu" and "tawaburu" appeared often in poems and songs associated with the asobi and that therefore the presence of these words in song 359 must also indicate that this song is about an asobi. However, the only occurrence of the two terms together in other lyrics in *Ryōjin hishō* are in songs that have not been associated with the asobi. For example, two songs under the *Hōbenbon* (The chapter on expedient means) rubric contain both verbs:

62   *byōdō daie no chi no ue ni   dōji no tawabure asobi wo mo*
         yōyaku hotoke no tane to shite   bodai daizu zo oinikeru
      Upon the grounds of the Undiscriminating Great Wisdom   even
         the games [jests] and playing of a child   gradually, as the seeds
         of the Buddha   they grow into the great bodhi tree.[74]

67   *hokke wa izure mo tōtoki ni   kono hon kiku koso awarenare   tōtokere*
         dōji no tawabure asobi made   hotoke ni naru   tozo toitamou
      Each part of the Lotus Sutra is august, but   to hear this chapter is
         particularly awe-inspiring,   is august   "even the games [jests] and
         playings of a child   attain Buddhahood," it says.[75]

The words "asobi" and "tawabure" appear once more, in the *Myōshōgon Ō bon* (The Śubha-vyūha-rāja chapter) section:

167   *tawabure asobi no uchi ni shimo   sakira ni manebin hito wo shite   mirai*
         no tsumi wo tsukusu made   hokke ni en wo ba musubasen
      Even amongst their games and play   those who are sharp-minded
         and wish to learn   until they exhaust their future sins   we
         shall let them tie their knots with the Lotus.[76]

---

74. Kobayashi Yoshinori et al., *Ryōjin hishō, Kanginshū, Kyōgen kayō*, pp. 22–23.
75. Ibid., p. 24.

The actors in this poem have been identified as Jōzō and Jōgen (Vimalagarbha and Vimalanetra), who "played" and showed the path of enlightenment to their father. It has also been suggested that the Buddhist term "yūge" (written with the characters for "asobi" and "tawabure"), "to wander about freely," indicated a state of free wandering, usually by buddhas and bodhisattvas; the connection between "play" in general and yūge was strong in this period, when child's play was sometimes seen as a path to enlightenment.[77]

Moreover, in song 167 the word "tsumi" appears together with the terms "asobi" and "tawabure." I see this not as evidence that the verbs therefore should be associated with sin in all cases, but rather that the verbs *can* coexist with tsumi in some cases. Since the verbs do not inherently suggest sinfulness, the concept of sin must be marked out clearly through the use of a separate word, "tsumi." In other words, "asobi" and "tawaburu" can function in various contexts and by themselves do not contain the implication of sin (as shown in songs 62 and 67).

Apart from the examples given above, the various forms of the words "asobu" and "tawaburu" appear separately in a total of 24 songs in the *Ryōjin hishō*. "Asobu" in its many conjugated forms and compounds appears twenty times,[78] of which thirteen describe the actions of animals (see below), six ap-

---

76. Ibid., p. 51.

77. Yokoi, *Chūsei minshū no seikatsu bunka*, pp. 86–87.

78. The following songs contain a form of the word "asobu," here translated as "play" or "wander":

123 "those who recite the Lotus Sutra . . . in wandering around they have no fear"

200 "all those who wander among these [worlds] / shall be friends of the lecture at Mount Gṛdhrakūṭa"

206 "the warbler in the city in Trāyastriṃśa / without deciding where to nest, it is at play like so"

269 " . . . descend and play / wander, oh (the deity) Great Generalissimo!"

276 "the Southern Shrine at the beach . . . in the seas of the ocean path he/she plays/wanders"

309 "these are no different from the pleasures of the Pure Land"

316 " . . . and on their treetops the cranes do play"

318 "in the ocean the ten-thousand-kalpa-turtle plays . . . "

319 "in the ocean the ten-thousand-kalpa-turtle plays . . . "

321 "the turtle that is drawn to the shining jewel-colored beach / after passing many kalpas does it now play"

327 " . . . let's play war games, / the deity of war!"

346 "playing by the riverbed are the 'letter birds' . . . "

pear in songs about deities or the Lotus Sutra, and one refers directly to the asobi in a "list" song of their favorite things. Forms of "tawaburu" appear four times,[79] including two referring to a child in the Hōbenbon section of the Lotus Sutra who builds a stupa out of sand, one about the twining of willow and wisteria, and one about a young hijiri that could have sexual connotations. Even in the last case, song 426, the verb "tawaburu" describes the intentions of a male hijiri: he declares that he will stray from the path of asceticism and lead a life of leisure/pleasure while he is young. This shows the verb is not reserved for the "sinful actions" of asobi women but refers more generally to "pleasurable" activities, which are occasionally contrasted with ascetic practices.

How we—that is, twentieth-century scholars of premodern Japan—view the concepts of asobi (to wander, to play) and tawabure (to play, to jest) must also be examined. In twelfth-century Heian Japan, "play" was an activity associated with the elite ruling class, deities who descended and wandered about, children, and animals. Playing was a luxury that was a privilege of the upper class and therefore was an important activity at court. In fact, banquets were often crucial arenas for the display of taste, talent, and wit, the "cultural capital" that was vital to securing the social and political favors of others. For precisely this reason, there were distinct guidelines for what kinds of "play" were appropriate during the era of *Ryōjin hishō*. Goshirakawa's

---

353 "the monkey kept at the corner of the stable / away from its leash it plays like so"

380 "things that asobi favor . . ."

387 "little birds that are intriguing . . . a mandarin duck, a kingfisher, a little grebe—they play by the river"

400 " . . . as the beach plovers play, dancing and wobbling"

407 "The Great Tang court is splendid, I hear . . . in the bedrooms, golden butterflies play"

408 "dance, dance, snail! . . . if you dance truly beautifully / I'll let you play even in the garden of flowers"

410 "what plays amidst one's head: head lice . . ."

438 "stay there, stay there, dragonfly! . . . I'll let children and youngsters play turning you in circles"

79. Songs that contain a form of the word "tawaburu":

11 "on the little willow / the wisteria flowers that hang down . . . intimate and playful . . . they sway"

68 "in the past, that even a child playing games / built a stupa out of sand . . ."

268 " . . . secluded in the mountains, [I] have practiced asceticism . . . the games of a child, even they [have merit]"

426 "I shall not push through as a hijiri . . . while I shall play around"

pursuit of imayō, a genre without the powers of tradition possessed by genres like waka poetry, was considered a deviant form of "play" and criticized as such.[80] Criticism of a genre within the activity of "play" should not, however, be confused with criticism of "play" as an activity.

Besides "asobu" and "tawaburu," two other terms that appear in song 359, "kodomo" (child) and "koe" (voice), deserve attention. The figure of a child can be found in many songs in *Ryōjin hishō*, but the word "kodomo" appears in only four other lyrics. Twice it refers to children in the Lotus Sutra (songs 72 and 73), and twice it is used in the phrase "my child," where the speaker is an old woman (songs 363 and 366). In all these instances, "kodomo" seems to be used to refer to a child of a particular parent, not a generic child as indicated by the term "warawa" or "dōji." The term "kodomo," along with the term "wagami" (my very body), lays a twofold emphasis on the personal quality of this song: my child, my body. Although Baba Mitsuko argues that "wagami" indicates a body-mind dichotomy in which the body, engaged in sinful activities, is chastised by the mind, which seeks the Buddhist way, she provides no real evidence for this reading.[81] Her suggestion that the words

---

80. See, e.g., *Hōgen monogatari*, which indicates that the retired emperor Sutoku described Goshirakawa as being devoid of knowledge in literary studies and as engaged in excessive "play"; contextualizing this comment with *Chūyūki*'s complaint that lower-class art forms were infiltrating aristocratic culture suggests that there were those in the upper class who considered a member of the imperial household's involvement in non-traditional arts a problem (Yasuda Motohisa, *Goshirakawa jōkō*, pp. 25–28). Also, *Gukanshō*'s description of Goshirakawa as an unsuitable choice for emperor because he had gained a reputation for excessively engaging in "play" can be interpreted not necessarily as a critique of "play" as such but of its presence in excess form (see Okami and Akamatsu, *Gukanshō*, p. 216).

81. For example, *Senzai wakashū*, a twenty-volume waka anthology commissioned by none other than Goshirakawa and compiled by Fujiwara no Toshinari around 1187–88, contains a poem by a woman identified as "asobi Todo":

819　　kazu naranu　　mi nimo kokoro no　　arigao ni
　　　　　hitori mo tsuki wo　　nagametsuru kana

　　　Unworthy of being counted　　this body—but my mind putting
　　　on　　a brave face
　　　all alone, at the moon　　I did gaze.

(Katano and Matsuno, *Senzai wakashū*, p. 247.)

The speaker presents herself as pretending to know the "proper way" to appreciate the proper poetic/aesthetic value of the moon. Although the phrase "kazu naranu" may seem like an expression of the asobi's admission of her own "lowliness," it is a common expression that "asobi tawaburu" and "wagami" together indicate the remorse of the asobi therefore remains unconvincing. Baba interprets "kodomo" to be a child of a "wretched," low-class parent like the asobi, a reading that further confirms her view of these women.[82] Since the term appears in the context of the Lotus Sutra, it seems more appropriate to view its usage here as simply indicating that the child is the speaker's, and perhaps even as an allusion to the enlightenment of the father through the playing of his children, Jōzō and Jōgen.

The term "koe," which I discuss above in the section on orality, appears as a single word (not in a compound) a total of twelve times aside from its appearance in song 359.[83] Seven of these instances refer directly to the chanting of sutras, and five to natural settings. In the latter category, three describe sounds that specifically evoke the Buddhist realm (for example, the bell of Gion shōja), and two appear in a landscape setting (the wind and a deer-scaring device). These examples show that the term "koe" indicates a sound emitted by a human agent only in the case of chanted sutras. This gives the line "playing children's voices" in song 359 strong overtones of relations to the divine.

What can be concluded from this discussion? Baba, like other scholars of Ryōjin hishō, devotes so much of her attention to establishing the verbs "asobu" and "tawaburu" in song 359 as indicators that the topic is the asobi that even though she mentions in passing that the verbs *also* refer to the passage in the Lotus Sutra about a child playing, she fails to notice that the very *subject* of the song is a child at play. The subject of the passage in the Lotus Sutra that contains the words rendered in Japanese as "asobu" and "tawaburu"[84]

---

appears elsewhere including the earlier *Shūi wakashū*, a collection from around 1005, in a poem unrelated to asobi:

984   *kazu naranu   mi wa kokoro dani   nakaranan*
          omoi shirazu wa   uramizaru beku
       Would my unworthy-of-being-counted body did not have a heart either;
          knew I nothing of desire,   there would be nothing to resent.

(Komachiya, *Shūi wakashū*, p. 281.)
The inclusion of poem 819 in an imperially commissioned anthology at the time of Goshirakawa's compilation of *Ryōjin hishō* shows again that the asobi's talents at waka composition continued to be taken seriously.

82. Baba Mitsuko, "Asobi wo sen to ya umareken," p. 19.

83. Songs 47, 117, 118, 171, 182 (twice), 189, 230, 304, 332, 429, and 434.

84. As understood by the composers of the songs of *Ryōjin hishō*; the actual Lotus Sutra passage contains only the character for "tawaburu," even though songs in *Ryōjin hishō* about

is a child, whose playing can be a foundation for attaining Buddhist enlightenment. Is it not possible, then, that song 359, which presents a child and the actions asobu and tawaburu, is indeed a song based on and in praise of the Lotus Sutra passage, not a song about an asobi lamenting her sins while alluding loosely to the Lotus Sutra passage? I suggest that past interpretations have forced a connection between the figure of the child and the supposed speaker, the asobi, by introducing the element of remorseful comparison between the sinful acts of flirtation and prostitution and the purity of the innocent children and that they have been blind to this alternative reading, which can explain the presence of the words and figures, because scholars have approached this poem with assumptions about prostitute/entertainers.

Why, then, is song 359 not included in the Lotus Sutra song group in the hōmon no uta Buddhist song section? There are two possible reasons: first, there are many other songs in the kamiuta section that refer to the sutra by mentioning specific terms or allude to Buddhist ideas or images in general. This song also points less directly to the passage in the Lotus Sutra than do songs such as number 67, which contains specific references including a quotation, and may have been placed elsewhere for this reason.[85] Second, an important feature of hōmon no uta is praise for a particular Buddhist deity, since they were often sung in circumstances that required the assistance of appropriate deities.[86] This suggests that song 359, which does not single out a specific deity for praise, did not belong in the hōmon no uta category and was therefore placed in a different section of the collection, even though it owes its topic to the Lotus Sutra.

Song 359 must also be read in the context of the sequence in which it appears: number 351 begins a series of songs that contain animal images, which

---

this passage all contain an additional character "asobu." The Lotus Sutra "Expedient Means" chapter has: "and children at play build mounds with little stones and as towers for the Buddha—these people shall all attain buddhahood." Also, in the "Simile and Parable" chapter, parable of the Burning House: "The goat cart, the deer cart, the ox cart, they are now all outside the gate, so you may play with them" (see Sakamoto and Iwamoto, Hokkekyō, 1: 114–15 and 164–65, respectively).

85. Takagi Yutaka (Heian jidai hokke bukkyōshi kenkyū, p. 295) also contends that in general, hōmon no uta follow sutra passages very closely, often expressing a sentiment directly in response to a passage or commenting on a particular passage. Song 359 may have been placed in the miscellaneous section since it did not fit these descriptions.

86. Ono, "Ryōjin hishō hōmon no uta no shinkō to hyōgen," p. 62.

continues until 358, a song that lists names of colors but ends with the image of a deer-patterned fabric and inserts the character of a son-in-law (one's child). Then 359 appears without any animal images, although, as illustrated above, the verb "asobu" is frequently used to describe the actions of animals, and therefore may relate this song to this sequence in this way; 360 resumes the animal imagery, picking up the deer image that appeared in 358. Both 361 and 362 contain animals but introduce the element of children and youth; this leads into the series on human children that starts with 363. This sequence suggests that song 359 plays a transitional role in the flow of images from animals to children.

As has been pointed out by Baba Mitsuko and other Japanese scholars, neither the speaker nor the subject of the first two lines of the song is identified. The reading "[are/were he/she/they] born in this world to play?" is ust as possible as "[am/was I] born in this world to play?" In my translation and interpretation of song 359, I have tried to reflect these ambiguities in an attempt to steer away from our modern notions about prostitution. My intent has been to reconsider past readings by examining motivations for interpretation. This is not to suggest, however, that song 359 prohibits its own recontextualization in which the word "asobi" becomes a pun on both the verb "to play" and women entertainers; as I noted above in this chapter, the genre of imayō begs for fluidity in interpretation from the moment a song is composed. I am proposing that the possibility of such a pun does not connote inherent sinfulness; rather, based on the numerous pieces of evidence discussed above, I argue that the song appears to be, above all, about children at divine play. The asobi who laments and recognizes her "sins" has largely been concocted by those in later generations who chose to contextualize it as such; the ambiguities of the song demand that we re-examine such assumed discourses so that all the marginalizing processes can be unveiled.

"Warera wa nanishite oinuran": The Nature of Remorse

Another song in Ryōjin hishō has been associated with the asobi's perceptions of their own sinfulness:

235   *warera wa nanishite oinuran*   *omoeba ito koso awarenare*   *ima wa*
       saihō gokuraku no   *mida no chikai wo nenzubeshi*

What have I been doing until old age?   thinking about it is indeed
sadly moving;   now, the Western Ultimate Joy's   Amitābha's
vows [we/I] shall concentrate upon.[87]

This song has been interpreted as the lament of an asobi named Tonekuro
(or Toneguro) and her hopes for the afterlife; the line "What have I been
doing until old age?" is commonly assumed to imply that the asobi is regretting the profession that she has pursued all her life.[88] This reading is usually
accompanied by the citation of passages in other texts in which this song appears. Here, I examine these texts in detail and discuss the significance of the
presentation of song 235 in *Ryōjin hishō*.

Ryōjin hishō kudenshū briefly mentions the Tonekuro story and song 235:
"The asobi Tonekuro was caught up in a battle, and at the moment of her
death, she sang "now, the Western Ultimate Joy's" and achieved ōjō."[89] This
passage appears in the section that lists the miraculous powers attained by
singing imayō songs. The emphasis is on the ability of imayō songs in general to induce ōjō; it does not comment on the characteristics of asobi
women. Furthermore, the line used to allude to the song, "now, the Western
Ultimate Joy's" (that is, rebirth in the Pure Land), appears in the middle of
the song; Goshirakawa does not refer to song 235 by citing the first line,
"What have I been doing to old age?" This contrasts with the preceding example of ōjō achieved through imayō: the courtier Fujiwara no Michisue
(1090–1128) had suffered repeatedly from high fevers. After he sings song 160
twice, his fever subsided.[90] In this case, song 160 is indicated by its first line,
"never, ever, in any way speak ill." The only other specific song cited in this
section is simply noted as "the song 'Shōtoku taishi,'" an unidentified number whose singing enabled a Shirogimi of Takasago, possibly another asobi,
to attain ōjō. The fragmentary lines used to allude to imayō songs seem to be
those that describe the "essence" of the song. Since song 235 is represented

---

87. Kobayashi Yoshinori et al., *Ryōjin hishō, Kanginshū, Kyōgen kayō*, pp. 68–69.

88. See, e.g., Baba Mitsuko, *Imayō no kokoro to kotoba*, p. 168.

89. Kobayashi Yoshinori et al., *Ryōjin hishō, Kanginshū, Kyōgen kayō*, p. 179.

90. *Yumeyume ikanimo soshiruna yo   ichiyo hokke no jujisha woba   yakuō
     yuse tamon jikoku jurasechi no   darani wo toitezo mamorunaru*
   Never, ever, in any way speak ill   of those who receive and uphold the
       One Vehicle Lotus;   Bhaiṣajya-rāja, Prādanaśūra, Vaiśravaṇa, Dhṛtarāṣṭra,
       and the ten rākṣasī   chant the dhāraṇi for their protection.

(Ibid., p. 179.)

by its third line about the Western Ultimate Joy, it is likely that Goshira-kawa perceived the significance of the story of Tonekuro to lie in her attainment of ōjō, not in her lament about her life.

In contrast, a more elaborate version of the story appears in *Hōbutsushū* (An anthology of treasures; written a few years after 1179), which was composed/compiled around the same period as the *Kudenshū*:

Tonekuro, an asobi of Kanzaki, through the years favored the ways of love; not knowing the name of the Buddhist Law, [she] crossed this world upon the waves on a boat. She spent [time] leaving herself up to the guests who came and went. When she was traveling to the western provinces accompanying a man, she encountered pirates and was stabbed in many places; when she was about to die, she stirred herself up to face westward and sang over and over the song:

> *warera wa nanishini oiniken   omoeba ito koso awarenare   ima wa*
> *saihō gokuraku no   mida no chikai wo nenzubeshi*
> For what have I grown to old age?   thinking about it is indeed sadly
> moving;   now, the Western Ultimate Joy's   Amitābha's vows
> [we/I] shall concentrate upon.

She simply became weaker and weaker and expired. From the western direction a faint sound of music was heard, and above the ocean billowed purple clouds, they say.

"Even if one does not concentrate solely on the Muryōju [= Amitābha] Buddha and also does not always plant many roots of goodness, if one follows the merits of practicing various good deeds and turns to face the Muryōju Buddha and hopes to achieve ōjō, this person at the time of his or her death shall be chosen to receive guidance," it says in the Daihōshaku Sutra. It is true that if a person concentrates upon the Muryōju Buddha, even if his or her merits are few, if he or she turns to face this Buddha, he or she shall achieve ōjō. What Gochūsho-ō [Prince Tomohira, 964–1009] wrote,

> even [one who committed] the ten evils, [Amitābha] still saves
> this is more [thorough] than a fast wind parting the clouds;
> to even one prayer he will always respond
> this is like the vast ocean which swallows up a tiny drop of dew

is in this frame of mind [that is, it contains the same essential meaning].[91]

This version of the story is strikingly different from the one in *Kudenshū*. Whereas in *Kudenshū* the details are kept to a minimum, *Hōbutsushū* opens with a contemptuous description of Tonekuro's lifestyle before her trip to

---

91. Koizumi et al., *Hōbutsushū, Kankyo no tomo, Hirasan kojin reitaku*, pp. 345–46.

the western provinces. The passage describing the circumstances of her ōjō is similar, but the author adds a passage from the Daihōshaku Sutra (The collection of sutras from the Great Jewel)[92] and Prince Tomohira's poem and argues that Tonekuro's story is an example of the "truths" expressed in these two texts.

In considering the differences between the two narratives, we must keep in mind the aims of each work. *Kudenshū* was intended to attest to the powers and traditions of the imayō genre and to legitimize its practice. *Hōbutsushū* is a work by Taira no Yasuyori (1145–after 1200?), a close retainer of Goshirakawa who is mentioned in *Kudenshū* as a skilled performer of imayō; he was exiled in 1177 to Kikai ga shima as a result of the Shishigatani Incident[93] but was later pardoned and seems to have led a quieter life until his death.[94] Yasuyori is thus a slightly younger contemporary of Goshirakawa and represents another viewpoint in the late Heian era. *Hōbutsushū* is a collection of setsuwa stories presented as a dialogue between a monk and an audience, arranged according to a definite outline established by the author. The stories aim through didactic means to illustrate the paths to Buddhist enlightenment. The focus here, then, is on the practice of Buddhism advocated by Yasuyori, or at least by the persona of the monk who tells the tales. Within this didactic framework, Tonekuro's story serves as evidence to support a teaching of the Daihōshaku Sutra, which states that even one who is not particularly meritorious can attain ōjō if he or she upholds this sutra for even a short while. To emphasize the omnipotence of this teaching, it was convenient to stress her "sinful" habits (especially from a Buddhist perspective), so that the message that even one who is as "lowly" as this woman can be saved comes forth clearly. This perspective appears in *Kudenshū* as well, yet the conflict of interests in *Kudenshū* makes its attitude toward the asobi ambiguous, whereas within the framework of *Hōbutsushū*, the asobi plays a more straightforward role.

Despite the judgments of the storyteller in *Hōbutsushū*, the song that Tonekuro sings still cannot necessarily be interpreted as a deathbed expression of remorse about her occupation. The first lines of the two versions

---

92. Sanskrit: *mahā-ratnakūta-dharmaparyāya-śatasāhasrika-grantha*.

93. On the third day of the sixth month of the first year of Jishō, six close retainers of Goshirakawa were arrested by Taira no Kiyomori for plotting to overthrow Kiyomori's regime. Of the six, four were exiled (see accounts in *Gyokuyō*, *Heike monogatari*, and *Genpei seisuiki*).

94. Koizumi et al., *Hōbutsushū, Kankyo no tomo, Hirasan kojin reitaku*, pp. 522–30.

differ: *warera wa nanishini oiniken* (*Hōbutsushū*), and *warera wa nanishite oinuran* (*Ryōjin hishō*). The change in meaning, however, is important in the overall interpretation of this song. Whereas the implication of the *Ryōjin hishō*'s version is "I wonder, what have I been doing all my life, until I have grown so old?," that of the *Hōbutsushū* suggests "for what purpose have I grown this old?" This seems an appropriate sentiment for an asobi who is about to die from wounds received in a pirate attack. In the *Ryōjin hishō* version, the speaker looks back at his or her life in general and sighs at the futility of it all, but the *Hōbutsushū* speaker cries out in frustration at having grown old (in this case, only to face death by assault) with no rewards at the end of life. In both cases, the answer is to call on Amitābha. Even within the marginalizing frame of the narrative, the song lyric itself remains resistant to a reading as an expression of remorse over one's sinful existence.

Two later works also present Tonekuro and song 235. Their notable lack of moral judgment indicates that this song continued to be presented in a variety of ways and was not caught in a teleological trajectory of increasing marginalization of asobi. One is the Zendōji-bon version of *Denpō-e ryūtsū*, a picture scroll about the monk Hōnen's life (dated 1237):

Also, the chōja of the same port lay ill in old age, and at the last moment when she sang an imayō song,

> nanishini warera ga oiniken   omoeba ito koso kanashikere   ima wa
> saihō gokuraku no   mida no chikai wo tanomubeshi
> For what have I grown to old age?   thinking about it is indeed
>   sad now,   the Western Ultimate Joy's   Amitābha's vows
>   [we/I] shall rely upon,

purple clouds billowed over the blue ocean, music was heard by people, and a wondrous fragrance wafted from her body as she achieved ōjō; thus now each of those who looked to the shōnin [Hōnen] for help said they hoped to make ties [with the Buddha] as she did.[95]

This work is characterized by its lack of condemnation of the asobi's profession, even though Hōnen's role in assisting her ōjō is emphasized, for obvious reasons. This portrayal is consistent with Imahori Taitsu's critique of scholars who conflate *Hōnen shōnin gyōjō ezu* with *Denpō-e*.

The final example is from *Jikkinshō* (ca. 1252), which contains another story about Tonekuro and her song (Chapter 10, Story 51).

---

95. Imahori, *Jingi shinkō no tenkai to bukkyō*, p. 208.

Tonekuro of Kanzaki was accompanying a man to Tsukushi when they encountered pirates. At the time when [she] received wounds everywhere and was about to die,

> warera nanishini oinuran   omoeba ito koso awarenare   ima wa
> saihō gokuraku no   mida no chikai wo nenzubeshi
> For what have I grown old?   thinking about it is indeed sadly
> moving; now,   the Western Ultimate Joy's   Amitābha's
> vows [we/I] shall conncentrate upon.

so she sang over and over and expired. At this time, in the west the sound of music was heard, and mysterious clouds billowed [they say]. Since her skill [in singing] was one that permeated her heart, she had sung imayō and had achieved ōjō. Attaining enlightenment does not depend on a particular deed; one should rely only on things to which one's heart is drawn in order to develop one's belief.[96]

The song sung by the asobi Tonekuro is a close variation of song 235 in the *Ryōjin hishō*.

The *Jikkinshō* narration emphasizes the marvelousness of Tonekuro's attainment of ōjō through singing imayō; there are no comments about the lowliness or the sinfulness of her status as asobi. I discuss the motivations and effects of *Jikkinshō* in Chapter 1; what is important in the present context is that this story appears in a chapter devoted to the literary and performing arts and their potential as means to attain political, social, and, here, religious advancement. The stories that follow it concern the composition of poetry and its effects on the attainment of ōjō. The preceding story is about non-ruling-class people in general, such as asobi, retainers, and wandering monks, whose poems were included in anthologies of poetry; these examples promote the idea of non-hereditary means of attaining power found throughout *Jikkinshō*. In addition, although the text "marginalizes" the asobi by proclaiming their "low" status in society, it places them among other marginalized groups and does not single them out as being particularly sinful. Here again, the song can be taken as a general commentary on one's life, not as remorse about one's pursuit of a particular profession.

In summary, the Tonekuro stories represent another instance of a modern overreading of asobi women's sinfulness. To claim that Tonekuro expresses remorse for a sinfulness universally recognized by society at the time is to focus on only one narrative about her life among many and to ignore

---

96. Izumi, *Jikkinshō*, p. 188.

the others. In neither song 359 nor song 235 do the lyrics position the asobi singing them as marginal. The songs in *Ryōjin hishō*, all authored by unnamed composers, are not transparent expressions of remorse by the asobi or any other group of women entertainers over their choice of profession or statements of the sinfulness of their lives. The figure of the asobi aware of her own incontestable "marginality" and "sinfulness," therefore, must be approached with suspicion; not only is it necessary to consider the ways in which such a trope was constructed in premodern texts, but also, in the case of the two songs examined above, it is vital that we closely investigate how recent scholarship in both Japanese and English has contributed to the petrification of otherwise dynamic processes of privileging and marginalization.

❧

In this chapter, I have attempted to expose the complex maneuverings of the compiler of *Ryōjin hishō*; I have also questioned the validity of twentieth-century scholars' claims that certain groups of women entertainers in the late Heian period were marginal beings by re-examining primary sources and paying particular attention to the declared motivations for marginalization or empowerment. I have argued not only that the marginalizing process is set into motion for specific reasons but also that the marginalizing process produces effects that are diverse, changing, and frequently contested or unrecognized. The example of these women shows that there is a need to reconsider scholarly approaches that either condemn a group as marginal and leave it at that (for example, Takikawa Masajirō) or promote a group as possessing some sort of intrinsic value because of their marginality (Saeki Junko); "marginality" should not be treated as an opaque and stagnant position. In light of these constructions, *Ryōjin hishō* cannot be read simply as a neutral collection of "historical" evidence about the practices of the times or an anthology of voices of the "common people." It is, instead, a site of contention of interested readings past and present.

The post–*Ryōjin hishō* history of the imayō genre and the women entertainers who sang these songs is usually told as a grim tale of decline.[97] The next major compilation of songs was the *Kanginshū* (ca. 1518). Although Emperor Gotoba was an ardent practitioner of imayō and a patron of women entertainers, and although imayō and the asobi continue to appear in texts

---

97. See, among many others, Fukazawa, *Chūsei shinwa no rentanjutsu*, pp. 132–33; and Kwon, "The Female Entertainment Tradition in Medieval Japan," p. 317.

after the time of Goshirakawa (for example, *Towazugatari* [An unasked-for tale; ca. 1306–13]) and the shirabyōshi continued to be patronized into the Kamakura period, no collection of imayō songs on the scale of *Ryōjin hishō* ever appeared again. *Ryōjin hishō* itself was lost until the beginning of the twentieth century. Ironically in light of Goshirakawa's ambitions, the text that was supposed to embody the pinnacle of imayō's success and popularity became inaccessible for many generations.

We must keep in mind, however, that other lineages of imayō presumably continued, and whether people at all levels of society at the time, including the asobi and the kugutsu themselves, considered *Ryōjin hishō* to be the definitive work in the genre or regarded Goshirakawa as the true and only master remains questionable. For instance, the lineage chart in *Imayō no ranshō* provides a glimpse into an alternative discourse. The chart suggests that indeed, as Goshirakawa had planned, his own line of imayō practice ended with him; with the compilation of *Ryōjin hishō*, which at once exalted and terminated the possibility of imayō's oral transmission, he succeeds in becoming the last authentic practitioner of imayō as *he* understood it. On the other hand, other master-disciple lines appear to have continued much longer than Goshirakawa's and may even have enjoyed more influence or popularity; due to the lack of surviving evidence, we can only speculate about them. The chart at the very least supports the argument that Goshirakawa's positioning of *Ryōjin hishō* as the definitive summation of the imayō tradition is, indeed, a carefully crafted presentation that has successfully managed to convince generations of scholars after his time. Taking Goshirakawa's words in *Kudenshū* as the only "truth" about the practice of imayō, its singers, and its lineage would be to buy into the notions that he sought to establish through this work: the importance and efficacy of imayō, his mastery of this technique and therefore his rightful position as the singular authority on it, and the securing of his own imayō ōjō. Goshirakawa's work must be situated in the context of these aims; his views represent one version of "truth" among many.

Part II
  Komachi

3 Authored Margins:
The Prosperity and Decline of Komachi

In Part I, I question the ontological status of the "margin" through detailed examinations of discourses about women entertainers and suggest that examining the processes of marginalization is a more productive endeavor than looking for static characteristics that define a "margin." In Part II, I focus on representations of the mid-ninth-century poet Ono no Komachi in the mid-Heian to the early Kamakura periods. This chapter investigates the workings of a particular marginalizing process and its resulting effect: the gendered construction of an authorial figure and, consequently, the texts attributed to her. I argue that texts categorized as "Heian women's writing," here the poems by Komachi, may be the end products of highly complex processes of construction of both the authorial figure and her supposed writings according to the agendas and strategies of later generations. To emphasize the constructed nature of "marginality" is not to trivialize the constructions as "fictitious" and therefore inconsequential; on the contrary, discursive constructions, when utilized by those with specific powers—such as poetry anthology compilers—can have a cumulative and lasting impact on not only the understanding of the marginalized figure by later generations but also the canon of premodern literature itself.

Commentators and scholars over the centuries have vigorously debated the details of Ono no Komachi's "life story." The sketchy consensus is that she was probably active around the mid-ninth century (the dates of her birth and death are unknown) and was well-known for her poetry; eighteen of her waka are included in the imperially commissioned *Kokinshū* (An anthology of waka past and present; ca. 905) anthology. By this time, she was already singled out as the only woman among the six representative poets of the ninth century. When Fujiwara no Kintō established the *sanjūrokkasen* (thirty-six poetic geniuses/immortals) around 1009 to 1012, Ono no Komachi was included as one of the *rokkasen* (classic six poetic geniuses/immortals). One "personal collection" of her poems, *Komachishū*, survives, but the date of its compilation is uncertain, and the collection includes a large number of poems that were probably not by Komachi. Most scholars believe that she served at court, although they differ on the exact nature of her occupation: the proposals range from *uneme*, a daughter of a provincial officer who served at court, to one of the imperial consorts of Emperor Nimmyō (r. 833–50).[1] Her life leaves much room for conjecture.

Since her lifetime, however, narratives about Komachi have been told and retold in a number of different genres. She is portrayed as an unparalleled beauty who was skilled at composing waka poetry but declined physically and materially in her later years.[2] In the Medieval era, the stories proliferated and became the subjects of well-known noh plays; in the Edo period and beyond, she appears repeatedly in popular stories and regional legends.[3] The first stage in this long history of legends about Komachi occurred, however, during the mid- to late Heian period. The two central tropes that take shape during this period are relevant in studying the relationship between women and marginalizing processes.[4]

Modern Japanese scholarship on Komachi, although diverse, is more sparse than one might expect, considering that she remains a household name to this day. Much scholarly effort has been dedicated to investigating the "true image" (*jitsuzō*) or "real life" of Komachi; since the details of her life

---

1. For a thorough discussion of the exact status and occupation of Komachi, see Tsunoda, "Ono no Komachi no mibun," pp. 47–53.

2. Katagiri, *Ono no Komachi tsuiseki*, pp. 6–7.

3. For a diagram of the development of legends concerning Komachi, see Maeda, *Ono no Komachi*, p. 316. Also, in the Edo period, Komachi was rumored to have lacked a vagina and was therefore said to be unable to have relationships with men; the relationship between her "favoring-the-ways-of-love" reputation and this opposite extreme would be a fascinating topic for future analysis.

4. I use the term "trope" throughout to indicate groups of stories that either constantly refer to a single "originary" text or share common characteristics crucial to a particular marginalizing representation. The intent is to genealogize, rather than to treat narratives as elements of a homogenous group, or, conversely, as unrelated products.

are nebulous, research has focused on delineating her biography through the poems attributed to her in *Kokinshū* and *Komachishū*, as well as through clues in waka commentaries and setsuwa collections, in an attempt to create a single authoritative and coherent narrative of her life. Representative works are Yamaguchi Hiroshi's *Keien no shijin: Ono no Komachi*,[5] Ueki Gaku's *Tamatsukuri Komachi to Ono no Komachi*,[6] Yokota Yukiya's *Ono no Komachi denki kenkyū*,[7] and Tanaka Kimiharu's *Komachi shigure*.[8] Such attempts to excavate the "truth" about Komachi's life tend to result in vague biographical speculations and give rise to questions about the possibility of such a reconstruction. An exception to this biographical approach is Kobayashi Shigemi's assertion that Komachi is a conglomerate figure embodying the oral storytelling traditions and the presence of miko shamanesses in the Ono lineage, which manifest themselves in stories about her.[9] Although this view takes into account the constructed aspect of Komachi's figure, the equation drawn between her narratives and the artistic skills possessed and maintained by the Ono and related clans ignores the questions Who was writing what and for what possible purposes? and What effects did the resulting text produce? Other approaches include compilations of "legends" about Komachi, which are valuable as reference sources but offer little analysis, such as Maeda Yoshiko's *Ono no Komachi* and Miyoshi Teiji's *Ono no Komachi kō-*

---

5. Yamaguchi Hiroshi, *Keien no shijin*. Although the existence of a Chinese model should suggest the constructed nature of Komachi's poems, Yamaguchi assumes that her poems closely mirror her life.

6. Ueki, *Tamatsukuri Komachi to Ono no Komachi*; this work proposes that Tamatsukuri Komachi was an actual person who lived about sixty years before Ono no Komachi. Ueki's evidence is generally ahistorical, and he does not regard Komachi's figure as a construction.

7. Yokota, *Ono no Komachi denki kenkyū*; a biographical investigation of Komachi.

8. Tanaka Kimiharu, *Komachi shigure*; an in-depth analysis of Komachi's *Kokinshū* poems together with biographical concerns. Other works include Kumagai, "Ono no Komachi no shinjitsu," pp. 24–32; and Asami, "Komachi henbō," pp. 12–34.

9. Kobayashi Shigemi, *Ono no Komachi kō*. Kobayashi ignores the fact that the various versions of the narratives about Komachi that appear in texts are not transparent manifestations of stories told by her kin; rather, they are mediated, motivated texts written and compiled by people outside this lineage group. The stories promote, negate, add and/or subtract aspects attributed to Komachi to suit different needs or aims. Kobayashi's treatment also tends to be ahistorical in its discussion of the professions of the Ono lineage, which was established long before the Heian period, since it is highly questionable whether their practices continued without change over the centuries. The author also assumes that polygamy necessarily bound women into an inescapably submissive role.

kyū. On the *minzokugaku* ("folk studies") front, in works such as "Josei to minkan denshō," Yanagita Kunio focused on the traveling female storytellers in later periods who told stories about Komachi.[10]

The most recent major Komachi scholar—who for the most part criticizes these past approaches—is Katagiri Yōichi, who states in *Ono no Komachi tsuiseki* that all representations of Komachi that people believed at some point to be true are worth studying (that is, although some scholars imply that only the search for her "true biography" is a valid endeavor, Katagiri proposes that the various "fictional" accounts of her life are also important as a subject of study).[11] He unfortunately claims that Komachi's "weak" figure "directly reflects the sorrow and distress of women in the mid-Heian era";[12] instead of asking who was constructing her figure in what particular ways for what purpose, he suggests that Komachi's poems simply echo the pitiable conditions of women that spontaneously gave rise to the tragic stories about her. He also reverts to "searching for the true Komachi" in another book.[13] On the other hand, in English-language scholarship, Sarah Strong has shown through her inquiry into noh pieces about Komachi and their sources that it is necessary to pay attention to the process by which specific gendered representations came into being.[14]

Using these recent views as a point of departure for my own investigation, I retain the idea that the figure of Komachi in the mid- to late Heian period is a conglomeration deriving from her poems, their interpretations, and narratives about her. I take this approach one step further by showing *how* and *why* certain representations came into existence. The importance of the narratives generated in this period lies not in their status as authoritative, undoctored accounts of her "actual life" (the very notion of a "reality" that preexists and stands outside textual production is itself problematic) but in the revelation of certain views on specific characteristics of women to be inferred from Komachi's constructed persona and actions. In this chapter, I argue that these characteristics are significant because (1) they are invoked, changed, and reinterpreted according to the textual setting, a process that reveals the non-uniform, fluctuating aspect of the marginalizing process; and

---

10. Yanagita, *Teihon Yanagita Kunio shū*, 8: 315–447.
11. Katagiri, *Ono no Komachi tsuiseki*, pp. 62–63, and *passim*.
12. Ibid., p. 106.
13. Katagiri, *Tensai sakka no kyozō to jitsuzō*, p. 237.
14. Strong, "The Making of a Femme Fatale," pp. 391–412.

(2) they had a significant impact on those responsible for literary attribution in this era. These individuals in turn contributed to the propagation of these characteristics and thereby reinforced their apparent "veracity."

Stories about Komachi found from the mid-Heian to the early Kamakura periods contain such repeated tropes as her unparalleled beauty, her literary skill, the waning of her attractiveness in her later years, her wandering in the Northeast, and her survival after death as a poetically inclined skull. The qualities that situate her figure at the center, both in the cultural and physical sense, are her physical attractiveness and poetic fame in the capital. As we shall see, these characteristics are repeatedly assigned to Komachi in the very stories that later result in marginalizing her figure. In fact, the texts seem to present these empowering qualities so that they can be shown to be ultimately ineffective and meaningless in the face of old age and poverty. I argue that this portrayal is a specifically gendered one in that the womanness of Komachi plays a crucial role in every instance. The reasons for such acts of marginalization can be located in both the religious and secular realms. On the one hand, authors interested in promoting particular Buddhist notions about material and sexual wealth found a convenient target in a particular representation of Komachi. On the other hand, texts catering to the newly risen ruling military class in the early Kamakura period could use her as a monitory lesson about choosing female companions.

Komachi's figure was marginalized through the discourse of female aging, which was woven into her legend by interested individuals and their texts in order to marginalize women who possessed that characteristic. Old age is not an essentially or inherently marginal category;[15] we must not take this for granted, even though the temptation may be great, given the marginalized status of senior citizens in a number of modern and historical cultures. If this category represents a marginalized state of being, as in the case of Ono no Komachi, then we must ask *why* it is represented as socially "marginal." In Komachi's case, this quality becomes marginalized because old age is deliberately associated with the loss of beauty and livelihood. I therefore argue that this quality is not itself "marginal" in the abstract; rather, it is polysemous. In certain contexts it serves to counteract the powers associated with a figure or a group. In this particular case, it is the ways in which such a characteristic was used in narratives about Komachi—

---

15. For example, the celebratory *okina*, manifested as an old man, is not necessarily socially marginal.

that this characteristic was configured in an attempt to negate the power of beauty and the resulting power of sexual attraction associated with her figure—that make it a marginalizing quality. The texts that marginalize Komachi through a portrayal of her aging draw selectively from certain pre-existing notions about old age and use them strategically to target her figure.

I begin with a close reading of passages and texts that tell one particular "story" about Komachi: in these works, Komachi is depicted as a woman who had been at the pinnacle of her wealth, both materially and physically, in her youth but became impoverished in old age and was forced to wander around as a beggar. I show that the different versions of this narrative come over time to domesticate Komachi's sexuality through the use of old age, here inseparably linked to physical decline and destitution. The early text *Tamatsukuri Komachishi sōsuisho* (The prosperity and decline of Tamatsukuri Komachi) does not focus on old age as a marginalizing quality that strips women of their sexual powers. Such a focus develops only in the later versions of Komachi's tale, which refer specifically to *Tamatsukuri* as their source of inspiration. This development indicates that in this case old age was a quality manipulated as capable of marginalizing precisely for the purpose of negating female sexual power. At the end of this section, I briefly discuss the images of women in old age as seen in texts from this period in order to assess portrayals of female aging in relation to Komachi's figure.

I then examine the selection and presentation of waka poems attributed to Komachi in imperially commissioned poetic anthologies as well as her "personal" poetry collection. Here, I show that the general trend toward the concretization of Komachi as a marginalized figure as seen in the narratives discussed in the preceding section can also be detected in these collections. I argue that these changes had important effects on the literary works attributed to her: there is a significant difference between the content of the poems credited to her in earlier poetry collections and those selected for inclusion in later collections. Such differences in the choices of compilers from different eras are deeply connected to the compilers' understanding of Komachi's character, and these variations in understanding interacted dialectically with the narratives about her life circulating at the time. Komachi's marginalization, therefore, was not simply a series of attempts by variously motivated individuals to domesticate her figure that had no lasting impact. In fact, the selections of poems as well as the narratives show that her marginalization had significant effects on her literary oeuvre because the link between this authorial figure and her literary works was made transparent by the editors of anthologies and by the authors of stories about her—that is, the poems were presented as telling a story about her "actual" life. By analyzing the transformation of the figure of Komachi as a literary producer, I problematize the ideas of authorship and attribution.

THE PROSPERITY AND DECLINE OF
ONO NO KOMACHI

The first trope I explore in detail is the presentation of Komachi as a prosperous woman who becomes a destitute hag forced to wander in search of sustenance. Since the earliest known text in which this trope appears is *Tamatsukuri Komachishi sōsuisho*, I refer to the group of writings featuring this trope as the *Tamatsukuri* "line" of texts. Hosokawa Ryōichi has proposed that the negative portrayal of Komachi reflects the historical rise of a "patriarchal" family system in the late Heian and Kamakura periods, in which single women were increasingly ostracized as an undesirable, unruly group that did not conform to the expected norms of marriage and family. He argues that the Pure Land Buddhism of this period attempted to implant in women the notion of their inherent impurity and sinfulness and thereby co-opt them into its religious paradigm by offering redemption.[16] Similarly, Enchi Fumiko argues that the male fear of a single woman without a husband or child contributed significantly to the unflattering portrayal of Komachi; she also asserts that an ideal beauty like Komachi had to be punished for the trials and agonies she caused men, even though such ideals were the constructions of the men themselves.[17] Although both readings are convincing, I would add that Hosokawa's "patriarchy" and Enchi's understanding of "men" as a category are monolithic, incontestable forces, and the assumption that "literature reflects history" assumes that "history," separable from "literature," is always the agent that acts upon the latter. Komachi's increasing marginalization was related not only to the development of familial "patriarchy" and male revenge but also to the question of how sexuality is located vis-à-vis old age. In the context of the works I discuss below, old age acts as a marginalizing quality because it is imbued with connotations of lack in the

16. Hosokawa, *Onna no chūsei*, pp. 218–80.
17. Enchi, "Ono no Komachi," pp. 126, 132.

economic sense (poverty) and the physical sense (loss of beauty). Furthermore, these "lacks," presented as inevitable, are significant precisely because
they serve to delegitimize and minimize the importance of the state in which
these qualities were present: beauty and sexual attractiveness made possible
in large part by economic prosperity (grooming, adornments, and clothing).
Below I discuss the tropes of beauty, material wealth, old age, and religion
and their presentation in *Tamatsukuri* and examine the ways in which these
narrative features are appropriated, emphasized, or even ignored in favor
of other characteristics in the later texts that refer back to *Tamatsukuri*'s
Komachi.

Tamatsukuri Komachishi sōsuisho

Tamatsukuri Komachishi sōsuisho (see Appendix, pp. 306–21, for a translation)
takes the form of a Chinese-style poem with a lengthy introduction. The
prose introduction is written in couplets of four and six characters, a style that
became popular in the Six Dynasties period (220–588), and the *zan*-style
poem of Buddhist praise is composed of 124 five-character lines.[18] The whole
work is said to be an explication of the Suffering of Old Age in the Buddhist
paradigm of the Four Sufferings (which also include birth, sickness, and
death) and is permeated by the ideology of *jōdo*, the Pure Land.[19] As many
scholars have pointed out, the text draws from a number of sources. The Chinese influence is obvious: the text itself claims that the poem is based on Bo
Juyi's "Qinzhong yin" (Lament of Qin; ca. 810), a series of ten poems about
prosperity and decline. We can also see influences of other poems by Bo Juyi
such as "Pipa xing" (Song of the lute; ca. 815). In addition, the list of foods in
the introduction is quite similar to the one in *Youxian ku* (Wanderings in the
cave of the immortals), a prose story by Zhang Zhuo (660–732), and elements
in the descriptions of Komachi's decline can be traced to such early works as
Zuozhuan and *Liji*.[20] Scholars have pointed out that the poem relies heavily on
the *Sutra of Meditation on the Buddha of Infinite Life* (*Kan'muryōju kyō*). They
also cite Japanese texts on which passages seem to be modeled: Genshin's (942–

---

18. Yamauchi et al., *Tamatsukuri Komachi sōsuisho*, p. 123. Specifically, this example of *zan* (poetry in praise of the Buddha) takes a *jie* (gāthā) format of regulated verse.

19. Tochio, "Tamatsukuri Komachishi sōsuisho," p. 29.

20. *Zuozhuan* (ca. 350 B.C.): *The Zuo Transmission*, an annotation of and addendum to the *Spring and Autumn Annals*. *Liji* (edited in the Han dynasty): *The Book of Rites*; one of the Six Classics.

1017) Pure Land paradigm as expressed in his work *Ōjō yōshū* (A collection of crucial texts for attaining rebirth in the Pure Land), which I discuss in detail in Chapter 4, and "Hinjogin" (Song of the impoverished woman), a poem by Ki no Haseo (845–912).[21] I refer to the latter, also influenced by "Pipa xing," in the following analysis.

Tamatsukuri was traditionally attributed to the monk Kūkai (774–835), the founder of the Shingon school in Japan, but many premodern commentators questioned this attribution, and almost all modern scholars reject it.[22] Most do agree, however, that it was probably written by a Buddhist monk profoundly influenced by the ideas of the Pure Land, possibly for *shōdō*, oral storytelling for the purpose of instructing believers,[23] in the mid-Heian period, and that it was well known by the late Heian period. The relevance of the name "Tamatsukuri" remains a mystery; it may be a place-name[24] or a clan name.

I discuss this text at length here since certain other narratives about Komachi, especially those of the late Heian period, mention that Ono no Komachi and the central figure(s) presented in *Tamatsukuri* were frequently considered one and the same. I illustrate some tropes presented in *Tamatsukuri* that become associated with Ono no Komachi's figure in this and other texts in order to show how certain features of the character "Komachi" found in this text became magnified or ignored in later stories. Overall, *Tamatsukuri* is important in that it presents two different versions of the character Komachi and is much less concerned (if at all) with the "sin" of Komachi's sexuality than are the later works that embrace certain details of

---

21. For a more detailed list of allusions, see Miyoshi, *Ono no Komachi kōkyū*, p. 220. See also Tochio, "*Tamatsukuri Komachishi sōsuisho*."

22. Scholars reject this traditional attribution since Ono no Komachi lived after Kūkai's death. Whether the Komachi of *Tamatsukuri* was in fact conceived of as being the same as Ono no Komachi at the time of the writing of this text is unclear; however, what is relevant to the discussion at hand is that the authors of the texts discussed below clearly assume that *Tamatsukuri*'s Komachi and Ono no Komachi are the same person.

23. Yamauchi et al., *Tamatsukuri Komachishi sōsuisho*, p. 125. However, Tochio ("*Tamatsukuri Komachishi sōsuisho*," p. 34) argues that in fact the surviving text may have been passed on exclusively in the Shingon tradition and read only by a limited audience. He does not present concrete evidence that this text was not used for shōdō; I proceed in this chapter, therefore, with the assumption that this work had at least some sort of audience outside an exclusive group of Shingon monks.

24. Well-known places called Tamatsukuri were found in Mutsu, Settsu, and Izumo provinces.

the story such as destitution and wandering but explicitly attribute the cause of her downfall to her love of love.

The introduction presents two characters: a wandering monk and an old, impoverished woman who we can assume is named Komachi because of the title of the work, although she is never addressed by that name in the text. The monk serves as the narrator who frames, in the prose introduction, the old woman's lengthy poetic monologue. The monk does not figure in the poem, which is presented almost entirely as a monologue by the old woman. The most striking feature of this pair of texts may be the differences in the details of the life of the protagonist, "Komachi." For the most part, scholars have tended to neglect these differences. One scholar who does address these differences, Watanabe Hideo, proposes that the two parts form an integrated whole, that the poem is an expansion of the tropes presented in the introduction, and that the two mirror each other neatly in that the introduction portrays the past and the present, whereas the poem addresses the present and the future.[25] Another scholar suggests that the two parts were written at different times by different authors and were joined in the mid-Heian, when the present title was given to the work to associate it explicitly with Komachi.[26] In light of this controversy, the "Komachis" in the two parts should not be equated immediately without question. A study of the differences between the two figures may help expose the multivalent discourses in this work. Below I therefore consider the introduction and the poem at first separately and then together.

The figure who appears in the introduction explains that she was born into an improbably wealthy family; her parents provide her with fantastic luxuries and plot to have her attain the status of empress. The untimely death of her entire family in her prime, however, leads to the complete reversal of her fortunes; she loses everything and is reduced to destitution and to seeking salvation in the Buddhist path. The exact timeline of her decline is unclear in this narrative, for decades must have passed between the death of her family and her meeting with the traveling monk; the "gap" is occupied in the poem, which describes her marriage to a hunter.

There is no general criticism of Komachi or women's "sexual abundance" in this particular narrative, despite the connections which are made between her figure and sexuality. The nature of Komachi's family occupation is sug-

---

25. Watanabe Hideo, "Ono no Komachi," pp. 80–81.
26. Tochio, "*Tamatsukuri Komachishi sōsuisho,*" pp. 30–32.

gested by the term *shōka* (*changjia* in Chinese): it is used for a household whose livelihood is singing and performance, with the women commonly engaged in prostitution.[27] The word *chang* appears in Bo Juyi's poem "Pipa xing";[28] since this poet's work is mentioned as an influence on *Tamatsukuri*, it is likely that this definition applies to the usage of the term here.

This text is the only one during the period covered in this chapter that names Komachi as a rough equivalent of the asobi, the subject of the two previous chapters of this book. Her association with the asobi, however, is evident elsewhere, as seen in *Shinsen rōeishū* (compiled by Fujiwara no Moto-toshi probably around 1107–23), which I note in Chapter 1: Komachi's poem from *Gosenshū* (ca. 950s, compiled by a committee) about weeping over a life spent on a boat appears under the *yūjo* (a Sinified reading of *asobi*) heading. It is possible that her poem was included in this section simply because its subject was wandering amid the waves, an image associated with the asobi. Even if this was the case, the development of Komachi's figure as an irogo-nomi, or one who favors the ways of love, in later stories suggests that Ko-machi was being associated, intentionally or not, with an abundance of sex-ual relations. Also, in the context of other works that focus on the asobi and old age, which I outline below in this chapter, it can be argued that "Ko-machi's loss of her [sexual] weapon is made more heart-wrenching since her beauty and sexual attraction were her livelihood."[29] Sexuality was becoming established as an important factor in Komachi's "downfall" legends, which later come to read her decrepitude as a result of her previous sexual over-confidence. Yet there is no condemnation of Komachi's sexuality on the whole in this text. We must also keep in mind two factors. First, the passage simply says that her performance/prostitution family was a wealthy and prosperous one. This reference represents at least a neutral attitude toward the family's business. Second, nowhere else in the introduction or the poem are there descriptions of her career as a singing girl. Even though the foun-dations of the legend that Komachi was an asobi or a promiscuous woman were built around this time, the contrast between her presumed profession, for which sexual attractiveness was vital, and the miserable state in which she finds herself in old age is implicit rather than explicit in *Tamatsukuri*. In-stead, the focus is on the issue of prosperity.

---

27. Morohashi, *Dai kanwa jiten*, 1: 840.
28. In Bo Juyi's poem, the term is *changnü*, or a woman who belongs to a *changjia*.
29. Saeki, *Yūjo no bunkashi*, pp. 161–62.

The details of her "downfall" are of particular importance to my argument. Even though the text states that Komachi was arrogant in the past and has now "fallen," she is portrayed as a victim of family ambition and misfortune; her parents indulge her in material wealth "beyond [their] station," turn down appropriate marriage prospects in order to achieve their goal, and leave her helpless at their death. The criticism, aside from the general attack on material wealth, is therefore focused not on Komachi herself but on her family.[30] The downfall of their plans may be a comment on the "presumptuousness" of an entertainment house in accruing so much property and hoping to marry into the imperial household. If "Pipa xing" was indeed a strong influence upon this text, then this reading is reinforced by the attitude expressed in Bo Juyi's poem: the speaker meets a pipa lute player upon a boat who tells him her life story. She had lived a luxurious life as a prosperous entertainer, but family tragedies coupled with the decline in her attractiveness forced her to become a merchant's wife. She criticizes the merchant for being concerned only with profit, and sadness is the prevailing mood. The introduction to the poem indicates that the speaker is being sent away from the capital in a demotion; the desolate state of the *pipa* player echoes his own misfortune.[31] The poem, then, is more an expression of bitterness over the turn of events in one's life than a didactic assertion that prosperity is inevitably punished by decline. After the deaths of her family, Komachi becomes an even more sympathetic character, as she gives away what little inheritance she has as offerings to the Buddhas and the souls of her deceased family. Komachi is presented less as a willfully indulgent individual and more as a good-hearted pampered "princess" who suffers a change in fortune because of the prideful plottings of her family and subsequently realizes the truth of the Buddhist way.

The narrative can also be read as a general cautionary tale for unmarried women: even the richest single woman can become impoverished almost instantly if she loses her family. Thus it is wise to prepare for such possibilities by realizing the vanity of material wealth and dedicating oneself to Buddhist

---

30. Maeda Yoshiko (*Ono no Komachi*, pp. 268–69) suggests that it was not overly ambitious for the family to hope that a prosperous woman entertainer would be able to enter the service of an emperor. The cases of Goshirakawa and Gotoba validate this statement, but since *Tamatsukuri* probably predates their reigns, it is not entirely clear whether Maeda's argument can be established in this case.

31. Uchida, *Hakushi monjū*, pp. 182–95.

practices. If "Hinjogin" was indeed a work that influenced *Tamatsukuri*, then this interpretation becomes even more plausible. Ki no Haseo's poem presents a woman who has become old and poor and proceeds to recount her life story. She had been brought up in a wealthy household, cherished by her parents. Suitors competed for her hand, but her parents decided to rely on a go-between and married the daughter to a good-for-nothing fool, on whom they spent a fortune. The parents then died, and the brothers of the daughter scattered; her husband also left. The household wealth declined steadily until she reached her current state. The poem ends with an admonition from the woman: "I say to the daughters of rich and noble houses of this world: in choosing a husband, observe his intentions and not his looks. Also, I beg the parents of the daughters of this world: write this down on a sash [i.e., do not forget this matter]."[32] The description of the protagonist's life is similar to that of Komachi's, especially up until her marriage to the unsuitable man. Her decline after the death of her parents also closely resembles that depicted in *Tamatsukuri*; the major difference between these two works is the extensive infusion of Pure Land ideas of transience into Komachi's story. The useless husband in this poem may be related to the figure of the abusive, meat-eating hunter who appears in the poem part of *Tamatsukuri*, discussed below. In any case, the message in "Hinjogin" is spelled out clearly and unambiguously; *Tamatsukuri* is less overt, but a similar cautionary tone—with a Buddhist twist—can be gathered from the progression of Komachi's life.

Tamatsukuri is ambiguous about Komachi's positionality within the text's moral economy. The attitude toward prosperity, which is crucially linked to Komachi's attractiveness, is highly conflicted. The introduction situates Komachi's physical beauty amid the material prosperity she enjoys. Her beauty is enhanced by, even predicated on, her wealth: grooming implements, makeup, jewelry, clothing. This intimate connection between material wealth and beauty makes the text's attitude toward wealth in general an important factor. The relationship between the Buddhist message of the vanity of material excess and the accumulated wealth portrayed in the text creates a definite ambivalence, if not contradiction, concerning the position of material wealth. Superficially, the message is clear: even the most extravagant luxuries have no meaning in life and may contribute to one's downfall later in life; therefore, one should follow the Buddhist path of renunciation.

---

32. Kakimura, *Honchō monzui chūshaku*, 1: 99.

Some Buddhist scriptures preach that culinary extravagance and luxurious surroundings can cause one to be reborn into the realm of the hungry ghosts.[33] However, if the author had intended to show the vanity of material possessions by presenting a character who had lost it all, the resulting effect is paradoxical. The lengthy and detailed descriptions of Komachi's extravagant lifestyle read like a catalogue of desirable but virtually unattainable products for the well-to-do. The numerous products of indulgence, painstakingly named, represent legendary and often unattainable objects, mostly of Chinese origin and many taken directly from works such as *Youxian ku*. The possibility of an early Heian woman of unclear origins who may have served at court possessing many of these items is questionable. In addition, the obscure characters used to describe these luxuries contain a strong element of both allusionistic and visual word-play.[34] Whether this enumeration actually served or was even intended to serve as a means to curb appetites for such fantasies of luxury is thus ambiguous; on the contrary, it may have defined the details of ultimate luxury and even stirred desires for the acquisition of such goods.[35]

Such an ambivalent attitude toward the material is reinforced in the passage "In the days when I toyed with the Luan bird mirror in my hands, I drew my eyebrows with blue-green liner, admiring my own appearance; when I receive the magic 'goose' jewel ball atop my head, the light from the white hair between the Buddha's eyes will drench me, and I will possess the moonlit Buddha-body." These lines draw a parallel between the beautifying of oneself through the use of secular implements and the illumination cast on one's body by the powers of the Buddha. This juxtaposition of images suggests, on the one hand, that beauty resulting from cosmetics is inferior to the attractiveness the body acquires from the supernatural glow of the Buddhist way. On the other hand, it also implies that the material pursuit of

---

33. Watanabe Hideo, "Ono no Komachi," p. 83.

34. Ibid., p. 82.

35. The idea that Buddhism played key roles in the trading and consumption of luxury goods has been proposed by Xinru Liu in *Ancient India and Ancient China*. Liu (pp. 175–76) claims that "Buddhist values created and sustained the demand for certain commodities traded between India and China during the first to the fifth centuries A.D." and that "Buddhism . . . affected the tastes and fashions of the urban population." Merchants traveled with Buddhist preachers, Buddhist concepts (such as the idea of the "seven jewels") inspired material desires in the well-to-do, and luxury items previously without religious connotations could become sacred (ibid., pp. 143 and 85).

beauty is somehow comparable to the Buddhist manifestation of radiance. Sensory splendor is equally present in both images. This passage exemplifies an overall sense that material wealth is an extension of physical attractiveness in that material possessions enhance, if not wholly represent, the effects of one's beauty. Therein lies the ambivalence: sensory beauty remains important in this particular Buddhist paradigm, yet the concept is intimately related to the material that the Buddhist paradigm seeks to transcend.

Furthermore, the loss of material possessions is also presented as a problem, for the old woman states that due to her lack of a proper robe to dye in nun's colors and food to offer to the Buddha, she has been unable to become a nun. Her previous offerings of her meager possessions immediately after her family members' deaths do not seem to have been acknowledged as adequate. This detail reinforces the idea that the concept of material possessions is neither simple nor clear-cut in this narrative; the passages seem to allude to the struggle between the justification of material offerings to Buddhist institutions and the rhetoric of renunciation and asceticism. *Tamatsukuri*'s conflicted discourse about material wealth, then, can be linked to its heterogeneous attitude toward Komachi's beauty and her resulting sexual power of attraction.

In the second part of the text, the poem, the central figure is an equally destitute old woman, yet the details of her story vary significantly from those of the "Komachi" of the introduction. The poem delves into her marriage to an abusive and crude hunter. The descriptions of her luxurious life as a young woman are quite short in comparison to those in the introduction, and there is much less of a sense of her complete indulgence in material wealth. The text focuses instead on her hardships and suffering; the message that she is being punished for an act committed by her or by her immediate family is not evident. In fact, the lifestyle criticized by the poem is not Komachi's but that of her hunter-husband. The most detailed "sinful" action in the poem is the hunter's killing of animals; portrayed in gruesome detail, it is highlighted as a grave offense against Buddhist ethical codes. Moreover, he is clearly described as a man who "had no talents in the arts"; this lack is highlighted by the descriptions of the wondrous performing arts in the Pure Land, which are illustrated at length toward the end of the poem. Komachi, on the other hand, remains a victim of his ignorant and tyrannical ways; at most she is a lesser accomplice in the sin of killing animals in that she participates in preparing the game for food and in consuming it. And there is no mention of her lack of appreciation or talent for the arts.

The issue of sexuality is not addressed overtly in the poem, but the text makes an elliptical comment through one of its main focuses, the bearing and rearing of children. In talking about her position vis-à-vis her parents, Komachi says at the very beginning: "What I want to tell Buddha is about my parent's debt of love," which suggests that one focus of the poem is the love given by parents to their children and the debt that the latter owe as a result. Within this framework, Komachi's love for her own child is presented as steadfast and strong despite the trials and sacrifices she must endure for his sake. The relationship between Komachi and her son is powerful but somewhat ambiguous: the process of childbirth itself is explicitly named as the cause of the loss of her youthful beauty, and she abandons grooming as she works hard to keep him clothed and fed. Despite her sacrifices, however, the child passes away and leaves her with only her altered appearance. This plotline indicates that bearing and rearing a child not only can be thankless, fruitless tasks but also can perhaps even accelerate the process of aging. They may therefore be undesirable precisely because of the text's conflicted yet insistent admiration of physical splendor. In other words, even though the overall rhetoric of transiency implies that any activity is futile, the persistent comments about the effects of motherhood on a woman's beauty, when read together with other passages concerned with physical attractiveness made possible by material wealth, suggest that in this text motherhood in particular becomes an impediment to the retention of beauty and therefore not necessarily a coveted or privileged way of life. Although it has been argued that after the Heian period motherhood became an increasingly important role for women with the solidification of paternalism and the significance of the ie family structure,[36] this mid-Heian text exhibits an uncertain attitude toward motherhood. Even though the ultimate goal of the work may be to illustrate the emptiness of all things, the emphasis on the futility of childbearing and child rearing may have had subversive effects.

The introduction and the poem may have been composed separately, but most scholars agree that the two were read as complementary parts of a single text by the mid-Heian period. *Tamatsukuri* can be read as a "life lesson" in two different ways. In the first lesson, two possible life scenarios for women are presented. The introduction shows the fate of a woman who does not

---

36. See Wakita, "Bosei sonchō shisō to zaigyōkan," pp. 172–203.

marry: without family support, it is extremely difficult for a woman to live on her own. The poem, however, shows the fate of a woman who does marry: if she marries the "wrong man" and she has no other family to turn to, her fate can be equally grim. The overall message might be this: married or unmarried, it is difficult for a woman to sustain prosperity.

The second lesson emerges from the balance of luxurious images described in the overall work. The lengthy passages in the poem praising the wonders of the Pure Land are the Buddhist, otherworldly counterparts of the material riches presented in the introduction. In the poem, jewels appear repeatedly in the landscape, as do wondrous birds, trees, and winds. Music forms an important component, as does visual splendor. These details are strikingly similar to those given in the introduction's descriptions of Komachi's prosperity in her youth. In this framework, then, it is as if the denial of the significance of one's possessions in this life is compensated by the promise of a luxurious landscape in the afterlife; perhaps the loss of material wealth is not a tragedy since it will reappear in the Pure Land. The virtual equation of this-worldly luxury with the sensory pleasures of the Pure Land paradoxically validates the former's glory, even if the intended effect was to show that the attainment of such a Pure-Land-on-earth would be punished.[37]

One might argue that the "promise of a paradise" as expressed in this text should be understood as a form of *upāya* (expedient means), but the multivalent effect that the text produces moves beyond the possible intentions of its author(s) through its complex and highly conflicting messages. The conflicting readings in each of the two parts as well as between the parts indicate the varying effects of the text's attempts at domesticating Komachi's figure. In summary, then, *Tamatsukuri* presents a non-judgmental view of Komachi's sexuality despite the presence of seeds of association between Komachi and her abundant powers of sexual attraction, a clashing view of the positive and negative aspects of the material wealth that enables her attractiveness, and a fairly sympathetic portrayal of Komachi as a victim of her family and her circumstances. Although it introduces female aging as an undesirable and therefore marginalizing force that acts on Komachi's figure, this Pure Land–influenced Buddhist narrative does not condemn her outright.

---

37. Tochio, "*Tamatsukuri Komachishi sōsuisho*," p. 37.

Setsuwa Collections and Waka Biography

After *Tamatsukuri*, the figure of Ono no Komachi as an old woman appears repeatedly in setsuwa collections and in brief passages in texts about waka poetry and poets. Below, I discuss a selection of such narratives that relate directly to the two tropes of old age and wandering, in order to show the changes in emphasis in depictions of Komachi: her representation takes a dramatic turn, as authors and compilers seek to marginalize both women's sexual and literary powers.

Fujiwara no Morifusa's (d. ca. 1094) *Sanjūrokunin kasenden* (Biographies of the thirty-six poetic immortals), which was probably written shortly after *Tamatsukuri*, contains a brief entry for Komachi. The passage says that she appears in *Ise monogatari* (Tales of Ise), an association that is relevant to the next chapter, and that she had become a nun.[38] Morifusa's claim that she entered a Buddhist order is significant, since the desire to achieve this state is expressed so prevalently in *Tamatsukuri*; yet as we will see below, later works that focus on Komachi as an old woman do not mention this at all. There is a shift in the emphasis of the narrative after this text: the subject of the story is no longer Komachi's desire for the Buddhist path but a concisely told tale of cause-and-effect in which Komachi's "transgressions" are punished.

Hōbutsushū (a few years after 1179), a self-consciously Buddhist didactic work written and compiled by Taira no Yasuyori, contains a reference to Komachi:

What Kōbō daishi [Kūkai] wrote in the text *Tamatsukuri* concerning the way Ono no Komachi became old and decrepit and ended up in poverty is indeed movingly sad. Left without clothing, she used her straw coat as sliding doors, and left without a mat, she used straw as her mat. She herself picked bracken in the fields and put them in a bamboo basket hanging from her arm. Remembering the past when she had favored the ways of love and was loved by others, there was not a time when she did not rain down tears.

> *iro miede   utsurou mono wa   yononaka no*
> *hito no kokoro no   hana nizo arikeru*

---

38. *Gunsho ruijū*, 4: 380.

That whose colors, unseen   yet change,   in this world—
is a flower   in one's heart, indeed.

This is a poem that she had composed in her youth.[39]

This story appears in Chapter 6, Section 5, Unit 7 of *Hōbutsushū*; the chapter describes the Six Realms, the section concerns the Human Realm, and the unit is devoted to examples of the Suffering of Desiring and Not Attaining, which is one of the Eight Sufferings.[40] At the beginning of the unit, Yasuyori states that this suffering, which is poverty, is the most unbearable of all sufferings. The focus in Komachi's story is presumably on her destitution. Her impoverished old age, however, is sharply contrasted to her youth, whose plentifulness is described solely in terms of having been full of amorous affairs. This polarization of poverty and a life full of love is an exception among the stories in this section, which tend to present *material affluence* as the opposite of destitution. The author's decision to emphasize Komachi's wealth of sexuality in her youth as positioned contrary to her lack of material sustenance in old age suggests that in Komachi's case her wealth was sexual; the accumulation of this capital was precisely what had to be shown to be a fruitless activity that resulted only in suffering in old age.

The fact that Yasuyori assumes that the figure in *Tamatsukuri* is Ono no Komachi the *Kokinshū* poet is significant; only a couple of decades earlier, this equation was regarded with a degree of skepticism, as seen in *Fukuro zōshi* (A bag of texts; ca. 1150s),[41] and it continued to be questioned in *Tsurezuregusa* (around 1330), which states that Kōbō daishi died too early for him to have written *Tamatsukuri* with Ono no Komachi in mind.[42] *Hōbutsushū*'s

---

39. Koizumi et al., *Hōbutsushū, Kankyo no tomo, Hirasan kojin reitaku*, pp. 137–38.

40. The Eight Sufferings are the sufferings of Life, of Old Age, of Illness, of Death, of Parting with Loved Ones, of Meeting with Those Who Harbor Resentment and Hate, of Desiring and Not Attaining, and those born from the Five Collections (the Material, Sensation, Representation, Conscious Formation, and Distinction).

41. Fujioka et al., *Fukuro zōshi kōshō*, pp. 490–95.

42. Kanda et al., *Hōjōki, Tsurezuregusa, Shōhōgen zōsui monki, Tannishō*, p. 229. Kenkō wrote in Section 173 that "the matter of Ono no Komachi is highly unclear. Her state of decline is seen in the text called *Tamatsukuri*. There is a theory that this text was written by Kiyoyuki, but [it] is listed in among the works of the Great Master of Mt. Kōya [Kūkai]. The Great Master had passed away at the beginning of the Jōwa years [the second year of Jōwa, 835]. Komachi's prime years happened after that; indeed, it is unclear." Komachi's figure is unstable even in this era. Another text that shows that Komachi had come to be associated with the figure in *Tamatsukuri* is in *Azuma kagami*, a "historical record" from the Kamakura period. In

explicit reference to *Tamatsukuri* as the authoritative biography of Ono no Komachi thereby consciously legitimated the previously ambiguous connection, even as it began to rewrite the "messages" of the earlier work. The manner in which the *Hōbutsushū* narrative spotlights Komachi's sexuality is very different from the primary concern of *Tamatsukuri*, which lists a vast array of material luxuries; instead of maintaining the earlier work's focus on material wealth, *Hōbutsushū*'s attention shifts to amorous abundance as a target for condemnation, which is directly related to the attempt to strip women of their sexuality as seen in other narratives about Komachi during this time and after. The passage presents her first as an amorous woman and then systematically destroys that reputation through the emphasis on her failure in a direct challenge to female sexual power.

Most important, Yasuyori here situates one of Komachi's poems from the *Kokinshū* in a way that appears to be a neutral explanation of its meaning but is in fact a contextualization of the poem according to his own judgment of Komachi's character. As it is presented here, this poem not only foreshadows her decline but also emphasizes the cooling of her lovers' feelings toward her. The focus is on the waning of Komachi's ability to maintain her suitors' interest. The actual circumstances of the composition of this poem will never be known, as no such explanations survive. The citing of this poem here serves a dual function: it links the poem to events in Komachi's life as constructed by Yasuyori and thereby gives his account of her life a feeling of legitimacy and authority. "Female experience," in this case, is clearly an interpreted context.

This marginalization of female sexuality—and by extension, Komachi's constructed figure—is most likely related to the positioning of her narrative within the overall text. *Hōbutsushū*'s premise is that a recluse happens to eavesdrop on a monk's late-night discussion of Buddhist truths with a handful of listeners at a temple hall. One particular audience member is highlighted: a young woman who engages the monk in a question-and-answer session, in which she asks about the treasures of the Buddhist law and the Six Realms of transmigration. It is in the latter section that we find the discourse of the Eight Sufferings and Komachi's story. The eavesdrop-

the entry for the eighth day, eleventh month of 1212, in a picture contest held at the imperial palace, a picture depicting the "prosperity and decline" of Ono no Komachi was shown (Kishi, *Azuma kagami*, 3: 192). This entry indicates that by the early Kamakura period Yasuyori's assumption had reached the mainstream.

ping narrator states that after hearing the monk explain these concepts and categories, the young woman was apparently moved to tears and asked how one could leave the Six Realms, which are composed only of suffering.[43] The narrator thereby situates the passage that marginalizes female sexuality as one that is aimed primarily at this woman. The "truth" of Komachi's life story has special significance in this context as a moral lesson for others of her sex.

By the time of the compilation of *Jikkinshō* (ca. 1252), the trope of Komachi's decline had been transformed (Chapter 2, Story 4):

When Ono no Komachi was young and favored the ways of love, the way in which she was fawned over by others was incomparable. In something called the [*Tamatsukuri Komachishi*] *Sōsuiki*, it seems to be written: "Even the wives of the King of Han and the Duke of Zhou or the queens of the Three Sovereigns and Five Emperors had not acted in such an indulgent manner." Since it was like this, for her clothes she layered the likes of brocade and embroidery, for her food she had prepared the delicacies of the land and the ocean, for her body she burned orchid-and-musk blend incense, with her mouth she composed poetry, and she looked down upon numerous men as base and hoped to become either an imperial consort or empress. While she lived like this, at seventeen she lost her mother, at nineteen her father died, at twenty-one she parted with her elder brother in death, and at twenty-three she was left behind by her younger brother; therefore she became alone and without kin, with no one upon whom to rely. Her extraordinary lifestyle degenerated day by day, her striking appearance declined each and every year, and those for whom she had felt fondness only avoided her. Her house became all broken down, the moonlight shining clearly, emptily—her garden grew wild with weeds. Since she had come to this state, when Fun'ya no Yasuhide went down to Mikawa province as a secretary-rank administrator and asked her to come, she composed something like

> wabinureba   mi wo ukikusa no   ne wo taete
>   sasou mizu araba   inan tozo omou
> So desolate   my body, like floating sad grasses   severed from their roots
>   if there were waters that beckoned   I should go, I think.

Thus she gradually became more desolate, and in the end she wandered among the fields and mountains. When she thought about her past, she must have regretted many deeds.[44]

---

43. Koizumi et al., *Hōbutsushū, Kankyo no tomo, Hirasan kojin reitaku*, pp. 144–45.
44. Kawamura, *Jikkinshō zenchūyaku*, pp. 154–56.

This narrative reinforces the connection between the figure of Ono no Komachi the poet and the protagonist of *Tamatsukuri*; the direct reference to the latter shows that this speaker considered the two characters to be one and the same. The differences between this version and her life as presented in *Tamatsukuri*, however, are significant. First, the *Jikkinshō* narrative claims that it was Komachi herself who arrogantly refused her many suitors and aspired to become an empress, whereas the earlier text unambiguously attributes this ambition to her family. Second, although the descriptions of her lavish lifestyle are similar in both texts, *Jikkinshō's* passage places a further emphasis upon her *irogonomi*, or favoring of the ways of love, which was not mentioned in *Tamatsukuri* but had appeared in *Hōbutsushū*. The very last line implies that these deeds of arrogance, indulgence, and sexuality were the direct cause of her downfall; this interpretation of "regret" is consistent with the other stories included in the same chapter of *Jikkinshō*, which also address indulgence as a bad deed. We thus see a shift in the portrayal of Komachi's figure from a victim of her family's social aspirations and example of the universal Buddhist truth of transiency to a deserving recipient of punishment for having toyed with men's affections and immersed herself in material wealth.

Even in the face of such strong marginalizing forces, however, textual slippages occur and allow one to read indications of resistance into the text. For example, wandering is presented in this passage as the final stage of Komachi's decline, which begins with the degeneration of both her lifestyle and her appearance after the death of her family. The poem attributed to her, which likens her to a floating blade of grass, reinforces this nomadic quality. This poem suggests, however, that she is willing to go to Mikawa to join Fun'ya no Yasuhide, although the narrator does not mention whether she actually did.[45] In fact, it seems that since the narrative continues to describe the downward trend in her lifestyle after the poem, she did not go to Mikawa. Living with Yasuhide would probably have reversed her fortunes, at least temporarily; the lack of mention of any such occurrence suggests that she refused his offer. Perhaps, then, she is prideful even in utter poverty; if

---

45. On the basis of the presentation of this poem in both *Kokinshū* and the standard version of *Komachishū*, most scholars agree that Komachi did not accompany Yasuhide (see Kamioka, *Waka setsuwa no kenkyū*, pp. 214–15). Tanaka Kimiharu (*Komachi shigure*, p. 44) proposes that the word *inan* may be a pun on "to say no," which would suggest that the poem rejects Yasuhide's offer.

she has chosen to remain poor rather than to be with a man, then this act can be seen as resistance. Her protests ultimately place her in dire circumstances and show the futility of such irreverent behavior, but the possibility of resistance places the poem in an unexpectedly disruptive framework.

How does the narrative about Komachi relate to the *Jikkinshō* as a whole? At first glance, it seems that the collection is not particularly misogynistic, nor does it directly attack women authors. On the contrary, figures such as Sei Shōnagon, Murasaki Shikibu, Izumi Shikibu, Akazome Emon, and others are mentioned in chapter 1, story 21, as elegant women attendants who served at court during Emperor Ichijō's reign (986–1011); this praise of mid-Heian court life is consistent with the rest of the work, which privileges courtly elegance and aesthetics. Why did Komachi in particular suffer from the textual treatment outlined above? A clue might be found in passages that discuss qualities desirable in a wife of the military class, the audience for the collection. There are numerous musings on this topic. Chapter 5, story 8, lists stubbornness, jealousy, and adultery among the reasons to divorce one's wife, and story 12 in the same chapter instructs women to be careful in choosing a mate and to follow parental instructions, since one's own deeds are often regrettable (note the irony here: *Jikkinshō* claims that it was Komachi herself who refused her suitors for marriage and encountered unhappiness as a result, whereas in the earlier *Tamatsukuri*, it was actually her obedience to her parents' ambitions that brought about her downfall). When choosing a wife who is not from the highest reaches of society, select not on the basis of appearance but rather with due regard for the "heart/mind" (Chapter 5, Story 7); in fact, since a beautiful woman is the root of unwanted attachment, one should hope not to come into contact with such a person (Chapter 9, Story 5). Furthermore, a wife should stand by her husband through hardship and poverty (Chapter 8, Stories 9 and 10), and her heart/mind should be at one with her husband's (Chapter 5, Story 14); she should care for him deeply and be led by him and be devoted to him even in the next life (Chapter 6, Story 21). The composite figure that materializes from these pronouncements is perhaps the exact opposite of Komachi's representation; she becomes a symbolic collection of characteristics to be avoided in a woman. If *Jikkinshō* was intended to be an instructional guidebook for young men of the new ruling military class, then Komachi is the epitome of the undesirable woman who will bring bad luck to her husband.

She is made to embody what the wife of a military-class man should *not* be: amorous, materialistic, and defiant.[46]

In these examples, we see a transformation of Komachi's figure from a victim of her family's social aspirations and the embodiment of the Buddhist truth of transiency to a deserving recipient of punishment for having thoughtlessly immersed herself in men's attentions and material wealth. The "proof" of this moral lesson is manifested by her poverty in old age; the marginalizing processes, variously motivated, attempt to erase past empowering—or at least ambivalent—discourses and re-read them according to the desired effects.

The Old Woman and Sexuality: Contextualizing Komachi's Figure in the Tamatsukuri Trope

A number of passages in various texts from the Heian and Kamakura periods depict the status of women in old age as the direct result of their sexuality. These narratives allow us to contextualize the particular portrayal and use of female aging in the stories about Komachi analyzed above. The previous examples exhibit general similarities with texts in which the attributes of old age were constructed to oppose and negate women's sexual power, either

---

46. Compare this narrative with the one found in *Kokon chomonjū* (ca. 1254, compiled by Tachibana no Narisue), another setsuwa collection from about the same time as *Jikkinshō*. The anthology contains a story almost identical to the one in *Jikkinshō* translated above. There is, however, one vital difference: in *Jikkinshō*, the last line reads: "When she thought about her past, she must have regretted many deeds," but the *Kokon chomonjū* version ends: "This story presents yet another example that lets us realize the way human beings are" (Nagazumi and Shimada, *Kokon chomonjū*, pp. 167–68). This comment, which does not refer to remorse for past deeds, states that Komachi's downfall is yet another illustration of the transient nature of human life; although the narrative does not present her life in a positive way, it nevertheless imparts a less critical tone by shifting the focus away from her particular case to the ways of the world in general. The contrast in the focus of these two works is probably related to the difference between the two collections: *Jikkinshō* explicitly displays its didacticism in its inclusion of Komachi's story in a chapter designed to condemn arrogant behavior and was compiled by a retired aristocrat-turned-monk who may have been more inclined to express condemnatory views on women's sexuality and material excess as hindrances to the smooth operation of the new ruling class's family structure. In contrast, the lay compiler of the not overtly instructional *Kokon chomonjū* places the passage in a chapter about waka poetry, and the collection contains narratives that affirm, as well as criticize, women's sexuality. The existence of these two versions thus confirms that the marginalization of sexuality is not an omnipresent or consistent phenomenon within even this short period of time.

in their youth (in these cases the potential for future decline was meant to serve as a deterrent to indulging in sexual activity) or in their old age. The appearance of these attempts to mitigate the threat of women's sexuality in legends about Komachi is not accidental; a woman reputed to have been un-paralleled in beauty who supposedly used that reputation to attract and ma-nipulate men was a most suitable target for showing that even the most beautiful woman must become repulsive in the end.

We have already seen in Chapter 1 examples of passages that correlate the aging of a woman and the loss of her sexuality. Poems in *Honchō mudaishi*'s section on the kugutsu include lines that attribute the scarcity of customers and the pity of travelers to the waning of a woman's appearance in her twi-light years. Poets project an ominous air onto these women entertainers' future by posing rhetorical questions about the uncertainty of their liveli-hood when they grow old. In these examples, old age is equated with the loss of a woman's power of sexual attraction; it is directly opposed to the women entertainers' youthful irresistibility. Furthermore, since physical attraction was often an important element in the professional success of these women, its decline would have serious consequences for their wealth and lifestyle. Old age for these women is presented as an inevitable future that not only will strip them of the ability to attract men but also casts a shadow over their current prosperity.

Similarly, *Shin sarugakuki*'s description of the sixteenth daughter harps on her unparalleled superiority as an asobi and sings her universal appeal. Im-mediately after this statement, however, the text comments, "Ah, while she is still young, she may pass her days selling herself, but after her colors fade, how will she spend the rest of her life?" This juxtaposition of the claim of the character's unquestionable and universal desirability and the taming of that power of attraction by the foreshadowing of its inevitable loss is effective precisely because she is depicted as being at the pinnacle of her profession; even the greatest asobi, who is capable of making any man succumb, will eventually become an ugly hag unable to support herself. The tempering of a woman's sexuality by focusing on a state in which she loses control of it is taken a step further in the death-decay scrolls, which are discussed in the next chapter. It is crucial to note, as I do in Chapter 1, that the depiction of a woman in old age did not *have* to take this path; stories about prosperous women entertainers who enjoyed the continued favors of powerful patrons did exist. That the *Tamatsukuri* trope seizes on the unflattering and disempowering visions of an old woman is therefore neither inevitable nor accidental; it is clear that the authors of such stories strategically selected the "prosperity and decline" narrative in order to achieve certain goals.

Female aging was used for purposes other than the mitigation of a youthful woman's sexual powers through the invocation of her inevitable decline; sexuality in old women also came to be ostracized as improper and laughable behavior. In *Shin sarugakuki*, for example, old women's sexuality is presented as pathetic and ridiculous. The first wife is described as someone who at age sixty has undergone physical decay yet still expects her husband, twenty years her junior, to pay sexual attention to her. She even worships deities of sexuality in the hope of reaping benefits. The language of the passage is untamed and vicious in parodying this old woman; the very idea that a woman may have sexual desires in old age is ridiculed. A particularly interesting moment is the following:

Her jealous eyes are like the coiling of a poisonous snake. Her angry face resembles a demon's furious stare. Her longing tears wash away her face powder. The flame of her grief burns the vermilion in her heart. She must shave and discard her snow-white hair and quickly take the shape of a nun. But she still clings to her dew-like life and becomes a living giant poisonous snake.[47]

The narrator is quite clear about what is proper for an old woman: she must rid herself of sexual desire, take Buddhist vows, and become a nun. The idea of a woman's timely retirement from sexual activity could be related to the (conjectured) practice among aristocratic women, especially imperial consorts during the early Heian period, of *tokosari* (leaving the bed), in which a woman stopped having sex at a certain age.[48] Fukutō Sanae proposes that becoming a nun, a process by which a woman sheds her sexuality, is an extension of this practice.[49] In light of the *Shin sarugakuki* passage and this practice, *Tamatsukuri* can be seen as a text that preaches the correct course of action by having a woman speak about her desire to become a nun.

Fukutō also suggests that the criticism expressed in this passage is directed at both old women and the newly popular worship of sex deities;[50] her

---

47. Shigematsu, *Shin sarugakuki, Unshū shōsoku*, pp. 15–17.

48. Kaneda, "Komachi to Ono shi," p. 113. However, the existence of this practice is controversial and still a subject for debate; see, e.g., Kudō, *Heianchō no kekkon seido to bungaku*, pp. 202–7.

49. Fukutō, *Heian chō no haha to ko*, p. 89; see also idem, *Heianchō no onna to otoko*, pp. 93–94.

50. Fukutō, *Heianchō no onna to otoko*, pp. 92–93.

reading would supply one motivation for the attack. She also contextualizes this text by placing it alongside other texts by women authors, such as Gen no naishi's comical and less than flattering portrayal in *Genji monogatari* and *Makura no sōshi's* (The pillow book) harsh criticisms of an older woman's pregnancy and her taking a young man as a lover. Fukutō concludes that although earlier texts such as *Ise monogatari* contain no trace of condemnation of older women's sexuality, by the eleventh century it was commonly portrayed as an unsightly, embarrassing phenomenon.[51]

Another text from around 1000 that portrays sexuality and an old woman is *Kūya rui* (A commemoration of Kūya), a biography of the monk Kūya (903–72) by the courtier Minamoto no Tamenori (d. 1011). An old woman whose "appearance has waned" lies ill outside a garden gate. After Kūya nurses her back to health, she says that her vital force is [blocked] and that she would like to engage in sexual intercourse with him. Kūya ponders her proposal and then finally consents. The old woman reveals her true identity by saying: "I am an old fox of the Shinsen garden. The Master is truly a Holy Man." She then disappears.[52] Kūya's willingness to engage in sexual relations with an old woman is used as proof of his sacred virtue; this example suggests that old women's desires for sexual activity could be regarded as being difficult to satisfy and highly unattractive.

The changes in attitude toward a woman associated with sexuality through her profession and her passage into old age and poverty are evident in the case of an old woman who was once a famous asobi named Higaki no ouna (the old woman Higaki), whose waka poem is included in *Gosenshū* (ca. 951):

[She] was living at a place called Shirakawa in Tsukushi, when the Senior Assistant Governor General Fujiwara no Okinori came for a visit. He stopped by, saying: "I would like some water"; so [she] brought out the water and composed this poem:

1220   *toshi fureba   waga kurokami mo   shirakawa no*
          mizuhakumu made   oinikeru kana
          Since the years have passed   my black hair, too,   like the White
          River, Shirakawa

---

51. Ibid., pp. 94–95.
52. Mima, "Kūya shōnin rui no kōtei," pp. 88–121.

I now have to get water there / my teeth have fallen out but are growing
back again[53]— I have gotten old.

At that place, she was a famous woman who loved poetry.[54]

The story of Higaki no ouna is told in much more detail in *Yamato monogatari* (ca. 951 as well) Story 126. Here she is described as a "very experienced woman who had spent her days elegantly" for a long time. She unfortunately suffered from the disturbance caused by Fujiwara no Sumitomo (d. 941); the burning of her house and looting of her possessions left her destitute. One day, Ono no Yoshifuru (884–967) tries to find her and meets a white-haired old woman fetching some water and returning to her shack. Someone identifies her as Higaki; Yoshifuru summons her, but she replies with the poem:

mubatama no   waga kurokami wa   shirakawa no
mizuhakumu made   narinikeru kana

The jet-black *mubatama* nut   my black hair—   at the White River
Shirakawa

I've come to have to get water there / my teeth have fallen out but are
growing back again   —I have reached this state.

This story is followed by four more brief anecdotes surrounding certain poems she is said to have composed.[55]

In both the *Gosenshū* commentary and the *Yamato* story, the old woman is represented sympathetically as a respected poet who enjoyed a sophisticated lifestyle but unfortunately fell victim to civil strife. Her decline is told without didactic overtones linking sexuality with eventual poverty. The narratives told in the "personal" collection of Higaki, *Higaki no ouna shū* (compiler unknown, ca. mid-Heian period), are substantially different. Even though overt didacticism is absent still, her "downfall" is not attributed to the unavoidable circumstances of war. Rather, her state is described as "desolation in old age": "[she] had become very old and had lost her dwelling place."[56] Old age is thus unquestioningly associated with poverty and decline; no further explanation was apparently needed.

---

53. Said to be an indication of aging.

54. Kifune, *Gosen wakashū zenshaku*, pp. 823–24.

55. Katagiri et al., *Taketori monogatari, Ise monogatari, Yamato monogatari, Heichū monogatari*, pp. 347–49.

56. Wakashi kenkyūkai, *Shikashū taisei*, 1, pp. 317–19.

A final example is *Ryōjin hishō*, the subject of Chapter 2 of this book, which contains a number of references to old age. Those songs that specifically name old women as subjects or objects emphasize that for women old age brings hardships and decline.[57] Even though old women's sexuality itself is not particularly criticized, the performative act of professional women entertainers singing about ominous futures for women indicates that the marginalization of female aging was being furthered by the very women whose sexuality was under attack from other directions: authors who were using the concept of old age as a weapon in the taming of female sexual power.

Around the time that Komachi's decline and misery in old age began to be explicitly presented as retribution for her youthful deeds, the marginalizing vision of old age was also being used to depict the lives of other women literary figures as impoverished and desolate. For example, Sei Shōnagon, the author of *Makura no sōshi*, appears in *Kojidan* (ca. 1212–15) as a demonic-looking aged nun whose broken-down shack is ridiculed by young aristocratic men; she retorts spiritedly by citing a Chinese proverb.[58] Sei Shōnagon's destitution in old age is established, even though she is portrayed as a still-active figure capable of putting young courtiers in their place. *Mumyō zōshi* (ca. 1198–1202) also states that Sei Shōnagon had no relatives to rely on and was forced to go to the country with her wet-nurse's child; longing for the past, she said: "I cannot forget [the men in] *naoshi* robes in the old days," as she wore rags and a patchwork hat.[59] Another case is that of Murasaki Shikibu, whom I discuss in the next chapter in relation to the tropes of women and death. Although conflicting depictions exist, it is clear that there were movements to transform famous female authors into victims of old age.

In establishing these examples as a context for reading the *Tamatsukuri* line of narratives about Komachi, I am not suggesting that for women old age was an essentially marginalizing quality or that poverty and decline were

---

57. For example, song 264 highlights the powers of professional monks in invoking the divine while emphasizing the ineffectiveness of an old woman's prayers; song 394 refers to women over thirty-five as being "no different from the lower leaves of maple trees"; old women (who refer to themselves by the pronoun *ouna*) with or without children can fare equally badly in their twilight years (songs 363, 366, and 397). Compare these to songs that portray old men: although these figures become targets of humor, the sense of unavoidable dejection, lack, and solitude found in songs about old women are not present. Old men's sexuality is targeted only when the object of their desire is beyond their reach (songs 382, 384).

58. Kobayashi Yasuharu, *Kojidan*, 1: 169.

59. Kuwabara, *Mumyō zōshi*, pp. 110–11.

inherent consequences of old age. Rather, I am proposing that in these specific instances old age was imbued with the aura of desolation and destitution precisely because it could be used to counter the forces of youthful sexuality and the economic prosperity that sometimes resulted from those forces.

THE GENDERED TRANSFORMATION
OF AN AUTHOR'S OEUVRE

As I hope to show, the marginalization of Komachi's figure in "biographical" narratives—although they are "virtual" in that they are constructions of specific historical and textual moments—had important implications for her poetry. The compilers of poetry collections equated her constructed "life" and "experiences" with a particular reading of her poems' contents and attributed to her other poets' works or neglected certain types of poems by her according to their understanding of her character. The stories analyzed above had a significant impact on literary circles of the mid-Heian to early Kamakura periods. In addition, we must keep in mind that her poems by no means necessarily represent the "way she really was." Various scholars have pointed out that Komachi often composed poems from the viewpoint of a persona; this convention may have derived from the tradition of Chinese poetry.[60] Her personas may have contributed significantly to the construction of her legendary figure, and claims for the "reality" of the character that can be discerned in her poetry cannot be substantiated. Komachi represents a case in which the figure of an author is not simply an individual who produces works that are passed down without change; the various interests behind the marginalizing narratives, such as the domestication of female sexuality, governed and molded the authorial figure called "Komachi" and her literary productions.

Komachi's poems can be found in two main categories of sources in the Heian period. The first is the imperially commissioned waka anthology such as *Kokinshū* (ca. 905; the first of such collections), and *Gosenshū* (the second of such anthologies, which was compiled in the 950s). Her poetry is absent in later collections until it reappears again in *Shin kokinshū* (A new anthology of waka, past and present; ca. 1205). The second type is her "personal" po-

---

60. Katagiri, "Saijo wo meguru jitsuzō to kyozō," pp. 12–15. See also Yamaguchi, *Keien no shijin.*

etry collection, *Komachishū*, of which there are two extant versions, both dating from around 1000. A discussion of all the poems attributed to Komachi is not within the scope of this chapter, and I limit my examination here to those poems and comments related to the *Tamatsukuri* trope.

I argue below that the selection and attribution of poems to Komachi in these collections correspond to the development of marginalizing tendencies found in the stories discussed above. Although the earlier collections contain poems that could be read retroactively as the germs of the "Komachi's prosperity and decline" narrative, her poetic persona remains polysemic. Tropes of aging and rejection—both on her and her suitor's parts—can be detected, but they are not presented within a discourse of marginalization that disempowers Komachi's figure through a particular understanding of female aging. In later works, however, the figure constructed through the choice of poems becomes more fixed along the lines of the prose narratives in terms of its emphasis on the tropes of old age, decline, and, ultimately, death. Also, the increasing prominence of the notion of failure in sexual relations again ties her figure to sexuality in a negative, disempowering manner.

Kokinshū *and* Gosenshū: *Tenth-Century Views*

Kokinshū begins with a famous *kana* introduction (*kanajo*), written by Ki no Tsurayuki (ca. 872?–945?), that includes a description and assessment of the poet Ono no Komachi:

Ono no Komachi is in the lineage of Sotoori-hime[61] of days past. [Her poems are] moving yet not strong. It can be said that [her poems] resemble a noble woman struck with an illness. They are not strong because they are poems by a woman.

> omoi tsutsu   nurebaya hito no   mietsuran
>   yume to shiriseba   samezaramashi wo
> Thinking   I went to sleep, so   I saw him, perhaps?
>   had I known it was a dream   I would not have awakened.

> iro miede   utsurou mono wa   yononaka no
>   hito no kokoro no   hana nizo arikeru

---

61. Sotoori-hime was the consort of the seventeenth emperor, Ingyō (dates unknown; perhaps mid-fifth century); described in *Nihon shoki*, Chapter 13. By the mid- to late Heian period, she was considered an incarnation of the deity Tamatsushima Myōjin (see the entry "Sotoori-hime" in Inui et al., *Nihon denki densetsu daijiten*).

> That whose colors, unseen   yet change,   in this world—
>   is a flower   in one's heart, indeed.
>
> *wabinureba*   *mi wo ukikusa no*   *ne wo taete*
>   *sasou mizu araba*   *inan tozo omou*
> So desolate   my body like floating sad grasses   severed from
> their roots;
>   if there were waters that beckoned   I should go, I think.

Sotoori-hime's poem:

> *waga seko ga*   *kubeki yoi nari*   *sasagani no*
>   *kumo no furumai*   *kanete shirushimo*
> My husband   will come visit tonight: the little-crab
>   spider's actions   already tell me so.[62]

The *mana* introduction (*manajo*), by Ki no Yoshimochi (d. 919), written in Chinese, also states:

Ono no Komachi's poems are in the lineage of Sotoori-hime of days past, but they are seductive yet weak. It is as if a sick woman had put on face powder.[63]

I cite these passages not for the purpose of discussing Tsurayuki's and Yoshimochi's views on Komachi but to note the poems and characteristics of Komachi that are found here and become important in later manifestations of her figure.[64] First, concerning the "lineage" of Sotoori-hime, the kanajo, unlike the manajo, fails to make explicit that it is Komachi's *poems* that are in the lineage (as opposed to herself). As numerous scholars have pointed out, this difference may be at the root of later interpretations such as the one found in *Kokin waka mokurokushū*, an annotated list of *Kokinshū* poems and poets by Fujiwara no Nakazane (1057–1118), that states that Sotoori-hime was Komachi's mother. Since Sotoori-hime was supposed to have been a beauty whose radiance shone through her clothes, Komachi's as-

---

62. Poem number 1110 in *Kokinshū*; the preface says: "The poem, which comes after the one that says 'omou chō / koto no ha nomi ya / aki wo ete' ("I think of you" / these word-leaves alone / withstand autumn tiresomeness; poem number 688); Sotoori-hime, alone, longs for the emperor."

63. Ozawa and Matsuda, *Kokin wakashū*, pp. 426–27.

64. In considering the negative descriptions of Komachi's poetic style, we must keep in mind Tsurayuki's interests in making such pronouncements. He has a stake in portraying older *Man'yōshū* poets such as Kakinomoto no Hitomaro and Yamanobe no Akahito as exemplary, and in his strategy he criticizes not only Komachi but the other *rokkasen* poets (see the rest of the *Kokinshū* prefaces; in English, see Helen McCullough, *Brocade by Night*).

sociation with this figure probably contributed to the establishment of Ko-machi's beauty,[65] which in turn provided the impetus for its negations through the usage of old age.

Second, the poems that Tsurayuki chose to exemplify Komachi's oeuvre in the kanajo presumably illustrate his argument that Komachi's poems are "weak." The second and third poems are used in *Hōbutsushū* and *Jikkinshō*, respectively, to illustrate Komachi's decline in her later years. In the *Kokinshū* context, however, they indicate the speaker's passivity and grief over changes in another person's heart and thereby exhibit the "weakness" that Tsurayuki may have intended to show, but they lack any association with Komachi's life or an explicit sign of decline. The first poem cited is about a dream, as are many of her poems in *Kokinshū*. It has been suggested that "Sotoori-hime's lineage" indicates that the poems are concerned with the tropes of distance from the object of one's love and longing, since according to the legend in *Nihon shoki*, Sotoori-hime had been placed far away from her spouse, the emperor, due to the jealousy of an older sister who was also an imperial consort.[66] Perhaps this sense of helpless passivity and longing also supported the notion of the poem's "weakness"; although such an interpretation of this poem is certainly contestable, Tsurayuki's subject position as a compiler and an aristocratic male must be kept in mind. This suggests that the "weakness" of Komachi's poems had not as yet been linked to or explained in terms of supposed events in the poet's life.

There are eighteen poems attributed to Komachi in *Kokinshū*; some of these appear in later anthologies. Their topics and attitudes are diverse; here

---

65. See, e.g., Maeda, *Ono no Komachi*, pp. 138–39; and Minamoto, "Komachi 'aname' se-tsuwa no keisei ni tsuite," p. 80. Also, concerning the relationship between Sotoori-hime and sexuality, almost two hundred years after the *Kokinshū* preface, Ōe no Masafusa's *Yūjo no ki* mentions that certain asobi women were "incarnations of Sotoori-hime" (see Chapter 1 of this book). Although this passage does not imply that Sotoori-hime was an asobi herself—if she was an icon of beauty at the time, it is possible that Masafusa was using her name in order to describe the attractiveness of asobi women—in the late Heian period the association between the imperial consort and women entertainers may have been established through passages such as this and may have heightened the sense that Komachi, in the "lineage" of Sotoori-hime, was somehow related to the asobi. Ōwa Iwao (*Yūjo to tennō*, pp. 287–90) asserts that since the passage in *Nihon shoki* states that Sotoori-hime was offered to Ingyō for one night at a banquet, her "temporary wife" status had come to be regarded as the origin of the asobi profession by the time of *Yūjo no ki*.

66. Takenishi, "Kokinshū, Narihira, Komachi, ōchō shūkasen," p. 62; Fujii, "Sotoori-hime no nagare," p. 95.

I discuss only those that address old age in order to examine the poetic "roots" of the *Tamatsukuri* trope. Two relevant portraits of Komachi emerge: the woman who loses her suitor(s) as she ages, and the fearless rejecter of men. *Kokinshū* does not imbed the poems within marginalizing narrative frames; however, the potential for marginalizing manipulation is present but not realized. In the first category, there are four poems:

113   *hana no iro wa*   *utsurini kerina*   *itazurani*
      waga mi yo ni furu   *nagame seshi mani*
    The color of the flower   has moved on by   in vain
      while I was gazing   at the long rain falling on my body in this world.[67]

This poem, probably the best known today due to its inclusion in the *Hyaku-nin isshu* (A poem each by a hundred poets) collection, was not particularly well known until the time of Fujiwara no Teika (1162–1241);[68] the rise in the popularity of this poem coincides with the solidification of Komachi's figure in the narratives cited above as an old woman whose appearance and status have declined. The interpretation of this poem has been a popular topic of debate among scholars. Some read "the color of the flower" strictly as a botanical description and thus deny the implication that it symbolizes the speaker's attractiveness; others insist that a symbolic reading is appropriate in that the phrase represents either a suitor's heart or the speaker's appearance. Both sides argue persuasively; what is important in the context of this chapter, however, is that at the time of *Kokinshū*, the interpretation of the symbolism of the flower may have been ambiguous, but the narrative feature of aging already exists.

A similar but less well known poem on aging that is attributed to Komachi in *Kokinshū* also appears in Section 131 of *Ise monogatari*:

782   *ima wa tote*   *wagami shigure ni*   *furinureba*
      kotonoha sae ni   *utsuroinikeri*
    Thinking now is the end,   upon my body the late-autumn rain of time
    falls and ages me, so
      even your word-leaves   have changed.[69]

---

67. Ozawa and Matsuda, *Kokin wakashū*, pp. 68–69.

68. Ibid., p. 69; also, the explicit association between the "color of flowers" and one's physical beauty was not made until Sōgi's time (1421–1502); see Akegawa, "Komachi densetsu no kōzō," pp. 43–53.

69. Ozawa and Matsuda, *Kokin wakashū*, p. 298.

The images here closely resemble those found in poem 113: the falling of rain that signals the passing of time (*shigure*), the verb *utsurou* (to change), and the awareness of her own body (*wagami*).

In another poem, the changing of a lover's heart is expressed:

822　*akikaze ni　　au tanomi koso　　kanashikere*
　　　wagami munashiku　　narinu to omoeba
　　　The ears of rice / my body's hope for reliance　　meets the autumn
　　　wind of tiresomeness:　　—how sad this is!
　　　—to think that my body　　has become useless.[70]

Here, "useless" does not necessarily mean old, but the word *munashi* can also indicate death. The speaking-skull poem I discuss in Chapter 4 starts with "the autumn wind," as does this poem; there may be a vague connection between the two poems. In the *Kokinshū* examples discussed so far, then, the topics of old age and death are addressed prominently in some poems but only indirectly in others.

All is not about degeneration and sadness in the passing of one's years, however. Compare the two poems above with another that contains the verb *utsurou* and the image of the flower:

797　*iro miede　　utsurou mono wa　　yononaka no*
　　　hito no kokoro no　　hana nizo arikeru
　　　That whose colors, unseen　　yet change,　　in this world—
　　　is a flower　　in one's heart, indeed.[71]

This poem appears in *Hōbutsushū*, examined in detail above. Note that here, the object that changes is not her own body but another person's "heart" or feelings. Any changes in her own condition are faintly implied at best.

A second trope in poems attributed to Komachi in *Kokinshū* is her defiant attitude toward her potential or actual suitors. The poem that appears in *Jikkinshō* in passages that claim to describe her old age and downfall into poverty is presented in *Kokinshū* without a contextualizing frame:

938　*wabinureba　　mi wo ukikusa no　　ne wo taete*
　　　sasou mizu araba　　inan tozo omou

---

70. Ibid., p. 310.
71. Ibid., p. 303.

So desolate   my body like floating sad grasses   severed from
their roots
      if there were waters that beckoned   I should go, I think.[72]

In the narratives discussed above, Komachi did not apparently go to Mikawa
with Fun'ya no Yasuhide, even though this poem suggests that she was so
miserable that she would have clung to any offer. Various explanations have
been offered to support this refusal. One interpretation of this poem is that
her reply to his offer was composed in a lighthearted, joking manner; both
parties understood that she would never accompany him.[73] Another interpretation is that the speaker implies that her roots have not yet been cut off
(that is, she has another lover); so this proposal is considered purely theoretically and had no practical possibilities.[74] Another possible implication of
the poem is that "I have become desolate indeed, since someone like you is
asking me to be a companion." This reading would indicate Komachi's wit in
putting her suitor in his place.[75] This poem in the context of *Kokinshū* is thus
not necessarily an indication of desolation and can even be read as resistance
or a tongue-in-cheek rejection.

This inkling of defiance as a characteristic attributed to Komachi's figure
can be read more strongly in the following poem:

623   *mirume naki   wagami wo ura to   shiraneba ya*
      karenade ama no   ashi tayuku kuru
      No chance for a meeting / the *mirume* seaweed   —such a melancholy
      bay, my body—   do you not know this?
      ceaselessly, the fisherman's   footsteps always come.[76]

The interpretation of this poem has been a subject for considerable debate.
Some scholars take *mirume* to mean "sightliness," or pleasing to the sight; *mirume naki*, therefore, is "unsightliness." Of those who uphold this reading,
some claim that the poem's speaker is a man, and the meaning thus "how can
she not think sad my unsightly state?" Others think that the speaker is a
woman (and therefore often Komachi herself), and change the gender of the

72. Ibid., p. 356.

73. Katagiri, *Tensai sakka no kyozō to jitsuzō*, p. 131.

74. Kobayashi Shigemi, *Ono no Komachi kō*, p. 204.

75. Baba Mitsuko, *Imayō no kokoro to kotoba*, p. 145.

76. Ozawa and Matsuda, *Kokin wakashū*, p. 245.

speaker and the subject of the question. Katagiri disagrees with both and proposes that *mirume* means "a chance to meet," citing the usage of this term in other contexts. This lack of a chance to meet may be the result of either circumstances or the speaker's decision to reject her suitor.[77]

The poem is significant for two reasons. First, the figure of the heartless woman who turns down an ardent suitor can be connected to the Komachi of the later versions of the *Tamatsukuri* trope. The narrative of rejection is developed much more fully in the Medieval period with the story of the Minor Captain Fukakusa, whose love for Komachi is tested when she sets him the task of visiting her every night for one hundred nights to prove his sincerity; on the ninety-ninth night he is unable to show up, and thus his entire effort comes to a futile end.[78] Second, the poem appears in Section 25 of *Ise monogatari*, in which it is presented as a reply to a poem by Ariwara no Narihira, who is pursuing a woman who sends him mixed signals. In later collections such as *Kokin waka rokujō* (Six volumes of waka past and present; ca. 980s), the comment preceding the poem—"he came but she would not see him"—suggests that she had ceased to be ambivalent and rejected her suitor. The association between Komachi and Narihira was an important factor in the development of the "speaking skull" trope to be discussed in Chapter 4. That storyline, which presents the meeting of Narihira, the rejected suitor, and the now-helpless and unattractive Komachi, can be read as Narihira's revenge for her coldness in this poem. As it stands in *Kokinshū*, however, Komachi remains an irreverent lover who is not explicitly described as suffering as a result of her resistance.

One more poem attributed to Komachi expresses rejection:

727 *ama no sumu*   *sato no shirube ni*   *aranakuni*
       uramin to nomi   *hito no iuran*
     I am not a guide in the village in which the fisher-folk live, but
       why is it that people only say "I saw the bay of reproach?"[79]

Katagiri speculates that this poem may have been one composed as part of a series of poems on the topic "fisher-folk" and therefore had no direct asso-

---

77. Katagiri, *Ono no Kamachi tsuiseki*, pp. 101–7.
78. See the noh play *Kayoi Komachi*.
79. Ozawa and Matsuda, *Kokin wakashū*, p. 279.

ciations with events in her life.[80] However, again, the poem presents people, probably men, who are resentful of Komachi; it remains open to the possibility of being embraced by later interpreters as "proof" that Komachi rejected lovesick suitors.

These analyses to the contrary, it is crucial to keep in mind not only that tropes of fleetingness and sadness over the changing state of things are common in waka poetry, but also that the poems cited represent only seven out of the eighteen attributed to Komachi in *Kokinshū*. The other eleven poems deal with different topics and representations of the poet's persona and oeuvre. Six concern dreams, mainly dreams of meeting a lover. These may have inspired her appearance in the dreams of others in the trope of the speaking-skull. Some of these poems present a woman speaker who travels along the dream-path in the hopes of seeing her beloved; this image is particularly powerful, since an aristocratic woman had relatively few chances to leave her dwelling place, let alone travel by herself on foot down a path. The dreamer is, then, a strong-willed woman who goes against custom, even if only in a dream.[81] The dream poems have also been read as an incantational act performed in order to realize a meeting with a lover.[82] Also, Komachi expresses explicit passion in poem 1030, in which she uses the image of a burning heart. These examples indicate that at this time the selection of her poems was still far from homogeneous.

This makes the selection of poems included in the setsuwa I discussed above all the more notable: in the *Tamatsukuri* narratives, the poems mentioned are numbers 797 (about the changing of the colors of one's flower-heart) and 938 (about a floating blade of grass willing to go any which way). They hint that the speaker—who is unquestioningly equated with Komachi herself in the narratives—suffered from declining fortunes and later was reduced to wandering about. The *Tamatsukuri* narratives thus exhibit extreme selectivity based on the characteristics ascribed to Komachi that the authors sought to highlight.

The next anthology to contain poems attributed to Komachi was *Gosenshū*. This collection lacks any introductory passage or preface, and the compiler's attitude toward her is unclear. Four poems attributed to her can be found in this collection.

---

80. Katagiri, *Tensai sakka no kyozō to jitsuzō*, pp. 222–223.
81. Ōtsuka, "Komachi no yume, Ōō no yume," pp. 182–83.
82. Tanaka Kimiharu, *Komachi shigure*, pp. 30–31.

The man's manners seemed to become increasingly uninterested:

779   *kokoro kara*   *ukitaru fune ni*   *norisomete*
      hitohi mo nami ni   *nurenu hi zo naki*
      Of my own free will   I have boarded a sad floating boat;   since
      I boarded it first
          there is not a single day   that I am not drenched by the waves.

When she was lost in thought, without a steady man:

1090   *ama no sumu*   *ura kogu fune no*   *kaji wo nami*
      yo wo umi wataru   *ware zo kanashiki*
      On the bay where the fisher-folk live,   the boat that rows   is
      without an oar above the waves;
          resentfully crossing the ocean of this world,   I am a sad existence.[83]

These two poems express grief over having to spend her days in uncertainty, one because her partner is not constant, and the other because her life is like an aimless boat. The floating and boat images in both poems reinforce the "rootless" image expressed in poem 938 of *Kokinshū*; the introductory notes tie the poems to specific circumstances of composition, and create a sense that Komachi's life and her poems have a transparent relationship: the latter is presented as direct "reflections" of the former. Also, the central concern of both introductory notes is her relationship (or lack of it) with a man; here we see that her figure is situated vis-à-vis a man and that she is unsuccessful in realizing the relationship. The presentation of these two poems, therefore, begins to display the development of poetic interpretation that equates Komachi's "life" with her poems.

    The third poem, part of an exchange made famous by its mention in texts such as *Yamato monogatari*, is the one sent by Komachi to the priest Henjō (816–90; poem 1196), to which the latter replies in an openly flirtatious manner (poem 1197):

Having paid a visit to a temple called Isonokami, the sun had set, so she thought, "I shall go home after sunrise" and stayed. Someone told her: "Henjō is at this temple"; so she composed [the following] in order to see how he would react:

1196   *iwa no ue ni*   *tabine wo sureba*   *ito samushi*
      koke no koromo wo   *ware ni kasanan*
      Upon the rocks   when I sleep, in my travels—   it is so cold;
          the robe of moss   won't you lend it to me?

---

83. Kifune, *Gosen wakashū zenshaku*, pp. 516–17, 724.

In reply:

1197   *yo wo somuku*   *koke no koromo wa*   *tada hitoe*
        kasaneba utoshi   *iza futari nen*
        There is only a single layer   of the robe of moss   which turns
        against the world;
                if I don't lend it and layer it, I would be unfriendly—   let the
                two of us sleep together.[84]

Modern scholars have interpreted this exchange as a reflection of Komachi's irogonomi.[85] The argument is that she was provocative in sending him a poem in the first place, but this practice may not have been unusual in the early Heian period.[86] Scholars seem to have bought into the preconception of Komachi's irogonomi by ignoring that fact that Henjō is much more aggressive and openly sexual, and that their interpretation may even be a latter-day misplacement/displacement of his irogonomi on her figure. In the exchange itself as presented in *Gosenshū*, her role as an instigator is downplayed.

The fourth poem (number 1361) is about the ocean, the topic of the first two poems above, but it has no overt connections with the tropes of love, old age, or wandering in poverty. In *Gosenshū*, then, although there are movements toward a strong association between supposed events in Komachi's life and the moods evoked in her poetry, the poems selected for inclusion still display diverse emotions and situations.

Komachishū: *The "Personal" Poetry Collection*

As mentioned above, Komachi's poems are subsequently absent from the imperial anthologies until *Shin kokinshū*: no poem attributed to her appears in *Shūishū* (ca. 1005), *Goshūishū* (1086), *Kin'yōshū* (Waka anthology of golden word-leaves; 1126–27), *Shikashū* (Waka anthology of flowering words; 1151), and *Senzaishū* (Waka anthology for a thousand years; 1188). This gap is filled

---

84. Ibid., pp. 807–9.

85. Araki ("Ono no Komachi no kōshoku setsuwa," p. 21) states that this exchange shows that Komachi had already been pegged as an irogonomi by this time; a similar view is expressed by Kobayashi Shigemi (*Ono no Komachi kō*, pp. 225–26). However, their reading remains questionable in that Henjō's poem is far more explicit in its sexual overtures than Komachi's and in that they arrived at this conclusion from an anachronistic analysis of Komachi's irogonomi. For other statements of this view, see Miyoshi, *Ono no Komachi kōkyū*, p. 234; and Katagiri, *Tensai sakka no kyozō to jitsuzō*, pp. 126–27.

86. Enchi, "Ono no Komachi," p. 119.

by the collection of Komachi's poems, *Komachishū*, which is included in Fuji-wara no Kintō's compilation *Sanjūrokunin shū* (An anthology of the thirty-six [poets]; ca. 1004–10). *Komachishū* probably came into existence around the year 1000, between the *Kokinshū/Gosenshū* group of imperial anthologies and *Shin kokinshū*; an examination of the text provides a rough picture of at least the early years of the formation of her figure through waka poetry. Katagiri Yōichi has suggested that the selections in *Komachishū* reflect the develop-ment of setsuwa stories about Komachi. My point is that such ascriptions are not curious coincidences or simple sympathetic "observations" about women in the mid-Heian period. Rather, they are motivated products of efforts to shape and mold a female author's oeuvre according to the aims and tastes of succeeding generations. I hope to demonstrate this through the use of specific examples.

There are two versions of *Komachishū*, the standard *rufubon* text and the shorter *ihon* text; both are thought to date from around the same period.[87] Both versions contain many poems elsewhere attributed to poets other than Komachi. Aside from shedding light on the interesting question of how a "personal" collection was defined and perceived in general,[88] this feature permits us to focus on the poems that are not by Komachi in order to ex-amine what kinds of poems were selected to represent or be associated with the conglomerate figure, Ono no Komachi. In fact, *Kokin waka rokujō* (980s), a non-imperial anthology compiled by an unknown individual, contains a poem falsely attributed to Komachi:

1046 *ōaraki no   mori no shitakusa   oinureba*
    koma mo susamezu   karu hito mo nashi
    The Ōaraki   forest's lower grasses   have grown old, so
    horses don't care for them   nor does anyone come to cut them.[89]

---

87. The dating of the versions has been a topic of debate among *Komachishū* scholars. The basic problem is that the earliest extant texts of both versions date only from the Kamakura period, although both internal and external evidence (such as Teika's selections in *Shin kokin-shū*) suggest that both versions were in existence at least by the eleventh century. See Katagiri, *Ono no Komachi tsuiseki*; and Shimada, *Heian zenki shikashū no kenkyū*, pp. 173–88.

88. Other shikashū such as *Akahitoshū* and *Yakamochishū* also contain similar divisions in the types of poems selected (Shimada, *Heian zenki shikashū no kenkyū*, p. 186).

89. Shinpen kokka taikan henshū iinkai, *Shinpen kokka taikan*, 2: 208, 242. Poem 1046 is explicitly attributed to Komachi. However, the same poem appears again in the same collec-tion as poem 3574, which is not attributed to her.

This poem has been traditionally interpreted as a humorous metaphor for the loss of a woman's sexuality in old age. It appears as poem number 892 in *Kokinshū* and is attributed to an unknown poet, but is identified as Ono no Komachi's in the *Kokin waka rokujō*. The change in authorship implies that the poem's trope of sexual decline with age was already beginning to be associated with Komachi's figure by the late tenth century.[90]

The standard version of *Komachishū* contains one hundred poems, with sixteen poems added based on "other sources." Katagiri divides the standard version of *Komachishū* into five parts and notes that almost all the poems attributed to Komachi in *Kokinshū* and *Gosenshū* are clustered in the first part, poems 1 to 45, whereas the other four parts contain mostly works that are either of unidentifiable origin or are identified in other collections as having been composed by *other* poets.[91] An examination of recurrent tropes in non–*Kokinshū*/*Gosenshū* poems in the first part and in the other four parts would therefore reveal to some extent the tropes that had come to be associated with Komachi's poetic oeuvre.

Poem 37, whose source is unknown despite its inclusion in the first group, contains the place-name Tamatsukuri bay (located in Mutsu province). This poem may have been attributed to Komachi due to the association between this name, its Michinoku location, and the text *Tamatsukuri*.[92] In the other four parts, poem 57 says that what the speaker had found sad about other people's lives is now part of her life; this sentiment strikingly resembles a passage in the introduction to *Tamatsukuri*: "Oh, how sad! In the past I had heard of a solitary widower . . . now, it is [= I am] a lonely single old woman." Similarly, poem 58 confesses that the speaker had thought that s/he would never see the day when her/his will would not be realized in this world.

Part three in Katagiri's division consists mostly of poems attributed to other poets in other texts. Of these poems, many present tropes of decline, powerlessness, and death. Poem 78 laments the speaker's lack of someone on whom to rely; in poem 88 the speaker is forgotten by the person who should be inquiring after him/her. Poem 96 evokes the image of "granny-discarding

---

90. Katagiri, *Ono no Komachi tsuiseki*, p. 66.

91. It has been suggested that poems by *asobi* women were incorporated into *Komachishū* (see Asami, "Komachi henbō," p. 22); this would be interesting, but there is no concrete evidence.

92. Katagiri, *Ono no Komachi tsuiseki*, p. 68.

mountain" to highlight the desolation in the speaker's heart. The desire to leave the world and to become a nun, as seen in *Tamatsukuri*, is expressed in poem 90. Longing for days long past is the topic of poem 95 and more explicitly of poem 110 of Katagiri's part four.[93] Lastly, poem 103 is found in section 155 of *Yamato monogatari*, in which a woman stolen away by a suitor to Michinoku is shocked by the change in her appearance over the years, composes this poem, and dies.[94] The same poem is found in *Man'yōshū* as poem 3807, where the explanatory text accompanying it mentions Mutsu province but not old age.[95] The trope of decline in physical appearance found in *Yamato monogatari* is consistent with the trends in the construction of Komachi's figure in *Komachishū*. The characteristics outlined above and the specific examples support the theory that *Komachishū* was engaged in a direct dialogue with contemporary stories about Komachi.

The ihon text is an even clearer illustration of the process by which Komachi's figure comes to be constructed through her poetry collection. The last three poems and their framing prose are especially indicative of the relationship between the narratives about her and her poetry. Interestingly enough, the poem central to the speaking-skull trope first appears in this text.

Around this time, of the person going down to/who is in Michinoku province, [she] asked, "When will you be back?" to which [he] replied, "Today or tomorrow I shall return."

> *michinoku wa*   *yo wo uki shima mo*   *ari to iu wo*
>   *seki koyurugi no*   *isogazaruran*
> In Michinoku   the "island for those sick of the world"   exists,
> I hear;
>   perhaps you will be in no hurry to cross   the barrier back to
> Koyurugi shore.

Saying this, [she] disappeared. Afterward, perhaps there was no one to look after her—she wandered around in a state of poverty.

[meaning unclear],[96] at an unexpected place there was a voice reciting a poem, so [he] fearfully drew nearer and listened:

---

93. Ibid., p. 178.

94. Katagiri et al., *Taketori monogatari, Ise monogatari, Yamato monogatari, Heichū monogatari*, pp. 389–90.

95. Kojima et al., *Man'yōshū*, 5: 244–45.

96. The passage is "*a wa de ka ta mi ni yu ki ke ru hi to*." Katagiri proposes that this phrase is a miscopying of "agatami ni yukikeru hito," meaning "the person who had gone to the prov-

> *akikaze no   fuku tabigoto ni   aname aname*
>   *ono towa nakute   susuki oikeri*
> The autumn wind   every time it blows   oh, my eyes! my eyes!
>   this is not Ono / a little field   but the pampas grass grows.

so it was heard; thinking this strange, [he] looked among the grasses, and Ono no Komachi beckoned him like a pampas grass charmingly. How was it that he knew who she was?

In the winter, she heard a traveler on the road say, "You look so cold; the way of the world is so fleeting." She suddenly composed:

> *tamakura no   hima no kaze dani   samukariki*
>   *mi wa narawashi no   mono nizo arikeru*
> [His] arm-pillow's   cracks, the wind blowing through it
> was cold—
>   a body is a thing   that grows used to such things, indeed.[97]

There are different views of the subtleties in this passage. One reading offered by Katagiri proposes that in the first poem, both Komachi and her lover are living in Michinoku when he decides to leave on a trip. Katagiri takes the apparition in the second poem to be the ghost of the deceased and suggests that the order of the second and third poems has been reversed.[98] Izumoji Osamu points out that the progression tells a tale much like the *Tamatsukuri* narrative of Komachi's decline. He shows that the "tamakura" poem appears in a story called "The Matter of the Magaridono Princess," number 28 in the first part of the collection *Kohon setsuwashū* (An old version of collected tales; ca. late Heian to early Kamakura, compiler unknown; a similar tale is also included in *Konjaku monogatari*, Chapter 19, Story 5) and that the plotline of a man parting with his lover and going away to Michinoku province, with the woman subsequently entering a state of financial decline and then composing/reciting the "tamakura" poem and passing away, can provide the framework for the reading of the *Komachishū* poem group. The result would be the following story: Komachi's lover leaves for Michinoku, making empty promises about a quick return home; she disap-

---

inces as an official" (Katagiri, *Ono no Komachi tsuiseki*, pp. 119–20), whereas Izumoji (*Setsuwashū no sekai*, p. 292) reads it more straightforwardly as "after not seeing each other for a while, the person visited the place to which [he] still felt an attachment."

97. Katagiri, *Ono no Komachi tsuiseki*, pp. 211–12. The "tamakura" poem appears in *Shūishū* as poem 901.

98. Katagiri, *Ono no Komachi tsuiseki*, pp. 115–17.

pears into obscurity after his departure, and when he finally returns to look for her, she is not at her former dwelling; there is only an apparition / his memory of her reciting a poem.[99] She has in fact died during wandering, after composing the "tamakura" poem.[100] Both scholars' views confirm that the tropes of abandonment by a person or persons upon whom one relies, poverty, lack of physical presence except as an apparition, and wandering relate this progression of poems to the *Tamatsukuri* trope. Similarly, Komachi is represented as a victim of a lover or a relationship gone sour. This positioning of her figure as a dejected partner in love can be interpreted as a disempowering force that unravels the powers stemming from her *irogonomi*. In other words, an illustration of her failure assures that her "arrogant" posturing in love and subsequent rejection of suitors result only in misery. All these emphases on Komachi's "decline" are evident in the poems newly attributed to her in *Komachishū*. This suggests the extent to which narrative tropes involving Komachi had come to influence—and be influenced by—the compiler(s) of this poetry collection.

Shin kokinshū: *Komachi Transformed*

It is not until *Shin kokinshū* in the early 1200s, compiled by a committee including Fujiwara no Teika, that Komachi's poems appear again in an imperial anthology. Although the neglect of her poetry in the collections between *Gosenshū* and this work is not extraordinary, considering the similar exclusion of other *Kokinshū* poets,[101] the transformation that takes place when Komachi's poems appear in the early Kamakura collection is significant. The choice of five of the six poems attributed to Komachi in *Shin kokinshū* illustrates the way in which the constructed persona that emerges from her poetry, which in *Kokinshū* and even *Gosenshū* was polysemic despite the presence of signs that presage later developments of her character, had narrowed to one intimately related to the tropes of degeneration, the passing of the years, and death—tropes that are precisely central to the narratives genealogized above, as well as those covered in the next chapter. This choice can be seen as an extension of the tropes that had become pronounced in

---

99. Izumoji (*Setsuwashū no sekai*, pp. 294–300) proposes that *aname aname* can mean "so unbearable, your heartlessness" if read as a shortened version of *a nameshi* ("oh, how unbearably heartless").

100. Ibid., pp. 286–310.

101. Kamioka, *Waka setsuwa no kenkyū*, p. 213.

Komachishū; in *Shin kokinshū*, the small number of poems selected attempt to streamline her figure into a unified representation: Komachi as the aging, failed lover. All but one of Komachi's poems in *Shin kokinshū* belong to the category of decline and dejection that I identified in the *Kokinshū* poems:

312   *fukimusubu   kaze wa mukashi no   aki nagara*
        arishi nimo ninu   sode no tsuyu kana
    The wind which blows and knots   is the same as those   from autumns past,
        but they do not resemble those days at all—   these dews upon my sleeve.

758   *aware nari   wagami no hate ya   asamidori*
        tsui niwa nobe no   kasumi to omoeba
    How sadly moving!   When I think that the end of my body: in the pale-green
        fields, ultimately,   will be the haze.

850   *aru wa naku   naki wa kazu sou   yononaka ni*
        aware izure no   hi made nagekan
    Those who exist will be gone,   those who are gone add up;   in such a world
        —oh, how sad!—until which day   will I continue to grieve?

1404   *wagami koso   aranu ka to nomi   tadorarure*
        toubeki hito ni   wasurareshi yori
    My body, indeed   is it even alive?   I only keep wondering and wandering
        since by those who should be visiting   I have been forgotten.

1802   *kogarashi no   kaze ni momijite   hitoshirezu*
        uki kotonoha no   tsumoru koro kana
    By the fallen-leaf winds   I have been turned red   unknown to others;
        for the leaves of sad words   to pile up—'tis the season.[102]

All these poems are tinged with a particular kind of grief: one that realizes transience, the sorrow of being forgotten by loved ones, the passing of the years, and death. Missing from the collection are Komachi's poems about burning passion and dreams, which occupied a major part of her oeuvre in *Kokinshū*; here, the figure of the poet is desolate and abandoned, much like the old woman in the *Tamatsukuri* trope. That these poems are taken from *Komachishū* is another consideration; all are poems attributed to unidentified

---

102. Tanaka Yutaka and Akase, *Shin kokin wakashū*, pp. 104, 225, 255, 409, 525.

poets in other anthologies. As I have outlined above, the "personal" collection itself seems to have been heavily influenced by the narratives about Komachi's supposed "life." In other words, there is a multitiered process of construction/marginalization evident here: poems attributed to Komachi in *Shin kokinshū* are based on those credited to her in *Komachishū*, despite their original appearance in other anthologies that do not attribute them to Komachi. *Komachishū*, in turn, is itself strongly influenced by numerous layers of narrative constructions. Of course, arguments about the changing tastes in poetry between the eras of *Kokinshū/Gosenshū* and *Shin kokinshū* should be taken into account in analyzing the differences in the types of poems selected in each collection. However, considering the similarity between the progression of thematic focus as seen in these waka collections and the transformations and trends we can trace in the development of Komachi's figure in prose narratives that claim to tell the story of her life, these changes cannot be dismissed as coincidental. The comparison of these anthologies suggests that the setsuwa construction of the character Ono no Komachi was reproduced in waka circles; it seems likely that her "dejected old woman" persona influenced the choice of poems attributed, which in turn contributed to the concretization of that trope.

The constructed aspect of the Komachi-as-old-woman trope in the *Shin kokinshū* poems becomes even more evident when we compare the representation of Komachi as an authorial figure in *Shin kokinshū* with that found in *Mumyō zōshi*, a critique of monogatari attributed to the Daughter of Fujiwara no Shunzei (around 1170?–1252). First, an allusion to Komachi is made in the very first passage, which describes the narrator, then an old nun, entering into conversation with the residents of a worn-down but aristocratic house. A woman from the house says about the nun: "Her appearance is so moving. What extent must be her devotional heart that at her age she engages in such visible hardships? [Her deed] is more commendable than Ono no Komachi's [flower basket] that hung from her arm."[103] The allusion to the story about the basket surely is a reference to *Tamatsukuri* and is presumably similar to the one in *Hōbutsushū*. The way in which the *Tamatsukuri* Komachi is invoked in this passage suggests that the residents of the house had an affirming attitude toward the hardships suffered by Komachi; that the legendary figure had wandered in her old age with a basket was a deed similar to the "commendable" action of the protagonist nun. The focus is on

---

103. Kuwabara, *Mumyō zōshi*, p. 10.

the piousness of engaging in ascetic practices even in old age; perhaps there is empathy as well, since the characters in the passage, the author, and Komachi were women of aristocratic background who could potentially suffer similar fates. The very fact that the narrator is described as an old nun, when the author herself was probably still young at the time of her writing, provides a hint concerning the location of her sympathies as well.

Mumyō zōshi then selects three poems from *Kokinshū* attributed to Komachi and frames them with a discussion among the women:

"Although there were many in the past who favored the ways of love and composed poetry, Ono no Komachi was the most [exquisite] in terms of her looks, appearance, manner of acting, and consideration, I think. That she composed:

> *iro miede   utsurou mono wa   yononaka no*
> *hito no kokoro no   hana nizo arikeru*
> That whose colors, unseen   yet change,   in this world—
> is a flower   in one's heart, indeed.

> *wabinureba   mi wo ukikusa no   ne wo taete*
> *sasou mizu araba   inan tozo omou*
> So desolate   my body like floating sad grasses   severed from
> their roots
> if there were waters that beckoned   I should go, I think.

> *omoitsutsu   nurebaya hito no   mietsuran*
> *yume to shiriseba   samezaramashi wo*
> Thinking   I went to sleep, so   I saw him, perhaps?
> had I known it was a dream   I would not have awakened.

These are truly the way women's poems should read, I feel, and I just break into tears," she said.

Then, there was another who said, "How one ends up in old age is so unbearable. Should even those who are not so [exemplary as Komachi] have to fall into such a state?"[104]

This passage is notable for its open commendation of Komachi's overall character ("looks, appearance, manner of acting, and consideration") and its citing of the third poem, which does not appear in any of the setsuwa stories that portray her as becoming old and impoverished or dying in a distant province. The range of Komachi's poetry provided in *Mumyō zōshi*, written around the same time as *Shin kokinshū*, generates a more diverse picture of

---

104. Ibid., pp. 107–8.

Komachi's oeuvre, and they are utilized to illustrate the exemplary character of Komachi both as a poet and as an individual. The passage also expresses chagrin and dissatisfaction that even someone of Komachi's capabilities fell into a wretched state in old age. Even though the mentioning of the "old age" trope reinforces the narrative of marginalization through its replication, the characters explicitly state their unhappiness and resentment with this discourse. The sympathy and admiration expressed by the two speakers in describing the deeds and fate of Komachi are important as a portrayal of women's attitudes toward her figure, if the author is indeed the Daughter of Shunzei. The conclusion for these women characters is that destitution and desolation in old age are neither deserved punishments for a woman who indulged in material wealth and sexual abundance in her youth nor natural consequences for someone of Komachi's talents, beauty, and stature. They regard her "downfall" as unusual and focus instead on praises for Komachi's lifestyle and poetry. The three poems are identical to those cited in the kana introduction of the *Kokinshū*, but they are contextualized quite differently here. Rather than criticizing them for being "weak," the last lines of the *Mumyō zōshi* passage exalt her figure as an admirable model if one were to "saturate the heart with the colors and fragrance." Authors and compilers clearly chose to highlight poems attributed to past poets for specific reasons; in turn their choices propagate or maintain particular representations of the poets.

Clearly, the trends and tropes present in the narratives discussed earlier in this chapter can also be found in poetic compilations; the relationship between the two genres is dialectic in that they develop the trope dynamically through mutual influence. These compilations are therefore far from being neutral grounds for the "transmission" of Komachi's poetry through the generations. The relationship between poetic collections and the setsuwa narratives is, of course, not monodirectional; these two categories are fluid and surely affected each other. This interaction and the very process of compilation, as we have seen above, indicate that the tradition concerning this poet was selectively and actively constituted at a date significantly later than the supposed date of its establishment. The fact that poems previously unassociated with Komachi (because they had been attributed to other identified or unnamed poets) came to be included in "Komachi's" oeuvre is a clear instance of the construction of an authorial figure and her repertoire by later generations. In this case, Komachi the literary figure becomes not the originator of texts but a symbolic magnet for texts that suit other people's (especially male compilers') perceptions of what she should have or could have written—this perception in turn is both strongly influenced by ideas about her supposed life and strongly influences those ideas. A close examination of the resulting set of chosen poems is crucial not because they provide a "true" insight into the "real" life of Komachi or the "nature of female experience" but because the compilers constructed specific narratives about her life and her character that are in keeping with the discourses that marginalize women's sexuality and literary clout. Michel Foucault has illustrated that the *function* of an author's name must be examined and that "the subject [/author] . . . must be stripped of its creative role and analyzed as a complex and variable function of discourse."[105] The figure of an author and authorship are constantly generated and changed according to the different interpretations of the significance of the authorial figure by others; an author can be a figure who is written and rewritten retroactively according to the interests and tastes of those who live in subsequent centuries. Moreover, the rewriting of the authorial figure can have important effects on the choices of works by that author and even lead to additions to that author's repertoire.

ɑʙ

In this chapter, I have focused on a group of texts in which Komachi's figure is constructed through marginalizing processes. By examining the discourse of female aging, I have shown that there was diachronic change in the stories about Komachi in related texts that portray old age, consisting in a generally increasing attempt to domesticate both Komachi's figure and women's sexuality. I then turned to waka poems supposedly composed by Komachi and included in collections from different eras. The increasing significance of the trope of old age in the poems suggests that the compilers of the collections were complicit in the project of equating the content of her poems and narratives about her "life story"; this maneuver both reinforced and was affected by the attempts at marginalization associated with the trope and shows that authorial attribution can be a highly constructive act. Motivated individuals or groups select the unsavory, undesirable aspects of old age and death, and these characteristics are assigned to Ono no Komachi, who stands for female sexuality in the stories examined above. This assignment marginalizes her, and this in turn vitiates the empowering characteristics she embodies.

---

105. Michel Foucault, "What Is an Author?" in idem, *Language, Counter-memory, Practice*, p. 138.

It is evident, then, that "female authorship" and "female experience" can be constructions of (male) members of later generations.[106] Does this process disempower female authors, and even negate the possibility of the category called "women's writing"? My answer would be both yes and no. In Komachi's case, biographical details and writings aside from the handful of poems attributed to her do not survive. In such cases, the question of female agency does become ambiguous and problematic. There is a great temptation to assume a cause-and-effect relationship between a female authorial figure and what has been understood traditionally as "women's writing," since the equation of a text with a gender in such cases augments the canon of "literature by women" and contributes to the list of female authors. My point is that such moves, if made hastily, can become complicit with the generations of mostly male agents who attempted to influence the formation of that very canon of "women's writing"; questioning female agency, therefore, is an attempt to render complex the processes through which such agency is created in the first place.

On the other hand, we should be able to consider how the construction of a female authorial figure complicates and adds nuance to the study of women's writing without discarding the notion of female agency altogether. The crucial issue is not whether women wrote in the Heian period—they most obviously did—but *how* a female author's figure and her writings were received, frequently intertwined, and discursively propagated in later generations. For example, I would argue that it was precisely the strength of Komachi's sexual and literary powers—which themselves were constructed and amplified by members of later generations—that made her the target of specific marginalizing processes. She became a convenient symbol to be dismantled through the rhetoric of gender and aging, which implied that even a beautiful and talented poet could suffer extreme material discomfort because

---

106. For example, interpretations of Komachi's figure played an important part in an interesting debate before World War II on the role of women in modern society. Kuroki Ruka proposed in *Ono no Komachi ron* (1913) that she should be the model for women of his time (early Taishō period) mainly due to her chastity (i.e., he chose to understand the trope of rejecting suitors as a sign of sexual restraint)—an ironic take on her character, since many prior texts claim that Komachi was abundantly amorous, and his interpretation of her figure received criticisms from a later scholar. This example illustrates the extent to which concerns contemporary to the scholar affect his or her interpretation of a historical figure—that is, the way in which representations of a particular figure are manipulated and given meaning according to specific interests of those constructing the representations.

of a loss of her beauty. As I discuss in the next chapter, other female authors who were not ascribed this particular combination of traits were subjected to different trajectories of marginalization or empowerment. It is important, therefore, to examine how each individual female author was represented over time, instead of making blanket assumptions about "women writers" as a collective agency.

4   Ghostly Margins:
The Death of Komachi

In the preceding chapter, I began the investigation of the figure of Ono no Komachi in Heian and early Kamakura texts and argued that a two-tiered process of marginalization—first of female aging and second of Komachi's sexuality through the negative discourse of old age for women—affected the canon of her literary productions to such an extent that the very idea of "authorship" is problematized in her case. In this chapter, I continue to examine discursive figurations of Komachi by turning to another textual construction based on the trope of Komachi as an old impoverished woman: stories that depict her post mortem as a poetically inclined skull. The texts that marginalized Komachi through a particular understanding of female aging targeted the sexual power she derived from her physical and material wealth. The works that cast her as a dead woman aim to vitiate two different characteristics: her power of poetic composition and her association with the culture of the capital.

In my continuing investigation of the "constructed margin," I argue not only that Komachi's figure was marginalized by using the discourse of death but also that the individuals who intentionally applied specific understandings of female death to her figure did not necessarily do so in order to marginalize her figure and her literary power. Instead, their textual productions, each of which arose from different motivations, produced marginalizing effects that were then co-opted by religious paradigms that seized on her figure as a convenient example of propagated "truths." As in the case of female aging discussed in the previous chapter, death is not *a priori* a "marginal"

status. In this two-part process, the discourse about dead women is imbued
first with unfavorable characteristics such as decay and impurity, and then
such concepts are selectively applied to Komachi's case in order to marginalize her physical being, which had slowly been separated from her poetic
capabilities, albeit without complete success, as we will see. Death is constructed both as an extension of the loss of sexual power because of aging
and as a passive, powerless state designed to force one to contemplate transience and the meaninglessness of sexual desire. Komachi's representation in
the group of texts that cast her as a corpse in varying states of decay is deeply
affected by this conception of death; the loss of her physicality parallels the
diminution of her powers of literary production. Furthermore, the same
texts locate her remains in an extreme northeastern province, as far away
from the capital as possible. Her figure is therefore physically removed from
the capital and its cultural arena. The textual politics surrounding Komachi's death therefore is this: the state of being deceased, so strongly associated with feminine marginalization itself, is applied to Komachi's case and
results not simply in a transference of the marginalizing qualities (such as
impurity) directly onto her figure but also in the separation of her role as
author from her physical body—that is, the effect is to de-emphasize her
poetic associations and highlight her corporeal, woman-ness through, paradoxically, the loss of her flesh.

The processes of marginalization, however, defy simplistic interpretations; the texts that disempower Komachi in the manner outlined above are
complicated and even challenged through other works in two ways. First, a
number of Komachi-as-a-speaking-skull stories credit her with full authorial
powers, and I argue below that this representation is an effect of the generic
concerns of these texts. Second, in discussing the striking discourse surrounding women's dead bodies, particularly in the context of specific Buddhist understandings, I focus on a case in which the "dead woman," who
is elsewhere represented as a repulsive and sexually unappetizing didactic
vehicle, arouses curiosity and even desire. The trope of the dead Komachi
therefore shows clearly the heterogeneous and nonuniversal aspects of marginalizing processes.

I begin my examination with a group of narratives that present Komachi as
a skull that calls attention to a pain-causing plant by reciting a poem. Here,
the issues of death and the female body are crucial; not only does her existence
as a skull deprive her irrevocably of the beauty that had been the source of her

sexual power, but she also is made physically helpless as an inert object. She is placed in a random field, in the northernmost province of Mutsu, far distant from the capital. In these works, she is credited only with the first half of the poem; in linked-verse fashion, it is completed by a man. What had been "her" poem in the poetry anthologies discussed in the previous chapter is partially attributed to a male protagonist. This removal of literary credit—so fluid and often problematic, as I have shown already and will illustrate again here—is carried to an extreme in later years, when Komachi's figure is detached from her poetry altogether and becomes a series of pictorial representations of female death, decay, and, consequently, desexualization. It is in these examples that we can see the Tendai / Pure Land Buddhist co-optation of her figure, already marginalized for different reasons in previous texts. Her representation comes to be used for the purpose of propagating particular conceptions about the Pure Land, namely the rhetoric of *fujō* (impurity) and *kusō* (nine aspects of decay). The separation of Komachi's physicality from her literary productions enabled the religious discourses of impurity and decay to focus solely on her objectified corporeal being without being distracted by any potentially redeeming features such as poetic talent.

I then complicate the picture by examining texts that attribute the poem entirely to Komachi and suggest that this counter-marginalizing representation, "intentional" or not, was an effect of the literary genres and aims of these texts. The studies and handbooks of waka poetry that included these stories were interested in the discussion of whole *tanka* poems (as opposed to *renga*, or linked-verse poems) or were particularly concerned with the issue of authorial credit. Finally, I investigate one example of the figure of the "dead woman" in a text from the early Kamakura period that points in a different direction: the possibility of the marginalized returning as unexpectedly empowered or desirable.

THE DEAD WOMAN AND THE POWERS
OF LITERARY PRODUCTION

This group of narratives presents Komachi as a poem-composing skull left in the middle of a field and calling attention to the pain in her eye socket from a growth of pampas grass. When we consider death as an extension of the trope of old age, these stories may be read right from the start as further attempts to marginalize the figure of Komachi by presenting her as a dead woman, as nothing but skull and bones; she is now completely stripped of the powers of beauty and therefore sexuality—or so it seems. In this trope, the powers of Komachi both as a poet and as a dead spirit are undercut. The marginalizing tendency proceeds beyond the negation of physical appearance in two directions: her full command over the authorship of her poem is denied, and she is placed as far away from the capital as was possible at the time. Whereas in the *Tamatsukuri* narratives poverty and old age play central roles in the pacification of Komachi's sexuality, these "speaking-skull" narratives work to undermine the prominence Komachi derived from her poetic and locational centrality and rewrite her role in relation to these sources of power. Once her figure has been rendered impotent, she can be utilized as an inert (and decaying) object of Buddhist meditation for the purpose of quelling heterosexual desire in men. Komachi becomes a character (albeit a crucial one) in stories in which the protagonist, Ariwara no Narihira, is a man and is credited with half of a poem. A renga exchange does not demean either party. However, when we consider the motivated maneuverings of authorship discussed above, as well as the existence of other stories in which Komachi is presented as the sole author of the poem and in which her ghostly spirit plays a more active role, the division of her poem and the attribution of one half to a male protagonist can be interpreted as an attempt to disperse her full literary prowess.

The reasons for this marginalization vary from text to text. In one case, Komachi's narrative is embedded in a complex explanation of the origins of a ceremonial detail that centers around the amorous exploits of Narihira; in this example, the desire to establish the relationship between Komachi and Narihira appears to have been the reason for linking the two figures through a renga exchange. In a second text, only a few famous female authors are discussed, and they are consistently shown to be marginalized figures whose full literary powers are not prominently displayed. In the last example, female authors are not targeted for disempowerment, and Komachi's story is raised as questionable hearsay; the effect, however, reproduces and reinforces the already present trope of Komachi as a physically helpless figure with diminished literary prowess. These passages, despite their varied nature, together create a strong effect: intentionally or not, Komachi is rendered as a female author whose connections to her supposed literary productions become tenuous. This effect paved the way for the next stage: the detachment of Komachi's figure from her literary productions in religious pictorial representations, which depict her in various stages of postmortem decay and do not refer to her poetry. The culminating effect is that the famous female author becomes an increasingly voiceless object lesson for the eradication of male sexual desire.

The crucial poem at the root of the speaking-skull narratives is known as the "aname aname" poem. Interestingly enough, this poem does not appear in any of the imperially commissioned waka anthologies and is mentioned first in the nonstandard ihon version of *Komachishū* (ca. 1000) examined in Chapter 3. The "speaking-skull" narratives, therefore, begin by departing from the selection of poems found in imperial anthologies; whether Ono no Komachi "really" composed the "aname aname" poem is clearly questionable. It is significant that certain compilers and storytellers chose to focus on this later addition as a poem composed by Komachi and then proceeded to re-move that very attribution by crediting half of it to another poet, Ariwara no Narihira. The author's oeuvre again proves to be a dynamic and unstable collection of texts that expands and contracts depending on how an author-ial figure is represented and for what purposes.

The last three poems and their framing prose in the ihon version of *Ko-machishū* are especially indicative of the relationship between Komachi's fig-ure and her poetry. In Chapter 3, I examine the progression of the "aname aname" and surrounding poems and their relevance to old age and decline. Here, I focus on the aspects of the poems relevant to the trope of Komachi as a dead woman. The poem in *Komachishū* reads as follows:

[meaning unclear],[1] at an unexpected place there was a voice reciting a poem, so [s/he] fearfully drew nearer and listened:

> akikaze no   fuku tabigoto ni   aname aname
>   ono towa nakute   susuki oikeri
> The autumn wind   every time it blows   oh, my eyes! my eyes!
>   this is not Ono / a little field   but the pampas grass grows.

so it was heard; thinking this strange, [s/he] looked amongst the grasses, and Ono no Komachi beckoned him/her like pampas grass charmingly. How was it that s/he knew who she was?[2]

In this passage, Komachi is cast as an apparition; perhaps she has been abandoned by the lover who encounters her in this form (the sequential nar-

---

1. See Chapter 3, note 96, pp. 165–66.
2. Katagiri, *Ono no Komachi tsuiseki*, pp. 211–12.

rative suggested by Katagiri and Izumoji, as noted in Chapter 3). On their own, however, the poem and the surrounding prose can also be interpreted as the story of a random traveler of unspecified gender who happens across Komachi's ghost. The issue of the deceased's identity is curious: on the one hand, the text clearly states that "Ono no Komachi beckoned him/her," yet it also makes this assertion unstable in two ways. First, the last sentence, "how was it that s/he knew who she was?" undoes the certainty of the identification. Second, the line "this is not Ono" suggests that, in fact, the apparition is not Komachi after all. The word *ono* can be explained as simple wordplay on "little field" and Komachi's surname, but this inclusion becomes significant when we compare it below to other possible puns and other textual instances in which this poem is invoked. The originary text, then, betrays its own logic of uncertainty about the apparition's identity. What, however, do specific narratives proceed to claim, despite this ambiguity?

Chipping Away at "Authorial Authority": Narihira the Enabler

The speaking-skull trope has been analyzed in two ways, neither of which addresses the issue of attribution. One scholar proposes that the identities of the actual speakers of the poems are irrelevant, since the poem is an incantational riddle-poem from the world of the deceased to appease Komachi's spirit.[3] Another scholar catalogues the variations within the trope but simply leaves matters at that.[4] By not considering the effects of Komachi's marginalization, these approaches miss crucial features in the development of her figure as a speaking skull. Close attention to the complexity of the processes of marginalization reveals that such discourses are neither necessarily teleological in their development nor consistent within a particular era. Differing degrees of empowerment and marginalization exist both within and outside a given time frame; such diversity and discursive conflicts indicate once again

---

3. Matsui, "Ono no Komachi dokuro eika kō," pp. 10–20. Saeki Junko (*Yūjo no bunkashi*, p. 174) also points out the incantational qualities of this poem. Similarly, Tanaki Keiko ("Komachi dokuro densetsu 'aname aname' kō," pp. 10–16) insists that the refrain is a variant form of *ainame*, a ritual in which a traveler who comes upon a sign of death by a roadside, such as a skull, would share his or her food with it; this is an interesting theory, but her evidence is either too indirect or anachronistic. Yet another theory is proposed by Izumoji (*Setsuwashū no sekai*, pp. 294–300): that *aname aname* means "it's unbearable, your coldness"; this alternative is connected with his reading of the poem in the *Komachishū* sequence described in Chapter 3.

4. Kamioka, *Waka setsuwa no kenkyū*, pp. 224–27.

that the states produced by the marginalizing process are neither static nor homogeneous and are instead motivated sites of dynamic and unresolved struggle.

Stories of skulls that speak can be found in sources that predate Komachi. For example, *Nihon ryōiki* (Accounts of the strange in Japan; ca. 810–24) contains two narratives with this trope. In one, a man pulls a bamboo shoot from the eye socket of a skull complaining of pains and is materially rewarded for his deed (Part 3, Story 27); stories that probably influenced this narrative are found in a variety of Chinese collections of strange and extraordinary tales ranging from *Shiyi ji* (Gathering remaining accounts, by Wang Jia, d. ca. 324) to *Soushen ji* (In search of the supernatural, by Gan Bao, fl. 320).[5] Although the Komachi stories are similar in the placement of the pampas grass in the eye socket of the skull, the role and gender of the person who pulls out the offending plant vary significantly, as we will see below. A similar narrative in which a kind deed is recompensed with the presentation of goods occurs in Part 1, Story 12, of the *Nihon ryōiki*, although the skull there does not speak. The most important aspect of both cases is the absence of a poem; the "aname aname" poem, which plays a crucial role in the positioning of Komachi in the "skull" narratives, has no counterpart in the *Nihon ryōiki* stories. This makes the centrality of poetry in stories involving Komachi even more striking.

Komachi's debut as a speaking skull is commonly believed to be the portrayal in *Gōke shidai* (The rulebook of Ōe family, ca. 1110) by Ōe no Masafusa, a lengthy handbook on the customs and traditional ceremonial procedures of the imperial court, as well as private rituals of aristocratic families. Widely used as a reference by members of the upper class who participated in and/or supervised such ceremonies, it contains detailed accounts of and instructions for such events.[6] Komachi's story appears in Chapter 14. The narrator relates that after Ariwara no Narihira's attempt to abduct the future Nijō empress failed,

the fifth-rank Middle Captain Ariwara no Narihira prepared himself to take the tonsure because he had wedded this empress[-to-be]; after that, in order to [give time to let] his hair grow back, he went to the province of Mutsu and headed for Yasoshima looking for Ono no Komachi's remains. When he was lodging at this

---

5. See, among others, Ishihara, "Kagakusho ni miru Komachi," pp. 39–40; and Maeda, *Ono no Komachi*, pp. 224–25.

6. Maeda ikutokukai sonkyōkaku bunko, *Gō shidai*, 3: appendix, p. 9.

island, all night long there was a voice, saying "the autumn wind / every time it blows / oh, my eyes! my eyes!" (*akikaze no / fuku ni tsuketemo / aname aname*). The next morning he went looking for it, and there was a skull with bracken in its eye sockets. The fifth-rank Middle Captain Ariwara wept and said, "It will not become Ono / a little field / in which pampas grass grows" (*ono to wa naraji / susuki oikeri*). He immediately gave it a burial.[7]

This is the first appearance of the "aname aname" poem in a story setting. The cryptic nature of this poem, especially the refrain "aname aname," has led to much speculation, as we will see below. In linked-verse fashion, Komachi recites the first part of the poem, and Narihira responds with the second half. If this story was devised after the poem appeared in a slightly variant form in the nonstandard version of *Komachishū*, then what is attributed entirely to Komachi in her poetry collection is here split in half, the latter half credited to a former male lover whose help is necessary for her to be buried properly. The precise reasons for the marginalization of Komachi's authorial powers in this passage are not obvious. Masafusa's handbook does not overtly denounce female writers, nor does it make religious proclamations that conflict with what Komachi's figure had come to symbolize. Rather, the details of her marginalization here might be unintended—that is, they are the products of an attempt to prioritize and foreground certain elements while downplaying others; intended or not, however, they generated important marginalizing tendencies that were amplified in years to come.

The passage appears in a section entitled "The Practice of the Empress's Outing in a Carriage," which starts by describing Fujiwara no Shōshi's (988–1074) outing to Ōharano on the outskirts of the capital. The narrative then shifts to the origins of outings to Ōharano by focusing on the entourage of the Gojō empress, Junshi (809–71). During this trip, Narihira supposedly sent a poem to the future Nijō empress, Kōshi, who is portrayed as having had an affair with him. The narrative shifts again, this time to Narihira's trip to Mutsu province, where Komachi's skull appears and the linked-verse *renga* exchange occurs. The narrative shifts abruptly for the third time to Narihira's affair with the priestess of Ise, probably Princess Tenshi (daughter of Emperor Montoku, r. 850–58); this liaison is said to have resulted in the birth of Takashina Moronao. The narrator states that to this day mem-

---

7. Kojitsu sōsho henshūbu, *Shintei zōho kojitsu sōsho*, 23: 407–8.

bers of the Takashina family refrain from visiting Ise, since Moronao was the product of a forbidden affair by a priestess who was expected to remain chaste. The section concludes by stating that it was this complex chain of events and associations that made people uneasy when Fujiwara no Sukenaka (1021–87) presented a picture of the Gojō empress's outing on the occasion of Shōshi's trip; presumably, people were apprehensive about Sukenaka's direct reference to a past outing that had had significant repercussions.

Komachi's story, then, is placed amid a rapidly flowing and changing narrative whose attention shifts from one incident to another; the one constant is Narihira. Komachi remains one of the many secondary characters, with an implication that Narihira may have had an affair with her as well, since the preceding and succeeding stories are concerned with his amorous exploits. Her role here is to serve as one of three examples that attest to Narihira's amorousness as well as his poetic skill; by attributing the second stanza of the "aname aname" poem to him, the text maintains his status as the protagonist of the passage. Furthermore, there is a certain sense of progression in Narihira's various productions: with Kōshi, he gives birth to an entire poem and suffers for his transgression by having his hair shaven off; with Komachi, he generates half a poem and assists a former lover (he is not punished but performs a pious act); and with Tenshi, he produces not a poem but a son, and it is his descendants who bear the consequences of his actions. Within the context of this progression, the placement of the linked verse exchange in the second position has meaning: Narihira's affairs are sequentially and thematically organized according to the extent of his literary output and his punishments. The renga exchange therefore plays a vital role in establishing an intimate relationship between Narihira and Komachi, as well as in constructing a complex but orderly narrative series about his affairs with three separate women.

Despite this lack of a strongly motivated discourse that marginalizes Komachi in particular, aspects of this passage had significant consequences for her figure. For example, Narihira's presence is notable in light of the fact that he is the presumed protagonist of *Ise monogatari*. The connection between Narihira and Komachi, two well-known poets from the early Heian period, is crucial in Komachi's association with sexual promiscuity. Although there are no earlier records of a meeting between the two, the explicit association comes from the unnamed role played by Komachi in *Ise monogatari*. In Section 25, there is a poetic exchange between Narihira and a character described only as *irogonominaru onna* (a woman who favors the ways of love).[8] Both poems appear in *Kokinshū*, which attributes the woman's poem of heartless rejection of an ardent suitor to Komachi (for a translation, see p. 158).[9] Whether the author of *Ise monogatari* intended to implicate Komachi as a "woman who favors the ways of love" or simply chose a random and convenient exchange from *Kokinshū* is unclear.[10] The significance of this passage lies in the result—the description *irogonominaru onna* came to be associated with Komachi. Also, in "Danjo kon'in fu" (A poem of a man and a woman in marriage) by Ōe no Asatsuna (886–958), the couple in the poem is linked to Komachi and Narihira in the passage "she is alluring, her manner like Ono no Komachi's / elegant in speech, he displays the Middle Captain Narihira's heart."[11] By the tenth century, the two poets were frequently paired, and Komachi was associated with sexual allure.

---

8. The exact implications of *irogonomi* in literary texts from the Heian period on have been much debated; the appearance of the term in *Ise monogatari* has been of particular concern. Among others, Sarah M. Strong ("The Making of a Femme Fatale") suggests that the implications were not necessarily negative at this time, and other scholars have a variety of views. A classic example is Origuchi Shinobu, who analyzes this quality as one possessed by a conqueror of lands, whose conquest of regional women was a symbolic display of dominance (see, e.g., Origuchi Shinobu's annotation of *Ise monogatari* in Origuchi hakase kinen kodai kenkyūjo, *Origuchi Shinobu zenshū/nōto hen*, 13: 214–15). Fukutō Sanae (*Heian chō no onna to otoko*, p. 9) states that it was in fact viewed as an undesirable quality in both men and women. Takahashi Tōru (*Irogonomi no bungaku to ōken*, pp. 52, 76–77, 80) proposes that the concept was intimately related to poetry and performance arts and was a characteristic not of the imperial line in power but those who were placed outside access to kingship; he says that when the term was applied to women, it usually was the case that these women were from the lower ranks of the aristocracy and that the quality permitted the transcendence of class distinctions. He also adds that the quality was criticized in both Confucian and Buddhist contexts. Imazeki Toshiko (see the chapter on Komachi in her book *"Irogonomi" no keifu*) asserts that although the term probably described connoisseurship, for women it inherently contained strong implications of tragedy of a magnitude much larger than in the case of men. In Komachi's case, the "original" implication of *irogonomi* as seen in *Ise monogatari* is not as crucial as the explicitly negative contexts in which it was placed in certain later texts that I outline in this chapter and in Chapter 3.

9. Ishihara, "Kagakusho ni miru Komachi," pp. 40–41. *Kokinshū* poem 623 ("mirume naki"). For more on Ono no Komachi as a heartless rejector of suitors as depicted in *Ise monogatari* and its commentaries, see Strong, "The Making of a Femme Fatale," pp. 391–412.

10. Katagiri, *Ono no Komachi tsuiseki*, p. 12.

11. Ōsone et al., *Honchō monzui*, p. 130.

Furthermore, two puns in Narihira's stanza invoke the trope of the "sexualized Komachi." First, "ono" is a possible triple pun on the name Ono, "little field," and also potentially "ax"; the ax may be a metaphor for sexual activity, as used in a poem attributed to Komachi in *Kokin waka rokujō*.[12] Second, the image of pampas grass conjures up sexual allure (as seen in the *Komachishū* passage, in which Komachi "beckoned [the narrator] like pampas grass charmingly"). Here, it is notable that this image is followed by yet another possible pun, this time on the verb "oikeri," which can mean "to have grown" and "to have grown old."[13] The phrase assigns sexual attractiveness to Komachi and then immediately sweeps it away: the pampas grass, charming in the past, has now grown old; there will be no ax (sexual activity).

In terms of distance from the capital, the northern origin of Ono no Komachi was suggested in the earlier work *Kokin wakashū mokuroku*, an annotated list of *Kokinshū* poems and poets by Fujiwara no Nakazane, from around 1118. Under Komachi, the entry first lists the number of her poems included in the collection and the categories in which they appear. This is followed by the brief description of her life: "Daughter of a district head in Dewa province. It is also said that her mother was Sotoori-hime. It is said she was called Hiyu-hime."[14] It is not entirely clear how she came to be established as a daughter of an official of Dewa province; some scholars speculate that the presence of members of the Ono lineage serving in some official capacity in the northern provinces of Japan had led to this view.[15] In any case, here we already see the association between Komachi's figure and the extreme north. The result is her physical removal from the capital, where she had served at court and had composed poems well enough received to have established her reputation as a representative poet of her time. She is no longer permitted to exist in this "central" space in which she earned her fame. Even though she still communicates with the male protagonist through waka poetry, an emblem of the cultural literacy of the capital, she needs someone who understands its prosody and its meaning—someone who can answer her to complete the poem and to bury her remains properly, someone from the capital—in order for her verse to have an effect. In other

---

12. See Chapter 3; poem 1,046 presents the image of "cutting grass" as a metaphor for engaging in sexual activities.

13. The actual verbs in their *shūshikei* forms are written *ofu* (to grow) and *oyu* (to grow old).

14. Saeki Tsunemaro, *Shinkō gunsho ruijū*, 13: 114.

15. Katagiri, *Ono no Komachi tsuiseki*, pp. 31–32.

words, Narihira's composing of the second stanza enables her burial and the signification and realization of her poetic gesture. The presence of this audience/enabler to understand and contextualize her stanza as waka poetry and to complete it with the declaration that her remains "will not become Ono / a little field" because of what he is about to do, which is to relieve her pain from the bracken and the wind by burying her properly, is mandatory in order for her to be free of her suffering, since she cannot save herself. Without Narihira's poetic response, her stanza would remain unfinished, without consequence (merely a complaint), and without an audience who can position it as a waka stanza; it is only through his reply/completion that the poem becomes "whole" and she is laid to rest.

Beginning in the early thirteenth century, the narrative about Komachi's skull came to be reproduced in various setsuwa collections; in them, the story becomes much more elaborate. The version in *Kojidan* (ca. 1212–15, compiled by Minamoto no Akikane) begins with the title "The Incident of Narihira Providing the Second Stanza for Komachi's Poem." The title makes it clear that Narihira is the main actor, not Komachi; the emphasis is on his adding a second stanza to her poem, and the fact that the poem is a linked verse. The narrative provides details regarding the circumstances of Narihira's departure:

When the courtier Narihira had kidnapped the empress at Nijō (before the start of her services at court) and was just about to leave, her brothers (the courtier Akinobu and others) caught up with him and took her back. At this time, it is said that they cut off Narihira's topknot. While he was waiting for his hair to grow back, he claimed that he was going to look at poem-pillows and left for East of the Pass (as seen in *Ise monogatari*).

At Yasoshima in Mutsu, he hears a voice reciting the same stanza found in *Gōke shidai*. He then "looked around following this voice, but there was nobody there; there was only a skull." He looks again in the morning and discovers the skull. "When he was thinking that this was quite extraordinary, someone said 'Ono no Komachi came to this province and died at this place. This is her skull.'" At this time Narihira is moved to compose the second stanza; the version in *Kojidan* is slightly different from that in *Gōke shidai*:

> *ono towa iwaji   susuki oikeri*
> it is not only in the little field / I will not say it is Ono   that pampas
> grass grows.

The story then ends right after the poem with the statement: "This place is called Ono. This incident can be found in *Nihongi*."[16]

This text differs from the earlier *Gōke shidai* passage in significant ways, even though both embody the marginalizing forces that posit death as a powerless state and assign divided authorship to a poem elsewhere attributed to Komachi alone. There are two main points of note. First, the way in which Komachi's identity is revealed and her poem is presented differ from the account in *Gōke shidai*: instead of Narihira looking specifically for Komachi's remains and finding them, in this narrative, the identity of the skull remains a mystery to him until a third person explains how the skull came to be where he had found it and to whom it belongs. Narihira comes upon Komachi's skull accidentally; it is just an incident in his life, not a purposeful quest on which he embarks. Second, in the *Kojidan* story, Narihira does not remove the offending plant from the skull's eye socket (or the narrator fails to mention it as a significant event), nor is there a description of his giving it a proper burial. In fact, the absence of a reference to Narihira's laying her remains to rest renders his stanza cryptic: what is the meaning of "it is not only in the little field / I will not say it is Ono"? The interpretation of this line has eluded scholars, but reading the passage in the context of Komachi's marginalization and comparing the versions in *Kojidan* and *Gōke shidai* permit the emergence of a possible dual—even triple—meaning. First, although Narihira finds Komachi's skull in Yasoshima and consequently "felt pity and was moved," the poem suggests that, in fact, pampas grass grows in places other than just this "little field," that is, the environs of Komachi's skull. In other words, suffering certainly exists at this place where Komachi is tormented, but it also exists elsewhere and everywhere; this connotation universalizes her specific suffering and thereby gives him an excuse not to aid her in alleviating her pain since no matter where one looks, there is distress.

Second, the other reading of "ono towa iwaji," "I will not say it is Ono," implies that Narihira refuses to believe that this is Komachi's skull. One could interpret this rejection as Narihira's disbelief that Komachi, the famed poet of the capital, had wandered to the extreme northeast to die in an open field; it does, however, grant him another excuse not to alleviate the skull's discomfort by removing the offending grass or giving it a burial. The third additional possibility is to read "ono" as ax and to remain attentive to the imagery of the pampas grass, as suggested above: one possible translation

---

16. Kobayashi Yasuharu, *Kojidan*, pp. 139–41. No such passage can be found in *Nihongi*.

would then be "I will not say it is an ax / the pampas grass has grown old." If the images of an ax and pampas grass were linked with the notion of sexual activity, then Narihira's denial of the skull "being an ax" can be read as his negation of Komachi's sexual appeal because she has grown old. He used to feel sexually attracted to Komachi; in her "old"—literally, postmortem—state, however, he denies the existence of her capacity to arouse desire—at least rhetorically. The nullification of sexual desire through the viewing of female corpses was an important part of Buddhist meditational practices, which I discuss below. In the *Kojidan* narrative, Komachi's skull becomes an object that inspires emotions and poetic creativity (but not sexual desire) in Narihira; he then leaves her to lament the pain.

In Chapter 1, we saw that *Kojidan* includes an empowering portrayal of an asobi chōja who reveals herself to be the incarnation of the bodhisattva Fugen. Here, the same text presents a woman in a much less potent manner. How might this phenomenon be contextualized? *Kojidan* presents a number of stories in which female characters play important roles, but named individuals who are famous female authors appear infrequently. When they do, the narratives about them tend to exhibit distinctly marginalizing tendencies. For example, Sei Shōnagon appears twice: once she is ridiculed by young aristocratic men in her old age, which is clearly described as "a state of decline" (*reiraku shitaru*), as mentioned in Chapter 3, and in another, as a nun, she so resembles a male monk that in order to escape being murdered, she reveals her genitals as proof of her womanhood (Chapter 2, Story 58). Izumi Shikibu is first mentioned briefly as the monk Dōmyō's love interest in a story that presents a dōsojin praising his sutra recitation (Chapter 3, Story 35); then she is involved in a poetic exchange with the monk Kūya (Chapter 3, Story 94). In the latter case, which simply lists the names of the poets and poems themselves without any framing narrative, her poem begs for his guidance so that she can follow the correct Buddhist path. Female authors who were well known at the time, therefore, are for the most part presented without reference to their literary capabilities; when they are credited with a poem, it explicitly asks for the aid of a more powerful male figure.

The women who are commended in *Kojidan* tend to be female characters associated with Buddhism, such as the empress devoted to the Lotus Sutra and the asobi who is Fugen incarnate. Famous female authors from the Heian period generally do not figure in such narratives, and when they do (as in the case of Izumi Shikibu), the passage is brief and not particularly full of praise. Even though the compilation is not a propaganda piece for Pure Land ideas—note the representation of an asobi with divine powers—the work as a whole promotes dedication to Buddhist principles, even though the manner in which such acts of devotion can be performed varies considerably. Komachi, here detached from any Buddhist associations and therefore not featured positively or prominently, is "buried" in a story about Narihira. *Kojidan*, therefore, illustrates the extent to which different motivations can generate both marginalizing and empowering discourses of female sexuality within a single text.

Mumyōshō, written by Kamo no Chōmei in the 1210s, includes a similar story titled "The Matter of 'Not Only in the Little Field / I Won't Say It's Ono.'" The most obvious difference is the presence of a framing device. The *Mumyōshō* narrative begins by stating, "According to a certain person" and ends with, "This is what a person said when there was a debate, and various speculations [were made] concerning whether Komachi of *Tamatsukuri* and Ono no Komachi were one and the same."[17] The story does not answer this question directly. The work discusses Heian female authors in a number of places but without marginalizing their creative capacities; thus the inclusion of Komachi's narrative cannot be explained easily as part of an overall trend or declared goals. Nevertheless, the narrative supports the theory that Komachi declined. The question is, "Were Tamatsukuri Komachi and Ono no Komachi the same person?" and the implied answer is, "Quite possibly—this is what happened to her after she became old and impoverished." In other words, although no definitive answer is given, it is clear that in *Tamatsukuri* an old woman named Komachi died in the northeast and became a skull.

Through the use of this frame, which alludes to her fate through the female aging trope, the old age and poverty already associated with her figure are linked with both abandonment and pain even after death, a situation alleviated by a male protagonist. Even though no overt criticisms or marginalizing comments about Komachi's character can be detected in the passage, the crucial association between *Tamatsukuri*'s Komachi and Komachi-as-skull is established here, albeit tentatively. This is a new development not seen in either *Gōke shidai* or *Kojidan*. It suggests that, unintended as it may have been, the *Mumyōshō* passage reinforced earlier marginalizing narratives and created new linkages that could be co-opted in future narratives to

17. Takahashi Kazuhiko, *Mumyōshō*, pp. 90–92.

further marginalize Komachi. A final difference between the *Mumyōshō* narrative and that in *Kojidan* is an expanded description of Narihira's musings before he sets off to Mutsu, which further emphasizes that this story is really about Narihira, not Komachi. In these ways, even a text without explicitly condemnatory statements can contribute to marginalization.

The focus of these narratives in a ceremonial handbook and setsuwa collections compiled by aristocratic men, then, is the male protagonist Narihira; Komachi becomes one proof of his sensitivity and perhaps a vehicle for his realization of transiency. The poetic credit given her is half that attributed to her in poetry collections such as *Komachishū*; the mechanism that allows the narrative to center around a male character is the reduction of a woman's literary powers. Together, a number of different contexts and motivations led to Komachi's marginalization. Indeed, they prepared the ground for the further marginalization and co-optation of her figure in a different direction: Buddhist discourses intended to eradicate male heterosexual desire.

Dead Women: Buddhism and the Suppression of Sexual Desire

The connections between the narratives examined above and a different genre of works that portray Komachi as a dead woman might seem tenuous, since the stories lack overt references to processes of decay and gruesome details of death, and Narihira does not appear in the visual representations. However, when we approach all these works with the issue of literary power in mind, their connections become more evident: both the setsuwa stories and the pictorial illustrations tend to separate Komachi from her role as creator of poetry and focus on her gendered corporeality. The attention of the reader and viewer is shifted away from her textual production and toward her "essential" nature as a woman.

The portrayal of Komachi as a decaying corpse is positioned within a religious matrix—works and visual images depicting the death of women and governed by certain Buddhist understandings of transience and desire. A woman's corpse is described in gruesome detail in order to strip her of the sources of her power to induce sexual desire in men: her physicality, her flesh. The human skeleton as the final state of the process of death and decay is an important part of this paradigm; it clearly links the trope of Komachi's skull with the objectified female body. I begin by examining the relationship between sexuality and death in the Buddhist context, as background for my subsequent discussion of the portrayal of Komachi the once-attractive poet as a rotting corpse in a Kamakura period painting designed for Buddhist meditation. The connection between stories about Komachi and Buddhist representations of death and the female body has already been suggested by Hosokawa Ryōichi,[18] among others; my aim here is to take such observations further by showing how the focus on Komachi's corporeality is inversely proportional to the invocation of her literary powers.

Two related concepts are central to the connection between women and death and decay. The first is the idea of fujō, or impurity, as identified most notably by the practitioners of Pure Land Buddhism. According to them, death and decay are proofs that the body itself is impure. As I show below, in the early Heian period, the image of a youthful figure who inevitably undergoes death and decay was not necessarily or explicitly female, but in the following centuries, women's bodies were used much more overtly to exemplify this impurity. The second concept is kusō, or the Nine Meditations; one focuses one's meditation on the nine stages of decay in order to realize the ephemeral nature of all things. The kusō were commonly described in a series of nine Chinese-style poems, each dedicated to one stage of decay. In textual and pictorial representations of kusō, the association between the corpse and womanhood appeared early; its later appreciation became more nuanced with the popularity of a kusō poem attributed to a Song dynasty Chinese poet, Su Dongpo (1037–1101). I will show that the discourse of fujō and kusō marginalized female bodies as repulsive objects unworthy of being the target of male sexual desire.

Early portrayals of death and transformation into a skeleton were presented within the general framework of ephemerality and were not gender-specific. The concept of *fujōkan*, or the meditative observation of impurity, appears early in the Heian period in *Ōjō yōshu*, a work by the monk Genshin (942–1017) promoting the achievement of ōjō (rebirth into the Pure Land) by chanting the nenbutsu, the recitation of the Amitābha's name. In the section entitled "First Great Pattern: Abhorring and Parting from the Impure Land," each of the Six Realms is described in terms of the evils and sufferings inherent in the category. The section on the Human Realm names three such aspects: impurity, suffering, and ephemerality, but the aspect given the longest elaboration by far is impurity. Genshin embarks on relentlessly detailed descriptions of the anatomy of the human body, listing bones, joints, tendons, organs, and vermin thought to inhabit the body. He

---

18. See Hosokawa, *Onna no chūsei*, pp. 219–71.

asks: "A body, as I have described, is completely rancid and impure, and due to its nature, it festers and rots. Who would actually cherish it and be proud of it?"[19] He claims that food is a source of impurity, since it turns into vile excrement after digestion, and then depicts the transformation of a corpse into bones and finally to dust. This description of decay is commonly believed to have contributed to the popularization of the concept of kusō. Genshin then states:

Indeed, know this: one's body is impure from beginning to end. One's beloved man or woman is also like this. . . . It is said [in Mohe zhiguan, Vol. 9, Part I] that "when one has not yet seen this aspect [of impurity], one's attachment is quite strong, but if one were to see it, desire would cease entirely." . . . [Mohe zhiguan] also says: "If one were to realize this aspect, then [one sees that] high eyebrows, green eyes, white teeth, or red lips are like putting powder upon a clump of excrement, or like putting on silk and damask upon a festering corpse. It is not fit to look at; how much the more so would [it be unfit to] draw one's body near it? There are those who bought the services of brahma-cārin[20] Mṛgalaṇḍika to have themselves be killed. How could one engage in kisses and embrace? Meditation like this is the rhubarb soup to cure the sickness of sexual desire.[21]

The text from which Genshin draws repeatedly in these passages is Mohe zhiguan (The great calming and contemplation), attributed to the Tiantai monk Zhizhe of the Sui dynasty (581–617).[22] The passage deals explicitly with the issue of sexual desire and contains graphic images designed to repulse the meditator and thus to curb sexual appetite. The overall message is that impurity is an inherent feature in all human bodies, regardless of sex. Although the references to powder and the like may apply only to women, Mṛgalaṇḍika is a man who was hired by a bhikṣu (an ascetic) who realized his own impurity to kill him. Mohe zhiguan presents this act in a positive light: Mṛgalaṇḍika is said to have been commended by a deity for his deed, and suicide by bhikṣus supposedly became popular.[23] The passage "one's beloved man or woman is also like this" further confirms this universality. In discussing the concept of fujō, then, Genshin focused not on the gendered body but on human impurity.

---

19. Ishida Mizumaro, Ōjō yōshū, 1: 56–57.
20. The first of the four life stages of the Brahmin.
21. Ishida Mizumaro, Ōjō yōshū, 1: 62–63.
22. Iwano, Kokuyaku issaikyō: shosōbu, 3: 1.
23. Ishida Mizumaro, Ōjō yōshū, 1; 355.

Another example of a gender-neutral vision of death and decay is a Chinese-style poem by Fujiwara no Yoshitaka (954–74) included in the *Wakan rōeishū* collection (ca. 1012) in the section entitled *mujō* (transience):

794   In the morning, the red face is proud in this world
     At dusk, it turns into white bones, expired in the outskirt field.[24]

This image parallels Komachi's decline from a "proud" state to bones scattered in a field. However, although the term "red face" (*kōgan*) can refer to a woman's beautiful face, it can also mean the ruddy complexion of a young man, and at least one annotator interprets this term in this way.[25] The term thus remains ambiguous in its gender, and the focus of the poem is the never-constant ways of the world and the transience of physical existence.

By the late twelfth century, impure flesh often came to be gendered, however. A story in *Hosshinshū*, by Kamo no Chōmei, a work heavily influenced by Genshin's text, relates the infatuation of the recluse-monk Genhin (d. 818) for a friend's wife after he catches a glimpse of her figure. He confesses his desire to his friend, who arranges for them to meet. Genhin gazes at her for two hours and then is able to leave without even approaching her since he has successfully performed a meditation on impurity. Chōmei comments:

For the most part, the structure of bones and flesh of a person's body is like a decrepit house. The system of the six digestive organs and the five vital organs is not any different from the coiling of a poisonous snake. Blood moistens the body, and tendons hold the joints together. It is merely a thin layer of skin that covers this all up, hiding these various impurities. Even if [one were to] put on white face powder and immerse oneself in the fragrance of incense, who would not recognize it as deceptive decoration? Food sought in the ocean and gotten in the mountains all changes into impurities after one night. It is like putting excrement into a painted urn and brocade upon a rotted corpse. Even if we were to wash it by tilting the great ocean, it would not be purified. Even if we were to burn sandalwood, the stench would return before long.

Still more, after one's spirit departs and life has come to an end, [the body] will be discarded by the foot of a mound. The flesh will bloat up and scatter in rot, finally becoming white bones; since enlightened people know this true aspect, they always avert themselves from it. It is said that "fools who indulge themselves in

---

24. Kawaguchi and Shida, *Wakan rōeishū, Ryōjin hishō*, p. 255.
25. Ibid., p. 284.

fleeting sensual pleasures and distract their minds resemble the insects in privies who are fond of excrement."[26]

Whole passages allude directly to those in *Ōjō yōshū*, but there is an important difference between the two texts. The descriptions of impurity in *Hosshinshū* are here placed exclusively in the context of meditation on a woman's body for the purpose of banishing sexual desire. What had been a basically ungendered discussion of the impure nature of all human flesh in *Ōjō yōshū* is transformed into a discourse of specifically and inherently female impurity. This ascription becomes even more blatant in a passage, discussed below, in *Kankyo no tomo*, which specifically names Komachi within the context of fujō meditation.

Although female bodies were presented as the root of evil desire that arose in men's hearts and must therefore be condemned, such rhetorical moves should not be understood as part of a simplistic and thoroughly pervasive discourse of oppression. Throughout the Heian and early Kamakura periods, monks of all ranks are depicted in narrative accounts as having affairs with women; in a number of cases, neither party was punished. Laws devised by aristocrats generally frowned on monks' marriages; those of the military class did not treat such incidents as anomalies or targets for criticism—although in the Kamakura period we begin to see instances in which women are blamed for igniting the flames of desire in men. Furthermore, stories in which monks confess that they had been expelled from their religious communities following affairs with women reveal that this explanation was used as an excuse for these monks to become true recluses, living away not only from lay society but from Buddhist organizations as well.[27] These

---

26. Miki, *Hōjōki/Hosshinshū*, pp. 181–82. Compare this tirade to Chapter 2, Story 92, in *Kojidan*: a monk falls in love with a woman attendant at court when he spots her from afar at Kiyomizu temple. He falls ill from longing and finally confesses to his disciples the cause of his sickness. They summon the woman in question, and she meets the monk without hesitation, despite his fearsome demonic appearance, and offers to help him. He thanks her for the visit and predicts that her offspring will reach the highest ranks of government and the Buddhist order; he then passes away. The narrative ends by noting that she came to gain the favors of Fujiwara no Yorimichi (992–1074), and her children attained the highest status in society. *Kojidan* as a whole does not particularly emphasize Pure Land ideas and tends not to be critical of women as a monolithic category. It is particularly notable that the narrative omits mention of women's fujō, does not blame her for attracting the attentions of the monk, and shows that, instead, she was able to reap great rewards from her ties with the monk.

27. See Ishida Mizumaro, *Nyobon—hijiri no sei*.

examples suggest that the rhetoric of the "sinfulness" of a monk's relationship with a woman was often manipulated to achieve specific goals. The impassioned arguments about the impurity of women's bodies are therefore especially striking for the severity of their pronouncements; this context is crucial for understanding Komachi's place within this discourse.

The related concept of kusō is illustrated by a series of poems attributed to Kūkai in chapter 10 of *Shoku henjō hakki seireishū hoketsushō* (or *Shoku henjō hokki shōryōshū hoketsushō*, commonly shortened to *Seireishū* [A collection on the soul]) called "Kusō no shi" (Poems on the Nine Meditations). This text describes the corpse's decay, often in gruesome detail, in terms of the nine stages of "newly dead," "bloating," "changing color," "scattering," "disarray," "linked bone," "linked white bone," "scattered white bone," and "becoming ash."[28] The fifth poem, on disarray, suggests that the corpse is female: "the beautiful face, also pussed and bleeding / the fragrant body, decayed away in vain."[29] The term *gyokugan*, or "beautiful face," was commonly used to describe a woman's face, for example, in Bo Juyi's "Changhen ge" (Song of everlasting sorrow). These poems create a definite link between a meditative exercise aimed at comprehending transience and the image of the woman's body in death as a repulsive tool used to realize that goal. There are, however, problems with this text's dating. The last three chapters (which include this poem) of the first redaction of *Seireishū*, which was compiled by a disciple of Kūkai, were lost and reunited with the first seven chapters by the monk Saisen only in 1079.[30] One scholar even speculates that the series of poems is a product of a much later era, since the extant version of this text is a copy from 1247.[31] Kūkai's *Sangō shi'iki* (The meanings of the Three Teachings) contains a similar passage that focuses on the decay of a woman's physical appearance,[32] but the surrounding chapter is devoted to a more general discussion of transience. Before the late Heian period, therefore, women played a role in kusō but were not necessarily the primary object of contemplation in the exercise.

Paintings depicting the nine stages of death and decay probably existed in the Heian period,[33] but in the Kamakura period, a noblewoman's figure be-

---

28. Watanabe Shōkō and Miyasaka, *Sangō shi'iki, Seireishū*, pp. 460–68.
29. Ibid., p. 464.
30. Ibid., p. 14.
31. Nakamura Tanio, "*Kusō shi emaki* no seiritsu," p. 167.
32. Watanabe Shōkō and Miyasaka, *Sangō shi'iki, Seireishū*, pp. 132–33.
33. Kawaguchi, "*Kusō zu*," p. 127.

gan to be explicitly associated in painting scrolls with the nine stages. The first frame in a picture scroll called *Kusō shi emaki* from the mid-Kamakura period by an unknown artist, for example, shows a living woman painted in a style similar to that found in the pictures of the thirty-six poetic geniuses popular in the early Kamakura period.[34] Perhaps the most interesting feature is that, to judge from the details of the portrayed stages of decay, the scroll seems to follow the poem "Jiuxiang shi" (Poems on the Nine Meditations) attributed to Su Dongpo as its sequential model rather than Kūkai's "Kusō no shi."[35] However, the kusō poems that most likely accompanied the pictures appear to have intentionally been removed at a later period.[36] The references in Su Dongpo's poem to eyebrow black suggest that the corpse may be a woman's, but a passage about a "red-faced scholar-official" who turns into white bone indicates that the gender of the corpse is not fixed. In its original form, the picture scroll may have exhibited potentially conflicting discourses between the clear visual identification of the corpse as female and the textual variation in the gender of the corpse. One might even speculate that the poems may have been excised because of this inconsistency between text and picture.

We can begin to detect associations between Komachi, death, and the powerlessness of female flesh at the end of the Heian period, when the gender of a dead body begins to play an increasingly important role in Buddhist discourse. For example, *Hōbutsushū* states in the "Suffering of Death" section: "The ox-headed and horse-headed torturers of hell cannot be moved to compassion even by the wondrous figures of Yang Guifei and Li Furen [two famous Chinese beauties]; the guards will not hesitate before the elegance of Sotoori-hime or Ono no Komachi."[37] On the one hand, this passage states that everyone is treated equally in the realm of hell, and elsewhere in the same work, Taira no Yasuyori cites, without mentioning gender, *Ōjō yōshū's* view of fujō that decay after death is proof of human impurity.[38] However, he also notes the ineffectiveness of a woman's beauty to mitigate her suffering in hell. In this way, the text can be linked to the trope of the "woman as an objectified target of meditation": the denial of a woman's physicality, a

---

34. Nakamura Tanio, "*Kusō shi emaki* no seiritsu," p. 170.

35. Ibid., p. 169.

36. Ibid., p. 166.

37. Koizumi et al., *Hōbutsushū, Kankyo no tomo, Hirasan kojin reitaku*, p. 89.

38. Ibid., pp. 301–2.

major source of her powers of attraction, as ultimately futile, suggests that a man's obsession with and attraction to such features is also empty.

A much more explicit ascription of impurity and decay to Komachi's figure is evident in a work that seems to have been heavily influenced by both *Hōbutsushū* and *Hosshinshū*. *Kankyo no tomo* (1222) is a collection of tales written by the priest Keisei for the imperial princesses. This text overflows with decaying flesh and the corpses of women in the many stories dedicated to this topic. There are many possible reasons for Keisei's obsession with decay, but his main point is that the physical body is ephemeral and not absolute nor permanent—and that female flesh is particularly impure and transient.[39] Part I, Story 20, is about a man who comes to realize fujō by looking at a skull and thinking that his wife is made of the same structure beneath her skin. He departs, promising his wife that if he reaches the Pure Land through the virtue of taking the tonsure, he will return to guide her there as well.[40] Part II, Story 9, is about a monk who falls in love with a noble woman who serves at court; by purposefully revealing her own fujō by conjuring a vision of rotting flesh, she deflates the monk's desire. Keisei comments:

When we look at records about the matter of Ono no Komachi, both her figure and her clothing are embarrassing to behold. Then how much the more so in the case of someone who is not particularly good-looking and lets her looks just follow the course of time—how can she be any different from this woman who serves at court [who has just displayed her fujō]?[41]

In this passage, Komachi's appearance in old age is explicitly associated with the concept of fujō; her decline is cited as proof that even a beautiful woman must decay and is therefore impure by nature. The focus in Keisei's work on women's death and decay is significant not only because it represents a shift away from the nongendered concept of impurity found in non-Japanese sources of Buddhist scriptures,[42] but also because it differs in this respect

---

39. See Harada, *Chūsei setsuwa bungaku no kenkyū*, 1: 340, and the rest of the chapter, in which he speculates why Keisei was so fascinated by the decay of the body by considering the priest's disfigurement in his youth, his remaining unmarried throughout his life, the unmarriageable status of imperial princesses, which required a banishment of sexual desire, and the many gruesome instances of death of family members that Keisei encountered in his life.

40. Koizumi et al., *Hōbutsushū, Kankyo no tomo, Hirasan kojin reitaku*, pp. 410–11.

41. Ibid., p. 443.

42. Pandey, "Women, Sexuality, and Enlightenment," p. 329.

from the previous texts, Ōjō yōshū and Hosshinshū, both of which exhibit a more universal view of impurity as an essential part of the human body.

The association between Komachi and decay develops further in pictorial works from this period. The scroll called Kusō shi emaki, discussed in the preceding pages, came also to be known as Ono no Komachi sōsui emaki in subsequent years. The portrait of the woman in the elaborate costume typically seen in pictures of "poetic immortals" and the images of the female body in various stages of postmortem decomposition now represented Ono no Komachi, not a generic and nameless figure.[43] The fact that she is portrayed as a rotting corpse may signify that she failed to achieve ōjō, since rebirth in the Pure Land was usually indicated by a lack of stench.[44] The transition from a generic female body to a named individual suggests that at least in certain media and genres, Komachi's marginalization was firmly established. Most important, the scroll presents only visual representations of a rotting corpse; there is no presentation of her poetry in this depiction. Her figure is completely detached from her works. Moreover, kusō poems were not waka but kanshi; Komachi, an "immortal" of the waka genre, is displaced from her medium and relocated into an (albeit absent) kanshi-related context, a genre usually not associated with the source of her literary power.[45] The elaborate discourses concerning women's essential impurity and their inevitable decay after death culminate in textual and visual representations of Komachi that do not refer to her literary skills at all; deprived of her poetic powers, her body becomes an object lesson about the nature of life as presented by Pure Land Buddhist rhetoric.

The narratives examined above in which Komachi is presented as a skull in need of aid are at least complicit with the growing consensus among aristocratic and religious men that Komachi, the famous poet, had undergone a decline (as shown in Chapter 3). Even though the motives for her portrayal

---

43. Tochio, "Tamatsukuri Komachishi sōsuisho shūshi no ki," p. 4; see plates 50 and 51 in Tōkyō kokuritsu hakubutsukan, Tokubetsuten: emaki. For another example, see also Chapter 3, note 42.

44. Hosokawa, Onna no chūsei, p. 253.

45. This is not to imply, however, that Komachi was familiar only with waka and not kanshi; on the contrary, scholars such as Miyoshi Teiji (Ono no Komachi kōkyū) suggest that she was quite knowledgeable about the genre. The point here, however, is that she came to be understood as an "immortal" within the waka context, and it is from this position of canonical centrality that her figure emanated authority; she did not derive such powers from her familiarity with kanshi works.

differ in *Gōke shidai*, *Kojidan*, and *Mumyōshō*, the overall textual effect, combined with the trope outlined in the *Tamatsukuri*-generated narratives, is a powerful trajectory of marginalization that strips this female author of her powers, both sexual and cultural/literary.

COUNTER-NARRATIVES

The processes of marginalization are highly complex, and a purely monolithic discourse of marginalization is, as I have tried to argue, difficult to find. Counter-marginalizing forces or slippages in discourse, intentional or not, problematize and ultimately resist totalizing efforts. An alternative selection of texts, upon first glance, appears to resemble the group analyzed above that present Komachi as a skull pleading with a living person to assist her in easing her suffering. A closer reading reveals, however, that Komachi is credited with the composition of a whole waka poem, and the location of her remains is not identified. These stories also assign a notably less passive role to Komachi's deceased spirit.[46] Even though these narratives date from the same period as the works discussed above, they make no attempt to deny her figure the full powers of literary authority, nor do they place her far from the capital. What could account for these differences? I will argue that they are not accidental, insignificant deviations within a single storyline in which Komachi is presented as a speaking skull, but that the generic as well as individual interests of the authors of these texts led them to focus on the poem *as a whole*. As a result, the creator of the poem, Komachi, becomes the one and only protagonist.

The first genre I will examine, *kagakusho*, or waka studies texts, consists of commentaries on previously composed poems and reference-style guides to composing poetry. The main concern of these texts is to annotate complete tanka poems, to discuss their details in a philological manner, and to note supposedly biographical facts relevant to the analysis of the poems. The kagakusho's combined interest in examining tanka poems and in clarifying specific words used in poetic composition through the use of examples helped generate more empowering narratives about Komachi as a skull. Second, I turn to two examples in which poetry is seen as the primary means for at-

---

46. The idea that either Narihira or Komachi plays the role of the main character in the speaking-skull stories is also discussed in Minamoto, "Komachi 'aname' setsuwa no keisei ni tsuite."

taining social recognition. Achieving fame through poetic composition meant that proper authorial credit was a crucial concern, and it is in this context that Komachi is associated with the "aname aname" poem in its entirety. I end with a brief discussion of one consequence of the marginalization of dead female bodies: in certain instances, dead female figures could exercise power in specific arenas.

Komachi as Protagonist: Kagaku Texts

The trope of Komachi as a speaking skull appears in *Waka dōmōshō* (A waka handbook for beginners), a waka commentary text by Fujiwara no Norikane dating to around 1118 to 1127. Most of this text is a dictionary of waka motifs and images, supported by examples from existing poems. The chapters are divided into many categories, such as "snow" and "moon" under the broader heading of "heavenly phenomena." The last chapter also discusses different genres of poetry and lists dos and don'ts of waka composition. The discussion of the "aname aname" poem presents a very different narrative from that in *Gōke shidai*. Komachi is the named main character, and Narihira does not appear. The passage is listed in section 7, under the category "grasses," which includes the image "pampas grass":

> akikaze no   fuku tabi goto ni   aname aname
>   ono towa naraji   susuki oikeri
> the autumn wind   every time it blows   oh, how painful! how painful!
>   it will not become Ono / a little field   in which pampas grass grows.

[This poem] is in *Ono no Komachi shū*. In the past, there was a person traveling through a field. S/he heard a voice reciting this poem like the sound of the wind. When s/he stopped and asked about it, s/he saw pampas grass growing out of someone's whitened skull. S/he removed this pampas grass, placed the skull in a purified location and went back. That night, in a dream: "I am that person called Ono no Komachi from long ago. I am happy and indebted," she said. So this poem was included in that collection [*Komachishū*], it is said. "Aname aname" means "oh, how painful!" [47]

In this story, Komachi recites the full poem herself and in a dream reveals her identity to the person who removed the offending plant from her skull before moving it to a "purified" location. Whereas in *Gōke shidai* the actions were attributed solely to Narihira and the skull remained basically a passive

---

47. Kyūsojin, *Nihon kagaku taikei bekkan*, 1: 248.

object, here the focus of the tale has shifted to the verbal power of the skull/Komachi, first in reciting the poem and then in the dream appearance. The traveler's gender, name, and the exact location of the field remain unknown. Furthermore, an explicitly male protagonist from the capital is not necessary for Komachi to obtain her goal; an anonymous, genderless passerby is all that is necessary for her poem to be heard, understood, and acted upon. This story extends the reach of waka poetry's influence beyond the realm of immortalized, famous poets such as Narihira, who was a necessary vehicle for reception in the texts examined above; waka is shown to be an effective and wondrous means of communicating with even a nameless traveler at an unspecified place.

The passage also insists upon citing the source for this poem; it refers to the *Komachishū* twice, once right after the poem and once toward the end. This careful genealogizing of the poem's origins may have led to the crediting of the entire poem to Komachi. Such an interest is in keeping with the generic concerns of kagaku texts in general. Komachi's character as an empowered figure, at least compared to her representation in the setsuwa stories outlined above, can be said to stem from this interest. It is ironic, of course, that this apparent concern for attribution and citation reinforced the validity of *Komachishū* as a reliable source for poems "by" Komachi, when, in fact, as we have seen, the collection is a thoroughly constructed representation of her oeuvre by later generations. Nevertheless, this example shows that *Komachishū*, a product of manipulative attributions, could become the origin of new tropes that empower an author.

One interesting detail, however, is that the wording of the poem differs slightly from the version given in *Komachishū*: "ono towa naraji" (it will not become Ono / a little field) in *Waka dōmōshō*, versus "ono towa nakute" (this is not Ono / a little field) in *Komachishū*. Why might a study of waka poems that appears to be concerned with accuracy, at least in citing the source of a poem, exhibit such variation? One possibility might be that since *Dōmōshō's* version is similar to the one found in *Gōke shidai* (the *ono towa* line is the same), the author chose to replace and supplement the poetry anthology's version with *Gōke's*, which was more consistent with the narrative framework: an assertive Komachi, determined that her remains "not become a little field," asks a traveler to move them to a more appropriate location. As in the case of Komachi as an impoverished old woman, an author's oeuvre and its details are prone to manipulation by members of later generations who mold literary products to suit their specific goals. Here, the story focuses on the figure of a "poetic immortal" who derives that status from her authorial authority, and the poem attributed to her serves to contribute to this goal.

The existence of both marginalizing narratives about the dead Komachi and the counter-marginalizing alternatives did not go unnoticed in the late Heian period; in fact, kagaku texts display a keen awareness of these contradictions and discuss them extensively. For example, there is a detailed comparison of the two contrasting groups of stories about Komachi as a speaking skull in the sixteenth chapter of Fujiwara no Kenshō's Shūchūshō (A handbook to put in one's sleeve; for a translation, see pp. 322–23), a waka commentary text from the 1180s. The work is devoted to explicating difficult terms used in waka by citing examples of past usages. The skull poem attributed to Komachi is mentioned for its unusual refrain, "aname aname," but the discussion develops into a comparison of the narratives in Gōke shidai and Waka dōmōshō. The entry first cites the poem's appearance in Gōke shidai and proceeds to give that collection's Narihira-centric account of the speaking-skull trope.[48] Kenshō does not leave matters at this, however; he then proceeds to retell Dōmōshō's story quite faithfully and asserts: "I say, the meanings of these two versions are different." He notes that one is a linked verse, and "in a later reign, Narihira added the second line," whereas "Dōmō says: 'one poem was heard in the voice of the wind.'" Kenshō then mentions the passage in Kokin wakashū mokuroku that casts Komachi as the daughter of a district head of Dewa province and adds: "For several decades [she] lived in the capital favoring the ways of love. But she returned to her home province to die. Therefore (her remains are in Yasoshima, perhaps?)."

The passage in Shūchūshō embodies the complexities of the kagaku genre and its interest in poems and poets: greatly concerned with literary details— the passage also includes notes about the differences in the types of plants that offend Komachi's skull, for instance—it calls attention to the variants in the attempts at marginalization. Although in the end, the narrative of Komachi's supposed love-favoring ways is repeated—notably without a condemnatory overtone—Kenshō seems to be looking desperately for a way

---

48. The last phrase of the Shūchūshō poem, however, reads: "susuki idekeri" (the pampas grass has come out) instead of "susuki oikeri" (the pampas grass grows / has grown old), which is how it appears in Gōke shidai; the omission of the reference to old age in this example suggests that there is a tendency here to limit the solidification of Komachi's figure as a marginalized trope.

to smooth out the problematic points of her stories, such as how Komachi's skull ended up in Yasoshima; he cannot simply put her there without a reason. Ultimately, he does not make interpretive pronouncements about the differences between the *Gōke* and *Dōmōshō* stories; he notes them but does not offer reasons for the variations. This late Heian comparison of variants suggests the extent to which the marginalizing processes detected in texts were considered to be neither universal nor unchanging by near-contemporaries.

Perhaps most striking, however, is the manner in which the "aname aname" entry is presented. Consistent with the format of the rest of the text, the passage first names the difficult term, then gives the "akikaze no" poem in its entirety before proceeding to discuss the *Gōke shidai* and *Dōmōshō* passages. The overall impression of the *Shūchūshō* narrative is that the poem is a tanka; the discussion of the two conflicting stories is more in the format of an extended annotation. Here again, the empowerment of a female literary figure and the destabilizing of marginalizing discourses arise from textual aims that were not directly related to the aggrandizing of female literary power.

Another set of texts empower the figure of Komachi-as-skull, but for a different reason: these texts are concerned about correct authorial attribution because of the belief that waka composition could help one gain social and cultural capital and thereby attain prominence. *Fukuro zōshi* is a waka commentary text written by Fujiwara no Kiyosuke in the 1150s. Under the category "poems by the deceased," it lists the name "Ono no Komachi" and cites the pampas grass poem in the following format (for a translation of the entire passage, see p. 323):

> akikaze no   uchifuku goto ni   aname aname
>   ono towa iwaji   susuki oikeri
> The autumn wind   every time it blows,   oh, my eyes! my eyes!
>   it's not only in the little field / I will not say it is Ono   that pampas
>   grass grows.[49]

The rest of the narrative proceeds in a manner similar to the one in *Dōmōshō*. This brief text is spare in its descriptions: neither the dreamer nor the location of the field is identified, and there are no explanations for the presence of Komachi's skull in an open field, unburied. However, unlike the ear-

---

49. Fujioka et al., *Fukuro zōshi kōshō: zatsudan hen*, pp. 432–36.

lier *Dōmōshō*, the sequence of the revelation of the poet's identity and the removal of the skull is reversed: Komachi identifies herself first in a dream that
shows visually that she is suffering from the pampas grass. She does not
merely wait for a random traveler to pass by and find her skull, which is reciting a poem in a wind-like manner; here, she chooses a specific individual,
induces an imagistic reconstruction of her environment in a dream, and succeeds in getting this person to remove the grass. Komachi is thus an active
participant in her own relocation. Furthermore, no mention is made of any
consequences arising from the dreamer's kind deed. The narrative shifts any
remaining focus away from the "someone" who helps the skull/apparition;
the central character is Komachi, whose name both begins and ends the passage. Unlike the account in *Dōmōshō*, this one does not name the collection
from which the poem is taken, but the strength of Komachi's character is
conveyed through these other means.

Within the context of this strong portrayal, we can reread the "aname
aname" poem once again. In the prose narrative, her dream apparition declares, "My name is Ono." The poem, however, negates the naming of Ono
with the line: "I will not say it is Ono"—what could this paradox imply? A
possible answer can be found in what is being denied by the name "Ono" in
the poem: the line states that the field in which the pampas grass grows and
has grown old is not Ono. Who is the "real" Ono? It is Komachi's apparition
itself. In other words, the poem and the narrative together suggest that
"Ono" refers to Komachi's ghostly figure, not the barren field in which her
remains lie; it is an assertion that her person is distinct from the insentient
earth and plants, especially the pampas grass that has grown old and lost its
power to attract. Although this reading reveals the complicity of this poem
with the discourse that marginalizes aging women as those who no longer
possess sexual power, it does suggest an alternative to the paradigms established by the Narihira-centric narratives. Indeed, "it's not only in the little
field" that such suffering can be found, yet it is Komachi who declares her
identity—and disclaims other identities—and succeeds in attaining peace
after death.

Fukuro zōshi, like *Mumyōshō*, contains a large number of narratives about
waka poems and poets. As noted above, the latter work presents an ambiguous yet complicit portrayal of Komachi; the implication is that after her decline in old age, she died in the northeast, and that it required a visit from
Narihira to complete her poem. What might account for the differences

between the two collections? One clue can be found in *Fukuro zōshi*'s apparent obsession with the attainment of fame and recognition through poetic composition. Scholars have pointed out that Kiyosuke, who was able to attain neither the poetic eminence nor the political prominence he had sought as an heir to the Rokujō line of the Fujiwara family (which had earlier produced such success), was using *Fukuro zōshi* as a vehicle through which to vent his frustrations and concerns. Among the primary topics of other stories in the collection are the achievement of fame and recognition as well as political advancement through the skillful composition of poetry and the problem of mistaken attribution, which could lead to misrepresentation even in imperially commissioned anthologies, the pinnacle of the waka canon at the time.[50] Stories about famous authors, both male and female, are also featured. In this light, it is possible that Kiyosuke carefully considered the authorship of the "aname aname" poem, and based on *Komachishū*, he decided that Komachi, a reputed poetic "immortal," was to be given full credit for the poem. In this case, the empowering narrative can be explained as being rooted in a general (as opposed to gender-specific) preoccupation with the potentials of literary power and authorship.

The second example of a work countering the marginalizing portrayals sketched in narratives that present Narihira as the protagonist is a text attributed to a female author dating from the early Kamakura period. *Mumyō zōshi* (ca. 1198–1202), a critique of monogatari attributed to the Daughter of Fujiwara no Shunzei (around 1170?–1252), is discussed in Chapter 3 as a work that espouses a view of Komachi that differs from those propagated in texts by male authors or compilers. The work contains the following passage on the "speaking-skull" trope:

In any case, [that Komachi became an old impoverished woman] makes us realize the unpredictable nature of this sad world, and it is moving. Even after becoming a corpse, she composed:

> akikaze no   fuku tabi goto ni   aname aname
>   ono towa iwaji   susuki oikeri
> The autumn wind   every time it blows,   oh, my eyes! my eyes!
>   it is not only in the little field / I will not say it is Ono / ax   in which
> pampas grass grows.

---

50. Nakamura Yasuo, "*Fukuro zōshi* zatsudanbu ni tsuite no kokoromiteki kaisetsu," pp. 498–512.

In a vast field, pampas grass was growing; [it blows in the wind and] this sound was heard. Thinking this pitiful, [a passerby] pulled out the pampas grass; that night, in a dream, I have heard that [the passerby] saw: "This skull is that of one called Ono no Komachi. Since the pampas grass hurt my eyes every time it swayed with the wind, I am so happy that [you] pulled it out and cast it aside. As a token of my appreciation, I will give you the ability to compose poetry well." The person who dreamed this was one called the Middle Captain Michinobu; I wonder if this is true? What other person [besides Komachi] would behave like this? If one were to saturate the heart with the colors and fragrance, this would be the way to be."[51]

This passage confirms the establishment of Komachi's figure as a beautiful and talented poet who fell into an uncommon state of hardship in her old age as well as the circulation of the "aname aname" narratives. By the time of *Mumyō zōshi*, these tropes seem to have been firmly entrenched, at least in certain circles. But the version of the skull story presented here is much closer to the ones found in *Waka dōmōshō* and *Fukuro zōshi* than those in *Kojidan* and *Mumyōshō* in that Komachi recites the entire poem and identifies herself in a person's dream. The differences between this story and those in *Waka dōmōshō* and *Fukuro zōshi* are also notable: here Komachi is a spirit with the power to reward kind human behavior with the ability to compose good poetry; ironically, this version, which appears significantly later than the ones in *Fukuro zōshi*, most resembles the speaking-skull story in the ninth-century *Nihon ryōiki*. Komachi's literary powers are emphasized not only through her own poetry but also through her capacity to share the powers of her talent with others. Even though the will to have the offending grass removed may not be as actively represented here as it is in *Fukuro zōshi*, the speaker suggests that Komachi's ability to compose poetry "even after becoming a corpse" was remarkable and thereby emphasizes her virtuosity.

Hosokawa Ryōichi suggests that the spirit's ability to reward the traveler could be a subversive rereading of the earlier images of Komachi in the "skull" narratives, which are products of an increasingly patriarchal society that deemed it desirable for a woman to be attached only to one man.[52] If the audience of *Mumyō zōshi* was female for the most part, Hosokawa's argument would be even more convincing: this text addresses a narrative about Komachi's life being generated by mostly male circles and presents a revisionist counter-narrative for the eyes of women. Overall the passage is a

51. Kuwabara, *Mumyō zōshi*, pp. 107–9.
52. Hosokawa, *Onna no chūsei*, p. 258.

positive assessment of Komachi's figure and stands in stark contrast to the descriptions and judgments of her life in other texts, mostly written by men. This elevation of Komachi by a female author should not be dismissed as a mere accident. Although it is possible that the author, as a descendant of Shunzei, was involved in the movement by the likes of Fujiwara no Teika to re-evaluate *Kokinshū* poets like Komachi,[53] the sympathetic attitude displayed here not only for her poetry but also for her life may not be simply a matter of poetics.

In fact, *Mumyō zōshi* as a whole can be viewed as a protest against the marginalization of female authors and authorship. Tanaka Takako reads the work as an attempt to improve the position of women authors in an increasingly oppressive era; more specifically, in the context of poetry, she argues that it is an expression of grief and resentment at the systematic exclusion of women from positions of poetic power, particularly as compilers of poetic collections (especially imperially commissioned anthologies) and judges of poetry contests. Tanaka claims that the Daughter of Shunzei perceived writing as the only way for an upper-class woman to achieve fame and that *Mumyō zōshi* was designed to catch the attention of the retired emperor Gotoba (r. 1183–98) in order both to advertise her own talents as a writer and to plead the case for women's writing in general.[54] The author's portrayal of Komachi as an empowered ghost can be placed within this context: it is the combination of Komachi's gender and her literary power that is crucial in this passage, and the attribution of the "aname aname" poem in its entirety to Komachi was an important component of the text's overall aim.

In summary, there are two possible explanations for the choice of either Narihira or Komachi as the protagonist of the speaking-skull story. First, the gendered author/compiler, as in the case of *Mumyō zōshi*, had significant motivations for promoting women's writing as a whole. Second, a collection's generic concerns sometimes complicated or even resulted in the countering of marginalizing tendencies. *Waka dōmōshō*, *Fukuro zōshi*, and *Shūchūshō* are kagaku texts, or studies of waka poems, and the overwhelming majority of the poems cited are tanka. *Dōmōshō* and *Shūchūshō* contain no examples of renga; in keeping with their concern for whole tanka poems, these works appear to be interested in the "aname aname" poem as tanka, not renga. If their compilers took the poem from *Komachishū*, which attributes it solely to Ko-

---

53. Kamioka, *Waka setsuwa no kenkyū*, p. 217.

54. See Tanaka Takako, "Chūsei no josei to bungaku."

machi, then they might have been inclined to keep the poem in its single-author format in order to remain consistent with their source. In the case of Dōmōshō, the drive to maintain the work's focus on tanka may even have created an empowering interpretation of a previously disempowering poetic presentation (as seen in Gōke shidai). The empowerment of Komachi as an active spirit can be read as a "by-product" of the compilers' literary interests as opposed to the main focus; yet this "by-product" played a significant role in combating the marginalizing representations of Komachi by other aristocratic men. These works contrast sharply with the previously cited passages in Kojidan and Mumyōshō, whose central concern is not the analysis of waka poems but the telling of stories; the author/compilers had no scholastic or gendered stake in keeping the poem whole.

Return of the Dead Woman

I have outlined in the preceding sections the ways in which women's bodies came to be portrayed as impure and loathsome due to their eventual decay, and how this discourse co-opted Komachi's figure as represented in a subgroup of the speaking-skull narratives for its own purposes. I end the chapter with a consideration of suggestions that the foundation of this marginalizing discourse—that is, the unattractiveness of women due to their impure/dead/decayed state—was not necessarily stable. The ultimate effectiveness of this image remains questionable, in fact, since the sexual desire induced by the female deceased comes to be an issue. Komachi's skull stories thus exist amid this complex discourse. As a female dead body, she is marginalized as the undesirable that aids men in ridding themselves of desire; yet the fascination with female corpses exhibited in some stories indicate that what is supposed to be undesirable can, paradoxically, be capable of feats not possible for living women and can even arouse desire. Beyond a certain point, decay and meditation on decay often seem to have undercut the very logic by which this type of contemplation operated. Although the examples below are not "about" Komachi, they point to the potential conflicts inherent in the discourse employed for her marginalization.

Nishiguchi Junko notes the increasing popularity toward the end of the Heian period of placing the bones of deceased women in sacred temple spaces that forbade the entrance of living women. She connects this trend with certain configurations of Buddhism associated with the Lotus Sutra which preached that a woman had to first lose her womanhood before she could attain ōjō and be reborn in the Pure Land. Examples of this line of thought can be seen in the *Ryōjin hishō* songs cited in the previous chapter. Nishiguchi concludes that in the skeletal state, a woman achieved a sexless existence and was thus permitted within the grounds of sacred mountain temples such as Hieizan and Kōyasan.[55] On the one hand, this belief marginalizes women in its pronouncement that a woman's body is a hindrance to rebirth in the Pure Land and that only after death can a woman be permitted to penetrate sacred grounds. However, we must also note the pivotal role played by the skeletal state in the achievement of ōjō. If becoming a skull meant a women could be reborn in the Pure Land and could enter a forbidden space, then that state becomes complicated if that dead woman can actually speak and act as an apparition—just as Komachi does in some of the stories discussed above.[56] She refuses to remain a silent pile of bones. In other words, through death, she successfully sheds the obstructions posed by her gendered existence, making her "equal" to men in a certain, albeit problematic, sense. She is, moreover,

---

55. Nishiguchi, *Onna no chikara*, pp. 16, 52, 80–83. She focuses on the popularization of a sutra called *Tennyo jōbutsu kyō* or *Tennyo shinkyō* (The sutra of the transformation of women for *jōbutsu*, or the Sutra of the transformation of women's bodies), as seen in accounts by Ōe no Masafusa, among others, which state that women can attain ōjō eventually by shedding their womanhood and that their role is valid because they are "mothers of the various buddhas" (ibid., pp. 105–11.) As I have noted in Chapter 3, the notion of women's *jōbutsu* (attainment of buddhahood) and ōjō is a controversial, with the debate between the possibilities of *sokushin jōbutsu* (attaining buddhahood in one's very body) and the necessity of *henjō nanshi* (changing into the form of a man). For more on this issue, see, among many works, Tanaka Takako, *Akujo ron*, pp. 183–88; Nagata, "Bukkyō ni miru boseikan," pp. 268–74; and Ōgoshi and Minamoto, *Kaitai suru bukkyō*. Also, Nishiguchi (*Onna no chikara*, p. 88) notes that the bones were most notably of women considered important to a family or a clan's roots and/or prosperity and were therefore often related to motherhood. If Komachi had come to be viewed as a non-mother by the time the speaking-skull stories materialized, then the familial significance of her bones would be diminished in this light. In addition, bones that had undergone cremation and bones that were the results of natural decay may have had different connotations of (im)purity. However, the very notion that a woman's bones could be considered a post-ōjō manifestation implies that Komachi's skull should not be interpreted only as a symbol of helplessness.

56. An analogous configuration might be the contemporary Taiwanese mode of worship that situates the dead flesh as *yin* ("disorder") and bones as *yang* ("order"); the skeletal state is one that has shed and therefore purified itself of the *yin* of bodily physicality and has ascended the steps of spiritual hierarchy and power (Sangren, *History and Magical Power in a Chinese Community*, pp. 137–38). This example indicates that flesh and bone can be differently empowered within a religious system.

powerful in death in some of the speaking-skull stories; her spirit possesses the ability to change events or people in this world.

Another example of ambiguity in the representation of a deceased woman occurs when she possesses the temporary power to create an illusion of her living self and therefore to attract men. Kubota Jun points out such a case in the setsuwa collection *Senjūshō* (probably ca. 1250).[57] In Chapter 7, Story 1, a Chinese emperor of the Liang court finds the sun setting as he is on a public mission in the mountains. He comes upon a solitary house, in which an attractive woman sits playing a harp. He spends the night there, only to wake up in the morning next to the remains of a woman. Startled, he rides his horse into the village to ask about the house, and a villager informs him that a young woman fond of playing the harp had died young; her ghost materializes at night. The crucial commentary by the narrator comes toward the end of the story: "Hearing this, I feel sort of frightened, but there is an element of sexual attractiveness" (*shikajika to kikite wa, nantonaku osoroshiku oboehabere domo, mata tsuyanaru kata mo haberubeshi*).[58] This comment is especially notable since the compiler of *Senjūshō* was probably a person well versed in certain aspects of Buddhist doctrine and may have been a monk.[59] An earlier story with a similar plotline is found in *Konjaku monogatari* (Chapter 27, Story 24), which is set in Japan. A husband returns home to his wife, whom he had abandoned, spends the night with her, and then discovers in the morning that he has been lying next to a corpse. After this discovery, he flees in terror.[60] In this well-known *Konjaku* story, however, there is no mention of the sexual attractiveness of the woman.

---

57. Kubota, "Gaikotsu no hanashi," pp. 96–97. Kubota also refers to another story about bones: Chapter 5, Story 15, presents the monk Saigyō, who is lonely in his reclusive life and conceives of a plan to collect dead people's bones in the field in order to construct a human companion (he does not succeed). Kubota argues that this story treats human remains merely as objects and not as meditative devices that expose the transient nature of this world as a whole and illustrates the collection's ambivalent view of skeletons (p. 101).

58. Yasuda Takako et al., *Senjūshō*, 2: 170–72.

59. *Senjūshō* was long attributed to Saigyō.

60. Mabuchi et al., *Konjaku monogatari shū*, 2: 268–72. Hitomi Tonomura ("Black Hair and Red Trousers," p. 145) notes two other stories from *Konjaku* in which "the decomposing female body, unlike the male, serves as a pedagogical symbol, a medium through which to convey the Buddhist messages of impermanence. A decomposing female body is a signifier for transmigration, the mutability of human life, and the fragility of physical beauty . . . the female body is used as an object lesson in spiritual training." She asks, "But what does it mean

Ironically, the *Konjaku* story, compiled slightly before the beginning of Komachi's skull stories, is presented simply as a "strange tale" in which the deceased woman is portrayed only as a martyr-like victim of her husband's inconsiderate behavior, whereas the *Senjūshō* story, compiled after Komachi's skull stories had undergone much development and meditations on women's corpses had become established, repeatedly dwells on the physical beauty of the ghost and mentions the alluring and arousing aspect of the tale. This comparison suggests that the attempt to marginalize women's sexuality by portraying their deceased physical bodies as repulsive may not have been entirely successful. In fact, in some instances, the dead female body and the ghostly apparition that can materialize from it, originally conceived of as the vehicle for banishing sexual desire, came to be the target of sexual desire instead. Kubota Jun speculates that the act of gazing at a skull in order to invoke what is supposed to be a festering female corpse may have only conjured up images of a living attractive woman and, in fact, that the spirit lost on its way toward enlightenment is not the one belonging to the skull but the one of the person beholding it.[61]

Another visual example is raised by Ikeda Shinobu, who examines the representations of female victims of battle in the picture scroll *Heiji monogatari emaki* (Picture scroll of the *Tale of Heiji*, ca. mid-thirteenth century). Ikeda points out that high-ranking women-in-waiting are portrayed erotically in death, with exposed body parts, and that this eroticism of female corpses exposing their flesh can also be seen in illustrations of Buddhist setsuwa that were meant to preach the impurity of the (gendered) flesh but actually contained sexually charged representations.[62] The reappearance of the very desire that was supposed to have been banished through meditation is reminiscent of Freud's "return of the repressed." The position of sexuality in Buddhism—here, heavily influenced by Pure Land discourse—is a complex one, since it is not monolithic or consistent over time, or across different schools of thought; condemnation of sexual activities is not necessarily or always a given. However, in light of the marginalization of Komachi's figure within the frameworks of fujō and kusō, it is important to keep in mind these other possibilities.

---

to illuminate the Buddha's truth consistently through the female body? Does it not configure the female body as an object of observation, an entity dissociated from her own humanity?"

61. Kubota, "Gaikotsu no hanashi," pp. 102–3.

62. Ikeda, "Kassen-e no naka no joseizō."

Indeed, it seems even doubtful that Narihira or any other male viewer/audience was able to escape from his sexual desires by looking at Komachi's skull; rather, the skull seems to have conjured up the image of the living Komachi. The very denial "I won't say it's [= the skull is] Ono" suggests that in order to dismiss the skull as not being Komachi's, the beholder had to call to mind a countering image of the "actual" Komachi. Most interestingly, such inklings of attraction can be found in the earliest text that presents the "aname aname" poem: the *Komachishū* passage, after citing the poem, states that "Ono no Komachi beckoned him like pampas grass charmingly." "Charming" (*wokashi*) suggests the ghostly yet still-present power of sexual attraction the deceased poet possessed over the narrator/male character. The results of marginalization can be quite different from those that might have been expected; such discourses cannot be claimed to be universally applicable or stable.

☙

Chapters 3 and 4 have sought to illustrate the ways in which motivated individuals or groups selected the unsavory, undesirable aspects of old age and death and assigned these characteristics to Ono no Komachi, who stands for female sexuality and literary power. This assignment marginalizes her by vitiating the empowering characteristics attributed to her. The trope of Komachi as an impoverished, old beggar woman contributed to the shaping of her oeuvre, and the stories that present her as a helpless skull who asks a male protagonist for assistance chip away at her powers of literary creation. Komachi's authorship is thus manipulated by later generations from two separate directions—through the selection of poems attributed to her and through the denial of authorship. The former are acts of addition that reproduce her supposed figure through an approach that equates poetic content with "authorial experience"; the latter are subtractive attempts to streamline and contour her "life story" and the poetry attributed to her. These attempts combined in the Heian and early Kamakura periods to generate dynamic, charged, and motivated definitions of the constructed figure named "Ono no Komachi."

The marginalization of Komachi through the linking of the "old beggar" and "speaking-skull" tropes has influenced the understanding of her figure up to the present day. For example, some scholars have pointed out that the concept of fujō can be seen in the poem of *Tamatsukuri Komachishi sōsuisho* in its description of death and decay and that its presence hints at the development of the other narrative tropes: the speaking skull, and her later portrayal as a decaying corpse.[63] However, the passage to which they refer is "The frosts have sealed in their bodies in the dim grave / the daylight exposes the corpses of the old grave mound"; this is a description of Komachi's parents' bodies and those around them in the grave mound and not of Komachi herself. If in fact later narratives construct and conveniently appropriate the trope of Komachi's impurity from this passage, then it is a clear case of the transference of characteristics: a deliberate misreading of the subject of impurity. This example, like those cited in Chapter 2, suggests that repeated instances of various constructed marginalizations can have significant influence on our reading of texts "by" and "about" Komachi; rigorous investigations of her textual presentations and representations are therefore necessary at every point, so that we can see both the motivatedness and the resulting effects of such discourses.

On the other hand, the speaking-skull stories in which Komachi plays a ghostly role show not only the constructed nature of marginality and disempowerment but also the complexities of marginalizing discourses. Marginalization does not develop in a strict diachronic progression; rather, these stories are characterized by synchronic variation, since both marginalizing and counter-marginalizing discourses that can be ascribed to motivations ranging from generic interests to feminist concerns can be read into them. The very discourses that marginalized women's bodies as undesirable are more heterogeneous than they might appear at first; such forces were complicated by paradoxical empowerment and even a resurgence of the desires they were designed to suppress.

In later centuries, Ono no Komachi's representations undergo further changes, many along the lines of the narratives discussed in Chapters 3 and 4. Lady Nijō's *Towazugatari* mentions Komachi's destitution. Other well-known examples include the noh plays *Sotoba Komachi* (Komachi at the grave-marker) and *Kayoi Komachi* (Visiting Komachi) (both ca. mid- to late fourteenth century), which present Komachi as an impoverished old woman and as engaged in a battle with a suitor she had rejected; a further examination of these plays would shed more light on the complexities of Komachi's marginalization and empowerment. In the late Muromachi and early Edo periods, collections of *otogi zōshi* (popular short narratives often accompanied by illustrations) include a selection called "Komachi no sōshi" (The story of

---

63. Watanabe Hideo, "Ono no Komachi," p. 84.

Komachi), and mid-to-late Edo period satiric poems, among others, represent her as lacking a vagina. Despite the many and varied attempts to marginalize Komachi's figure, legends about her have remained popular to the present day. There are still locations throughout Japan that claim to be the site of Komachi's grave. Her popularity through the years may be regarded as a sort of resistance against the forces that have wanted to marginalize her figure or the very reinforcement of those forces through the spread of views that position her as marginalized. Her continued presence is most likely a combination of both; a precise contextual and textual examination of each historical setting would be necessary to evaluate the phenomenon.

I will end with two questions and possible answers. First, why was female sexuality, or the power of women to attract men, singled out for marginalization? One obvious answer is that this attraction was an impediment to the achievement of Buddhist enlightenment for men. Desire was a threat since it could stand in the way of ōjō, and the source of desire in men had to be negated or domesticated so that it could be controlled. The motivation to contain this power may also have been related to a social configuration of the period; as suggested by Hosokawa, a woman's ability to attract many men could have been troublesome for the patriarchal family system, which was on the rise in the late Heian to early Kamakura periods. This system demanded that a woman be attached to only one man and that military-class men seek wives who fit the aims of the (male-controlled) ruling class. But although such motivations are important, they do not guarantee a consistent or convincing effect, as we have seen in cases such as Senjūshō.

Second, why was Komachi chosen as a target? I see two reasons. First, she had been constructed as a beautiful, highly attractive woman, who could reject suitors at will. The power to reject is complicated, since it can be construed in a number of different ways, such as chastity (Kuroki Ruka's interpretation), arrogance, or coyness. It is, however, a power that she had over men; she could not be made to follow their wishes. This uncontrollable power to attract was precisely what had to be domesticated in both the Buddhist and patriarchal paradigms. Second, Komachi was established as a poet of considerable literary status, since she was the only woman included in the rokkasen. There are two reasons why this literary clout needed to be undermined. On one hand, the ability to compose waka skillfully was an essential part of social intercourse, which included relationships between men and women; an artist who could utilize this medium fully thus had a great advantage in the arena of sexual negotiations. Komachi's reputation of literary power, therefore, greatly enhanced her attraction. On the other hand, the marginalization of this woman author can be placed in a larger context. As mentioned before, Komachi is not the only famous Heian female literary creator who figures in tales about decline in old age and death; especially from the Medieval period onward, figures such as Sei Shōnagon, Lady Ise, and Izumi Shikibu come to be associated with such tropes. This marginalization of deceased women authors includes Murasaki Shikibu, who appears in the "Do Not Speak Lies" section of Chapter 5 of *Hōbutsushū*: "Recently, Murasaki Shikibu, due to her sin of having created *Genji monogatari* using empty words, had fallen into hell and found the suffering unbearable; she thus appeared in a person's dream, whereupon poets gathered and copied sutras in a day and offered them."[64] This brief passage led to the production of a whole series of texts in the Kamakura period and a noh play, *Genji kuyō* (Praying for Genji), whose purpose is to deliver her from hell. In a later text called *Yotsugi monogatari* (Tales of the successive reigns), written by an unknown author in the mid- to late Kamakura period, the narrator states that Murasaki Shikibu's father, Tametoki, was the author of *Genji monogatari* and that his daughter had merely filled in the details.[65] If the figure of Komachi faced marginalization through strategic attacks on her locational/ cultural and literary centrality, the figure of Murasaki Shikibu suffered from the denial of her status as author altogether. This is clearly a case in which a famous woman writer is posthumously stripped of her literary power, either through the denunciation of the literary activity as a sin or crime or by crediting a male author with her work. Even amid what seems to be a patent trend toward the marginalization of women authors in general—during the Medieval period contemporary texts by female authors appear to have been less canonical than texts by women writers had been in the Heian period— the "how" and "when" of canon formation are, of course, crucial in considering this issue. It is important to examine each individual case closely in order to delineate the details of marginalizing processes in all of their complexities. Heian women's literary power may have been slowly but surely dismantled through a strategic attack on the figures of the authors themselves, but the web of motives and effects that produced such a trend was far from monolithic.

---

64. Koizumi et al., *Hōbutsushū, Kankyo no tomo, Hirasan kojin reitaku*, p. 229.
65. Zoku gunsho ruijū kanseikai, *Zoku gunsho ruijū*, vol. 32, part II, p. 157.

Part III
    Hashihime

5 Return of the Margins: Polygyny, Longing, Demon

Whereas Parts I and II address, respectively, the representations of a group of women and a female literary figure who are both well known and well studied, this chapter deals with a relatively obscure figure. For many generations scholars and the reading public have assumed that the asobi and Ono no Komachi actually existed as historical figures (despite the problems that arise from such assumptions); Hashihime, by contrast, has been perceived as a deity and/or a fictional character since her first appearance. In the previous chapters, I try to reveal the constructedness of "historical figures"; here, I concentrate on the relationship between the construction of a "fictional figure" and "historical" practices. Also, whereas the preceding chapters outline generally increasing tendencies toward the disempowerment of female figures through marginalization, the central figure of this chapter shows that marginalization can, paradoxically, empower a figure in certain complex ways, which then put into motion further reactions and attempts at re-marginalization.

The literal translation of "Hashihime" is "bridge lady," and some scholars claim that it is a generic term for female bridge deities.[1] The focus of this chapter is a particular Hashihime at Uji, a location southeast of the Heian capital. The development of poetry and prose on the figure of Hashihime of Uji proceeds in what appears at first glance to be two strikingly different

---

1. Mainly those scholars who follow Yanagita Kunio's views; for Yanagita's scholarship, see the following note.

directions. Hashihime initially appears in mid-Heian texts as a woman who spends lonely nights waiting for her lover to visit. Although this image continues to be reproduced into the Kamakura period and beyond, another representation also emerges: that of Hashihime as a fierce *oni* (demon).

Past Japanese scholarship has interpreted stories about Hashihime in a number of ways. Although Yanagita Kunio's works are fraught with controversy, he was one of the first modern scholars to address her figure. He argued that Hashihime was originally one of a pair of water/river deities, one female and one male. However, as times changed, only the female deity remained popular, as her status as a divine figure underwent "deterioration" (*reiraku*), and she was reduced to a *yōkai* (monster).[2] Some later scholars see

---

2. Yanagita, *Teihon Yanagita Kunio shū*, 26: 342–43; see also ibid., 5: 214–29. Yanagita's theory that the yōkai are kami who have experienced decline has been criticized as too general and inaccurate; see Komatsu, "Yōkai: yamanba wo megutte." Yanagita (5: 228) also proposes that Hashihime belongs to a pair of deities, one female and one male, whose images were placed at bridges. He argues that since it was inappropriate for a couple to be disturbed, especially if they were divine figures, there was a belief that the space they occupied would not be invaded by others. The pair of deities thus functioned as protectors of a community's boundary, and the two faces of Hashihime—one a benevolent water deity who pines for her mate, the other a fear-inspiring demon—developed in hope that the former would apply to the community and the latter would manifest itself to invaders from the outside. This theory can be critiqued in two ways. First, although spotty evidence exists from the mid-Heian period that pairs of deities were installed at crossroads (as seen in *Honchō seiki*, *Fusō ryakki*, and *Konjaku monogatari*; see Sasamoto, *Tsuji no sekai*, pp. 51–52), which many scholars argue share the same marginal/supernatural quality as bridges, and a picture scroll from the twelfth century depicts a small shrine at the foot of a bridge (as seen in *Nenchū gyōji emaki*; Sasamoto, *Tsuji no sekai*, p. 61), Yanagita's argument remains ahistorical. Although it is not impossible that Hashihime was worshipped in the manner that Yanagita suggests, there is no direct evidence from the period under investigation. Second, his assertion that couples formed a union which should not be disturbed is also speculative. Although it may be possible that Hashihime was part of a pair at some point in time, the fact that by the time the "pining wife" trope appeared she was a solitary figure must be taken into account; in other words, if Yanagita's speculation is correct, then a textual "decoupling" must have occurred before Hashihime's first known appearance in *Kokinshū* in 905, which presents her alone and waiting for her lover. If this is the case, then the male deity of the pair must have sunk into oblivion by that time, the spiritual power derived from the union must have dissipated, and Hashihime at Uji had taken on a significance of her own as the sole protector of the bridge. The "decoupling" would therefore have further emphasized the importance of her solitary state as well as her own power as a deity; these qualities are important in the discussion below. Instead of focusing on the nebulous proposition that bridge deities as a pair functioned as protectors, as Yanagita does, I find it more fruitful to explore the significance of Hashihime as a single female deity.

the "pining wife" trope as a depiction of the tragic death of a fisherman and the grief of his widow, with longing on both sides as its central theme, and claim that the narrative developed from the worship of water-deities in the manner suggested by Yanagita.[3] Others prefer to approach her figure purely as a female deity waiting to be joined in a sacred union with a male deity.[4] Yet another theory states that Hashihime is the deified figure of a miko responsible for pacifying the sometimes-harmful powers of the river.[5] Concerning the transformation of women into demonic figures in the Medieval period in general, one scholar suggests that since women were suffering from unprecedented and complex social oppression, their demonization represents recognition of and sympathy for the many resentments they harbored. This in turn created the compassionate need to save these pitiable women, usually through the Buddhist path.[6] Finally, Yoshikai Naoto, who has conducted perhaps the most thorough investigation of narratives about Hashihime, carefully divides them into different storylines and basically treats them as independent developments in different genres of writing or performance.[7]

None of these scholars, however, has dealt directly with the possible reasons for the existence of two distinct images of Hashihime, nor with the implications of the different portrayals of her. The contrast between the pining wife/lover and the ferocious demon may suggest at first that the two Hashihimes of Uji are different beings altogether. As I attempt to show below, however, the two manifestations of Hashihime are in fact closely related. This becomes clear when we examine the figure in conjunction with the practice of polygyny and the consequent marginalization of jealousy: Hashihime represents a double movement in the oppressive construction of the female figure in a polygynous order. The oppression of women to which I refer is not a generalized situation; Hashihime's case involves a particular class of women involved in a specific marital or relational configuration. On the one hand, the waiting woman is aestheticized and deified into an elegant poetic trope that conveniently erases the disruptive forces of polygyny such

---

3. See, e.g., Noguchi Hirohisa's entry on "Hashihime" in Inui et al., *Nihon denki densetsu daijiten*, pp. 709–10; and Kuwahara, *Chūsei monogatari no kisoteki kenkyū*.

4. Kobayashi Shigemi, *Ono no Komachi kō*, pp. 368–69.

5. Kondō, *Nihon no oni*, p. 188.

6. Baba Akiko, *Oni no kenkyū*, p. 217.

7. Yoshikai, "*Hashihime monogatari no shiteki kōsatsu*," pp. 105–34.

as jealousy and domesticates her suffering. On the other hand, the undesirable emotion of jealousy is transformed into the marginalized, shunned figure of a demon. In the latter case, however, the marginalized returns to threaten the well-being of those who inhabit the center—that is, men (and women) who reside in the capital—through its demonic capacity for violence; demonization leads to both vilification and empowerment. The final pacification and marginalization of the demonic, furthermore, results in the denial of women's capacity for violent physical acts. In discussing the issue of polygyny as a potential site for dissatisfaction for women, I am not suggesting that monogamy is a timeless, necessarily desirable, or morally correct configuration of heterosexual relationships; rather, I wish to focus on the process by which representations of a woman's supposed "experience" of polygyny become marginalized and manipulated in the textual arena.

Marriage and female-male relationship configurations in the Heian and Kamakura periods have been the subject of scholarly debate for some time. It appears to have been the norm for a man to have multiple female partners, at least among aristocratic and other upper-class circles, during the period in which the texts discussed below were produced. For the purposes of this chapter, I use the term "polygyny" to refer to the social expectation that this relational configuration was practiced without negative legal consequences or social ostracization. Recently, there has been some controversy among scholars over the details of marriage structures in the upper class. Takamure Itsue, a major figure in this area of study, has asserted that marriages in the Heian period were polygynous but uxorilocal and that women had significant power in a marriage, even though after this period "patriarchal" forces (i.e., those that disempowered women socially, economically, and politically) overwhelmed this system.[8] Some scholars in the 1990s have critiqued her view, however. Kurihara Hiromu claims that the uxorilocal state was only temporary for a married couple.[9] Kudō Shigenori argues that Heian society was not legally polygynous, since a man was allowed to "marry" only one woman, even though he may often have been involved in a number of relationships with women, some of whom may have borne his children and/or been supported economically by him.[10] A full discussion of marriage configurations in this period is beyond the scope of this chapter, but a few fac-

---

8. See, e.g., Takamure, *Nihon kon'in shi*.
9. See Kurihara, *Takamura Itsue no kon'in joseishizō no kenkyū*.
10. See Kudō, *Heianchō no kekkon seido to bungaku*.

tors are relevant. First, in general, scholars assert that an upper-class woman's position in marriage became more restricted starting in the mid- to late Heian period, as seen in trends such as increasing economic dependency on the husband because of changes in inheritance patterns, a decline in the divorce rate, which suggests the stigmatization of repeated couplings and de-couplings, and the appearance of terms designating a woman's involvement with a man other than her husband.[11] During the same period, the trope of the pining wife/lover becomes increasingly aestheticized, and the jealous demon begins to appear. The term "polygyny" is even more applicable to the Kamakura and later periods, when scholars are in general agreement that in-creasingly, upper-class women were expected to be faithful to one husband whereas men could engage openly in affairs or concubinage.[12] Second, al-though the narrative of the decline in women's status in marriage is convincing at one level, it is important not to assume a transparent cause-and-effect rela-tionship in which a "historical reality" acts on "literature," which "reflects" it; the picture is much more complicated. For example, we should remember that polygyny did not eliminate the possibility that a woman could have rela-tions with more than one man. Representations of such cases exist through-out the mid-Heian to the Kamakura periods.[13] Even though I focus on poly-gyny in this chapter, forgetting this aspect (which is so notably absent from stories about Hashihime) would skew our understanding of female-male sexual relationships in this era. As we shall see, one of the poetic invocations of Hashihime in *Genji monogatari*, a work by a female author, occurs in the story of a woman who is having simultaneous affairs with two men.

---

11. Sōgō joseishi kenkyūkai, *Nihon josei no rekishi: sei, ai, kazoku*, pp. 67–78. See also Wakita, *Nihon chūsei joseishi no kenkyū*.

12. For example, Tabata Yasuko (*Nihon chūsei no josei*, pp. 18–20) discusses the notion of *teijo*, or "model woman," in the Kamakura period. During this time, the term was used to de-scribe women who were devoted to their male partners. Tabata points out that although *teijo* did not refer to women who abstained from a second marriage (as was the case in the Edo pe-riod), there was no corresponding term for men; she therefore concludes that husband-centric ideas of partnership were on the rise.

13. Hitomi Tonomura ("Black Hair and Red Trousers") notes examples from *Konjaku monogatari* and states that "marriage, as such, was not necessarily a male-centered institution at this time" (p. 136) and that "women's plural sexual relationships seem commonplace, even if polyandry is not" (p. 138), despite strong implications of inequality (men can have two "wives" but women only have "affairs" outside marriage, etc.). As for representations in the Kamakura period, *Towazugatari* is often cited as an example of a portrayal of a woman's engagement with multiple partners.

Given the already unstable grounds of the "historical practice" of polygyny, the question this chapter addresses is this: *How* does the trope of
Hashihime configure polygyny and its players? My aim is to focus on the
process by which representations of a woman's supposed "experience" of polygyny are constructed and marginalized in various texts. Joan W. Scott has
critiqued the use of "experience" as unmediated "factual evidence" in the
study of history:

> [Studies that remain within the epistemological frame of orthodox history] take as
> self-evident the identities of those whose experience is being documented and thus
> naturalize their difference. They locate resistance outside its discursive construction,
> and reify agency as an inherent attribute of individuals, thus decontextualizing it. . . .
> The evidence of experience . . . reproduces rather than contests given ideological
> systems.[14]

In her challenge to the use of "experience" as a privileged kind of evidence,
Scott refers primarily to accounts by individuals of their "own experiences."
But her point is also relevant in considering the vision of Hashihime's "experience" constructed by upper-class men operating within the polygynous
system. The position of "woman in polygyny" is thus formulated through
these textual attempts and naturalized through repetition. The question of
historicity, text, and experience is particularly pertinent since the great majority of scholars of Japanese women's history utilize works such as *Genji
monogatari* and *Kagerō nikki* (The Kagerō diary, by the Mother of Michi-
tsuna; ca. 974) as unproblematic evidence of women's experiences in polygyny. My point is not that such "fictional" texts are ill-suited to the study of
"history"; rather, I begin with the premise that all texts discursively construct
ideological systems and locate individuals within them, and that it is necessary to pay attention to the process of this construction.

In addition to polygyny, two spaces inextricably linked with Hashihime—the place called Uji and bridges—are relevant to the analysis of texts
in which she appears. Minzoku studies have focused on the liminal functions
of particular geographic locations, including these two, and topoi were
constructed around them before and after the first known appearance of
Hashihime.

Uji was an important location long before the Heian period. It was also
the site where Uji no Waki Iratsuko had taken up residence; he was a son of

---

14. Scott, "Experience," p. 25.

Emperor Ōjin (active late fourth–early fifth centuries) and may have committed suicide or been killed in a succession struggle, which eventually resulted in his older brother's becoming the next emperor.[15] Uji no Waki Iratsuko was later deified as the kami of the Rikyū shrine,[16] who came to be portrayed as Hashihime's lover in waka commentary works in the late Heian period. Uji therefore had an association with the loss of power by a figure who withdrew himself from or was defeated in an imperial struggle.

Genji monogatari's "Uji chapters" probably popularized the location and the construction of its image as a desolate location difficult to reach from the capital. For example, when Kaoru first visits the Eighth Prince at Uji, he is surprised by the roar of the rushing waters and the fierce winds. In this text, Uji cannot be contained as merely an aesthetically rustic location; there is a sense of wilderness coupled with sadness and melancholy, a pun on the name.

Furthermore, toward the end of the Heian period, Uji became prominent as one of the more notable arenas for battles and therefore bloodshed during the Genpei wars. This association between warfare and Uji is important when we consider the genre of texts that present Hashihime as a fierce demon, such as *Heike monogatari* (The tale of Heike; various versions ca. thirteenth–fourteenth centuries) and *Soga monogatari* (The tale of Soga; ca. fourteenth century). Both belong to the category of *gunki monogatari*, or narratives that center around military events and battles.

---

15. Ishihara, "Uji no denshō," pp. 16–19. Ishihara uses *Nihon shoki* as his main source. The chapters on Emperor Ōjin and Nintoku state that Emperor Ōjin wanted Uji no Waki Iratsuko to succeed him instead of his older brothers Ōsazaki no Mikoto and Ōyamamori no Mikoto, but the latter revolted against this decision after his father's death. A battle ensued, and Uji no Waki Iratsuko emerged victorious. He and the remaining brother, Ōsazaki no Mikoto, attempted to yield the title of emperor to the other, and Uji no Waki Iratsuko committed suicide out of his belief that Ōsazaki no Mikoto was more fit to rule and that a younger brother should not become the ruler over his older brother. Ōsazaki no Mikoto grieved over his brother's death, and Uji no Waki Iratsuko resurrected himself momentarily to assure him that he would tell the spirit of his father, Emperor Ōjin, that his older brother was a more suitable choice for emperor. Ōsazaki no Mikoto took the throne as Emperor Nintoku (see Sakamoto Tarō et al., *Nihon shoki*, 1: 362–88). *Kojiki* also tells of the same struggle but simply states that Uji no Waki Iratsuko died young while he and his brother each claimed the other to be the rightful successor (see *Kojiki*, chapter on Emperor Ōjin; Ogihara, *Kojiki*, pp. 151–67).

16. Ishihara, "Uji no denshō," p. 16.

Uji was also the site of large-scale tombs and functioned as a gravesite for the Fujiwara clan.[17] One example of Uji's association with death and the afterlife is Fujiwara no Yorimichi's Byōdōin, a villa-turned-temple built in 1052, which was inspired by Pure Land teachings and intended to re-create Amitābha's welcoming of the deceased into the Western Pure Land.[18] It has been pointed out that spaces designated to hold "impure" objects, such as the dead, were not necessarily themselves spaces originally demarcated as "impure." In fact, such special spaces seem to have had the power to contain and even purify the impure agents that entered them.[19] In this sense, Uji would have been regarded not simply as an inauspicious site of death and decay but as a space that had the power to neutralize death and even to assure a happy afterlife. The *makurakotoba* (pillow word) for Uji in waka poetry is *chihaya-buru*, or "the kami showing their power"; this further suggests that Uji had an association with the divine.

The combination of Uji as a perceived place of "wild nature" and its special religious connection might have been enough to ensure its importance in the minds of upper-class residents of the capital, but Uji was also popular throughout the Heian period and beyond as a site for aristocratic retreat, especially in the form of country villas. Perhaps the most famous is the estate owned by the regent Fujiwara no Michinaga (966–1027), which was later transformed into Byōdōin by his son Yorimichi. During Michinaga's lifetime, it was a site for elaborate banquets and a convenient stop en route to and from the Fujiwara family shrine at Kasuga.[20] The courtier Minamoto no Takakuni (1004–77) is said to have spent time at Uji collecting stories, according to the preface of *Uji shūi monogatari* (Tales gleaned at Uji).[21] Certain descriptions of the location suggest that it was not always perceived as an untamable place. For example, Fujiwara no Akihira's *Unshū shōsoku* (Model letters from Izumo; ca. 1060s) narrates an elegant upper-class outing to Uji; the scenery is beautiful, and poetry is recited. He then notes that a boat with

---

17. Amino et al., *Ama no hashi, chi no hashi*, p. 192.

18. Moriya, *Geinō to chinkon*, p. 10.

19. See Yamamoto Kōji, *Kegare to ōharae*; he discusses the problem of purity and impurity associated with specific spaces extensively.

20. Nakajima, "Uji no sekai—Hashihime no maki—," p. 40.

21. The preface suggests two meanings for the title *Uji shūi monogatari*: (1) Tales gleaned at Uji and (2) Tales of the Uji chamberlain (a Chamberlain Toshisada [unidentified, fl. second half of the twelfth century?] is said to have possessed the original version of the text at one point; *shūi* is the Chinese equivalent (*shiyi*) of the Japanese post of chamberlain [*jijū*]).

asobi women singing imayō songs came forth.[22] This passage indicates that an outing to Uji was an established aristocratic practice and that the asobi who benefited from the patronage of the aristocrats practiced their profession in Uji as well as at such better-known haunts as Eguchi and Kanzaki.

The composite textual image of Uji is thus multifaceted but clustered around certain distinct themes. It was marked by physical marginality due to its distance from the capital, which contributed to its association with a "wild" rusticity, yet it was a crucial node in transportation to and from the capital and had a special significance for the Fujiwara family. Both death and the afterlife operated as key components of Uji in the aristocratic world, but the members of the aristocracy did not hesitate to spend their leisure time there. Uji, within the aristocratic paradigm of the time, appears to have been a place that was accessible enough to enable the enjoyments of the capital culture (such as banquets) yet just remote enough to conjure up images of wilderness, mystery, death, and the divine. It can be understood as a kind of defamiliarizing territory: Uji belonged to the capital's imagination and observed its protocols for the most part, yet there was always the possibility of the familiar going awry. As we will see below, this characteristic is analogous to the one ascribed to Hashihime's two faces: domesticated and dangerous. The further association of Uji with wartime bloodshed in the late Heian period linked the location with violence, which becomes a significant aspect of Hashihime of Uji.

The construction of the bridge at Uji seems to have taken place well before the Heian period. A stele describing the history of the Uji bridge, probably dating from the early Heian period, states that it was built in 646 as a deed to gain merit by a Buddhist monk named Dōtō.[23] The Uji river is described as a rapid and treacherous body of water, and the stele explains that Dōtō had undertaken the task of bridge building "so that [sentient beings] can cross over to the shores of enlightenment."[24] *Nihon ryōiki* (ca. 810–24) has the same account but identifies Dōtō (Totŭn) as a monk from Koguryŏ (Part I, Story 12). Similarly, Chapter 19, Story 31, of *Konjaku monogatari* relates that Dōtō built the bridge, probably with the help of a heavenly

---

22. Shigematsu, *Shin sarugakuki / Unshū shōsoku*, pp. 173–74.

23. Called *Ujibashi no hi*, the stele itself has been lost, but its inscription was recorded in works such as *Fusō ryakki*. The upper third was supposedly excavated in the Edo period.

24. Amino et al., *Ama no hashi, chi no hashi*, p. 106.

being.[25] Texts indicate that throughout the early to mid-Heian period, the Uji bridge, which was made of wood and was about 90 meters in length and 5 meters in width, had to be replanked regularly because of storms and floods. However, by the time of *Ishiyamadera engi* (The *engi* of Ishiyama Temple),[26] a picture scroll from the fourteenth century, construction techniques seem to have improved greatly, and the Uji bridge had become a more permanent structure.[27] The bridge was under the jurisdiction of the central government in the early Heian period, but in the eleventh century, lack of funds forced the government to rely on provincial governors to repair it; by the late Heian period, money for repairs seems to have been collected by monks from the public.[28] More evidence of ties between this bridge and religion can be found in ceremonies celebrating the completion of repairs in 1283, which involved two hundred monks and the building of a thirteen-story stupa.[29] The supernatural, therefore, was an important part of bridge building at Uji at least as early as the mid-Heian.

A number of recent scholars have focused on bridges. It has been pointed out that pre-Heian conceptions linked the two homophones *hashi* "border" and *hashi* "bridge," and that in works such as *Man'yōshū* and *Nihon shoki* (Chronicles of Japan; ca. 720), bridges could span vertical spaces—between heaven and earth, for instance—as well as horizontal spaces.[30] Bridges were also known as sites of fortunetelling (*hashi-uranai*);[31] this activity suggests that the space marked by a bridge was thought of as having access to the supernatural world. The practice of offering human sacrifices to ensure a successful bridge building is also evident in some texts, although this does not seem to have occurred regularly.

---

25. Yamada Yoshio et al., *Konjaku monogatarishū*, 4: 123–24. In addition to the examples listed above, other works such as *Shoku nihongi* state that the monk was Dōshō, not Dōtō; later accounts often confused the two (see Yoshikai, "Hashihime monogatari no shiteki kōsatsu").

26. *Engi* refers to narratives that present the origins, history, and/or special powers of a religious establishment.

27. Oyamada, *Hashi*, pp. 33–39.

28. Gomi, *Inseiki shakai no kenkyū*, p. 206.

29. Ōta, "Chūsei no minshū kyūzai no shosō," p. 73.

30. Oyamada, *Hashi*, pp. 10–11.

31. Specifically, the Modori-bashi at Ichijō, which is the setting for some of the Hashi-hime-as-demon stories, is mentioned in the mid- to late Heian period as a place where *hashi-uranai* took place (Ōta, "Chūsei no minshū kyūzai no shosō," p. 66).

Beyond these observations, *minzokugaku* scholars who study the social significance of marginal spaces and their otherworldly characteristics such as Amino Yoshihiko, among others,[32] have proposed the importance of certain "border" or "marginal" (*kyōkaiteki*) spaces in late Heian and Medieval society. These spaces functioned as locations in which the human was represented as interacting with the supernatural. Amino argues that such spaces include bridges, which were placed under the jurisdiction of provincial governors in the early Heian period but were managed by the central government through the *kebi'ishi* (guards/police) by the end of that period; bridge construction was often executed by imperial command. He suggests that bridges, like other spaces such as roads, passes, ports, and graveyards, were "nonrelated" (*muen*) to anyone in that they could not be owned by an individual before the Heian period, and that these were consciously delineated as "public" spaces administered by the central government during the Heian period.[33] Documents from the eleventh century also suggest that bridges served as markers of village boundaries and therefore did not actually belong to a particular village.[34] Namihira Emiko argues that certain spaces such as the borders of villages and crossroads were seen as dangerous or impure; such spaces permitted the appearance of extraordinary beings, which necessitated rituals to ensure the safety of humans who infringed upon these spaces.[35] Similarly, bridges were sometimes thought to be places where vengeful spirits of those who had died in water-related accidents materialized and harassed passersby[36] and were conceived of as a "liminal" space that marked the mediating boundary between the everyday and the "other world."[37] These assertions that certain places with access to the supernatural realm were located within the bounds of everyday life—bridges served important transportational functions along with roads and riverbeds—is consistent with the many narratives, especially those from the Medieval period,

---

32. For a discussion of views similar to Amino's, see Yamada Naomi, "Kyōkai no bungakushi," pp. 1–23.

33. See Amino, "Kyōkai ryōiki to kokka." Also, for the concept of the "public" or "nonrelated spaces," see Amino, *Muen, kugai, raku*. A similar view of riverbeds and bridges being spaces where the human interacts with the divine can be found in Sasamoto, *Tsuji no sekai*.

34. Nishigaki, "Hashi, kyōkai, hashiuranai," pp. 135–37.

35. Namihira, *Kegare*, pp. 191–227.

36. Ōta, "Chūsei no minshū kyūzai no shosō," pp. 64–65.

37. Ishizaka, "Ōchō no 'hashi,'" pp. 23–32; she cites and agrees with Akasaka Norio's theory in his work *Ijinron josetsu* (1985).

that portray such "otherworldly" spaces as hell and the underwater dragon-king's palace as fairly close to the human habitat, such as immediately under a shrine or just off the coast.[38] The validity of each of these theories can be debated, but the general consensus of scholars who study the role of such spaces in society is that bridges were associated with the extraordinary and therefore were appropriate as the stage for supernatural occurrences.

The act of building a bridge was also associated with the divine, as I have indicated above. Bridge construction was often a part of kanjin activities by Buddhist monks and hijiri (holy men); "kanjin" is defined as "a drive for contributions from the general public."[39] In the early Heian period when the central government had full control over bridges, taxes were used for their construction and repair, but kanjin hijiri took over the task for the most part after the Heian period, and such activities seem to have been funded through kanjin as well as through tolls.[40] The devotion of time and money to bridge building by religious figures has been interpreted as evidence that bridges were considered sacred spaces, suitable for the appearance of super-natural beings or the sacralization of the groups of people associated with them.[41] Kanjin activities were most prominent in the Medieval period, but as pointed out by Amino Yoshihiko and Gomi Fumihiko, the idea that build-ing a bridge was an offering to the Buddhist order appears earlier; this is suggested by the comment on the Uji bridge stele that the bridge was built in the hope that such a beneficial deed would enable sentient beings to be led to buddhahood. The symbolic transposition of building a bridge from one side of a river to the other and from this world to the afterlife seems to have played an important part in the association of bridge building with Bud-dhism, and those who contributed to the kanjin hijiri probably did so to "tie a knot of relation" with these hijiri and to make an offering to the dead.[42]

The link between bridges and the supernatural goes beyond those who were involved in their construction or repair. For example, a piece of a well-known bridge could serve as an offering to the Buddha. Chapter 3, Story 10, of Uji shūi monogatari tells of a poet called the Mother of Haku (Haku = Prince Yasumoto, d. 1090) who offered a piece of a famed waka topos, the

---

38. See Tokue, "Setsuwa kara mita takai."
39. Goodwin, Alms and Vagabonds, p. 1.
40. Amino, "Kyōkai ryōiki to kokka," p. 330.
41. Ibid.
42. Nei, "Hashi to kanjin hijiri," pp. 272–75.

bridge at Nagara, to a monk.[43] Bridges also frequently served as meeting places for the human and the supernatural; among many such occurrences, one example is found in chapter 4, story 13, of the same collection. It describes the meeting on a bridge of a monk and a person afflicted with a skin disease who has a deep knowledge of the dharma. The ill person disappears, and the monk wonders if it was not a manifestation of some sort.[44] A number of the narratives involving demons to be discussed below are set on bridges.

Within this association between bridges and the supernatural is the category of supernatural women and bridges, which is exemplified by Story 22 in Chapter 27 of *Konjaku monogatari*. A woman at Seta bridge entrusts a mysterious box to a man to carry to another woman at Osame bridge in Mino province. He is forbidden to look at the contents, but his jealous wife, who suspects that the box is a gift for another woman, opens it to find eyeballs and penises inside. The man takes the box to Osame bridge quickly, but the woman who meets him there knows that he has peeked inside. He returns home but dies shortly thereafter. The story ends with a warning for wives against jealousy.[45] I address the issue of jealousy below, but the important feature of this story here is location of the two strange women at their re-

---

43. Kobayashi Chishō, *Uji shūi monogatari*, pp. 148–49.

44. Ibid., pp. 192–92. Other examples that link bridges with the supernatural are *Konjaku monogatari*'s narrative about a "holy person" who repairs the bridge at Toba and holds an extravagant dedicatory ceremony by inviting famous monks from Mt. Hiei and Mii temple and entertaining them with music and dance (Mabuchi et al., *Konjaku monogatari shū*, 4: 79–80, 217). The *Konjaku* version of Dōtō's building of the Uji bridge noted above also presents bridge building as an offertory activity, complete with the help of superhuman beings. Accounts of other early figures associate the building of bridges with superhuman capabilities; Minamoto no Tamenori's *Sanbō-e* (ca. 984) notes that E no Ubasoku (a.k.a. En no Gyōja), the semi-mythical founder of the Shugendō school (dates unknown; active late seventh–early eighth centuries), commanded *kijin*, or "demon deities," to construct a bridge connecting Mt. Kazuraki and Mt. Kimpu—a virtually impossible task, since the distance between the two mountains spanned several *li* (Izumoji, *Sanbō-e*, pp. 74–75; also, Yamada Yoshio, *Sanbō-e ryakuchū*, pp. 133–38). The next story describes incidents in the life of the monk Gyōgi (668–749), here identified as Bodhisattva Gyōgi; among his compassionate deeds listed, there is the mention: "When it came to difficult paths, he built bridges and constructed dikes to enable crossing. When he spotted good places, he erected halls and constructed temples" (Izumoji, *Sanbō-e*, p. 77). Tales about these two figures are included in various other story collections, such as *Nihon ryōiki*.

45. Mabuchi et al., *Konjaku monogatari shū*, 4: pp. 79–83.

spective bridges. The uncanny contents of the box, as well as the fact that the woman at Osame bridge knows instantly that the box had been opened, point to these women's more-than-human identity. They are not explicitly named as bridge deities or even demons, but their association with the supernatural is clear. Annotators have claimed that these women were probably bridge-spirits like Hashihime.

When we take all these elements into consideration, both the particular place called Uji and bridges in general possess a certain sense of the out-of-the-ordinary that is still familiar and accessible. These geographically "marginal" locations at the outskirts of the capital (which in fact were central to society in the sense that activities ranging from everyday transportation to burial took place in these locations) were also constructed as conceptually marginal: as places that permitted encounters with events or beings that belonged to the extraordinary, nonhuman realm.

The association of the figure of Hashihime, the bridge deity, with Uji was firmly established by the late Heian period. The first known appearance of Hashihime, in a *Kokinshū* poem, clearly names her as "Hashihime of Uji," and waka handbooks associate her strongly with Uji and bridges. One example is Fujiwara no Kiyosuke's *Waka shogakushō* (A handbook of waka basics; ca. 1169), a basic manual for waka composition that includes lists of categories of objects and place-names found in waka poems. Under the entry "bridges," it cites "the Uji bridge: from Hashihime"; under the category "kami deities," it lists "Hashihime (a protective deity of bridges; also called *hashimori* [bridge guardian])," and under "rivers," it notes "Uji river: there are wicker fishtraps, there is a bridge, compose as Hashihime."[46] An example from a later date is *Yagumo mishō* (Explanations of the eight clouds; ca, 1235–42, by retired emperor Juntoku), also a waka handbook; under "famous places—bridges," it lists the Uji bridge first and notes that the usage comes from *Kokinshū* and that it is associated with Hashihime.[47] The association between Hashihime and Uji, then, had become standard by the time many of the stories that I examine below were authored. The strong association of this female figure with the marginalized and unstable topoi of both Uji and bridges suggests that she was ripe for identification with the divine as well as with certain marginalized qualities associated with the feminine. On the one hand, both her divinity and her locational marginalization could serve to

---

46. Sasaki, *Nihon kagaku taikei*, 2: 231, 211, 226.

47. Kyūsojin, *Nihon kagaku taikei bekkan*, 3: 408.

show that even those occupying the outer circles of the social imagination could conform to the demands of the social "norm" for certain groups: the marginalized figure becomes the aestheticized model of a woman in a polygynous situation. On the other hand, the marginalized figure was a convenient repository for "female" emotions such as jealousy deemed undesirable in the practice of polygyny, yet the ambiguity contained in the locations associated with this particular figure left room for the supernatural to cause havoc.

AESTHETICIZING POLYGYNY:
THE PINING WIFE

The figure of Hashihime, who comes to accumulate ascribed qualities of divinity, geographical marginalization vis-à-vis the capital, and the violence associated with Uji and bridges, exhibits a curious course of development that reveals the motivated aspect of her constructed figure. The associations that converge at the Uji bridge are combined in different ways according to the effects authors sought to produce. I first examine the trope of the supernatural woman who is presented as pining away for her husband/lover by focusing on waka poetry and commentary, which are mostly attributed to men. I then closely analyze passages in *Genji monogatari* that contain references to Hashihime in order to show the presence of resistances in the understanding of her figure by a female author. I end this section with a brief look at some later texts; the distinct shifts in the interpretations of her character in these texts show how at every textual moment, her figure is molded to convey different aims.

Waka Poems and Waka Studies by Aristocratic Men

The earliest reference to Hashihime occurs in a waka poem, and it is this genre and discussions about this genre in which the trope of the female bridge deity filled with longing for her absent love develops extensively in the Heian period. I therefore begin my investigation of Hashihime with these texts. I argue below that this figure becomes increasingly deified as she becomes more explicitly associated with polygynous situations and as her longing is aestheticized further. Interestingly enough, such aestheticized visions of Hashihime are products of male aristocrats who themselves generally practiced polygyny in courtship and marriage; they clearly had a personal stake in portraying a complicit female figure who longs only for one male partner.

The first known appearance of the figure of Hashihime occurs in *Kokin-shū* (ca. 905) poem number 689, by an unidentified poet:

> *samushiro ni   koromo katashiki   koyoi mo ya*
> *ware wo matsuran   uji no hashihime*
>
> Upon a narrow grass mat   laying down her robe only
> tonight, again—
>   she must be waiting for me,   Hashihime of Uji.[48]

This poem's specification of Uji established the association between Hashihime and the cultural implications of the place Uji. Her figure in this poem is that of a lonely woman awaiting her lover's visit. All annotators of the poem point out that the act of laying down only her own robe means that she is readying a single bed for a solitary night's sleep; a night spent with her loved one would involve two robes. The circumstances of the speaker have been interpreted in various ways. Some have posited a traveler thinking about his wife at home;[49] others have seen in the phrase "uji no hashihime" (Hashihime of Uji) a pun on "uchi no hashi hime" (my noble, beloved wife).[50] These readings, however, have overlooked an important element in the poem in light of the later developments of Hashihime stories: namely, the portrayal of a particular configuration of a relationship between a man and a woman.

There are two separate but related approaches to this poem, depending on whether we read the pun into the poem. First, let us consider the poem without the pun, since none of the early annotators of this poem whose works I explore in detail below mentions it (the first to do so is Kamo no Mabuchi [1697–1769], in the Edo period). The speaker, presumably a man, speculates about the actions and feelings of this Hashihime, but the circumstances of their current separation remain unexplained. Without the pun, the speaker's pining for Hashihime is only implied in the poem; her waiting is clearly illustrated, but his own thoughts are left obscure. This effect con-

---

48. Ozawa and Matsuda, *Kokin wakashū*, p. 267.

49. Ibid.

50. Takeoke, *Kokin wakashū zenchūshaku*, 2: 338–40. This pun was first pointed out in *Kokin wakashū uchigiki* (an annotation of the *Kokinshū* by Kamo no Mabuchi, ca. 1764), and Takeoke expresses his agreement with the earlier annotator. Ishihara ("Uji no denshō," p. 24) also agrees with this interpretation.

trasts with the surrounding poems, which voice pining and longing in the first person; poem 689 instead creates a distance between the speaker and the emotion, since the emotion is felt by someone else. In other words, although the reader may be tempted to believe that the speaker reciprocates Hashihime's longing for him, the poem itself does not necessarily indicate such a return of feelings. To the contrary, the speaker may have wearied of her earnest longing for him, or perhaps he even feels guilty since he has already moved on to someone else. These readings may sound extreme, but the fact remains that the poem does not directly convey the speaker's attitude toward Hashihime's waiting.

If we accept the pun on "Uji no Hashihime" and "my noble, beloved wife," the feeling of the speaker becomes clearer. If he calls her his "beloved," then presumably he is thinking of her fondly as he imagines her pining for him. However, there still remains the question of the relative positioning of the man and the woman in this poem. Even though the male speaker of the poem refers to his wife as "beloved," he is still the one who imagines that his wife is longing for him earnestly. The image of a woman pining solely for the speaker may be called the product of a self-flattering "male" imagination;[51] one might even go so far as to say there is an attitude of superiority in the way he pities the poor woman who awaits only him. Polygyny necessitates that the many wives be faithful to one man (at least theoretically); thus the wife who waits earnestly for only her husband was a reassuring and convenient creation, if not delusion, on which male hearts could rest. As I note above, texts from this period suggest that women could have multiple lovers as well; the image of a singularly devoted wife allowed for the aversion of one's attention from, or even denial of, such activities. Most important, the poem portrays the unequal relationship between the male speaker and the female object: she can only wait for him in loneliness, and he is the actor who can choose whether to visit her. All these elements problematize the figure of the "pining Hashihime" presented in traditional scholarship.[52]

---

51. By "male" imagination, I refer not to a monolithic or essential imagination of the male sex, but to an imagination that privileges the (here, heterosexual) male position.

52. Two other poems by unidentified poets in *Kokinshū* mention Uji as a location, although Hashihime herself is not named in them:

825   *wasuraruru*   *mi wo ujibashi no*   *naka taete*
       hito mo kayowanu   *toshi zo enikeru*

Ise monogatari contains a variation of the "samushiro ni" poem that does not name Hashihime but is relevant to the development of her figure because the attached story addresses a polygynous situation:

> samushiro ni   koromo katashiki   koyoi mo ya
>   koishiki hito ni   awade nomi nemu
>
> Upon a narrow grass mat   laying down only my robe
> tonight, again—
>   the one for whom I long   I do not meet; shall I sleep alone?[53]

Section 63, in which this poem is included, is intended to prove the egalitarian quality of Ariwara no Narihira's sexual attention. An old woman whom Narihira had seen once composes this poem, and he spends the night with her out of sympathy. The narrator praises Narihira's actions by stating that this incident shows the fairness with which he treated his women; whereas other men did not show affection toward women they no longer favor, he was considerate of the feelings of a woman he did not even care for.

Although this poem does not allude directly to Hashihime, the potential significance of the story is twofold. First, the composer of the poem in this story is a woman, who succeeds in gaining the attention of a man through its

---

> My forgotten   body, so sad, like the Uji bridge   severed in the middle—
>   with no one crossing back and forth,   the years have passed.

904   chihayaburu   uji no hashimori   nare wo shizo
>   aware to wa omou   toshi no enureba
>
> The bridge guard of Uji   —where the *kami* show their power—   so familiar
> to me,
>   I consider dear to my heart   since so many years have passed.

Poem 825 is about parting, and the pun on *uji*, which points to both the place-name and "to be sad," becomes a popular one as Uji comes to be associated with poetic melancholy. The themes of a love that has ceased and the forgotten person are not entirely unrelated to Hashihime, especially since later annotators and poets focus on the absence of her partner, as we shall see below in the text. The image of the ephemeral bridge is standard in waka poems; the trope "floating bridge of dreams" exemplifies the emphasis on the unstable and impermanent condition of bridges (Oyamada, *Hashi*, pp. 13–14). This bridge at Uji, severed in the middle, is more than unstable; the love is thus not just unsteady but finished. Poem 904 appears to be an expression of fondness for the familiar face of a bridge guard, but as we shall see below, the phrase "uji no hashimori" becomes replaced by "uji no hashihime" in many of the waka commentary texts that discuss Hashihime.

53. Katagiri et al., *Taketori monogatari, Ise monogatari, Yamato monogatari, Heichū monogatari*, pp. 164–66.

recitation. This contrasts with the *Kokinshū* version whose speaker/persona is a man wondering about a woman. If the two poems are related, then either the old woman has cleverly shifted the subject of the poem to herself and thus avoids the situation in which Hashihime is placed in the *Kokinshū* poem, or this poem is the "original" poem to which the *Kokinshū* poem alludes, in which case the latter represents a male (voice)'s appropriation of the poem's content.[54] Second, the praise Narihira receives for the fair distribution of his affections could be related to the theme of jealousy, which is developed in the course of the different versions of Hashihime narratives. Since he treats his women fairly, he is successful at navigating the potentially treacherous waters of polygyny.

In the tenth century, the figure of Hashihime in waka poems remained close to the one portrayed in *Kokinshū*, and the association of her figure with the divine was more clearly established. The following are examples found in *Sanekatashū*, the "personal" collection of poems by Fujiwara no Sanekata (958?–98).

When [I] had gone to Uji with this and that person, Fujiwara no Kagemasa wrote this down on a lid of a cypress-bark food container and sent it over:

22   *hashihime ni   yowa no samusa mo   toubeki ni*
      sasowade suguru   karibito ya tare
      One should ask Hashihime about the coldness of the night—
          who is the heartless hunter that passes by without a greeting?

23   *hashihime ni   sode katashikan   hodo mo nashi*
      kari ni tomaran   hito ni taguite
      I do not have the time to lay down a single sleeve for Hashihime—
          since I am together with a fleeting love/hunter.

At Uji, when [we] were dozing off upon a floating bridge above the waters, under the moon deep in the night the voices were amusing, and the Middle Captain Nobukata said:

57   *ujigawa no   nami no makura ni   yume samete*
      Upon the Uji river's   waves, my pillow,   I awoke from a dream—

to which I said:

---

54. Since the exact date of *Ise monogatari*'s completion is not clear, it is difficult to assess whether the old woman's poem alludes to the *Kokinshū* poem or the *Kokinshū* poem is in fact an allusion to the one in *Ise monogatari*.

> yoru hashihime ya i mo nezaruran
> at night, Hashihime must be unable to sleep at all.

At the Uji villa, to a certain woman:

198 *hashihime no* *katashiku sode mo* *katashikade*
   omowazaritsuru *mono wo koso omoe*
  Even Hashihime's singly laid sleeve is not laid out;
   unexpectedly I am lost in thought.[55]

These poems suggest that, as understood by Sanekata and his acquaintances, Hashihime is a female deity who lives by or in the Uji river. She is someone to whom respects should be paid when passing by her territory, and poem 23 paints the picture of a ritualistic laying-down of a single robe for her sake. As in the *Kokinshū* poem, this image of a single robe laid down for sleep alludes to her loneliness and longing. Poem 198 refers pointedly to the expectation of the male speaker that a woman would be waiting for him, as Hashihime waited for her lover; this time, he is surprised that this is not the case.

In the twelfth century, the focus of the "pining Hashihime" trope moves more directly toward polygyny, and the stories come to be told mainly in texts that annotate waka or teach about various aspects of them. Such texts, kagakusho (examples of which are discussed in previous chapters), began as written accounts of orally transmitted commentaries, anecdotes, and interpretations of waka poems that had been passed down in a family. Although a kagakusho's intimate connection with a single family suggests that the interpretations were of private nature in that individuals' interpretations were marked as such, during the late Heian period, these texts were also concerned with delineating a "traditional" interpretation, as we shall see below. In other words, these texts were not simply the "private opinions" of courtiers but were designed to teach the correct anecdotes and commentaries based on precedents. The anecdotes, or setsuwa stories attached to waka poems, therefore played a crucial part in the transmission of a traditional understanding of the poems.[56]

All the earliest examples of these works that discuss Hashihime at length come from one branch of the Fujiwara family, the Rokujō Fujiwara. *Ōgishō*

---

55. Inukai et al., *Heian shikashū*, pp. 186–263.
56. Yamada Yōji, "Kagakusho to setsuwa," pp. 155–62.

(ca. 1135–44), a waka commentary by Fujiwara no Kiyosuke, presents the earliest known description of an "old story" called *Hashihime monogatari*.

61   *samushiro ni   koromo katashiki   koyoi mo ya*
        ware wo matsuran   uji no hashihime

    Upon a narrow grass mat   laying down her robe only
    tonight, again—
        she must be waiting for me,   Hashihime of Uji.

This poem is found in something called *Hashihime monogatari*. In the past, there was a man with two wives. The first wife had a craving for seven-colored seaweed during her menstruation. He went to the seaside to look for it but was abducted by the dragon-king [and died]; the first wife went looking for him on foot, and one night when she was staying at a hut on the beach, she happened to meet him. He came from the seaside, reciting this poem. He explained the situation and disappeared at dawn. The wife went home weeping. The second wife heard the story and went to the same place to wait for the man; he appeared, once again reciting this poem. The second wife, in a fit of jealousy that he should abandon her in his thoughts and adore the first wife, flung herself at the man. The man and the hut vanished like snow disappearing. Since this is an old *monogatari*, I will not note it down in detail. According to the collection,

        chihayaburu   uji no hashihime   nare wo shimo
           aware to wa omou   toshi no enureba

        Hashihime of Uji   —where the *kami* show their power   so
        familiar to me,
           I consider dear to my heart   since so many years have passed.

This poem was also composed with this incident in mind. Since this man had snuck around behind his first wife's back, it seems that he composed this poem by associating the older person with Hashihime. *Chihayaburu* (the kami show their power) here indicates that since the man and woman are from the days of old, they are deities. Also, everything has a kami that protects it; this is what is called a *tamashii* (soul). Therefore it can be understood that a deity who protects bridges is called Hashihime. Since kami are things of old, [the poet] associated the elderly person with [the kami]. I understand that [the deity] is called Hashihime of Uji. It is common practice to call kami deities by names such as *hime* (lady) and *mori* (protector). Sahohime, Tatsutahime, Yamahime, and Shimamori are all kami.[57]

There are three important points in this passage. First, compared to the earlier references to Hashihime, the divine aspect of her figure becomes clearer

---

57. Sasaki, *Nihon kagaku taikei*, 1: 332.

and more explicit in this discussion. There are many possible reasons for emphasizing her divinity, but in light of the issue of polygyny, one answer might be that the projection of certain human practices on the "lives" of deities was a way to legitimize the practice by constructing its universality. By showing that even female divinities spend their time waiting for infrequent visits by their male partners, polygyny in the human realm is naturalized.

Second, the exact nature of *Hashihime monogatari* remains unclear, since it has not survived to this day. Scholars have debated the form and content of this lost text, as well as its relationship with the *Kokinshū* "samushiro ni" poem.[58] I have interpreted the *Kokinshū* poem without referring to *Hashihime monogatari*, since the evidence for its existence at the beginning of the tenth century remains nebulous. However, in the case of *Ōgishō*, the crucial question is not How long has this *monogatari* been in circulation? but What is the significance of its appearance in this particular text in this manner? The most significant answer: the passage explicitly places two women in a polygynous configuration. The narrative contextualizes two *Kokinshū* poems: nos. 689 ("samushiro ni") and 904 ("chihayaburu"), anchoring the relationship between Hashihime's figure and polygyny as the "correct" setting for these poems. Specifically, poem 689 is embedded within a narrative of a husband's speculation about his first wife's feelings, and the subject of poem 904, who was *uji no hashimori* (bridge guard at Uji) in the *Kokinshū* version, has been transformed into *uji no hashihime* (Hashihime of Uji) in *Ōgishō*. This transformation changes the poem's reading from the expression of fondness for a bridge guard with potentially non-sexual, homosexual, or heterosexual (from the point of view of a woman) overtones in the *Kokinshū* version to one that is decidedly heterosexual and understood as being from the point of view of a man within the context of the *Ōgishō* narrative.

Third, the passage puts forth a particular vision of the positionality of women in a polygynous situation. Let us examine how each woman is represented. The first wife expresses what might be considered an unreasonable or at least difficult request by asking for seven-colored seaweed during a state that is explicitly associated with the condition of womanhood (menstruation). The text then shows that this desire eventually causes the loss of

---

58. See, e.g., Kyūsojin, "Kofudoki itsubun 'uji no hashihime' sono ta ni tsuite"; and Yoshikai, "*Hashihime monogatari* no shiteki kōsatsu."

her husband to the dragon-king; she must pay dearly for her "womanly" cravings. The first wife, however, is redeemed through the act of looking for her missing husband, and she is rewarded by his apparition who recites the poem from *Kokinshū* that I discussed above. Through the poem, she is constructed as a woman who pines after her husband night after night, even though in this case, the chances for his return look quite slim. In other words, the first wife is situated by the narrator as one who searches earnestly for her lost husband *and* is situated by her husband as one who continues to pine for him faithfully. She is doubly constructed as the root of one problem and the solution to another: although she makes the mistake of material desire, she is given an opportunity to serve as an exemplary wife.

The second wife enters late in the story as an imitator of the first wife. She waits for her husband on the same beach, but he emerges from the ocean reciting the same poem, presumably because he was under the impression that his first wife had come for another visit. The second wife becomes jealous, and it is this jealousy that causes the instant disappearance of the husband's apparition. In this way, the second wife is pitted as the antithesis of the first wife, who is cast as a compliant polygynous subject: the second wife is *not* the patient pining wife in the poem, and she is *not* the one who occupies her husband's approving thoughts. Consequently, she is penalized by the loss of her husband altogether.

The narrative thus presents the situation that led to the composition of the "samushiro ni" poem in a way that finds the cause of the man's disappearance in the women's actions: the first wife contributed to the first instance of loss, and the second wife explicitly caused the husband's second disappearance through her inappropriate behavior. The lonesome "pining wife" positionality represented in the poem is therefore not a result of the husband's neglect but of the women's own mistakes, and a woman who does not fit easily into that positionality is duly punished. The husband's figure remains curiously passive and is left blameless in the creation of the longing figure of Hashihime.

Fujiwara no Kenshō (ca. 1130–?), the younger brother of Kiyosuke, also authored two waka commentary texts, the first edition of which is called *Kenpishō* (Kenshō's secret handbook; 1179–83) and the second, re-edited, edition, *Shūchūshō* (ca. 1185–93). Both texts contain the same discussion about Hashihime of Uji, and the theme of Hashihime-as-kami is further emphasized and expanded:

Uji no Hashihime

> *chihayaburu* *uji no hashihime* *nare wo shizo*
> *kanashi to wa omou* *toshi no henureba*
>
> Hashihime of Uji —where the *kami* show their power— so
> familiar to me,
> I consider dear to my heart/sad since so many years have passed.

Kenshō says that Hashihime of Uji is called Hime Daimyōjin (the great lady kami) and is the name of the kami who lives underneath the Uji bridge. To this kami's place, a kami named Rikyū (detached palace) comes every night; it is said that as a sign that Rikyū is on his way home, at dawn there are sounds of the waves of the Uji river rising high. . . . A monk named Ryū'en claims that this poem was composed by the deity at Sumiyoshi when Hashihime of Uji was his wife. I wonder if this is true? The Uji bridge is said to have first been constructed in the second year of Taika during the reign of Emperor Kōtoku by the monk Dōshō. Sumiyoshi, on the other hand, has been in existence since the age of the deities. The claim that [the Sumiyoshi deity] started to have relations with Hashihime after so many years seems dubious. However, an annotation of *Kokinshū* says that [Hashihime of Uji] is also Hamahime (lady of the beach) of Uji. Some people say that the matter [of the relationship between the Sumiyoshi deity and Hashihime] took place before the bridge was constructed.

After this section, Kenshō cites in full the story of the two wives and the husband who is kidnapped by the dragon-king, naming *Ōgishō* as his source. At the very end, he adds:

I say, concerning Hashihime of Uji, *Hashihime monogatari* sounds too fictional. The matter about Hime Daimyōjin, however, seems fitting for both of these poems.[59]

It is significant that one of the partners of "Hashihime the bridge deity" is the Rikyū deity, who is most likely Uji no Waki Iratsuko, discussed above. This imperial prince, a tragic figure who was ousted from power and resided in a marginal location away from the capital, forms a relationship with Hashihime, another deity associated with the marginalized/liminal because of her connections with bridges and the location of Uji. More important, however, is the possibility that both the Rikyū and Sumiyoshi deities had engaged in simultaneous or successive relationships with Hashihime. Al-

---

59. For *Shūchūshō*: Kyūsojin, *Nihon kagaku taikei bekkan*, 2: 131–32; and for *Kenpishō*, ibid., 5: 17–19. "Both of these poems" refers to the "samushiro ni" and "chihayaburu" poems; see the discussion of *Ōgishō*.

though Kenshō does not focus on this configuration explicitly, its existence is notable in light of the issue of polygamy surrounding the figure of Hashihime. The polygynous story of *Hashihime monogatari* is here tempered by the stories of a polyandrous Hashihime Daimyōjin. Kenshō even declares that the latter is more believable than the former. Even among siblings, we can observe conflicting views about the interpretation of Hashihime's figure at this point.

Toward the end of the twelfth century, however, the focus of waka annotators shifts to the figure of the first wife in *Hashihime monogatari* as a pining wife. *Waka iroha* (The ABCs of waka; ca. 1198) by Jōgaku also lists the *Kokinshū* poem "samushiro ni" and gives an account of two wives almost identical to the story in *Ōgishō*. However, it omits the second section of the *Ōgishō* version, which starts with the poem "chihayaburu." *Ōgishō*'s statements about the divinity of Hashihime are condensed into two lines at the end in this narrative: "Hashihime is a guardian deity of bridges. She is also called *hashimori*."[60] This abbreviation of the story's reference to Hashihime's divinity can be interpreted as a result of the firm establishment of her figure as a kami by this time; if her figure was generally accepted and well known as a guardian deity of bridges, there would perhaps have been less of a need to expand on the details of her divine origins. On the other hand, as it is found in *Waka iroha*, the story concentrates on the Hashihime-as-pining-wife figure and does not mention the visits by the Rikyū and/or Sumiyoshi deities; the text focuses almost exclusively on the retelling of *Hashihime monogatari* and therefore the wives' misery as a product of their own actions.

Shin kokinshū (ca. 1205) continues the theme of Hashihime as a lonely figure who spends her nights without her lover. The popularity of her figure among poets at this time is evident from the large number of poems in "personal" poetry collections from this period as well.[61] Below I give some representative poems that name her explicitly in *Shin kokinshū*:

420   *samushiro ya*   *matsu yo no aki no*   *kaze fukete*
       tsuki wo katashiku   *uji no hashihime*

—Fujiwara no Teika

    Upon the narrow grass mat,   the night spent waiting, the autumn
    wind of tiresomeness blows deep;
        laying down a single moon,   Hashihime of Uji.

---

60. Sasaki, ed., *Nihon kagaku taikei*, 3: 223.
61. See Yoshikai, "*Hashihime monogatari no shiteki kōsatsu*," p. 116.

611   Composed according to the topic "frost upon a bridge":

    katashiki no   sode wo ya shimo ni   kasanuran
        tsuki ni yogaruru   uji no hashihime

                                                —the monk Kōshō

    Her singly laid   sleeve, she must be layering   upon the frost
        apart at night due to the moon,   Hashihime of Uji.

636   At the place where there is a painting of the Uji river on the sliding door at
Saishō Shitennō temple:

    hashihime no   katashiki goromo   samushiro ni
        matsu yo munashiki   uji no akebono

                                    —retired emperor Gotoba

    Hashihime's   singly laid robe   upon the narrow grass mat
        —the night spent waiting in vain—   dawn at Uji.

637   *ajirogi ni   izayou nami no   oto fukete*
       hitori ya nenuru   uji no hashihime

                                —former Archbishop Jien

    The sound of the waves   caught up in the winter fishtrap   grows
    later with the night;
        has she fallen asleep alone?   Hashihime of Uji.[62]

Compared to the poems in *Sanekatashū*, which emphasized Hashihime's divinity as much as her longing, these poems are concerned almost exclusively with the loneliness and waiting experienced by Hashihime; her status as a deity becomes much less significant. For example, poem 420, like earlier poems about Hashihime, portrays Hashihime as one who waits in vain for a visit by her long-absent lover. There are, however, some notable departures; such changes emphasize the characteristics of devotion and pitifulness even further. For instance, the use of the phrase *aki no kaze*, which is a pun on "autumn wind" and "wind of tiresomeness," clearly suggests that Hashihime's partner has already grown tired of her, yet she continues to spend nights waiting for him. This poem also aestheticizes her situation by replacing her singly laid robe with a single moon. The text removes the material symbol of her anticipated sexual encounter and instead renders it into an intangible and reified entity, the moon, which is closely associated with waka aesthetics as well as Buddhist salvation. In these ways, Hashihime's desertion becomes an elegant snapshot of melancholy: she is now a lover so

---

62. Minemura, *Shin kokin wakashū*, pp. 148, 198, 204.

devoted to her partner that she pines for him despite the deepening "winds of tiresomeness," and her story may even be read as a Buddhist allegory of blindness to the sadness of attachment. Poem 611 deliberately adds frost to the picture since its topic is "frost upon a bridge"; this extra element makes Hashihime's lonely situation even more desolate and cold. Despite such hardships, she seems to continue to play her role as pining lover, hoping that one of these nights her beloved will pause for a visit. Furthermore, her partner's absence is blamed upon the moon; granted, a visit on a brightly-lit night would be too obvious and rather unartful,[63] but on the other hand, it is a convenient way to deflect her partner's lack of attentiveness—it can be construed as an excuse among the ranks of directional taboos, which also helped men in avoiding visits to women they did not wish to see on a particular day. This poem thus emphasizes Hashihime's devotion by showing her perseverance in difficult conditions and forgives the man for his negligence by shifting our attention to questions of social (or religious) propriety. The changes in her representations over two centuries are evident in this comparison; the aestheticization and poeticization of her pining seem to have reached a new level among these poets.

Kenchū mikkanshō (Secret corrections to Kenshō's annotations; ca. 1221) by Fujiwara no Teika contains a substantial annotation of the "samushiro ni" poem. Along the lines of earlier works such as *Ōgishō*, *Kenpishō*, and *Shūchūshō*, he mentions the various stories associated with Hashihime: the two theories about Hashihime's relationships, one with the Rikyū deity and the other with the Sumiyoshi deity, and *Hashihime monogatari*. In this work, however, he seems determined to reconcile all these strands in order to establish a single figure of Hashihime, the bridge deity. Twice he insists that "there is only one (*ittei*) Hashihime of Uji" and that the story of the two wives is also that of the deity Hashihime. Furthermore, he notes that when he had heard this story being told during his youth, he had "felt sadly moved by it and shed tears."[64] The text thus exhibits an impulse to consolidate the

---

63. Some annotators interpret the line "apart at night due to the moon" as "since the moonlight is so bright, the male deity has not visited recently." If Hashihime's lover was a kami as suggested by the waka commentary texts dating from around the time this collection was compiled, he would have been afraid of being seen. On the other hand, since Hashihime's divine nature is not highlighted in *Shin kokinshū*, it is also possible to read the poem as being applicable to a human character as well.

64. Kyūsojin, *Nihon kagaku taikei bekkan*, 5: 226–28.

scattered portrait of an important poetic figure; Hashihime becomes established as both a deity and a tragic heroine.

Teika's efforts to bring together the various narratives about Hashihime and to pinpoint her figure seem to have had some effect, as seen in the case of *Iroha wananshū* (A lexical anthology of waka trouble-spots; author unknown, possibly a Tendai monk; ca. mid-Kamakura period), which contains a version of the story almost identical to the one told in *Waka iroha*.[65] However, other narratives continued to develop. One example is a passage in *Bishamondōbon kokinshūchū* (An annotation of the *Kokinshū*, Bishamondō version),[66] by an unknown author dating probably from the late Kamakura period, which cites the following poem:

503   *omou niwa   shinoburu koto zo   makenikeru*
       iro niwa ideji to   omoishi mono wo
       My thoughts of longing—   in suppressing them   I have failed;
       even though I had thought to   prevent their colors from surfacing.

The annotator contemplates various possible authors of the poem and raises Hashihime of Uji as a candidate. The narrative proceeds to tell a story similar to *Hashihime monogatari* outlined above,[67] with three major differences. First, although polygyny remains a strong factor in this story (there is no mention of a second wife who existed before the husband's disappearance, but the husband is explicitly described as having become the dragon-king's son-in-law), the element of jealousy is excised. The first wife, upon witnessing her husband emerge from the dragon-king's bejeweled palanquin, sadly gives up hope of recovering him from the grips of his new wife/life. Hashihime is represented as a docile and unthreatening participant in the polygynous system who does not protest against her fate. Second, perhaps as a reward for this commendable behavior, Hashihime is ultimately reunited with her husband, even though it is not clear whether the joining occurs in this

---

65. Ibid., 2: 488.

66. The passage itself cites *Yamashiro no kuni fudoki* as the source of this story, but no such passage can be found in the original version of the *Fudoki* (commissioned 713); the current compilation of *Fudoki itsubun* draws this very passage from *Bishamondō* for the citation of the Hashihime story (Akimoto, *Fudoki*, pp. 29–30, 418).

67. Yoshizawa, *Mikan kokubun chūshaku taikei*, 4:135. The annotator states that according to some, Ariwara no Narihira recited this poem but changed the second half into *au ni shikaeba / samo araba are* (if I can see you, then / come what may — I care not); this is the version that appears in *Ise monogatari*, story 65.

life or the next. Third, the composer of this poem is not the husband but Hashihime herself. In other narratives that present the "samushiro ni" poem, the male speaker thinks to himself that Hashihime must be waiting for him; in this passage, however, Hashihime herself voices her "thoughts of longing" for her husband. There is no longer any question about Hashihime's pining. In all of these ways, she comes to play the desirable model of the woman-in-polygyny.

The marginalizing discourse, however, was not monolithic. An interesting twist to the portrayal of Hashihime can be found in the collection *Fūyō wakashū* (probably compiled by Fujiwara no Tameie, ca. 1271), vol. 13, "Love," section 1, which presents the following poem by a fictional emperor:

When the empress was in Uji, [he] composed this:

> *katashiki no   sode wa ware nomi   kuchihatete*
> *tsurenasa masaru   uji no hashihime*
> The single laid-out   sleeve—mine alone   has fallen apart;
> her heart grows colder,   Hashihime of Uji.[68]

Here, the tables have been turned: instead of the trope of the waiting Hashihime, it is the speaker who pines for her. She is no longer a woman waiting for her lover's visit; in this poem, she is the one who makes him lay down a single robe/sleeve as he spends his nights without her. His feelings are not returned, since she is the coldhearted one who has caused his robe/sleeve to become tattered. The change in her character can be explained as part of the poet's clever and surprising technique in which he makes an allusion yet presents it with a new twist, thereby catching the attention of the reader or listener. Similar techniques are found in examples cited earlier: *Sanekatashū* poem 198, in which a man is surprised that his lover has not, in fact, spread the "singly laid sleeve," and *Shin kokinshū* poem 637, which casts a doubt (albeit slight) whether Hashihime has, in fact, fallen asleep alone (as opposed to with some other person). However, such transformations of Hashihime's figure from an idealized waiting woman to a woman who remains unresponsive to a man's courtship can also be read as another manipulation of the female figure within the symbolic matrix of female-male relationships. Hashihime's figure moves from the convenient and docile to the difficult and resentment-arousing, qualities undesirable in a polygynous configuration. In this way, these attributes are related to jealousy, another

---

68. Kokumin tosho kabushiki kaisha, *Kōchū kokka taikei*, 23: 141.

obstacle to the smooth operation of polygyny and such texts associate the "pining-lover" trope to Hashihime's other side, the jealous demon.

Finally, a collection called *Sandai wakashū* (An anthology of waka on classified topics), probably compiled during the Kamakura period, quotes a *Hashihime monogatari* along much the same lines as the one found in *Ōgishō*, with an added twist to the plot. After the second wife causes the disappearance of her husband, she regrets it deeply and throws herself into the Uji river; her vengeful spirit becomes the great kami Hashihime.[69] The naming of the second wife as Hashihime-the-deity is curious, since the story does cite the *Kokinshū* poem "samushiro ni," which presents the figure of Hashihime-the-pining-wife, when the husband appears out of the ocean to converse with his first wife. In effect, this narrative contains two Hashihimes: the pining first wife and the jealous second wife, who share the same name. Here, we see a further transition in Hashihime's identity, hinted at earlier in a somewhat similar instance of confusion found in *Ōgishō*, from a lonesome figure perpetually longing and waiting for her lover to the jealous woman who is transformed into a violent vengeful spirit. As Yoshikai Naoto has pointed out, the second wife's act of throwing herself into the Uji river and then emerging as a spirit is strikingly similar to the metamorphosis of a nobleman's daughter who immerses herself in the same river in order to become a demon named Hashihime of Uji, which I address in detail in the next section.[70] The dates of the earliest version of Hashihime-as-demon storyline and *Sandai wakashū* are nebulous enough that we cannot know which came first, but this example strongly suggests that the two sides of Hashihime were intimately related.

What could account for the discursive figurations of Hashihime that we have encountered so far? Certainly, it is the case that waka as a genre produced numerous aestheticized pining-lover tropes. In this sense, Hashihime is not an exception. On the other hand, we must remember that almost all the examples outlined above were authored or edited by aristocratic men; the notable exception is the *Kokinshū* poem that marks the first known appearance of Hashihime, which is attributed to an unknown poet. Since these men were, generally speaking, practitioners of polygyny, one might be able to read a motivation, conscious or not, in depicting Hashihime's figure in this particular way. The aestheticization of her pining figure is not an accident;

69. Yoshikai, "Shūi *Hashihime monogatari*," pp. 64–65.
70. Yoshikai, "*Hashihime monogatari no shiteki kōsatsu*," p. 128.

the desire to depict an objectified, harmless female figure can be read into the stories, especially when examined in conjunction with the demon stories that represent the other side of the coin, the simultaneous existence of the suppressed fear of the domesticated polygynous configuration gone haywire. Furthermore, we can see that even within the parameters of waka and discourses surrounding it, tropes with instabilities and ruptures that anticipate or allude to non-waka narratives begin to appear. As I note above, the pining-wife trope is neither uniform nor consistent. Hints of anxiety (a cold-hearted, resistant Hashihime) and Hashihime's possible involvement with multiple partners suggest that all was not calm under the dominant discourse of the aestheticized female lover.

Murasaki Shikibu and the Trope of Hashihime

One example of disruption is evident in a text written by a female author in the mid-Heian period. Her rereading and subversion of the trope of the pining woman, which was just beginning to be established in her time, indicates the potential for gendered resistance by an author whose social class practiced polygyny. Hashihime is perhaps best known for her mention in Murasaki Shikibu's *Genji monogatari*. The figure first appears in the chapter named after Hashihime, in which Kaoru succeeds in viewing from afar the two daughters of the Eighth Prince, who lives in Uji. He then sends a poem to the older daughter, Ōigimi:

> hashihime no   kokoro wo kumite   takase sasu
>   sao no shizuku ni   sode zo nurenuru
> Hashihime's   thoughts, I gather;   plunged into the shallows,
>   the oar—by its drops of water   my sleeves have been drenched.

Ōigimi replies:

> sashikaeru   uji no kawawosa   asayū no
>   shizuku ya sode wo   kutashihatsuran
> Back and forth,   the "river boss"[71] of Uji   morning and night;
>   their drops of water   have drenched my sleeve into shreds.[72]

---

71. I.e., the head of the oarsmen who row the boats that cross the Uji river; also a reference to Ōigimi herself.

72. Abe Akio et al., *Genji monogatari*, 5: 141–42.

Annotators have pointed out that the Hashihime to whom Kaoru refers is a bridge deity. Like Ōigimi, she seems to be a tragic figure and wins Kaoru's sympathy, partly because of her isolated, country surroundings, as suggested by the description of simple brushwood-carrying boats crossing the river that immediately precedes his poem. In addition, his allusion to the *Kokinshū* poem "samushiro ni" by naming Hashihime implies that Ōigimi, like Hashihime, has been spending lonely nights without a lover. In this way, he hints at his desire for courtship, and Ōigimi's response, which imbues Kaoru's sleeve image with even greater sorrow, seems to suggest that she agrees with Kaoru's assessment of her lonesome situation. However, she subtly shifts the central image of the poem from Hashihime to the boatrowers. She thereby dilutes the resonance of a woman without a lover and focuses instead on the sadness that derives from the rustic scenery immediately before their eyes. This maneuver on her part can be interpreted as a foreshadowing of her future resistance to Kaoru's pursuit.

Hashihime next appears in the "Agemaki" chapter, when Niou becomes involved with Nakanokimi. He composes the following poem while trying to convince her that although it may be difficult for him to visit a remote place because of his social position, he is still thinking of her:

> naka taen   mono naranakuni   hashihime no
>   katashiku sode ya   yowa ni nurasan
> Even though it is not   as if we would part,   Hashihime's
>   singly laid sleeve   will be damp in the night.

To which Nakanokimi replies:

> taeseji no   waga tanomi niya   ujibashi no
>   harukeki naka wo   machiwatarubeki
> "We will not part—"   with this as my only hope,   the Uji bridge
>   so far in distance,   can I wait for your crossing for so long?[73]

The perspective of Niou's poem is quite similar to the *Kokinshū* "samushiro ni" poem in that the speaker, a man, speculates about the feelings of a woman he has left far away. Here, however, we have a woman's reply to this male stance, and she does not simply echo his sentiments. Instead, Nakanokimi turns the focus from the image of a woman waiting obediently for her lover's visit to the resentful voice of that woman herself. Her poem sug-

---

73. Ibid., p. 274.

gests that the "waiting woman" does not always wait in tears day after day, and that one day she may even cease to wait.

In the "Ukifune" chapter, Kaoru recites the *Kokinshū* poem "samushiro ni" while thinking about Ukifune during a gathering at court. When Niou overhears this, he becomes annoyed that he has so formidable a rival, goes to Uji, and whisks Ukifune away to a hidden house, where they are able to spend time in seclusion. Ironically, the conjuring of the representation of a faithful woman waiting for her man here serves to deepen Ukifune's involvement in a polyandrous relationship. In this instance, the recitation of the poem instills a feeling of competition—perhaps even jealousy—in a man, which is an interesting contrast to later developments of Hashihime's figure in which female jealousy plays a prominent role, as I show below.

The final appearance of Hashihime in *Genji* represents the ultimate reversal of the *Kokinshū* poem's stance. After Ukifune's disappearance, Kaoru desires the First Princess in the "Kagerō" chapter, yet he still thinks: "Even now, so sad in my heart, how Hashihime renders my thoughts in disarray!" as he longs for Ōigimi, now long dead.[74] Hashihime, who was supposed to be pining for her man, is now the cause for a man's unattainable pining instead.

Although a thorough analysis of the Uji chapters is beyond the scope of this book, two points are relevant to the construction of Hashihime as a pining wife, especially since *Genji* is the only text written by a woman in the mid-Heian to early Kamakura periods that contains significant references to her figure. First, all the poems that directly name Hashihime are either composed or recited by male characters. When her pining figure is invoked in delicate moments of courtship negotiations, it is used to speak on behalf of the women who are courted—that is, Hashihime's stance is forced on the female characters as part of their experience and emotions, when in fact they might feel quite differently.

Second, the artificiality of the trope and the presumptuous and strategic nature of male views on what women "must be feeling" is brought into light through the women's responses. Their replies suggest that the pining-wife trope was not accepted without resistance. Ōigimi's response appears to be the most straightforward, but she skillfully turns the focus away from Hashihime in her poem. Nakanokimi questions Niou's assumption that she will quietly spend lonely days thinking only of him; she wonders how long she will be able to wait for his visit solely on the strength of his promise not

---

74. Abe Akio et al., *Genji monogatari*, 6: 249.

to end the relationship. Presented with the image of the ever-faithful, ever-patient woman crystallized into the figure of the pining Hashihime, Naka-nokimi raises the possibility of the end of a woman's patience, the hint that one day she will tire of acting like Hashihime. Her response is to reject a product developed, if not entirely created by, "male" imagination. In the next sequence, Ukifune herself neither hears Kaoru's recitation nor responds to it; the poem serves only to fan Niou's rivalry and jealousy. Hashihime thus functions here to escalate the attentions of men directed toward one woman; this is an interesting reversal of polygyny, since in this case, it is Ukifune who is seeing two men. This textual moment that re-presents the "original" reference to Hashihime (the "samushiro ni" poem) is therefore a notable subversion of both previous and subsequent readings of her figure; the passage can be interpreted as an attempt to reread and re-create the tradition of Hashihime-as-pining-lover. However, the limitations of polyandry under the system of male-female relationships presented in *Genji* are delineated by the fact that Ukifune ultimately cannot sustain a relationship with both men and has to take Buddhist vows. The last appearance of Hashihime presents the reversal of the gender of the person who longs and the person for whom longing is felt, since Kaoru is left in a permanent state of "laying down a single robe" when it comes to Ōigimi, even though he continues to have other affairs. The manipulations of Hashihime's image in *Genji* thus represents a departure from earlier conceptions of her figure in ways that subtly critique the practice of polygyny as presented in the work overall.

Later Medieval Discourses: Critiques of "Attachment"

Hashihime continued to appear as a pining-wife figure in narratives in subsequent eras. After the Kamakura period, the main theme of stories that mention this side of Hashihime changes from polygyny to women's victimization; this victimization is in turn obscured by the notion of improper attachment. The noh play *Eguchi* (attributed to Kan'ami, ca. 1332–84) presents a famous asobi named Eguchi no kimi as well as other asobi who lament their sinfulness and attachment to this world and finally become transformed into the bodhisattva Samantabhadra. As I note above, in the eleventh century Uji was known for having asobi. In a monologue describing her sadness over the fleeting nature of her relationships with her clients, Eguchi no kimi says, "Also, Uji no Hashihime—she waits for the person who has no plans for a visit; this is similar to my own situation, how sad."[75] The asobi then talk about the need to rid oneself of attachment, from which Hashi-hime is presumably suffering. The problem, then, lies with Hashihime and the asobi, who still hold attachment to their heartless clients; there is no blame placed on the men who positioned them in situations of longing in the first place. Here, the pining lover metamorphoses into a self-correcting en-tity who eradicates the possibility of troublesome emotions and transforma-tions on her own accord: she pines, she self-criticizes, and she self-pacifies into a benevolent bodhisattva.

Chapter 11 of *Taiheiki* (An account of the great peace; multiple authors; fourteenth century) mentions Hashihime of Uji in a story about three pairs of husbands and wives who committed suicide during the Nanboku wars. The husbands died in their castle, and the wives rowed out to sea and threw themselves into the waves. The husbands' ghosts subsequently importuned travelers passing through the area to row them out to sea so that they could be reunited with their wives' ghosts. As they approach the area where the wives drowned, burning flames arise from the waves. Attachment is once again the crucial focus of this narrative; at the end of this story about parting and longing, the narrator says: "Our country's Hashihime of Uji pined for her husband and drenched her singly laid sleeve in the waves. These are all wonders of the long-ago past and are found in old records. That these inci-dents in front of one's eyes appear to be real—the extent of this delusional attachment is indeed deeply sinful."[76] In *Taiheiki*, the three wives obey the orders of their husbands who planned their suicide; this is also the case in the story immediately preceding this one. The men themselves may have been casualties of the circumstances and politics of their era, and interest-ingly enough, the husbands are the ones represented as the main "pining" figures. The women, however, certainly appear to be silent victims, here no longer of polygyny but of male-initiated wars. The victimization of these women is marginalized and made obscure through the reference to Hashi-hime's longing, which is presented as sinful attachment.

The next instance is a story from *Shintōshū* (Collected tales about the kami; ca. early fifteenth century, compiler unknown; possibly by an oral sto-ryteller in the Agui school). In "The Matter of the Great Kami Deity Hashihime," a man passing by a bridge site at Nagara with his wife and his

---

75. Koyama et al., *Yōkyokushū*, 1: 266.
76. Yamashita, *Taiheiki*, 2: 173–78.

child suggests that a human sacrifice of someone who is wearing a light-yellow divided skirt with white patches at the knee would lead to the successful construction of the bridge. Unfortunately, he happens to be wearing that very outfit, and the official overseeing construction of the bridge forces the entire family to sacrifice itself. The wife composes a poem before she leaps to her death saying that if he had kept quiet, this calamity would not have befallen them. She subsequently becomes Hashihime when people feel sorry for her and worship her as a deity.[77] The plotline does not resemble any of the pining Hashihime stories discussed above, and the introduction clearly states that although there are many bridge deities named Hashihime, such as the ones at Uji and Yodo, this story will be about the Hashihime at Nagara. As in the *Taiheiki* example, however, the victimization of a woman by a man is the central focus of the narrative. She is made to suffer because of his extraneous and ill-timed comment. If Hashihime of Uji had been established over the years as a helpless woman at the mercy of a man, Hashihime of Nagara is also a recipient of male oppression, from both her dim-witted husband and the bridge official, who is presumably male.

The last example is an otogi zōshi picture-scroll called *Hashihime monogatari* (author unknown; Muromachi period, 1336–1573), which elaborates on the plot of early pining-wife stories that present a husband who is lost at sea and two wives who go looking for him. The most notable change in the expansion in light of the issues of polygyny and jealousy is found at the end of the story, in which the two wives voice their resentment toward each other. Hashihime, the first wife, regrets having told the second wife about her meeting with the husband and laments the second wife's stupidity, which caused the departure of the mediator who had enabled the missing husband to appear. The second wife in turn repeatedly expresses her anger toward the husband who seemed to be thinking only about the first wife.[78] The two women are pitted against each other in the game of resentment, as the focus of each woman's anger ultimately turns to the other and away from the social practice of polygynous marriage that placed them in positions with high potential for suffering. Needless to say, the historical circumstances of this text are vastly different from earlier works such as *Ōgishō* that first intro-

---

77. Watanabe Kunio and Kondō, *Shintōshū/Kawanobon*, pp. 25–29; and Kishi, *Shintōshū*, pp. 113–15.

78. Yokoyama and Matsumoto, *Muromachi jidai monogatari taisei*, 10: 309–15.

duced *Hashihime monogatari*. The discourse of polygyny had undergone numerous transformations throughout the centuries, and the changes in the narratives themselves indicate the different concerns that had arisen over time, even though Hashihime's figure continued to stand for the constructed female figure placed in a polygynous situation.

THE OTHER SIDE OF POLYGYNY:
THE JEALOUS DEMON

Above, I outline developments in the discursive construction of Hashihime as a deity who is a pining wife or lover and propose that the aestheticization of this waiting-woman figure can be read as a domestication of neglected lovers or wives in a polygynous situation. Below, I turn to the other possibility that results from this neglect: the figure of a woman who becomes a threatening demon out of jealousy and resentment. I first outline the characteristics of demons relevant to Hashihime's case, especially the notion that demonic women appear in instances of polygamous relationships. I then examine a number of narratives whose main theme is jealousy in order to establish how jealousy came to be intimately associated with the "feminine" and to explore its various consequences: physical empowerment, revenge, punishment, regret, or lack thereof. The examination of the "demonic" and "jealousy" will reveal the extent to which the configuration of polygyny played crucial roles in the materialization of both categories. Hashihime emerges from this context as an unusually empowered female demon who channels her jealous polygyny-born rage into extreme capacities for dangerous physical power. I conclude with a discussion of her empowerment and propose potential reasons for the dialectic remarginalization of her figure in later narratives.

Defining the Demonic: Violence, Gender, and the Marginalized

Several crucial characteristics of demons as seen in a number of setsuwa collections are relevant to the figure of Hashihime-as-demon. Some scholars have proposed that the demonization of women can be understood in general as an expression of male fear of the feminine and feminine power, which is both uncontrollable by men and incomprehensible to them.[79] Although

---

79. See, e.g., Komatsu, *Ijinron*, p. 120.

this interpretation offers a way to read texts that demonize women, it does not define or adequately address the construction of "feminine powers" as "uncontrollable" or "incomprehensible." As I show below, demonic transformation in the case of Hashihime did not reflect a generalized fear of the "feminine" but was associated with a particular social practice and the construction of the role of women in that practice in an attempt to marginalize certain undesirable "feminine" tendencies. Another scholar asserts that in the Heian period, demons were becoming differentiated from other supernatural powers such as the kami, and that at this stage, they were not necessarily malignant beings. Rather, they often were used to explain strange phenomena or were in part representations of people who led lives that went against the grain of "normal" society, such as those who resided outside ordinary communities (in the mountains, for example), those expelled from a community for some reason, and criminals.[80] This approach tries to reveal the "true" identity of demons, yet it overlooks the motivated aspect of the texts it cites. Why were such people or groups of people portrayed as marginalized figures? With these issues in mind, I will outline some important characteristics of demons and show that the issue of gender and the configuration of relationships were crucial in defining the demonic. Demonized women were portrayed as possessors of sexual capital and the potential for polyandrous relationships—the exact opposite of the configuration presented in the Hashihime-as-pining-deity trope—as well as the capacity for trickery and violence.

A thorough investigation of demons in literature from the mid-Heian to mid-Kamakura periods is beyond the scope of this chapter; the focus here is on those characteristics of oni (demons) relevant to the discussion of Hashihime. The character for oni is the same as the Chinese word gui, and Heian ideas about the physical appearance of demons were heavily influenced by both Chinese and Indian depictions of demons,[81] although there are debates concerning the origins of the word's usage in Japan.[82] Their position vis-à-vis human society was complex; first and foremost, they were ostracized. Ryōjin hishō song 339 curses:

> ware wo tanomete konu otoku   tsuno mitsu oitaru oni ni nare   sate hito ni
> utomareyo

---

80. See Baba Akiko, Oni no kenkyū.

81. Kondō, Nihon no oni, p. 15.

82. For a discussion of Origuchi Shinobu's views on the word oni and its earliest uses, see Baba Akiko, Oni no kenkyū.

> May he who made me count on him and failed to come see me   be turned
> into a demon with three sprouting horns   and be shunned by every-
> one else![83]

A story discussed in detail below tells the story of a woman who turns herself into a demon in order to kill her lover but is unable to return to her human shape and must live in hiding; the fact that the narrative represents her
as being forced to conceal her form from the world suggests that demons
were understood to be marginalized by human communities. Demons also
appear most frequently in marginalized spaces, such as bridges and abandoned huts. One interpretation of a certain group of demon stories is that
they are cautionary tales against wandering into certain spaces marked as
dangerous.[84] If this theory is valid, then demons in certain circumstances
would have functioned as shunned beings whose very presence could cause
people to flee in terror.

Even though often ostracized, demons were powerful in many ways.
Chapter 27 of *Konjaku monogatari*, which is devoted to stories about unusual
supernatural phenomena, such as spirits, demons, and foxes, is a good starting point for an examination of demons. First, the narratives about demons
are almost always characterized by graphic violence and frightening detail;
these qualities contrast with stories about other forms of supernatural beings, who are sometimes humorous and for the most part harmless.[85] Some
scholars go as far as to claim that oni are by definition beings that try to affect humans in a negative way, in contrast to kami, who bring positive effects.[86] Second, demons in these *Konjaku* stories storm through the capital
itself, whereas stories about foxes and other spirits tend to be set in the
provinces.[87] Furthermore, demons appear not to recognize the limits of

---

83. Kobayashi Yoshinori et al., *Ryōjin hishō, Kanginshū, Kyōgen kayō*, pp. 96–97.

84. Murai, "*Konjaku monogatari*," p. 73.

85. A story towards the end of the chapter contains the following passage: "Thinking
about it now, [we can see that the incident described in the story] must have been a fox's
trick. . . . After the three men left the inn, there were no frightening occurrences. Had it been
an actual oni demon, they could not have been unharmed at the time of the incident or afterward" (Mabuchi et al., *Konjaku monogatari shū*, 4: 156). This passage suggests that foxes may
trick, but they do not have the capacity for violence possessed by demons.

86. Komatsu, "Yōkai," pp. 337–38. This polarization is a bit extreme, for there are kami—
such as Hashihime herself—who seem to possess both qualities.

87. Murai, "*Konjaku monogatari*," p. 71.

social class and rank; in their singular drive to harm—usually to consume—their victims, they affect even those who hold high positions at court or in the imperial household. Finally, unlike *tengu* (a goblin-like being with a long nose and wings) and foxes, which are usually depicted as occupants of a supernatural world who make only occasional forays into the human world, demons are often transformed human beings.[88] Demons were thus powerful and feared as well as shunned yet had intimate connections with the human world.

Gender plays an important role in the identification of both the victims and the perpetrators in demon narratives. Women appear frequently both as victims of demonic appetites[89] and as demons themselves, but it is the latter to which I turn my attention, since it is the role played by Hashihime of Uji. Demons often disguise themselves as attractive and seductive women in order to lure unsuspecting passersby. Story 13 in Chapter 27 of *Konjaku monogatari*, which relates the tale of the demon at the Agi bridge, is repeatedly cited as an early prototype of the Hashihime stories found in *Heike monogatari*. This passage presents what later becomes a familiar trope: a demon disguises itself as a beautiful woman in order to ensnare a male victim. When the protagonist first encounters the demon, one look is enough to entrance:

It was not easy to see from a distance, but it seemed that in the middle of the bridge, there was someone there. [He] looked at it with trepidation, thinking "this must be the demon"; she wore a deep purple unlined robe over a soft, light lavender robe and a long crimson divided skirt. She was covering her mouth, and the way the woman's eyes looked drew sympathy. How she cast a quick glance [at him] was also moving. It seemed that she had not gotten there of her own will but was left behind by someone; she was leaning on the railing of the bridge, but when she saw that someone else had come by, she looked embarrassed yet happy. Upon seeing this, the man lost his senses and thought, "I shall gather her in my arms and take her away with me on this horse"—he thought her so dear that he nearly fell off his horse.[90]

This demon in the guise of a woman is a seducer of men, albeit an unsuccessful one since the man manages to escape her snares by banishing desire and ignoring her plea for help. She catches his attention with her attractive

88. Tanaka Takako, *Akujo ron*; see esp. the chapter "Oni ni toritsukareta 'akujo': Somedonokō to kurai arasoi."

89. See, e.g., *Konjaku monogatari*, chap. 27, story 8, in which a demon disguises itself as a man in order to approach a woman and succeeds in eating her.

90. Mabuchi et al., *Konjaku monogatari shū*, 4: 53–54.

appearance and her helplessness; his reaction is to want desperately to take her away with him. Had he not heard rumors about demons who appear at this location, he would probably have succumbed to his desires. As he makes his escape, the demon gives chase, but he had prepared for such an encounter by smearing oil on his horse's rear so that no demon could get a firm grip. The demon/woman gets its revenge later, however; it visits the man disguised as his younger brother. By telling him that their mother has passed away and they must talk in person, the demon succeeds in entering the man's house despite his resolve to bar entrance to anyone. After conversing for a while, the demon suddenly attacks the man, and they struggle fiercely. The man begs his wife for a sword, but since the demon is still disguised as the brother, she thinks that her husband has lost his mind and refuses. The demon bites off the man's head as it returns to its original shape in triumph. The text ends with a caution against women who are too "correct"; had the wife not insisted that her husband not battle his brother with a sword, he might have survived. The women in this story function only to harm the male protagonist: the woman/demon attracts his attention through the arousal of desire, and the wife, albeit unintentionally, enables his death. The demon-as-woman is a particularly important double, since it implants in people's minds the frightening possibility that an attractive woman might be a carnivorous demon.

Similar encounters between a man and a woman/demon can be found elsewhere. For instance, Story 28 in Chapter 12 of *Konjaku monogatari* is a particularly didactic tale about the efficacy and importance of the Lotus Sutra. It features the narrow escape of a man who loses his way and accidentally asks a woman in a seemingly abandoned house for help; she becomes a demon who pursues him and consumes his horse.[91] *Shūi ōjōden* (Collected biographies of those who have achieved rebirth in the Pure Land), a collection of stories by Miyoshi no Tameyasu (1048–1139) about people who achieved ōjō, has a tale whose plotline closely resembles that of the *Konjaku* narrative; however, the description of the woman-as-transformed-demon is much more elaborate in this later text. The *Konjaku* story does not give a physical description of the woman and portrays the man as the one who initiates the interaction by disturbing the woman with his plea for aid. *Shūi ōjōden* calls her a "beautiful woman" who actively lures him into her house. The story begins with the explanation that the male protagonist had been traveling on government duty

---

91. Yamada Yoshio et al., *Konjaku monogatari shū*, 3: 171–73.

when he was "captivated by a demon and lost his composure." The man then enters the woman's house and thinks: "In the depth of the mountains, there is [this] gorgeous woman. In the outskirts of the capital, I have yet to see such a woman. Perhaps this is the *rasetsu* [Sanskrit: rākṣasī] cannibal-demon?"[92] The demon is here made into an object of beauty, who in turn is demonized because of her beauty, her solitary state, her aggressive luring, and her marginal location outside the capital. In fact, it is almost as if the man wills her into her demon shape, since the transformation occurs immediately after he thinks that she might be a demon and tries to leave. The association between attractive woman and demon is established as a male fear. This demon is ultimately banished, albeit temporarily, since the powers of the Lotus Sutra dispel her, and the man eventually attains rebirth in the Pure Land.

In these examples, demons of unspecified gender impersonate attractive women in order to trap men. Demons and women are also linked in the trope of women, particularly older women, becoming demons. Two examples of such transformations can be found Stories 15 and 22 in Chapter 27 of *Konjaku monogatari*. In both examples, hunger is the drive that ultimately reveals the demon's identity; the would-be victims narrowly escape their fate either through early detection or skillful martial maneuvers. Story 22 is especially bitter since the woman who turns into a demon "because of her old age" tries to eat her own child. A warning toward the end of the story states that "all parents who grow old become demons and try to eat their children." Although the warning seems to cover both mothers and fathers, since this story is the only one among those included in this chapter in which a parent tries to kill a child, the fact that the demon is a mother leaves a strong impression. As is the case with Ono no Komachi, the marginalization of an old woman in this manner is also significant within the discourse of gender. The fear that a mother may change into a demon and threaten the life of her own child can be read as a further development of the woman-as-a-threatening-figure; the story shows not only that an attractive female stranger can turn out to be a demon but also that a female member of one's own family can suddenly change from a comforting presence to a violent and harmful one. The demon, therefore, can represent either the harmful excesses of female sexual capital that men must be careful to avoid or the uncanny transformation of a familiar female figure into a suddenly unknown and violent entity. As we shall see, both of these dangers play key roles in the Hashihime-as-demon narratives.

---

92. Inoue and Ōsone, Ōjōden, Hokke genki, p. 340.

In another significant body of texts, the female characters, represented as demons or as having interactions with demons, are implicated as involved with more than one male partner. The linking of the demonic with women in polyandrous situations in the mid- to late Heian period suggests that such relationships were beginning to be regarded as problematic; this is especially true in the cases of imperial consorts. The demonization of women who involve themselves with more than one male partner can be viewed as yet another side of the pining-Hashihime trope and potential conflict inherent in it, in which the woman is, at least for the most part, the obedient partner in a polygynous situation.

An early example of the demonized polyandrous woman can be found in Story 58 in *Yamato monogatari*, in which Taira no Kanemori (fl. late tenth century) calls the granddaughters of an imperial prince oni when he sends them a waka poem as a gesture of courtship:

> *michinoku no   adachigahara no   kurozuka ni*
> *oni komoreri to   kiku wa makoto ka*
> In Mutsu province,   in Adachi field,   at a place called Kurozuka
> there hide[s a] demon[s],   I hear; could it be true?[93]

Kanemori asks for the hand of one of the daughters, but her parent declines his offer on the grounds that she is too young and says that perhaps at a later date a marriage might be possible. He returns to the capital without success; some time later, the daughter, who had married another man in the meantime, comes to the capital. He sends her a reproachful poem that expresses resentment over her "betrayal":

> *toshi wo ete   nurewataritsuru   koromode wo*
> *kyō no namida ni   kuchi ya shinuran*
> The years have passed,   drenched through and through   is my sleeve—
> after today's tears   they will crumble away.[94]

---

93. Katagiri et al., *Taketori monogatari, Ise monogatari, Yamato monogatari, Heichū monogatari*, p. 290. Another instance of the likening of women to demons can be found in *Ise monogatari*, story 58, in which a man jokingly calls a number of women gathered around a shabby hut "demons."

94. Katagiri et al., *Taketori monogatari, Ise monogatari, Yamato monogatari, Heichū monogatari*, p. 291.

A modern commentator argues that the daughters are likened to demons because of the legend that demons lived in Kurozuka and that Kanemori alluded to demons in jest.⁹⁵ Although this view may be valid, the significance of the relationship between gender and demonization should not be over-looked. Unlike most of the pining-Hashihime narratives, this story is about one woman and two men, and the man poses himself in the poem as the one who had been pining for the woman for a long time only to find out that she had married another man. In this case, the desirable woman/demon is thus the one who makes her lover wait for her in vain; somewhat akin to the *Fūyō wakashū* example discussed above in which Hashihime had turned into a coldhearted woman, the woman/demon is here the one who hurts the man in a multi-partner relationship. The woman, therefore, is literally demonized as the agent who has caused this surge of rhetorical sorrow in the man; al-though an element of lighthearted jesting can be read into the poem, the story exemplifies the important trope of the demon-woman.

Another notable group of narratives concerns demons vis-à-vis women related to the imperial family and the configuration of polyandry. These are relevant to the topic of this chapter in that they illustrate the extent of de-monic figures' involvement in the question of heterosexual relationships. One such tale that presents the full effect of a demon's ferocious appetite is Story 7 in Chapter 27 of *Konjaku monogatari*, which discusses an affair be-tween Ariwara no Narihira and an unnamed woman. Although her identity is not made clear in the story, by the time of *Konjaku monogatari*, the story of Narihira's abduction of Fujiwara no Kōshi (842–910, consort of Emperor Seiwa, mother of Emperor Yōzei), who later comes to be called the Nijō empress after she becomes an imperial consort, seems to have been well known.⁹⁶ Narihira hides his forbidden love in an abandoned mountain storehouse, and the woman is eaten by a demon of an unspecified gender. In a gruesome scene of discovery, Narihira finds only her head remaining.⁹⁷ This story has been interpreted as Narihira's punishment for trying to ab-

95. Ibid., p. 290.

96. See, e.g., Ōe no Masafusa's *Gōke shidai*, mentioned in the previous chapter. Also, Ōka-gami (author unknown; ca. eleventh century) notes this affair and wonders how she had man-aged to become a consort despite her involvement with Narihira (see Matsumura, *Ōkagami*, pp. 20–21).

97. Mabuchi et al., *Konjaku monogatari shū*, 4: 38–40. Also, although Narihira's attempt to hide the Nijō empress appears in *Ise monogatari*, story 6, as well, the portrayal of the demon's deeds is not nearly as graphic in the earlier text.

scond with a future imperial consort; the "demon" is identified as a composite picture of Kōshi's older brothers, who took her back.[98] Although this view takes into account the political and social configuration in which Narihira was involved, it tends to underplay the significance of an empress's being the victim of a violent attack by a demon. According to the *Konjaku* story, the woman dies a horrible death; if she is supposed to represent or allude to Kōshi, then the woman who is supposed to become the mother of the next emperor dies even before she is given a chance to become a consort. In other words, the demon terminates the possibility of future liaisons with other men, as well as—interestingly enough—the imperial line. Her fate in the *Konjaku* story, therefore, can be read as retribution for her affair with Narihira, and the demon serves to terminate any potential for a polyandrous configuration. In addition, Kōshi's association with multiple male partners does not end with Narihira; she suffers a fall in social status in her later years, as *Fusō ryakki* (by Kōen, completed between 1094 and 1107) notes that she had lost her title of former empress in 896 due to an affair with a monk.[99] Kōshi is, therefore, a woman who is portrayed as having met (demonic) resistance and suppression in her attempts to have relationships with more than one man—be it at one time or in succession.

Story 7 in Chapter 20 of *Konjaku monogatari* presents an incident in which a powerful hijiri is called to cure an imperial consort, the Somedono empress (Fujiwara no Meishi, 826–99; mother of Emperor Seiwa), of possession by a spirit. Upon successfully completing his task, he happens to see the empress's beautiful figure and falls prey to desire. After being captured during an attempt to satisfy his sexual drive, he dies with the intention of being reborn as demon; he succeeds and returns to achieve his original goal repeatedly.[100] This story and the previous one about Narihira and the Nijō empress (who marries Somedono's son) show two contrasting approaches to the interactions of high-ranking women with demons. In chapter 27, story 7, the woman is viciously murdered and consumed by a demon, whereas in chapter 20, story 7, she becomes the target of a hijiri/demon's overwhelming sexual drive. Japanese scholars have frequently examined the latter story in particular and offered different interpretations. Minamoto Junko proposes that the Somedono empress's story is actually about the love that blossoms

98. Baba, *Oni no kenkyū*, pp. 52–58, as seen in *Ise monogatari*, Story 6.

99. Tanaka Takako, *Akujo ron*, pp. 121–22. Kōshi regained her status posthumously in 943.

100. Yamada Yoshio et al., *Konjaku monogatari shū*, 4: 155–58.

between the hijiri and the empress; he is overcome by his love, and despite the apparent criticism that such an act is inappropriate, the narrative "recognizes (*mitomeru*) the love between a man and a woman."[101] Tanaka Takako, by contrast, reads the story as a politically motivated rape incident; she asserts that the narrator blames the victim (the empress) and not the rapist (the hijiri) in an attempt to portray the woman as a temptress who has the potential to destroy men.[102]

Although both readings offer convincing perspectives, if we approach this story through the question of polygyny and polyandry, a related but different possibility emerges. When the hijiri turns into a demon and visits the empress, the narrator states that the demon cast a spell over her and caused her to lose her mind so that she smiled and willfully let the demon through the curtains to sleep with her. Thereafter, repeated references are made to the empress's abnormal state of mind as the affair with the demon continues. For a woman of high rank to engage in an extramarital affair and to escape the fate of Kōshi, she apparently had to be described as having lost her senses due to a supernatural force. In other words, the untamable powers of the demon created the possibility of an empress's sexual engagement outside her marriage; here, demonic mind-control functions as an excuse for polyandry, and she is able to retain her social position and remain alive. These two *Konjaku* stories, then, show that demons could play crucial parts in the enabling or disabling of polygamous situations.

In summary, these narratives indicate that demons were often characterized by their marginalized status in society, that their ferocious power threatened the very existence of human beings who came into contact with them, and that their female manifestations, either as a transformed state or as an originary form, represented the violent dangers of sexual and familial relationships.[103] In contrast to the pining-Hashihime trope, the demonic Hashihime is freighted with a different set of loaded contexts; the female demon becomes an emblem of physical violence and sexual excess that result

---

101. See Minamoto's chapter "Nihon bukkyō no seisabetsu," in Ōgoshi, Minamoto, and Yamashita, *Seisabetsu suru bukkyō*, p. 108.

102. See Tanaka Takako, "Oni ni toritsukareta 'akujo': Somedonokō to kurai arasoi," in idem, *Akujo ron*.

103. In addition to the instances noted above, interactions between female characters and demons were often portrayed as being deeply connected to polyandrous configurations and sexual transgressions on the part of women.

in either the succumbing of male victims to demonic trickery or the possibility of multiple-male-partner relationships.

Jealousy and Transformation: Two Paths of Consequence

Many Heian and early Kamakura period narratives present women's jealousy and consequent transformation and can be studied to investigate why women's jealousy was marginalized into the demonized. These narratives exhibit different attitudes toward the transformed manifestation of female jealousy. Some passages criticize the combination of women, jealousy, and the demonic, and the female protagonist encounters an unhappy ending. In those that feature non-demonic transformations, in contrast, the emphasis is more on the fear-inspiring powers of jealous female rage, and there are no attempts to undercut those powers through overt criticisms of the woman or of jealousy. These subtle but significant differences indicate that narratives about jealous women transformed did not have a monolithic and inevitable plotline. A demon born of jealousy seems to have been an important target for criticism, yet at least through the early Kamakura period there was ambivalence over the fate of the female characters who had transformed into beings other than a demon.

I begin with a narrative that presents resentment as the cause of transformation and ends tragically. The sheer physical powers of the female demon in this story are tempered by the distinctly moral judgments voiced by the character herself regarding the nature of women and jealousy. Story 3 in the second part of *Kankyo no tomo* (ca. 1222, attributed to the priest Keisei; for a translation, see pp. 324–25) is entitled, "The Matter of a Deeply Resentful Woman Who Became a Demon While Still Alive." This text is often cited as a predecessor of the Hashihime-as-demon stories and is therefore worth a detailed examination here. This narrative is about a woman who purposefully changes into a demon because of her resentment against a man. The exact circumstances of his estrangement from her are somewhat complex. At the beginning, the woman seems to mistake his infrequent visits due to distance for neglect, yet he grows wary of her after she becomes suspicious, and her family calls him "no good" after she disappears. The man may not have necessarily been involved in a polygynous relationship; resentment, however, arises in her heart at a furious pace, and she refuses to eat. She then decides to take matters into her own hands. "One day she took a nearby bucket full of syrup, put her hair up in five sections, and smeared the syrup upon her hair and let it dry so that it resembled horns. Nobody knew this was happening. She then put on a crimson divided skirt, and after nightfall she secretly ran away and disappeared."[104] What happens after her departure is a telling indication of the perception of demons by the narrator: the woman cannot return to her original human shape. Embarrassed by her shape, she must live in hiding. This representation is in line with those in the demon stories discussed in the preceding section; literally marginalized from society, living in the ceiling of a decrepit hall in the middle of a field, the demon-woman must make herself invisible and commit antisocial acts in order to survive. The narrator even speculates that this demon-woman is not destined for any happiness after her death. Miserable in both this world and the next, the woman who harbors resentment against a man is shown to lead a thoroughly undesirable existence.

She makes the following confession to the villagers who burn her hiding place in order to force her to appear:

"I am the daughter of such-and-such a person of a certain place. A regrettable feeling arose in my heart, and I did this and that, and I left. I eventually killed the man who left me. After that, I could not return to my former appearance, and I was wary of people's eyes; without anywhere to live, I have been hiding in this hall. As it was like this, the living body is a wretched thing—I could not bear it when I became hungry. Everything was painful; my suffering has been indescribable. At night and during the day, I felt as if the inside of my body was burning up, I was regretful and felt useless without end. What I wish for is that you promise to gather together and carefully copy the Lotus Sutra in a day, offer it, and pray for me. Also, if among you there are those who have wives (and children), you must tell them what I have told you—preach to them that they must never let rise the thoughts which arose in my heart." The demon then wept and flung herself into the flames and died.[105]

In this narrative, the woman-demon herself denounces her own deeds and transformed state and finally takes her own wretched life while begging that other women be warned not to follow her path. The woman-demon, powerful enough to kill the man whom she resented—an event described only briefly and without detail—is shown to be, in the end, an entity that must be destroyed, either by others or of her own accord. Her physical capacities are truncated both textually and through her own self-critique.

---

104. Koizumi et al., *Hōbutsushū, Kankyo no tomo, Hirasan kojin reitaku*, p. 422.
105. Ibid., p. 424.

A different trope emerges in narratives that deal with jealousy and transformation but lack explicit moral pronouncements about women's jealousy, do not necessarily mention negative consequences for the transformed character, do not focus on her remorse, and do not specifically define the protagonist as a demon. Although the previous example indicates that resentment could be presented as an undesirable emotion that causes frightening transformations resulting in the tragic ending of the woman who harbored the emotion, other stories from the same period show that different paths were possible. A jealous woman could, for example, become a powerful spirit who mercilessly takes revenge on those who had caused her suffering and emerge unremorseful and virtually undisturbed. Even though she is forced to undergo an unintended and undesirable transformation due to jealousy, she is able to acquire certain supernatural powers that affect others. One important feature of these narratives is that the transformation does not involve becoming a demon; however, the earlier Hashihime-as-demon narratives I investigate below belong more to this category than to the previous one of jealousy and transformation with a tragic ending, and these tales indicate that precedents for non-negative endings do exist.

Story 23 in Chapter 27 of *Konjaku monogatari*, although it does not mention the word *oni*, is placed amid stories that deal with demons. This tale concerns the vengeful spirit of a living woman who kills her husband. A man of the lower classes is traveling east from the capital, and at a crossroads (a key space for the emergence of apparitions) he meets a woman standing alone in the middle of the night, much in the way that demons disguised as attractive women present themselves. She begs him to lead her to a particular person's house. He goes out of his way to take her there; and she thanks him, tells him her address, and disappears. He senses something strange about this encounter and discovers next morning that the man of the house has been killed by the spirit of his estranged wife. The traveler then drops by the woman's house, and she expresses her gratitude by providing him with a feast and gifts. The story ends there with an explanation by the narrator that the victim's wife "had resented his leaving her and turned into a living vengeful spirit in order to kill him. Therefore, women's hearts are fearsome things—so it is passed down in the various stories, I hear."[106] The woman in this story does not turn into a demon, but the elements of jealousy and her power to kill a man whom she resents are clearly established. Not only does

---

106. Mabuchi et al., *Konjaku monogatari shū*, 4: 75–79.

she express no remorse over her deed, but she rewards the person who helped her carry out her task. The narrator voices fear of "women's hearts" but does not make an attempt to bring this fear under control by making derogatory comments about jealousy per se. Nor is any mention made of the jealous woman's fate; the woman attained her goal, without punishment, as far as the narrator was concerned.

Hosshinshū, which criticizes women's jealousy quite directly,[107] nonetheless contains a passage that addresses jealousy without negative commentary. In a story called "The Matter of a Servant of the Shijō Empress Putting a Curse on a Person and Becoming a Beggar," a certain woman, a former servant of an empress, becomes involved with a man who promises to take her to the provinces when he becomes a governor. She believes him, and after an elaborate send-off by her employer and her colleagues, she waits for him to come get her at her house. He never materializes, and she discovers that he has left for the provinces with his primary wife. The former servant becomes enraged and embarrassed about what other people will think. She visits Kibune, just as Hashihime is said to have done, and prays that the primary wife be killed in return for her own life or a miserable existence as a beggar. The primary wife does die a month later, and the former servant becomes a beggar. The narrator explains that she did not regret her downfall since her wishes had come true; only in old age did she wonder why she had done such a deed and had disqualified herself from attaining enlightenment in this life and the next, but "there is nothing to be done."[108] No "moral" is spelled out here concerning the supposedly jealous and therefore sinful tendencies of *all* women, nor is there an encouragement to feel regret over such vengeful deeds. Rather, the narrative focuses on the satisfaction of revenge, and the candid comment at the end, "there is nothing to be done," suggests that even a regretful heart—the previous story to the contrary—is useless.[109] One in-

---

107. See chapter 5, story 3: "The Matter of a Mother Becoming Jealous of Her Daughter and the Mother's Fingers Turning into Snakes."

108. Miki, *Hōjōki/Hosshinshū*, pp. 368–70.

109. A somewhat similar example is *Kojidan*, Chapter 2, Story 93, in which a first wife, angry at being abandoned by her husband, goes to Kibune to pray that he be made a beggar. Her wishes eventually come true, but upon hearing about his destitution, she brings him some food and recounts the past, sometimes weeping and sometimes resentfully. The husband merely says at the end, "I understand." Here again, neither the woman nor her deeds are criticized by the narrator, and there is even a sense of resignation and comprehension at the conclusion.

teresting point is that in this narrative, it is the deity at Kibune who commits the act of revenge on behalf of the woman who comes to pray there (who herself does not undergo an immediate transformation); this contrasts with the Hashihime-as-demon trope, in which the deity assists the transformation of a woman into a demon so that she herself can be the executor of vengeful acts. Hashihime's role as the key agent of physical violence therefore becomes even more notable in this context; she is a demon who takes matters into her own hands.

A further example of jealous vengeance is found in Chapter 20 of *Kokon chomonjū* (ca. 1254, compiled by Tachibana no Narisue). A jealous woman turns into a snake because her husband, a monk, has entered an affair with a shirabyōshi dancer. One night, when he is in bed with his new lover, he feels as if he is making love to his first wife even though he is obviously with the dancer. He feels rather strange, when all of a sudden a snake crawls out of nowhere and bites onto his penis. The monk finally cuts off the snake with a sword and throws it away in a river. He falls seriously ill afterward. The first wife dies soon after the incident, and the last comment by the narrator is "this is a frightening incident."[110] This is a clear case of a polygynous situation giving rise to jealous transformation. Whether the first wife willed the change of her own form into a snake is not mentioned, but she viciously attacks her husband as a snake, targeting his offending body part, the cause of her jealousy. She succeeds in making him fall gravely ill. The narrator does not embark on an anti-jealousy tirade, and there is no monologue by the wife regretting her deeds; there is simply an expression of fear in the conclusion. Although the act of revenge was committed in exchange for her life, her success is noted without reference to the supposedly deplorable behavior of jealous women. She is also the agent who carries out the revenge in a transformed state (as opposed to a deity who carries out the act on behalf of a client); however, perhaps the snake, since it is less physically menacing than a demon, did not have enough power to commit the act and still survive herself.

Finally, among the possible alternatives to the kind of discourses found in narratives that marginalize demonized resentful women, one well-known example illustrates that the demonization of women did not escape criticism, especially by the very gender that suffered from such characterizations. A critique of the trope of the woman-as-demon can be found in poem 44 of

---

110. Nakazumi and Shimada, *Kokon chomonjū*, pp. 538–39.

Murasaki Shikibu shū (Murasaki Shikibu poetry collection; compiled by Murasaki Shikibu, ca. 1012–17):

Upon seeing the picture of a scene in which behind the unsightly appearance of a woman possessed by a spirit, a young monk is tying up the former wife who has turned into a demon, and the husband is chanting a sutra in an attempt to get rid of the spirit:

> naki hito ni   kagoto wo kakete   wazurau mo
>   ono ga kokoro no   oni ni ya wa aranu
> To blame matters   upon the deceased   and feel ill-at-ease:
>   is this not, in fact, due to the demon   in his own heart?

The reply:

> kotowari ya   kimi ga kokoro no   yami nareba
>   oni no kage to wa   shiruku miyuran
> It is as you say;   since your heart   is in darkness,
>   the shadow of the demon   you do see clearly.[111]

Murasaki Shikibu makes a keen observation concerning the tension in a multipartner relationship: since the trope of a jealous first wife who turns into a demon is circulating in certain circles, a man is able to blame his own difficulties with his current wife on troubles brought on by his deceased wife. The first wife serves as a scapegoat, and the real demon is "in his heart"; Murasaki Shikibu has also imagined that the man feels uncomfortable about the entire situation, since he is at least somewhat aware that he is doing something wrong. The reply poem, perhaps composed by Murasaki Shikibu's woman-in-waiting according to the annotator, can be interpreted as an expression of agreement with a further ironic twist. She suggests that Murasaki Shikibu is indeed correct, but that the author of *Genji monogatari* can have this insight only because her own heart is in darkness, where demons dwell. The exchange, therefore, is at once a critical exploration of the woman-as-demon trope and an expression of exasperation that such a critique can be made only by someone who is unhappy and discontent. The significance of this passage lies in its concern with the strains and resentments that polygyny produces; Murasaki Shikibu notes that the representation of the wife as a demon is a product of the polygynous man's actions and feelings in his own heart. The passage, therefore, confirms the existence of the trope of the jealous, demonic woman even as it undercuts it.

---

111. Yamamoto Ritatsu, *Murasaki Shikibu nikki, Murasaki Shikibu shū*, pp. 131–32.

All the narratives about women's jealousy and transformation examined above are concerned with anger, resentment, and revenge. Narrators often express fear of jealousy because of these emotions and the physical displays of violence—such as mutilation and murder—that frequently accompany them. The violent acts disrupt the system of polygyny and society in general, and there are stories that attempt to control the situation by criticizing such acts. Other stories simply leave them after noting the narrator's fears. The potential for disruption thus seems to have been an important concern in many texts from this period, even though the reaction to that potential ranged from attempted containment to simple awe. Demons, however, were singled out as particularly dangerous and powerful transformations, first, because they could carry out the act of revenge themselves, and second, because as noted in the previous section, they were intimately linked to polyandrous possibilities that challenged the polygynous system at its most fundamental level. Demons therefore needed to be further marginalized in some way, through the discourse of moral denouncement or by portraying the tragic consequences of jealousy.

Hashihime as Demon: The Power of the Jealous Woman Unleashed

Where should the demonic Hashihime be located within the complex web of discourses about "female jealousy" and demonic beings? One advantage that Hashihime enjoys over other women turned demon is that the earlier narratives about her empower her greatly. She is an extremely strong and violent demon with a capacity for merciless violence. She feels no compunction for her deeds, nor does she suffer retribution. This portrayal has even more impact when considered in light of the narratives outlined above: unlike the *Kankyo no tomo* narrative (which many scholars see as a major influence on the Hashihime-as-demon trope), Hashihime meets no known tragic end, and she is not made to play the role of a mouthpiece for moral lessons about women and jealousy as general categories. Unlike narratives that show jealous women relying on the powers of deities to perform acts of revenge on their behalf or those that show the transformed being as insufficiently powerful to survive the wreaking of revenge, Hashihime is a mentally and physically capable agent who emerges successful in her endeavors.

The dangerous, unremorseful nature of this Hashihime is in complete contrast with her pining-wife trope. This polarization can be understood in two ways. First, it can be read as attempt to vilify women's jealousy in a polygynous situation as a threat with no redeeming features; unlike the "tragic ending" transformation trope, which leaves open the possibility that the reader might feel sympathy for the jealous women who regret their deeds, the violent, inhuman demon named Hashihime is a frighteningly clever and strong monster with no redeeming qualities in the eyes of men whom she tries to victimize. The creation of Hashihime's demonic figure involved a number of manipulations of the characteristics of demons and jealous women; the result is a figure who inspires only fear, the demon one can truly despise. Second, the capacity for physical violence embodied in the demonic Hashihime can be interpreted as an effect of concerns stemming from the genre as well as the text's intended functions. The passages below are taken from works in the gunki monogatari genre. Texts in this category routinely valorize strength, triumph, and heroic acts of violence; I will argue that Hashihime's powers stem, at least partly, from such generic concerns. Furthermore, one of the purposes of the first example below was to pacify the spirits of the deceased by glorifying their achievements; Hashihime's empowerment could be interpreted as part of that goal. Later narratives diverge from the empowering portrayal. As we shall see below, the production of the powerful, threatening manifestation enabled her violent and forced domestication in later texts driven by changing generic concerns.

The earliest known text that portrays Hashihime of Uji as a demon is *Yashirobon Heike monogatari* (*The Tale of Heike*, Yashirobon version).[112] Since *Heike* developed as both a written and an orally transmitted work, a number of different versions exist today, but *Yashirobon* is thought to be one of the older versions of *Heike*, possibly dating from the early to mid-thirteenth century.[113] Hashihime appears in "Tsurugi no maki" (The sword chapter), part I, which relates anecdotes about two treasured swords passed down in the Minamoto family. One of the swords, named Higekiri (beard-cutter), is

---

112. A passage in an annotation of *Kokinshū* called *Kokin Tameieshō* by Fujiwara no Tameie (1197–1275) supposedly states that a kami called Hashimori (bridge guardian) originated as a female demon who had immersed herself in the Uji river for one hundred nights out of jealousy so that she might remove the offending second wife. This passage, however, is found only in an Edo-period work called *Yamashiro meishoshi*, which claims that it is an excerpt from *Tameieshō*; the existing version of *Tameieshō* does not contain this passage (see Yoshikai, "*Hashihime monogatari* no shiteki kōsatsu"). Since the attribution cannot be fully established at this point, *Yashirobon* remains the earliest work to introduce Hashihime as a demon.

113. For a more detailed discussion of the nature of Yashirobon vis-à-vis other versions, see Hyōdō, "*Yashirobon no isō*," pp. 76–82.

the focus of the tale about Hashihime. This section of the chapter begins with the mysterious disappearance of large numbers of people during the lifetime of Minamoto no Raikō (948–1021).

When inquiring about this matter [of the mysterious disappearances]: during the reign of Emperor Saga [r. 809–23], a certain nobleman's daughter became so jealous that she went to pray to the great kami at Kibune. She entered a seven-day prayer retreat, wishing that she soon be transformed alive into a demon, so that she might harm the woman/women of whom she was jealous. According to the sign [from the kami] that appeared: if she wanted to become a demon, she should change her appearance, go to the riverside at Uji, and immerse herself for twenty-one days; she would then turn into a demon. The woman, overjoyed, returned to the capital and went to a place where no one was around; she divided her long hair into five segments and pasted pine resin on them, twisting them up into five horns. On her face, she put vermilion, and painted red lead oxide on her body. She wore a metal ring upon her head and lit pine torches, one of which she held with her mouth. After the night deepened and people became few, she ran out onto Yamato street and headed south. From her head rose five burning flames. Of those who happened to see this sight, there was none who did not lose their wits, take to bed, and die. In this manner she reached the riverside of Uji, where she immersed herself for twenty-one days. With the help of the great kami at Kibune, she soon was transformed alive into a demon. She is also called Hashihime of Uji, I understand. After becoming a demon, she caused the disappearance of the relatives of the woman/women who had caused her jealousy, the relatives of the man who had shunned her—not limiting her choices to high or low, not discriminating between men and women. When she wanted to take away a man, she changed her form into an attractive woman, and when she wanted to take away a woman, she changed her form into a man. In this way she caused many to disappear, and the people's fears were so immeasurable that throughout the capital, after four o'clock in the afternoon visitors were not let in, nor did people go visiting.[114]

The unnamed daughter of a nobleman thus succeeds in a willful transformation out of jealousy induced by a polygynous relationship. She becomes a demon so powerful that the entire capital is terrorized. Uji must have had some significance in the ritual of changing one's form into a demon, since she first travels north to Kibune, where the kami tells her to head all the way south to Uji. Kibune shrine, also located by a river, is the place where Izumi Shikibu is said to have gone when she had been forgotten by a

---

114. Satō and Haruta, *Yashirobon Heike monogatari*, 2: 542–44.

man;[115] this narrative can be found in various guises in such texts as *Goshūi-shū*, *Toshiyori zuinō*, and *Mumyō zōshi*. Kibune seems to have acquired a reputation as a place for women to consult the deity about problems with neglectful men; Uji had apparently become significant as a location where it was appropriate to express one's jealous anger and where supernatural transformations were possible. These details reinforce earlier discussions in this chapter about Uji as a marginalized and supernatural space suitable for demonic transformation, or a defamiliarization of polygyny.

The narrative develops along lines similar to those of the *Konjaku* story about the demon of Agi bridge. One day, Watanabe no Tsuna, one of the four most prominent retainers of Raikō, is delivering a message for his lord. Raikō, worried about Tsuna's safety at night, lends him the Higekiri sword for protection. At the eastern end of the "Turning Back" bridge at Ichijō Horikawa, Tsuna encounters: "a woman a bit over twenty years of age, skin as white as snow, wearing a very appealing lined 'plum' robe, a sash across her chest, and an amulet pouch; there was a sutra inside her sleeve. Without a companion, she was heading south all alone."[116] As in so many texts, the solitary and attractive woman/demon, here one who seems to need the protective powers of an amulet and a sutra, draws the attention of a man. She asks Tsuna to take her to Gojō; he agrees immediately and takes her up onto the horse with him. She then says that she does not need to go to Gojō after all and that he could take her directly to her house, which is outside the capital. When he accedes to her request, she suddenly changes her shape

---

115. Poems 125 and 126 of *Izumi Shikibu shū*:

When she was forgotten by a man, she went to pray at Kibune, and upon seeing the fireflies at Mitarashi river:

> mono omoeba   sawa no hotaru mo   wagami yori
>   akugare izuru   tama ka to zo miru
> So lost in thought,   even the fireflies in the valley   seem like my spirit
>   escaped from my body   and wandering about

[The kami's] reply:

> okuyama ni   tagirite otsuru   takitsu se no
>   tama chiru bakari   mono na omoiso
> Deep in the mountains,   in the shallows of the waterfall   rushing down,
>   the spirit-waterdrops shatter and splash;   do not be so lost in thought.

(Nomura, *Izumi Shikibu nikki, Izumi Shikibu shū*, p. 129.)

116. Satō and Haruta, *Yashirobon Heike monogatari*, p. 544.

into a demon, saying: "The place I am going to go is Mount Atago!" She grabs Tsuna by his topknot and begins to fly toward the mountain. Tsuna, however, was apparently prepared for this turn of events; he calmly draws his Higekiri sword and slices off the arm of the demon. He lands safely with the demon's arm still attached to his topknot.

Like the main character in the *Konjaku* narrative, Tsuna begins a seven-day retreat in order to avoid the demon's revenge. However, whereas in *Konjaku* the demon had disguised itself as the man's younger brother, *Heike*'s Hashihime disguises herself as Tsuna's aunt, who had raised him as if he had been her own son. After lengthy exchanges between the demon/aunt and Tsuna that reveal the eloquence of Hashihime through her skillful rhetorical manipulation of Tsuna's emotions and his sense of filial piety, she succeeds in making him let her into his house and show her the demon's arm. As soon as she sees the arm, she snatches it away, resumes her demon shape, and flies away into the sky. Unlike the *Konjaku* story in which the man is ruthlessly slaughtered by the demon, in this version Tsuna remains unharmed, the text explains, because of the powers of the Niō (Vajra-pāṇi) sutra he had been chanting during his retreat. The section ends with the comment that the Higekiri sword was renamed Onimaru, since it had been used to cut off the arm of an oni demon.

This story, which marks the first known appearance of Hashihime as a demon, has a number of significant points. First, the social position of the woman who turns herself into a demon is made clear—she is "a certain nobleman's daughter," a person of some rank. Again, men of this class were among the primary practitioners of polygyny; this detail adds believability to her unfortunate situation, and the identification of her social status brings this chilling story uncomfortably close to the upper class.

Second, Hashihime, who had transformed herself into a demon in order to seek revenge on those who had caused her to become jealous, is a cunning manipulator of relationships with the opposite sex. This masquerade raises a frightening possibility of uncertainty in a heterosexual relationship: Could the person to whom one is attracted be, in fact, a demon who will take away one's life? The answer is "yes" in Hashihime's case; her figure renders sexual attraction a realm of potential horror. Right after her transformation, she fluidly masquerades as either a man or a woman depending on her prey and attracts her victim's attention by posing as a member of the opposite sex. She then focuses on a particular man's position vis-à-vis the different women in his life. She first becomes an attractive young woman in order to lure Tsuna into her trap. When that approach fails, she exploits to the fullest extent the relationship between a son and a mother figure who had reared him. Here, the uncanniness of a nurturing mother figure turning into a demon resembles the *Konjaku* story outlined above about an old-woman-turned-demon who tries to victimize her son. Hashihime's extensive monologue that causes Tsuna to break the observance of his retreat shows that this demon is powerful not simply because she has terrifying physical capacities for violence but because she is able to use psychological manipulation and verbal skills to achieve her goals.

Third, the sheer extent of Hashihime's power as a demon is an important feature of this story. Immediately after her transformation, she systematically targets her prey and carries out her revenge against those who had caused her suffering, although it is left ambiguous whether she harmed the man who had caused her suffering or the "other woman/women" who had made her jealous; snatching away their loved ones was perhaps her method of revenge. Hashihime so terrifies the capital that people are afraid to venture outside after a certain hour. Although Hashihime suffers the loss of her arm and succeeds in retrieving it but not in committing an act of revenge against Tsuna (she may have had no interest in revenge since Tsuna is not explicitly named as a practitioner of polygyny), she still escapes with the arm and presumably reattaches it and becomes once again the powerful demon that she was before. The fact that she is cast as a nobleman's daughter from the early 800s who continues to wreak havoc nearly two centuries later suggests that this is not a being who can be expected to die according to a human life cycle, and that she could very well be alive for many years to come. There is no mention of her fate or whereabouts after this incident, and there is certainly no mention of any Buddhist-influenced remorse and repentance or a tragic ending of her life. Hashihime's fate as a woman-turned-demon from jealousy, therefore, is exceptional when we consider the narratives cited above that focus on both the power of the woman-demon/avenger *and* her eventual demise. She is a fear-inspiring, merciless demon through and through; only Tsuna's superhero-like character aided by the powers of the Niō sutra permit his survival.

Why is Hashihime so powerful? Why depict a woman who derives her power from the resentment she feels against the reigning relationship configuration, polygyny, as someone so unstoppable? *Yashirobon*'s departure from other narratives that either cast the jealous-woman-turned-demon as a recipient of deserved punishment or place non-demonized female characters in empowered states but not at the level of Hashihime (who is able to terrorize an entire city and remain unharmed) is of crucial concern. There are two possible explanations. First, the passages I have cited that are not specifically about Hashihime are parts of setsuwa collections whose rhetoric is often heavily didactic, whereas her story in the *Yashirobon Heike* is placed within a text with different concerns. The gunki genre is very much concerned with the details of battle and focuses on impressive displays of both physical and mental powers that can lead an entire clan to victory or failure. In this context, the glorification of Hashihime's cunning and violent powers is consistent with other stories of valor and strength. In other words, the figure of Hashihime in *Yashirobon* can be understood as an effect of the text's interest in depicting heroic and awe-inspiring demonstrations of power. Second, if, as has been argued, the reciters of the *Heike* stories, the *biwa hōshi*, were responsible for exorcising the vengeful spirits of those who had died in battle,[117] then one could interpret Hashihime as one of the vengeful (although not exactly deceased) who must be appeased through the telling of his or her story; furthermore, the reciters had little direct class-based (they were not part of the polygyny-practicing upper-class) or other incentives to portray her as one who is ultimately defeated. In fact, if *Heike* characters on the losing side were often portrayed heroically in order to appease their spirits,[118] the representation of a powerful Hashihime could have been the result of a similar motivation in that it was hoped that the picture of an untamable demon could pacify her vengefulness.

If this was the case, then the attempt to ultimately pacify a vengeful spirit involved an intermediate and paradoxical stage in which the spirit was necessarily greatly empowered; without aggrandizement, spirits seeking revenge would not be satisfied with the way in which they were represented and could not be exorcised. Following this logic, it would have been necessary to generate a vision of Hashihime as an extremely powerful being before she could be successfully removed. In this manner, the wrath of the jealous woman, a terrifying "side-effect" of polygyny, comes to be vividly articulated; even if this powerful wrath is invoked as a "by-product" in the process of

---

117. See, e.g., Fukuda, *Chūsei katarimono bungei*; for discussions of monogatari's relationship to exorcism, purification, and ōken (kingly authority), see Hyōdō, *Ōken to monogatari*.

118. Yamashita, *Katari to shite no "Heike monogatari,"* p. 75.

exorcism, her terror-causing presence becomes repeatedly and firmly grounded with every recitation.

If the docile, pining Hashihime of waka poetry constructs the women in polygynous relationships as uncomplaining participants in that configuration, the demonic Hashihime of *Yashirobon* establishes the "worst-case scenario" of polygyny even as she is supposedly being pacified. Through her character, both faithful longing and jealous rage come to be ascribed as "experiences" of the "woman-in-polygyny." In turn, these ascriptions become targets for criticism and generate further attempts to control such disruptive features, which have been naturalized as inherent to the female sex.

These arguments are reinforced when we examine subsequent versions of Hashihime's struggle with a male figure who wields a famed treasure-sword. In later versions of *Heike monogatari*, such as the *Hyaku-nijukku-bon* from the late Kamakura period, the story is told along lines quite similar to the version in *Yashirobon*, although it condenses a number of details, especially the extended dialogue between Tsuna and his aunt. This diminishes the eloquence displayed by Hashihime-in-disguise and shifts the focus toward her physical prowess. This shift implies that the trajectory of the *Heike* stories about Hashihime followed the gunki genre's tendency to valorize violence. Further changes occur in the centuries to follow: the story about Tsuna's encounter with a demon is retold in the noh play and otogi zōshi *Rashōmon*, but the identity of the demon in those narratives is no longer Hashihime but a male demon from Mount Ōe. What remains consistent over time is the demon's power, not the gendered agent of that power.

Another, slightly later text in the gunki monogatari genre illustrates another possible reason for the portrayal of Hashihime as a powerful demon and depicts her figure in a considerably different manner. *Soga monogatari* (author unknown; ca. fourteenth century) also mentions Hashihime of Uji in a struggle with a sword, but this time the details differ significantly from the *Heike* versions:

At that time, Hashihime of Uji was on a rampage, taking people away. At dusk one day, when Minamoto no Yoshi'ie [1039–1106] had gone to Uji, just as people had said, the waves of the river had become rough as there crawled up onto the bridge a beautiful woman of about eighteen or nineteen who then tried to drag Yoshi'ie off of his horse into the river. The sword in question pulled itself out and cut off Hashihime's bow-arm. [Her] powers insufficient, she jumped into the river, and after that, the troubles at Uji subsided. Due to this, the sword in his possession was named Himekiri (lady-cutter).[119]

It has been pointed out that this story is related to the one in *Sandai wakashū* cited above in which a vengeful spirit called Hashihime goes on a rampage.[120] The differences between this passage and the ones in the *Heike* versions clearly illustrate the particular way in which, as well as the extent to which, the powerful demon presented earlier has been domesticated. In this story, the struggle takes place between Yoshi'ie and Hashihime at the Uji river, her home territory. Unlike the *Heike* versions in which her frightening powers are still untamed at the end of the story, in *Soga* she is completely pacified at her dwelling place, and her activities cease after this incident. The striking maneuverings of relationships with members of the opposite sex as displayed in the *Heike* versions of Hashihime are completely absent here; instead of arousing attraction by posing as a beautiful woman and thereby luring her victim to take her upon his horse, here she simply tries to drag Yoshi'ie off his horse by force. She therefore becomes merely a physical threat (albeit an uncanny one still) that can be overcome with strength, with a little help from a supernatural sword; she is no longer a being who causes fear and suspicion in one's very relationship with others in society. Furthermore, her gender is clearly marked to the end; whereas in *Heike*, the sword was renamed "Onimaru" after the oni demon, here it is renamed "Himekiri," or "lady-cutter." The malign supernatural manifestation is therefore unmistakably identified as a woman. This Hashihime, therefore, is a disempowered spirit, stripped of her demonic powers and her ability to play mindgames, completely defeated by a man and his sword, to be commemorated only in the name of the sword that marks her pacification. The demon who had been vilified in earlier texts is now brought to "justice."

The omission of an explicit explanation of Hashihime's "background" or an explanation of her origins means that her association with polygyny-induced jealous rage and transformation is made tenuous. At first glance, this detachment might appear to empower jealousy: since Hashihime's figure comes to represent only physical power (divorced from the question of jealousy) and its taming, her domestication does not necessarily signal a

---

119. Ichiko and Ōshima, *Soga monogatari*, p. 306. This edition is based on a kanabon version; kanabon most likely date from the late fourteenth century and may have been edited by Buddhist monks.

120. Yoshikai, "*Hashihime monogatari* no shiteki kōsatsu," p. 128.

pacification of jealous revenge per se. On the other hand, with the power of agency—that is, the capacity for physical violence embodied by Hashihime in *Yashirobon*—brought under control, what remains unaddressed, unresolved, and in limbo is precisely this question of polygyny and the problem of jealousy. Stripped of the strength to carry out violent acts of revenge, this female character has lost her means to resist and subvert oppressive relationship configurations.

Since *Soga* was recited just as *Heike* was, most likely for the same purpose of pacifying the vengeful spirits of the dead, and since both are usually classified as gunki because of their attention to matters of martial triumph and heroism, questions regarding the reasons for differences in the degree of Hashihime's marginalization arise. This concern is especially valid because *Soga* reciters may have included itinerant female performers; Why did they disempower Hashihime? I offer two answers in an attempt to explain the differences. First, it is important to consider the function of the Hashihime story within the two narratives. In *Heike*, the Sword Chapter serves as an explanation why the Minamoto (also called the Genji) emerged victorious over the Taira (also called the Heike); the accomplishment of this great feat is attributed to the marvelous sword. If one of the aims in the recitation of *Heike* was to appease the spirits of the dead Heike, showing that past Minamoto warrior-heroes such as Tsuna were not invincible (witness his trouble with demons) and claiming that the Heike's loss was due to the powers of a sword (as opposed to, for example, superior strategic planning by the Minamoto) could have been seen as effective means for vindication. In *Soga*, Hashihime appears in a similar explanation of the wonders of a particular sword, but the sword is presented to Soga no Jūrō, one of two brothers who engage in a vendetta to avenge their father. Her story is embedded in a monologue that tries to illustrate the marvelous nature of the sword that will be used against a powerful government official; for this purpose, the ease with which the sword cuts down a troublesome spirit becomes important. In addition, whereas in *Heike*, Hashihime's transformation from human to demon is described in detail, in *Soga* she is presented as a demon from beginning to end. This lack of mention of the details of her attachment to this world perhaps meant that there was no need pacify her spirit in the same manner as was necessary for vengeful spirits; in other words, since *Soga* portrays her simply as a propagator of annoyances and not as a transformed being with a past full of anger and a desire for vengeance, she does not require the complex process of exorcism through glorification that other vengeful spirits demand.

Second, *Soga* exhibits specific characteristics that do not necessarily take aim at Hashihime or female empowerment per se but affect them nevertheless. As has been noted by many scholars, in general the earlier texts in the gunki genre tend to portray two warring factions with relative fairness, but later texts increasingly deal with a single figure or a family and often concentrate on heroicizing or aggrandizing the accomplishments and moral statures of the protagonist(s).[121] *Heike* and *Soga* conform to this model: the *Heike* presents both flattering and unflattering portrayals of the Minamoto and Heike clans, and *Soga* is intent on depicting the two brothers, Gorō and Jūrō, as rightful avengers of their father's murder. This change in focus partly explains the shift in Hashihime's portrayal: whereas in the earlier work, she is one among many disparate characters, both winners and losers, upright or evil, in the later work, her figure is subordinate to the monolithic narrative of the brothers' vendetta. The differences between the two extant versions of *Soga* reinforces this theory; the *kanabon*, which contains the passage cited above, greatly favors the brothers' side and omits details given in the *manabon* version that flatter the "enemy" side. The impression imparted by the kanabon, therefore, is that all the blame is to be placed on the murderer of the father and that the brothers are heroes who corrected a wrong. Hashihime is employed as a device to glorify the implement with which the brothers commit the long-delayed task.[122]

Hashihime's example shows that there is no simple or consistent equation between a literary producer/presenter's gender and her/his sympathies for a story's characters who share that gender. *Soga* might subvert "authority"—the shōgun Yoritomo and his government—through the glorification of a vendetta against a high-ranking official, but it does not privilege the powers of a female demon through the story of Hashihime. The demon, formally represented and understood as a powerful being in *Heike*, is now marginalized for the purposes of extolling the protagonists of the narrative. On the other hand, it shows that the empowerment of a female figure can be unintentional in that it may be a side-effect of the overall generic and textual aims, but even such unintended displays of female powers incite later marginalizations of these powers. In other words, what might appear to be a

---

121. See, e.g., Kitagawa, *Gunki monogatari kō*, pp. 9–10.
122. Amano, "Denkiteki sekai e no keisha," pp. 144–47.

feminist representation of a female demon might not be a product of authorial intentions but a textual effect, or by-product, that nevertheless has significant ramifications. *Yashirobon* names the direct cause of Hashihime's transformation as jealousy born out of a polygynous situation; intentionally or not, her empowerment and capacity for violence are firmly established.

Furthermore, if we suppose that the Hashihime-as-demon narratives interacted with one another as they developed over the centuries, then we can see a dynamic and dialectic continuum of marginalization, empowerment, and marginalization. Jealousy was marginalized, ascribed as "feminine," and feared in a polygynous context; the fear contributed to a woman's demonization, which in turn caused supernatural empowerment; then that power was pacified and tamed (intentionally or not) so that jealousy was containable again. This example clearly illustrates that marginalization is a complex and ongoing process that can create a character who is shunned and feared by society yet possesses differing degrees of power depending on her placement vis-à-vis previous texts that tell her story.

&cs;

I end my discussion of Hashihime with an examination of three noh plays from the Medieval era. The first, *Hashihime*, was possibly written by Zeami (1363–1443). This play begins with the appearance of the commonly found character of a traveling monk. He has completed a retreat at Kibune and is passing through Uji on his way south, when he meets a woman who claims that she is a local villager. She explains that Hashihime is the name of the protective deity of the bridge he just crossed and that she is one and the same as the deity at Kibune. Hashihime, she adds, has been repeating the cycle of rebirth as a human being and as a deity. Asked to elaborate on Hashihime's story by the monk, the villager proceeds to create an elaborate vision of Hashihime as a lonely, pining woman waiting for her lover, and recites the *Kokinshū* poem within this context. She then admits that she is none other than the ghost of Hashihime, who has turned into a demon of resentment, and disappears. She rematerializes in the shape of a demon; she explains the process by which she transformed herself into her present shape and expresses her embarrassment. After describing her permanent wandering status, she disappears again.[123]

---

123. Haga, *Yōkyoku sōsho* 3: 115–18. When Hashihime appears for the second time in her demon shape, she recites the following poem:

This text establishes an unambiguous cause-and-effect relationship between Hashihime's two tropes: she is a pining lover who becomes resentful of her abandoned, solitary situation and turns herself into a demon. By quoting the "samushiro ni" poem in the play, the melancholy Hashihime of waka aesthetics is fused with the violent demon of gunki narratives. The play exorcises this conglomerate figure through the acknowledgment of this threatening figure, the admission of embarrassment by that figure, and the enactment of her disappearance at the end. These moves assure that the demon-born-out-of-polygyny is properly recognized as such and pacified.

Two other noh plays that do not feature Hashihime as a character nevertheless help place Hashihime in a larger context. These plays deal with women as demons, and the context of polygyny is once again foregrounded. In both instances, the female demon is an angry woman seeking revenge for the suffering she experienced in polygynous relationships. These examples therefore bring the issue back to Hashihime's first representation as a woman caught in polygyny and remind us of the potential for disruption present in such conditions.

Demons or demonic transformations are found in several noh plays; *Kurozuka* (also known as *Adachigahara*) in particular, possibly by Zeami or Konparu Zenchiku (1405–ca. 1470), combines both the woman/demon and the gruesomeness of violence found in the earlier setsuwa works outlined above. A group of *yamabushi* (mountain ascetics) reach a place called Adachigahara (Adachi field) in Mutsu province, where they ask for a night's lodging at a woman's house. She provides them with hospitality and leaves the house to fetch firewood for the guests; before leaving, she forbids them to look inside her bedroom. A yamabushi breaks his promise and peeks inside, only to find human carcasses piled up to the ceiling. The group flees, and the woman turns into her demon shape out of anger at their betrayal

---

samushiro ni   koke no koromo wo   katashikite
  ware wo matsuran   uji no tabibito
On a narrow grass mat   laying down   your robe of moss only —
  you must be waiting for me   traveler of Uji.

This poem alludes to the "samushiro ni" poem yet twists it around so that the male monk is now the one waiting for Hashihime to materialize. This textual moment, which subverts the trope of the pining woman in polygyny by turning the tables, undercuts the overall discourse of Hashihime's regret and embarrassment, and illustrates once again that slippages can occur in an otherwise marginalizing discourse.

and chases after them, but the yamabushi chant their spells, weakening her and expelling her from their sight.[124] The play mentions the poem from *Yamato monogatari* noted above and turns the metaphorical usage of the woman-as-demon in the earlier work into a cannibalistic woman/demon, only to have a group of men exorcise her in the end. Whether her transformation was inevitable and whether the yamabushi would have suffered the same fate as the corpses had they obeyed her are left unclear; the yamabushi imposed themselves on her, and she was treating them kindly until they broke their promise. One approach that may shed an interesting comparative light on this play is to read it with the narratives about Ono no Komachi in mind. There are a number of similarities: the location named in this text is in Michinoku province, where Komachi's skull is said to have been placed, the female protagonist has grown old, and she is living a solitary and destitute life, longing for the better days of the past. There is one major difference, however: in Komachi's case, her sexuality has been tamed through the portrayal of old age, but the woman of Kurozuka has instead acquired a collection of corpses. These bodies have been interpreted as symbols of mental scars acquired in past relationships,[125] but they can also be regarded in a more straightforward manner. The sex of the corpses is not specified in the text, but the sex of the yamabushi suggests that perhaps her other victims were men as well; if they were mostly male, then this woman/demon is a manifestation of the possible alter ego of Komachi—that is, the solitary woman who could not be pacified in old age, the lonely woman who takes revenge on the conflated target of men who neglected her and permitted her to become poor and alone and the male sex in general. Whereas Komachi is represented as quietly wandering around in utter poverty asking for Buddhist salvation, this *Kurozuka* woman actively harms those of the same sex as the people who abandoned her. Like Komachi, however, even this fear-inspiring figure is tamed in the end.

Defeat of a woman who becomes a demon occurs in another noh play from a later period. The first half of the plot of *Kanawa* (The metal ring; author unknown; probably fifteenth century), closely resembles the *Heike* passage about the metamorphosis of a woman driven by jealousy and the desire for revenge into a demon who is strikingly similar to Uji no Hashihime. *Kanawa* does not name the demonic transformation as Hashihime, but the

---

124. Koyama et al., *Yōkyokushū*, 2: 137–52, 275–80.
125. Baba Akiko, *Oni no kenkyū*, p. 226.

"shape of the beautiful woman," the first wife of a man who had neglected her in favor of a second wife, becomes "a demon of resentment" at Kibune shrine; some of these details are shared by Hashihime as well. This woman acts out an *uwanari-uchi*, or the practice of a first wife beating the second wife, upon a straw doll; she moves on to a doll representing her husband, but the powers of prayer of the Onmyō (Yinyang) master who has performed a ritual for the husband weakens the demon and causes her final disappearance.[126] The play does not indicate whether the demon was successful in murdering or seriously harming the second wife; the Onmyō spells seem to have affected the demon only when she tried to beat the husband-doll. Here, the only person who emerges unharmed is the man, who, through his multiple relationships with women, had caused pain and anger in the first wife; the two wives, on the other hand, suffer greatly from his deeds without any redemption.[127] Most important, this work makes explicit the process of exorcism that lay outside the textual boundaries in the *Heike* passage: whereas in the latter, the demon was represented within the text as a powerful being who was (it was hoped) pacified through the performance of that text, *Kanawa* incorporates the performance of exorcism within the text itself. Exorcism in this play, therefore, is a *double* process: the staging of the play functions exorcistically, and the play itself contains the enactment of exorcism. This configuration presents two layers of security; the malign threat is definitively pacified, even though she claims that her disappearance is only temporary. The emphasis on the play as a juggernaut of pacification may hint at a rivalry between noh performers and *Heike* reciters: the double exorcism can be read as an advertisement of the play's extra efficacy compared to

---

126. Itō Masayoshi, *Yōkyokushū*, 1: 320–28.

127. Another noh play from the same time period, *Momijigari* (attributed to Kanze Nobumitsu [1435–1516]), presents demons in the disguise of beautiful upper-class women on an outing to view fall foliage. Taira no Koremori is wined and entertained by them and falls asleep, drunk. The demon/woman leaves him in order to undergo transformation, but upon leaving him, she says, "Dozing while waiting for the moonrise, the dew upon the singly laid sleeve is deep; do not awaken from your dream" (Koyama et al., *Yōkyokushū*, 2: 426). A deity appears in Koremori's dream to warn him of the true identity of the women, and he succeeds in defeating the demons in a battle. The reference to the singly laid sleeve suggests an allusion to Hashihime; the woman, described as being sad and lonely at the beginning, laments that promises / sexual liaisons are fleeting. This figure, who embodies female resentment against female-male relationships, is mercilessly slain, and the play ends with the line "[Koremori's] power is indeed fearfully [strong]!"

the single exorcism in the *Heike*. We may find a similar logic at work in the noh tradition itself: since the earlier *Hashihime* is less self-conscious in its display of exorcism, *Kanawa*'s flaunting of its pacificatory powers helps distinguish later noh from its predecessors by virtue of being "better and stronger." This feature may have appealed to the upper-class (polygynous) patrons of the arts, and contributed to the further flourishing of noh.

In this chapter, I have tried to read the two contrasting discourses about a particular "fictional" character in relation to the practice of polygyny in the upper class. Both the pining-female figure and the ferocious demon have the same name, Hashihime of Uji. These two aspects of her character are not simply random qualities brought together by accident; rather, they represent different characteristics ascribed to a woman who is made to suffer because of a relationship with a man. Hashihime, associated with the locationally marginalized from her first appearance, undergoes both further marginalization and periodic empowerment due to her particular position in the textual flow of the various representations of female-male relationships. I have shown that the pining-wife trope can be interpreted as an increasing tendency to aestheticize and domesticate the figure of the ideal lover/wife in a polygynous situation, yet instability and the potential for conflict are always present in the image. In Hashihime's demonic representation, jealousy was isolated for ostracization through its inseparable connection with the demonic because jealousy and resentment were crucial emotions that upset the peace of a polygynous relationship. A figure who embodied jealousy was presented as a target of detestation, which in turn allowed for the creation of a powerful and unsympathetic monster. This dangerous demon Hashihime is quelled in *Soga*, and other nameless women-demons come to be pacified repeatedly in noh plays. The question of jealousy and polygyny continue to haunt and produce marginalizing and empowering narratives long after the thirteenth century. The complex dialectic relationship between marginalization and empowerment weaves dynamic webs that entangle the specific textual production of gender.

To stop at the conclusion that there was a "male plot" in the construction of Hashihime's figure, however, might be too straightforward an analysis. In fact, the two Hashihimes also simultaneously contributed to the construction of *male* desire and positionality within the polygynous system as well as, ultimately, the system itself. In the pining-lover narratives, the man is represented as the agent who is desired and grants visits (which are usually not too frequent) at his will, perhaps even a heartless man who has only vague pity for the woman to whom he had already blown "winds of tiresomeness." The male position is repeatedly generated as a distancing and objectifying one: in poetry, the man wonders with fair certainty that his lover is pining away, or he is even sometimes transformed into an omniscient narrator who paints a picture in which the woman is definitely pining away for her absent lover. In *Hashihime monogatari*, the man becomes almost a passive bystander who stands apart from and above the trials and tribulations of his faithful female partners. Indeed, the figure of the waiting woman and the man whose visits are infrequent may sound extremely familiar, naturalized, and "real" precisely due to their repeated appearance in texts that situate the woman and the man within polygynous relationships in this manner. In order for the logic of polygyny—that is, one man visiting multiple women—to function successfully, those exact positionalities must be presented and received as the norm. Texts that present the pining-wife trope are therefore at once complicit with and responsible for the maintenance and amplification of the vision of polygyny in smooth operation. This does not preclude narratives from being both complicit and subversive, however; the example of *Genji monogatari* cited in this chapter illustrates that the trope of the pining woman can be invoked *and* reworked as a critique of polygynous practices.

In the "demon" narratives, on the other hand, the man is situated as a victim overshadowed by a dangerous force; it is not entirely clear whether it is possible to prevent what is presented as the unlucky predicament of having selected a lover whose jealousy fuels ferocious rage. In these ways, jealousy and a man's ordeals in dealing with this problem also come to be naturalized as being part of the polygynous system. This "explanation" displaces the potential problems that polygyny can generate solely onto so-called female jealousy and then attempts to attribute this quality to a supernatural being, who can then be exorcised. The discourse, however, has loose ends: it permits, in turn, the existence of a violently empowered woman-demon and casts the man in a defensive role, the recipient of her wrath. In this manner, the trope of Hashihime of Uji constructs the "experience" of women and men in polygyny, outlines the boundaries and the expectations of its practice, and points to the ways in which such constructions nevertheless fail to render seamless the system they legitimate.

Epilogue

This book begins with the question "What is a margin?" Throughout, I have attempted to outline the contours of specific instances of textual marginalization that constructed each separate instance of a "margin" and the resulting textual effects. I have also suggested that these effects, although constructed, nonuniform, nonmonolithic, and certainly nonuniversal, could accumulate and produce further and broader consequences. It is these effects and consequences to which I turn in this last section to conclude this discussion of the relationships between gender and marginalization.

The three parts of this study address different targets and qualities singled out for marginalization: the representations of women entertainers varied according to generic concerns or desires for religious enlightenment, Ono no Komachi was portrayed as an impoverished wanderer or as a skull in a geographically peripheral location in an attempt to domesticate her sexual and literary powers, and Hashihime was pacified both through her aestheticization and through the taming of her demonic capacity. In each of these examples, marginalizing processes produced effects that affected gendered powers which were not necessarily the direct targets of criticism in each instance. In other words, the marginalization of one figure and her associated characteristics led to the indirect yet significant lessening of some of her other powers.

For example, in the case of women entertainers, the power that was diminished stemmed from their sexuality; this move was accomplished in two ways. First, during the eleventh through early thirteenth centuries, these women were marginalized through analogies to certain Chinese sources that described "barbarian" peoples and through the ascription of "sinfulness" to their very existence by rival Buddhist practitioners. The sexual powers of the asobi and kugutsu became associated with discourses of the "peripheral" and "sinful" through the presence of these concepts in texts that supposedly "described" their lifestyle and "expressed" their views; consequently, such marginalizing processes resulted in the diminishing of female sexual power in these texts. Second, another layer of marginalizing tendencies appears in modern Japanese- and English-language scholarship on women entertainers. Twentieth-century scholars assume the "marginality" of these women as a fact and interpret songs attributed to them in a manner consistent with such assumptions. Female sexual power, again, comes to the forefront: Why might these scholars tend to view prostitution as *a priori* "marginal" and easily imagine the profession as having generally been considered "sinful"? Scholarship proves to be inseparable from its context; modern or contemporary understandings of prostitution marginalize, intentionally or not, the female sexual powers of Heian and early Kamakura women entertainers.

What might have been some of the effects of textual marginalizations during the tenth to early thirteenth centuries? Scholars have argued that changes in the Medieval period suggest that women entertainers were increasingly ostracized from society in more obvious ways that manifested themselves in legal, political, and social formations.[1] But this approach, which stresses temporal comparisons, is fueled by a desire to narrate a continuity between women entertainer/prostitutes from the Heian period all the way to the *mizushōbai* ("sex industry") women of today.[2] This idea of a continuous group lineage encourages certain modern scholars to apply contemporary notions about prostitution to the figures of the asobi and kugutsu. It is, however, difficult to argue that oppressive measures in later centuries are based completely on textual claims made in earlier times. Is it possible to talk about "effects" without resorting to the idea of seamless continuity? As an alternative, I suggest that such diverse individual marginalizing processes produce effects, each of which creates different understandings of the marginalized; it should be possible to study them without claiming an unbroken lineage for women entertainers.

---

1. See, among others, Amino, *Chūsei no hinin to yūjo.*

2. See, e.g., Takikawa Masajirō's works, which present sporadic anecdotal analogies between, for instance, the asobi of the Heian period and prostitutes in contemporary Japan.

In the second example of Ono no Komachi, the gendered power that suffers is literary. The history of her figure exhibits both indirect and straightforward attempts to domesticate the power held by female authors. First, I have illustrated the ways in which a female author's oeuvre was posthumously created and re-created through interpretations of her constructed figure. In this case, the empowering qualities of physical attractiveness and literary and cultural capital attributed to Komachi are domesticated through particular understandings of old age; the marginalizing processes generate a complex web of consequences, such as the molding of the types of poems credited to her. The narratives about her figure directly attack overindulgent material prosperity and sexual abundance through the invocation of their consequences (poverty in old age) and do not take their aim at female literary power per se; however, what is affected as a consequence of the complex process of marginalization is in fact her literary power. Komachi's authority over what becomes transmitted as her literary production is not only impaired but thoroughly eradicated by the attribution of poems that fit later compilers' notions about the sorts of poems that would be appropriate in light of her constructed "life story." Second, the texts in which Komachi is presented as a poem-reciting skull include more explicit attempts at mitigating female literary power, with the emphasis shifting to a male protagonist and their insistence on removing half of the credit for her poem to him. This maneuver is taken even further in visual representations that completely divorce Komachi's corporeality from her literary productions. The examples countering such attributions do suggest, however, that such discourses remained highly dynamic and unstable.

The problem of authorial attribution and the construction of literary oeuvres is related to the concept of canon formation at a more general level. It is important here not to conflate the more recent acts of canon formation since the Edo period[3]—which have chosen to exalt a select number of texts attributed to women for specific purposes (such as nationalistic concerns), while excluding most female authors from the canon of Medieval literature—with canon formation during the Heian and early Kamakura eras from which the texts discussed in this book date. Komachi's example shows not only that we must examine closely how and why literary canons have been created in recent years, but also that we need to be cautious about as-

---

3. For discussions on canon formation, see Harootunian, *Things Seen and Unseen*; and Brownstein, "From Kokugaku to Kokubungaku."

sumptions that treat a literary product from much earlier times as static units awaiting the selection processes of later generations. In other words, "ancient" texts are not unchanging objects that become subject to the manipulations of modern canon-formation processes; rather, it seems more useful to conceive of the "canon" as an unstable and motivated construction from the moment a text is created. The very notion of a bounded literary oeuvre should be reconsidered.

Finally, the case of Hashihime displays the efforts to contain and nullify successful demonstrations of female physical power or a woman's capacity for violence. Chapter 5 outlines the ways in which problems rooted in the system of polygyny (such as the often-neglected female lover/spouse and potential explosions of jealousy) were narratively domesticated through the rendering of Hashihime's figure both as a woman pining away for her lover and longing for his visit and as an initially powerful and ferocious demon born out of jealous rage who is pacified in later texts. In other words, in this example, textual efforts to control problems generated by the system of polygyny lead to two ways of suppressing women's ability to cause physical harm to others: one, the denial and avoidance of such powers through a focus on a female figure's imagined aestheticized longing, and two, the recognition of the powers of a woman-turned-demon who eventually succumbs to superior (male) forces. This negation is significant when we consider the particularly prominent roles violence and physical prowess play after the Genpei wars, the establishment of a military government in Kamakura, and the recurring instances of unrest throughout the provinces in the years to follow. Compared to the Heian, which is discursively situated as having been relatively peaceful, these features of the Medieval era become even more striking. In such an age, the discourse of military might and individual strength and heroism appears, and social, political, and even religious powers are equated the capacity to achieve victory through violence. With a few exceptions, women are conspicuously missing from such narratives. The denial of women's physical powers suggests that the potential rewards that could be reaped from such a display were also unavailable to them. Hashihime's example shows how two seemingly different arenas of marginalization—polygyny and militaristic rule—can converge; the webs of marginalizing processes sometimes spread to unexpected places, and this in turn demands that we examine specific historical moments through an approach that considers many different discourses simultaneously.

Appendix

Appendix:
Translations of Selected Texts

Note: Parentheses indicate commentary in the original text; brackets mark my addition.

CHAPTER I

A. *Kanbun Writings About the Asobi and the Kugutsu*

1. *Yūjo [= asobi] no ki*

From the harbor at Yodo in Yamashiro province, go west one day floating upon the great river;[1] this [place] is called Kaya.[2] There is not one who travels back and forth on the three roads San'yō, Saikai, and Nankai who does not take this path. The river winds south and north, here and there and at the villages it divides its flow, as it heads toward Kawachi province. This is called Eguchi. Perhaps it is Aju pasture of the Bureau of Medicine, the Ōba holding of the Housekeeping Office.

When one reaches Settsu province, there are places such as Kanzaki and Kashima. People's houses continue endlessly, their gates all lined up and their doors all in a row. The singing women form groups; poling small boats, they reach the travel ships and offer bedroom companionship. Their voices halt the clouds in the valley, and their melodies linger in the waterside

---

1. The Yodo river.
2. Another name for Yamazaki.

breeze. There is no one who passes by who does not forget all about one's home. The reeds on the sandbar, the petal sprays of waves—from old men fishing to traveling merchants, the bows and sterns of the boats form lines in a crowd, and it is as if there were almost no open water. It may be that under heaven, this is the most amusing place.

Eguchi was started by Kannon. There are Naka no kimi, [missing characters], Koma, Shirome, and Tonomori. Kashima sees Miyagi as their originator. There are Nyoi, Kōro, Kujaku, and Tachimaki. Kanzaki takes Kakohime as their *chōja* [leader]. There are ones like Koso, Miyako, Rikimyō, and Koji. Every one of them is a reincarnation of the Kushira [kokila] bird,[3] and a later incarnation of Sotoori-hime.[4] From high court nobles at the top to commoners at the bottom, there is no one whom they do not lead into their woven bamboo bedding and cast favors upon. Or, they become wives or concubines and are cherished until their death. Even a wise man or a gentleman does not escape from such deeds. Sumiyoshi in the south and Hirota in the west are established as places to pray for business. Hyakudayū, who is especially worshipped, is the same as Sae no kami. If we were to count them one by one, their numbers would reach one hundred thousand. They are good at seducing the hearts of people. Also, these are the customs since the days of old.

During the Chōho years [999–1004], Higashi Sanjōin[5] went to worship at Sumiyoshi shrine and Tennō temple. At that time, the prime minister-priest[6] cast his favors upon Kokannon. During the Chōgen years [1028–37], Jōtōmon'in[7] also went on an outing. At that time, the Uji prime minister[8] patronized Naka no kimi. During the Enkyū years [1069–74], the retired emperor Gosanjō went to this temple and shrine also. Those like Komainu and Koushi lined up their boats and came over. People talked about deities and immortals. These were the auspicious events of recent years.

It is said that a high-ranking courtier or a person of refinement who travels to Kaya from the capital in order to patronize an asobi will love a person of Eguchi. Provincial governors and those below in rank who enter the river

---

3. A bird native to India known for its beautiful voice.
4. See Chapter 2 for details.
5. Senshi, mother of Emperor Ichijō (r. 986–1011).
6. Fujiwara no Michinaga (966–1027), brother of Senshi.
7. Shōshi, consort of Ichijō.
8. Fujiwara no Yorimichi (992–1074).

from the western provinces will love a person of Kanzaki. This is because they all take up with whom they first see. What [the asobi] obtain is called *danshu* [their "fee"]. When it is time to divide [their loot], their sense of honor goes away, the color of anger arises, and large or small disputes become no different from brawls. They cut raw silk into measured lengths, or divide rice grains into portions. Or perhaps there are rules like that of Chen Ping's on "dividing the meat fairly."[9] Those maidservants of good families who stay in boats going up and down the river are called *tanzen* and also "amateur asobi." They get small amounts of gifts, which they use to maintain their daily livelihood. Here, there are the names Keihyō and Tōken. It is according to practice that they command the boats and are paid a part [ambiguous passage].

Even though [a piece about the asobi] can be seen in Gō no Kanrin's preface,[10] I am only recording other things now.[11]

2. *Kairaishi no ki*

Kairaishi have no established places to live and have no houses to protect. Casting a tent [yurt] with felt curtains, they move about, following the water and grass. These resemble the customs of the Northern Barbarians. The men are all adept at the bow and ride horses and make hunting their task. They can also make a pair of swords fly up into the air, juggle seven balls, and make peach-wood dolls dance and have them fight a match. Their ability for making [the dolls] do things that living people do closely resembles the games of turning fish into dragons and beasts. Changing pebbles into money and plants into animals, they [characters missing] well the eyes of people. The women put on "sad-face" makeup, do the "bent-at-the-hip" walk, and smile the "toothache-smile"; donning vermilion and wearing white powder, they sing songs and provide licentious pleasures and thus seek to charm. Their parents and husbands do not [admonish them]. Often they run into travelers, but they do not shun an evening's joyous rendezvous. The fees they receive are such that they are offered embroidered clothes, brocade robes, golden hairpins, and boxes all worth a thousand pieces of gold; there is not one who does not marvel and store them away. They do not plow even one *se* of rice fields, nor do they pick even one branch of mulberry. In this

---

9. A reference to the "Chen Changxiang shijia" chapter in *Shiji*.

10. Ōe no Mochitoki's *Yūjo wo miru*; see Chapter 1.

11. Yamagishi, *Kodai seiji shakai shisō*, pp. 153–56.

manner, they do not subject themselves to prefectural officials, none of them is a regular dweller, and they are naturally equivalent to "drifters." They do not recognize even the royalty at the top, nor do they fear provincial governors. They take not having any taxes and levies as their lifetime enjoyment. At night they worship the hyakugami, beating drums, dancing, and yelling, praying for its aid in bringing good fortune.

In the eastern provinces, those groups at Mino, Mikawa, and Tōtōmi are the most rich and powerful. Groups in Harima in San'yō and Tanba in San'in rank next. Groups in Saikai are at the bottom. Famous kugutsu are Komi, Hiyu, Sanzensai, Banzai, Kogimi, and Magogimi. They move the dusts of Han E,[12] and their echoes surround the beams. Those who hear them wet their hat strings and cannot keep themselves at rest. Song types such as *imayō, furukawayō, ashigara, kataoroshi, saibara, kurotoriko, tauta, kami-uta, saouta, tsujiuta, mako, fūzoku, zushi,* and *beppō* are countless. [These singers] are indeed exceptional under the heavens. Who can possibly not feel compassion toward them?[13]

B. *Kanshi on Kugutsu in* Honchō mudaishi

1. *Kugutsu* (The puppeteers) by Hosshōji *nyūdō*[14]

The kugutsu have often come and gone since the past;
across ten thousand *li* they set up new dwellings.
Divining for the night's lodging, singing alone in the mountain on
    a moonlit night,
they search out [human] traces and never stay put in the misty
    fields of spring.
In her prime, in the flowering capital she basks in her fame and favor;
in her twilight years, she tends the wormwood-roof hut in [his] absence.
Customers en route and travelers on their way avert their eyes in
    pity from afar;
this is indeed due to hair that is white and a face empty and wrinkled.

---

12. Refers to a legend found in Chinese works such as *Liezi* (attributed to Lie Yukou in the Warring States period, but actually probably written in the Wei or Jin dynasty) and *Dushi tongdian* (by Du You, Tang dynasty). Han E is presented as a singer whose beautiful voice lingered in the beams; another singer, Yu Gong, is said to have moved the dust on the beams with his singing. This narrative is the origin of the title *Ryōjin hishō*.

13. Yamagishi, *Kodai seiji shakai shisō*, pp. 157–59.

14. Fujiwara no Tadamichi's (1097–1164) religious name.

2. *Kugutsu* (The puppeteers) by Fujiwara no Sanemitsu (n.d.)

Ah, the kugutsu, those tricksters, crazy folk—
in their own world, grief and joy are all the same [as in ours].
Divining for lodging in the mountains and rivers, in remote places,
they are deeply resentful that old age has come upon their voices and looks.
Traveling and wandering, they completely forget the three-wheeled task;[15]
they don't practice matters of the world, giving themselves to the ten
    thousand *li*.
Travelers en route mingle their collars with them; how can they detain
    them?
When the clouds brighten [at dawn], they know they are off into the
    autumn wind.

3. *Kugutsu* (The puppeteers) by Fujiwara no Mototoshi (1060–1142)

Under the autumn moon, I come out of the pass and head toward a
    faraway city;
the kugutsu come in a crowd and get in my way.
Exchanging promises at the traveler's inn, there is a touch of frost at twilight;
singing, they stay at the station, while the moon goes down.
The eyebrow green, the red powder, all for the sake of her job;
with beautiful songs and the Chu dance they seduce one's emotions.
The piece is finished—filled with pity I take leave of these wandering folk;
[two characters missing] facing them, the promise of a lifetime.

4. *Kugutsu* (The puppeteers) by Fujiwara no Atsumitsu (1063–1144)

Under the tent, they nurture women entertainers to make their living;
the mountains serve as wind screens, the moss is their mattress.
Their dwellings are as among the Xiongnu, they have no fixed place;
their songs are passed down—on the beams there is leftover dust.
At the traveler's inn the moon is frigid, in the evening in search of customers;
at the old shrine the storm blows cold, in the morning they make an offering
    to the gods.
It is hard for them to follow the footprints leading to Chaste
    Woman Gorge,

---

15. The three wheels that support this world: wind, water, and gold; thereby meaning "this world." "Task" indicates the practice of agriculture and residing in a fixed place. In other words, the *kugutsu* "forget" (i.e., do not practice) the everyday work of ordinary folk.

below the "looking out for the husband rock" they try divining for a mate.

By the woven brushwood fence in autumn the flowers wilt, and crickets
    sense the night;

at Aohaka grasses are sparse, and horses await for spring (the place in Mino
    province where the kugutsu live is said to be called Awohaka).

To linger quietly beside the short fence in talk and laughter is fine,

[but] do not enter into intimacy from a fleeting moment's thought.

5. *Kugutsu* (The puppeteers) by Fujiwara no Shigeaki (n.d.)

Those called kugutsu, where are they?

They are always on the move, they never have leisure to think.

At the outskirts they move from place to place, they have no fixed dwelling;

in their travels they sell their charms, longing for success in bed.

In luster they glisten like cherry and peach trees in the spring rain,

in powder they compare to orchid and melilot in the autumn wind.

In the green fields the grasses are deep, they set down a village;

at the mirror-mountain under the cold moon, they divine for a hometown.

They sing some songs in order to make a living;

as a favored woman for a night, she melts her customers' bowels.

What will they do after their years spent in these tents?

Their beautiful appearances will change and depart, wounding their hearts.

6. *Kugutsu* (The puppeteers) by Nakahara no Hirotoshi (n.d.)

The kugutsu, these folk, they follow no codes of conduct,

it is known that there are many women among them.

Rush-thatched eaves they raise near the mountains and forests,

their woven bamboo doors often follow the water-grass as they move from
    place to place.

When travelers come, secretly they feel joy in their hearts,

when people on the road pass on by, they look at them [disappointed].

Singing "Breaking off the Willow Branch," this is how they make
    their livelihood,

they don't pick mulberries for a living, they don't produce off the land.

The arching moth-brows are thin like the waning moon,

the splendid cicada-wing hair hangs down like clouds at sunset.

The fragrant promise of a thousand years—for what husband and wife?

One night's ties their destiny, they must suddenly part.

Those who sell love in Tamba province, they forget about their ugliness (the
    kugutsu women of Tamba province are all said to be unsightly);

those who are famous at Akasaka, many have mustaches around their
mouths (among the kugutsu women of Akasaka in the Mikawa province,
there are many who have mustaches. They are called the *kuchihige-no-kimi*,
so it is said).
They apply rouge and put on powder only seeking to flirt,
so that they may gain favor they pray repeatedly to the kami and
local deities.

7. *The Kugutsu Magogimi* by Ōe no Masafusa (1041–1111)

Traveling on a boat I met her, and my tears were never stinted;
her songs were like a string of beads, they truly rang "ling-long."
Her green-black moth-brows are thin, she wears a gossamer silk robe—this
is on the outside;
her skin like a red jewel, so supple; this is inside her brocade sleeve.
Clouds pause; her voice's reverberating reaches the moon in the clear river
of stars,
the melody flutters up the dust and draws the wind over the painted beams.
Her fame and talent are like this, but her fate is also like this—
why is it that for so many years she has followed tumbleweed?[16]

C. Setsuwa About Asobi

1. *Shōkū and the Asobi-as-Fugen's-Incarnation*: from *Jikkinshō* (Chapter 3, Story 15)

Shōkū shōnin [holy person] of [Mount] Shosha prayed night and day so
that he might see a living Fugen; one night, exhausted from chanting the sutras, clutching a sutra and leaning on his armrest, he fell asleep and had a
dream, which said that if he wanted to see a living Fugen he should go see
the leader of the asobi at Kanzaki. After he woke up, he thought this dream
very strange; he went there and reached the house of the leader. They were
having a banquet and dancing with the duty officers. The leader sat at the
front, beat the *tsuzumi* drum, and kept the beat of the *ranbyōshi*. The lyrics
went, "At the Mitarai shores in Murozumi along the Suō sea / the winds do
not blow but little waves rise." The shōnin went to a quiet corner to worship
and pay respect and stared intently [at the chōja]. At this time, the chōja
suddenly appeared in the form of the bodhisattva Fugen, riding a white ele-

---

16. Toyoshima, *Gunsho ruijū*, 9, bunpitsubu/shōsokubu, pp. 15–16; and Homma, *Honchō mu-daishi zenchūyaku*, 1: 192–208.

phant with six tusks, and from between its eyebrows light shone upon both monk and lay, men and women, both base and noble. Then an indescribably wondrous voice came forth, "In the great ocean of Truth and the Undefiled, even though the winds of the Five Dusts and Six Desires do not blow, there is not a moment when the waves of various relations and True Suchness do not rise." Finding it difficult to hold back his tears of emotion, he opened his eyes; she returned to her form as a woman singing "Murozumi along the Suō sea." When his eyes were closed, her shape appeared as the bodhisattva and performed the teachings of the Buddha. Like this, he bowed in reverence over and over and was about to leave, crying, when the chōja suddenly left her seat and approached the shōnin through an alley. Saying "Do not talk about this with others," she died immediately. An extraordinary fragrance filled the sky, and the scent was strong. Since the chōja had died, the banquet's mood fell low, and [people] shed endless tears of sorrow. The shōnin drowned himself even more in tears, so much so that he got lost on his road back home. Since this chōja was the kind of woman to favor the ways of love, who would have known that she was the incarnation of the bodhisattva? This example shows that the compassionate vow of the buddhas and bodhisattvas [is such that] they use *upāya* [expedient means] to teach sentient beings, and they take various forms to instruct; these forms are not base. This shōnin is a person of no learning. When the Junior Archbishop Eshin [= Genshin] and Archbishop Danna [= Gaku'un] came over to discuss the dharma text, to their question "Can the person who attains enlightenment alone reach the place of the Buddha?" he answered, "To reach or not to reach, this does not matter; it is profitless [to ask]." When they said, "Only by debating the dharma gate shall the eyes of wisdom open. We came because we thought that would not be possible in this kind of countryside." He answered, "This dharma gate was opened by Fugen who came here." At this time, Eshin could not halt the thoughts to follow him in reverence and worship, so he prayed and said to Danna, "Recite words of praise for this hijiri."

> "The colors of my body are like the Golden Mountain
> orderly and majestic, it is indescribable.
> It is as if amidst pure lapis-lazuli
> the true golden image appears,"

so he recited and worshipped.[17]

---

17. Izumi, *Jikkinshō*, pp. 59–60; and Kawamura, *Jikkinshō zenchūyaku*, pp. 189–94.

2. *The Asobi at Muro:* from *Kankyo no tomo* (Part 2, Story 2)

The matter of the lady at Muro awakening her desire to follow the Buddhist path after being forgotten by Kenki.

Was it in the Middle past, the Middle Counselor Kenki[18] had been in love with an asobi from Muro and had exchanged serious vows, but for some reason [their relationship] withered, and he sent her back to the inns at Muro.

This woman said this to her mother: " I didn't intend to come back here, but I thought, while you are alive, how can I not return? So I have come back to my hometown against my will. Even though I am here, I shall no longer behave as I did before;[19] please understand." Thus she never left her house, and she always purified her mind and chanted the nenbutsu prayer. Her parent[s] criticized her, but after a while they no longer said anything. Meanwhile, day by day the state of the household began to decline beyond words. However, she showed no signs of concern.

As the days passed like this, the mother became ill and died. The family had reached a state in which even the bell that was to be rung every seven days could not be managed [because of poverty], so they could do nothing but cry hard all the time. Even the few servants who had remained used the taboo as an excuse and scattered away somewhere.

Matters continued in this way until the eve of the forty-ninth day. That evening, there was a boat that came by full of things all piled up. This woman had one lowly person accompany her and boarded this boat. This boat was that of a low-ranking retainer of the Middle Counselor who had been sent to the country and was on his way back to the capital. Anyway, this owner of the boat was stunned and said, "This is the boat of such-and-such person; how can I let you on board? Certainly you know . . . ?"

[She,] saying "I know. What problem is there?" boarded [the boat]. Now, on the next morning, he had her take fifty units [of money]. This woman, leaving home, said, "My filial offerings to my parent have been completed today," and cut off her hair and left it behind.

She then performed the various Buddhist rituals of that day and distributed [her earnings] among those who served her daily; as for herself she be-

---

18. Minamoto no Akimoto (1000–1047); took the tonsure after death of retired emperor Goichijō.

19. I.e., as an asobi.

came a nun that very day and secured a quiet place and followed Buddhist practices strictly.

Now, as for the retainer on the boat, he went up to the capital and reported to the Middle Counselor, "There was this and that matter." [The Middle Counselor], said: "Ah, in that case, indeed it is that she who seemed to be a superior person [before] still remains a good person now. It is a pity that you had her take so little. If it were to happen again, have her take one hundred." His tears welled up.

When one becomes such an asobi person, this is a result of deeds from past lives; and no matter what it may be, to decide that a peripheral existence is worthless and futile is unprecedented. Those who are forgotten by someone else all pile up resentment upon resentment and place more sins beside sins. To try hard to forget these thoughts and to use them as a means to escape from this sad world—this is indeed splendid. I have heard of many examples in which a person who seemed quite marvelous, because she/he could not endure the resentment in his/her heart, her/his fearful name became famous afterwards; but to actually regard this world as something to be avoided—this especially is without precedent.

I even think that since *Ōjōden*[20] indicates that the Middle Counselor was an extraordinary achiever of ōjō, in the above incident perhaps he first blew the autumn winds of tiresomeness to dye even a sleeve that could not be ruffled [i.e., it would seem in character for him to have begun to express a waning of his interest in her precisely in order to bring forth the color of enlightenment to a person who otherwise would never have awakened].[21]

3. *The Asobi at Muro*: from *Senjūshō* (Chapter 3, Story 3)

The asobi of Muro casts away this world.

In the past, at a place called Take no oka in Harima province, there was a nun who lived in a hut. She used to be an asobi at Muro, and since her appearance was not bad, she was courted by the Middle Counselor Akimoto of the Daigo Genji and had lived in the capital for about a year. For some reason, things came to an end, and after she returned to Muro she did not again behave like an asobi, so it is said.

---

20. *Zoku honchō ōjōden*, compiled by Ōe no Masafusa.

21. Koizumi et al., *Hōbutsushū, Kankyo no tomo, Hirasan kojin reitaku*, pp. 419–21.

One day, she saw someone who served the Middle Counselor aboard a boat going from the western provinces to the capital. She cut off her hair, wrapped it in paper from Michinoku province, and wrote this:

> tsuki mo sezu   uki wo miru me no   kanashisa ni
>   ama to naritemo   sode zo kawakanu
> Endlessly   seeing suffering   due to this sadness
>   I have become a nun, but   my sleeves are still not dry.

So she wrote, and after she threw it upon the boat, she concentrated solely on attaining enlightenment, and at this place she set up a hut and lived there deep in reflection. The Middle Counselor, upon seeing this, shed tears like falling raindrops.

Now, this nun did nothing but chant the nenbutsu prayer night and day, and finally she attained ōjō, which she had sought; there were many people who came and worshipped her [former dwelling]. At the remains of her hut are round wooden posts, decayed—the pillars show the disintegrated wood, which remains to this day. The few wooden joints that had been planted straight make one feel moved. One can't help thinking about how she lived. She was so far removed from villages, her womanly heart unsuitable—in any case, she must have put the hut together, in whatever odd fashion. How did she secure her food? Over and over, this makes one feel so moved. Among women, those who become asobi like this do not feel too deeply about their skills, which are loathed by others, but [this nun's] mind was such that she concentrated upon the sadness of this world and devoted herself [to worship]. I feel that this is extraordinary.

This Middle Counselor was also an extraordinary person who attained ōjō, so it says in an ōjōden ["biographies" of those who have achieved ōjō], so perhaps it is true. An uninterested heart was shaken [by being let go by him], as if the "autumn winds" blew in this world. Now again, I think that they must have become a happy pair of newborn bodhisattvas, and for some reason this is very moving.[22]

---

22. Yasuda et al., *Senjūshō*, 1: 59–61.

D. *Yamato monogatari* (Section 145)

The Teiji emperor [Uda; r. 887–97] went down the river. Among the *ukareme*, there was one called Shiro. He summoned her, and she arrived. Many high court nobles and audience-room courtiers and princes had all gathered there, so she had placed herself far away. "That you have placed yourself so far away, compose a poem about it," [the emperor] said; thus she quickly composed one:

> *hama chidori   tobiyuku kagiri   arikereba*
> *kumo tatsu yama wo   awa to koso mire*
> The beach plover—   there is a limit to how far it can fly, so
> the mountain with clouds rising   [it] does regard as that hazy
> Awa.[23]

so she composed; [the emperor] was very much impressed and gave her rewards.

> *inochi dani   kokoro ni kanau   mono naraba*
> *nani ka wakare no   kanashikaramashi*
> If only [my] life   were something   that could be controlled
> why would parting   be sad at all?

The poem that goes like this is also one which was composed by Shiro.[24]

CHAPTER 3

A. *Tamatsukuri Komachishū sōsuisho*[25]

When I was going down the road, on my way, while I was walking down the path, by the path, off the side of the road, there was a woman. Her face was gaunt, her body thin and tired; her head like frost-laden mugwort, her skin like a frozen pear. Her bones stood out sharply, and her tendons were pro-

---

23. Like the beach plover, which is unable to fly to the mountain in Awa and can only gaze at it from afar, Shiro cannot approach the emperor too closely and can only look at him from a distance.

24. Katagiri et al., *Taketori monogatari, Ise monogatari, Yamato monogatari, Heichū monogatari*, p. 365.

25. The annotations to this text are based in large part on Tochio, *Tamatsukuri Komachishi sōsuisho*.

nounced; her face had blackened, and her teeth had yellowed. Naked, without any clothes; barefoot, she had no shoes. Her voice trembled, she was unable to speak; her legs weak, she was unable to walk. Having already exhausted her food, it was difficult to obtain meals in the morning and evening. All the rice bran and rice mixed with its hull were gone, and her fleeting life was uncertain.

On her left arm hung a broken basket, in her right hand she held a torn straw hat. Off her neck hung a single bundle, and on her back she bore a single sack. What was in the sack? A soiled robe. What was in the bundle? Dried millet and beans. What was inside the straw hat? Black arrowhead from the rice paddies. What was in the basket? Green bracken and fiddleheads from the fields.

Her robe, ripped at the shoulder, hung down at her chest, and her straw raincoat, torn around the neck, hung around her hips. In the middle of the road, bent over she walked almost like a crawl, and on the streets she wandered to and fro.

I asked this woman, saying: "Which place are you from? Which family's child are you? From which village do you come, from which province have you arrived? Do you have a father and a mother? Have you no children? Have you no siblings? Do you have any relatives?"

The woman answered, saying: "I am a child of an entertainer's household,[26] I am from a wealthy and prosperous family. When I was at my peak, my arrogance was extreme; now that I have fallen, my sorrows are deep. I was not yet sixteen, but my fame was equal to three thousand.[27] Adored within the splendid curtains, I never walked outside. Loved within the jeweled blinds, I never went beyond the gates. In the morning, I faced the Luan bird[28] mirror and primped myself by drawing moth-brows; in the evening I took the phoenix hairpin and perfected my glossy beauty by putting my hair up like cicada-wings. In addition, I never went without white powder on my face, nor did I ever stop using rouge on it. My peach-blossom face flowered

---

26. Cf. Bo Juyi's "Pipa xing"; also, "Gushi shijiu shou" (included in *Wen xuan*), second poem: "I used to be the daughter in an entertainer's household, now I am the wife of a dissolute man."

27. An allusion to Bo Juyi's "Changhen ge," in which Yang Guifei (719–56, tragic consort of Xuanzong and a famed beauty) is described as having been lavished with the emperor's attentions at the expense of three thousand other women at court.

28. A mythical bird akin to the phoenix.

in the dew; my willow hair was combed by the wind. My arms were plump, the jade bracelets tight; my skin gleaming, my brocade clothing pulled taut. My radiant face was like lotus blossoms floating amidst the waves at dawn; my pliant hips were easily mistaken for willow branches stirred in a spring wind. Not giving Yang Guifei's[29] flower-eyes the time of day, neither did I consider Li Furen's[30] lotus-eyelashes any competition.

I would not wear a robe if it was not like cicada-wing silk; I would not eat food unless it was rice as white as fangs. Brocade embroidered robes were many in my orchid bedroom; gossamer damask silk robes were overflowing from the cassia palace rooms. My pale yellow sleeves fluttered, as if colorful clouds floated around jade-green peaks; my sleeve's hem sparkled, resembling green waves rolling onto a blue beach. My damask and gauze robes shone upon the earth, and their luminous colors unfurled heavenward. My night dress was soft as rabbit fur, and my sable fur robe was soaked crimson and indigo, its colors rich. My cicada-wing shift and my spider-web skirt were dyed blue-purple, their colors fine. The light shone upon the Qilin[31]-engraved bracelet, and the incense burned fragrant over the mandarin-duck bedding.

The clouds by the Wu Gorge[32] were always upon my collar, and the whirling snow by the Luo River[33] was always in my sleeve. The thin silk socks, the damask silk shoes, collected upon the matting made of "dragon-hair" rush; the pale yellow silk footwear, the silken footwear, lined up by the edge of the ivory bed. Fragrant incense burned ceaselessly, brilliant colors overflowed everywhere. My face, beautifully alluring, was the same as the flower petals opening up, laden with dew. The fragrance, smelling splendid, was no different from orchid and musk scents scattered by the wind.

Ladies-in-waiting, servants both male and female, flanked me left and right; servant men and boys surrounded me front and back. The house was decorated with jewels and jade, and my room was garnished with red and beautiful jewels. The walls were plastered with white powder, and the fences were painted with vermilion and blue-green paint. The eaves were embed-

---

29. See footnote 27.

30. Consort of Emperor Wu of the Han dynasty (r. 140–87 B.C.).

31. A mythical beast with a wolf's head, a deer's body, an ox's tail, and a horse's hoofs; *kirin* in Japanese.

32. One of the Three Gorges along the Yangzi river in present-day Sichuan, associated with a female deity in Song Yu's (290–223 b.c.) poems "Gaotang fu" and "Shennü fu."

33. A river that runs through Luoyang, also associated with a female river deity in Cao Zhi's (192–232) "Luoshen fu," which was modeled on Song Yu's poems (see note 32).

ded with amber, and from the screens hung pearls. Curtains were decorated with halcyons, and the coverings were embroidered with purple swallows. Mica layers were streamed across the windows, and crystals were floated by the door. Corals lined the floors, and on the terraces, agates were inlaid. The light of the red candles graced the nine-branched candlesticks and filled the hall; the blue-purple musk incense embraced a hundred flowers as it permeated the room.

In all things, I did as I pleased, and my myriad thoughts all came into fruition. In dress, I was indulgent, and in drinks and food, I was thoroughly satiated. The red grains of plain rice were steamed in a jade steamer and served in a golden bowl, and the clear brew of green wine filled vermilion jars and was ladled into bejeweled goblets. As for fish marinated in vinegar, I would not put it in my mouth it if it was not the fatty part of red carp; as for vinegared fish, I would not taste it if it was not the gills of the red sea bass. Yellow gibel wrapped in a leaf and baked, green trout grilled, yellow Gui fish[34] tossed in dressing, yellow eel seethed and frozen. For the boiled dish with vegetables, trout of the eastern rivers would be used, and for soup, sea bream of the northern ocean would be cooked. Dried salmon, dried gray mullet, salted eel, tuna marinade, quail soup, wild goose meat pickled in salt, dried phoenix meat, pheasant stew. Goose gizzard, bear paw, rabbit thigh, great deer's marrow, dragon brain. Boiled abalone, toasted clam, baked octopus, roasted sea cucumber. Crab claw, snail intestine, turtle tail, and crane head. Placed upon a silver plate, laid out upon a golden table. Served on a bejeweled bowl, put upon a footed tray flecked with gold and silver.

Also, the delicious fruits from the heavenly peaks were collected, and the delectable vegetables from the spiritual marshes were gathered. The five-colored melon of the eastern gate,[35] the seven-colored eggplant of the western window.[36] The eight-per-bunch apple of Dunhuang,[37] the five-clump plum of Huanghuan.[38] The pear of Duke Zhang of Taigu,[39] the apricot of

---

34. *Siniperca gill.*

35. According to *Youxian ku*, a passage in *Hanshu* (in the biography of Xiao He) says that Zhaoping planted melons outside the Eastern Gate of Chang'an after the fall of the Qin and his loss of rank.

36. Not an allusion; created as a parallel for the "melon of the eastern gate."

37. Cf. *Youxian ku*, in which these apples serve as a parallel for the melons.

38. Huanghuan is a fictitious name created as a parallel for Dunhuang. The plum is an allusion to the five-pitted pear found in *Youxian ku*.

39. An allusion to Pan Anren's "Xianju fu" (Jin dynasty, 265–420).

King Zeng of Guangling.[40] The immortal cassia of the King Father of the East,[41] the sacred peach of the Queen Mother of the West.[42] The peppers of Weinan, clumped like a cow's udder, the dates of Zhaobei, like a chicken heart.[43] The dried persimmon from Mount Tai and Hua peak,[44] the dried chestnuts of the splendid hills and beautiful heights. The red mandarin oranges from south of the mountains, the blue-green citrons from north of the gorges. The white water chestnuts from east of the Yellow river, the green arrowheads from south of the Yangzi river.

All the myriad delicacies named above are rare in flavor and magnificent in scent. Even the queens of the Three Sovereigns[45] and the Five Emperors[46] had not been indulgent to this extent. Even the wives of the Lord of Han[47] and the Duke of Zhou[48] did not spoil themselves this much. My prosperity was in excess, my rewards beyond my station.

Thus at the beginning of the three months of spring when the warbler sings, I toyed with the snow-laden plum blossoms under the curtains early in the morning; at the end of the ninety days of autumn when deer cry, I gazed at the dew-laden chrysanthemums within the screen late in the evening. I awaited the season of flowers to take up the jeweled brush and composed waka poems about the crimson cherry blossoms and the lavender wisteria; I would welcome a moonlit evening by playing a harp with golden strings, making wondrous music with the crane harp and dragon flute. As my mouth blew into the phoenix flute, the dust on the beams swirled,[49] its voice indescribable. I took the wine cup made of nautilus shells; the moon in the sky fell [into the wine cup] with a still shining.

---

40. Possibly a mistake for "the King of Chu"; allusion to apricots unidentified.

41. Husband of the Queen Mother of the West.

42. A female deity; the peach, notable for its delicious taste and its size, ripens only every three thousand years.

43. Weinan (the south of Wei) is here given as a parallel for Zhaobei (the north of Zhao). The peppers and dates are taken from *Youxian ku*.

44. Mount Tai is located in present-day Shandong province, and Hua peak in Shaanxi province. The allusion that refers to persimmons in these areas is unidentified.

45. The Three Sovereigns are Fuxi, Shennong, and the Yellow Emperor (Huang di).

46. The Five Emperors are Shaohao, Zhuanxu, Gaoxin, Yao, and Shun.

47. Probably Emperor Wen (r. 179–157 B.C.).

48. Son of King Wen of Zhou (eleventh century B.C.); assisted King Wu in the destruction of the Shang and the establishment of the Zhou dynasty, later served as regent for King Wu's son, King Cheng.

49. An allusion to wondrous voices making dusts on the beams fly; see note 12 above.

Thus the children of the emperor and courtiers fought day and night to propose marriage to me; the rich and noble guests all competed to set a wedding date. Despite these wishes, my parents did not permit them, and my brothers would not hear of it. Their only ambition was to make me an empress, and they had no intention of letting me be a wife of an ordinary family.

However, at seventeen I lost my caring mother, and at nineteen my compassionate father passed away. At twenty-one my older brother expired, and at twenty-three my younger brother died. My sorrowful wails like the cries of a lone crane resounded in the skies and echoed faintly; the parting voice of the migrating wild goose was heard in the western reaches, and my despair was heartfelt. In the morning I shed tears alone in the house; in the evening I felt stomach-severing pain under the lonely eaves. Serving women ceased to wait on me; serving men stopped working for me. The riches began to disappear, and my clothing and food became coarse. The house began to deteriorate, and the wind and frost crept in during the darkness. The gate and door were already in disrepair, blocked by the wild grasses and trees. Bramble and brier grew thick inside the courtyard; foxes and badgers lived in the back. Bats made their dwelling in the eaves, and crickets made themselves at home on the wall. The light of fireflies abundant; the sound of thunder rang through. The root of happiness had already withered as the leaves of trouble grew of their own accord. The household wealth was rapidly exhausted, and I was left alone as an impoverished orphan. Any leftover grains I gave as offering to the Buddha; any remnants of silk cloth I gave as offering to my deceased parents in return for their former love for me. What little remained of my inheritance, I sold it all; what property happened to be still left, I sold every last bit.

Oh, how sad! In the past I had heard of a solitary widower, left alone in the household. Now, it is a lonely single old woman, wandering around the streets. Rather than loitering around the world of people in vain, leading a life of shame, what would be better than returning to the Way of the Buddha and practicing virtuous deeds for the sake of the afterlife? As I humbly see it, gold hairpins and jeweled bracelets cannot serve to decorate the Buddha; embroidered clothes and silk collars are no use as a nun's robe. With this, I want to shave off the random lengths of my frost-colored hair and to avoid the place where the Six Dusts[50] settle; I shall shave off what little re-

---

50. Form/color, sound, smell, taste, touch, [distracting] thoughts; these "dusts" obstruct the mind's path to the Buddhist Way.

mains of my snow-colored hair to in order to return to the border of the Three Treasures.[51]

In the days when I toyed with the Luan-bird mirror in my hands, I drew my eyebrow with blue-green liner, admiring my own appearance; when I receive the magic "goose" jewel ball atop my head,[52] the light from the white hair between the Buddha's eyes[53] will drench me, and I will possess the moonlit Buddha-body. I should of course become a nun and return to the way of the Buddha, following monks' example by listening to the dharmas. However, I have no robe to be dyed, no food to give as offering. Even though I only want to [follow this path] with one mind, I have yet to be able to rely upon the Ten Powers.[54] I pray to the various Buddhas, please lead this lonely body to salvation, and so on . . . ."

I heard these words, and I myself have quoted what she said. I looked up to the blue skies and wept sadly, and under the white sun I lay down and sang sorrowfully. Thinking about it indeed: riches and nobility are distributed by heaven, and the color of clouds in the east, west, south, and north are unstable. Love and enjoyment are human feelings, but the voice of the wind of birth, old age, illness, and death is ever-changing. I say to aging women: Who can maintain one's riches and status forever? I want to say to lonely old widows: Whose child is able to spend many years in comfort?

Therefore, I have studied from the *shi* of Content-with-heavenly-will's "Qinzhong yin," and learned from the *fu* of Fortunate-earth's "Lushang yong."[55] I made the rhyme according to the old style and have chosen new content to compose a poem in this manner.

---

51. Buddha (the enlightened), *dharma* (the teachings), *saṅgha* (the monkhood).

52. An allusion to a *maṇi* (magic jewel) swallowed by a goose; see vol. 82 of *Fayuan zhulin* (A Tang dynasty Buddhist encyclopedia compiled by Daoshi; see Teiser, "T'ang Buddhist Encyclopedias," pp. 109–28).

53. One of the thirty-two aspects of the Buddha.

54. The Ten Powers of the Buddha: (1) the power to distinguish between the reasonable and unreasonable, (2) the power to know the relationship between karmic deeds and retributions, (3) the power to know the meditations, (4) the power to know the superiority and inferiority of the nature of sentient beings, (5) the power to know the wishes of sentient beings, (6) the power to know the truth about sentient beings and all phenomena, (7) the power to know to which realms sentient beings have gone, (8) the power to recall the past lives of oneself and others, (9) the power to know where sentient beings will be reborn, and (10) the power to know the methods to attain enlightenment.

55. Content-with-heavenly-will (Letian) is Bo Juyi's *zi*, or "style name"; Fortunate-earth (Xingdi) is probably Cao Zhi, according to Tochio. "Qinzhong yin" and "Lushang yong" have

One hundred twenty-four rhyming couplets:[56]

> By the roadside there is an old woman
>> her appearance so very feeble.
> Her vital force completely exhausted
>> her face completely gaunt.
> On her body, ragged clothing like leaves in the wind
>> in her mouth, she rarely even eats flowers laden with dew.
> In the summer she does not make up her eyes beautifully like
> lotus blossoms
>> in the spring she does not draw her willow-eyebrows.
> Her crane-feather colored head is like frost-laden mugwort
>> her back, spotted like blowfish, resembles a frozen pear.
> She bends her crown over to comb her hair falling on her temples
>> she scratches her head to pick out her remaining whiskery hairs.
> In walking, she is ever more feeble
>> in her ways she looks so exhausted.
> "The bitterness! Having been separated from my father and mother
>> many times the seasons have come and gone.
> How sorrowful! Having parted from my parents
>> many years have arrived anew.
> The frosts have sealed their bodies in the dim grave
>> the daylight exposes the corpses of the old gravemound.
> The pines grow old, the wind rustles through
>> the mugwort thrive, the snow falls starkly white.
> My heart burned out, my entrails already about to be severed
>> my blood-stained tears stream down first.
> Snapping my fingers, my eyelids refusing to close
>> deep in navel-biting regret, I can't think, chin propped in hand.
> My chest and liver are pulverized, yet still grief remains
>> my stomach and gall are shattered without a trace.
> What I want to tell the Buddha and speak to the monk
>> is about the debt of love I received from my parents.

---

only tenuous connections with the content of the poem that follows, according to Katagiri, *Ono no Komachi tsuiseki*, pp. 49–50.

56. In actuality, there are 131 rhyming couplets. The discrepancy may be due to changes that occurred across versions.

As I was spending my years as a lonely widow
    I married a hunter.
The hunter had two wives
    I [solitary concubine] did not have a single maidservant.
The two wives cursed each other in prayers
    and I alone grieved over myself.
As I spent my days in sorrow
    I gave birth to a boy.
The boy looked beautiful
    but my body declined in shapeliness.
I did not lament over my gaunt figure
    but thought of the plump face of my child.
My skin was full of boils and bruises
    my bones and muscles hurt everywhere.
My eyebrow-black, long abandoned with my mirror
    in my jasper box, a jeweled mirror in long disuse.
In the autumn frost I combed my white hair
    by the waves of dawn, I washed my yellowing wisps.
My lips chapped, rouge could not moisten them
    my face wrinkled, my powder not smooth.
When I was rich, I used to play in the depths of a wealthy house
    when I was noble, I had played around by the little fence in the
    women's quarters.
Under the moonlight I smiled faintly
    in front of flowers I strolled languidly.
The embroidered curtains of brocade and gold yarns
    strands of jewels decorated the [curtain] panels.
The carriage with phoenixes crossing their wings
    the horse-cart drawn by fast horses all lined up in a row.
But in poverty, it is difficult to continue my dew-like existence
    being lowly, it is easy for my looks to wane.
After sunset, I slept by an abandoned back gate
    when mornings came I lay down by the broken doors.
The mandarin ducks' wings did not touch
    the flounders' fins were not next to each other.[57]

---

57. The implication is that the husband and wife did not get along. An allusion to Luo
Yuan's text Erya yi (Song dynasty, 960–1279), which states that flounders always travel in pairs.

For my child to wear, I went begging for baby clothes
    for my husband to wear, I went looking for thread and fabric.
I stayed by my husband as the purple swallows do[58]
    I loved my child as the pheasants do.[59]
The eggs and baby pheasants lived in the depth of the nest
    the pair of swallows were by the old fence.
The fence tilts and they cry, "nan-nan"
    the nest tips over and they chirp, "zi zi."
Unlike the pheasants and the swallows,
    husband and wife argued constantly.
Thinking about the eggs and baby birds
    mother and child often comforted one another.
When my child grew thinner, I was at a loss
    if my husband was angry, what could I do?
When clothing was poor, I let him beat me with a cane
    when food and drink were coarse, he would hit me with a whip.
The husband had no talents in the arts
    the wife was righteous but was the poorest of the poor.
He had no interest in household matters
    I was inadequate at managing household funds.
In the old days, I had been keen about everything
    now, I was no good at anything.
The fisherman rows out in the autumn waves
    the weaving-woman weaves in the frost at dusk.
On the green fields the plow has been long abandoned
    on the dark planting mounds the hoe has been left for a while.
In the meager paddies, rice is sparse
    in the barren fields, wheat is scarce.
Hunting our only livelihood,
    unable to save even a little bit.
Eating hoofed animals of the forest to pass a day,
    being helped in passing the days by the winged animals
    over the fields.

---

58. An allusion to, for example, Yü Jianwu's poem "He Jin Anwang yongyan shi" (Liang dynasty, 502–57), which describes pairs of swallows as being inseparable.

59. An allusion to Ma Rong's "Changdi fu" (Eastern Han dynasty, 25–220).

For a morning meal, the geese and duck of the marshes,
    in the evening kitchen, the great deer of the peaks.
Tough tendons fill the jars and bowls
    brain and fluid crowd the cups and platters.
The stinking rotten meat of animals that run
    the smelly fat of birds that fly.
The raw stench scatters over one's lips
    and the foul odor lingers in the nostrils.
The sin of one's life is limitless
    the suffering after death is incomparable.
I wish to part with the Six Dusts
    and want to receive the Three Treasures.
Bats lived in the weathered house
    foxes and badgers made their dwelling in the torn-down abode.
Crickets chirping loudly hung onto the wall
    cicadas cried by the back door.
Black snakes looked in the lattice window in the moonlight
    poisonous snakes lined up along the cloud-shaped beam.
Thorn bush and spiny orange are difficult to cut away
    wormwood has not yet been trimmed away.
By the old threshold the sad winds arise
    by the desolate window the tear-dews pile.
Suffering I spent many years
    grieving I passed myriad hours.
Gone, never to return: my peak years
    here, never to leave: my decayed figure.
The moonlight shines less brightly
    and the color of frost is colder.
My remaining days almost gone, so few
    my years left to live so short, how many more?
I pray to the heavens for riches and nobility
    I pray to the earth for joy and prosperity.
I look for the auspicious grasses in the blue gorges
    I seek the rare herbs in the green peaks.
In the past, there were no true words
    now as before, there are only lies.

Lying starved, we seek wondrous medicines
    sick in bed, we ask for a good doctor.
Removing my snow-white hair I shall return to the Buddha
    shaving my frost-colored hair I shall become a nun.
Shedding the clothes dusty from the roots of desire
    I will wear the dharma-robe of the absolute.[60]
Grieving over the cycle of reincarnation in the Six Realms[61]
    pitying the coming-and-going to the Three Paths.[62]
My parents have gone ahead, I have fallen behind
    my child died from illness and my husband also passed away.
My parents gone, I have nowhere to turn
    my husband and child dead, I have no one to rely on.
Happiness in front of me is not worth anything
    I will focus solely on the joys in my afterlife.
The only thing to abhor is defilement
    and what I wish for is the absolute.
Autumn nights are deep and endless
    spring days are leisurely and slow.
Wiping my tears I lie in self pity,
    my stomach torn, I get up and smile bitterly.
My sleeves are hardly ever dry
    in the long nights I often stand up my pillow.[63]
My sorrow overflows from my heart
    the anger in my soul fills my chest.
Forever continuing to make offerings for the sake of ōjō,[64]
    immediately making food for the awakening of faith [and
    becoming a nun].

---

60. An existence that does not owe itself to karmic causes.

61. Hell, hungry-ghost, animal, *asura* (deities at endless war), human, *deva* (a form of heavenly being).

62. The three evil realms of hell, hungry-ghost, and animal.

63. Instead of putting her head on the pillow laid normally and going to sleep, unable to sleep she stands it up on its side and leans on it.

64. Rebirth in the Pure Land after one's death.

"Fishing for the Heart Fish" in the Ocean of Wisdom[65]
>"running the Mind-Horse" to the Dharma Castle.[66]
The august wind blows refreshingly
>the dharma rain falls comfortingly.
The wisdom sun's rays are bright
>the colors of the clouds of compassion are clear.
In life after life, if the teachings are correct,
>then in generations we shall rely upon [the Buddha] undoubtedly.
Quickly bidding farewell to the *sahā* realm[67]
>rapidly I will visit the gardens of Ultimate Joy.[68]
I will have the two reverends[69] as my friends
>and make my master the one Buddha.[70]
For the color of flowers I shall fold the thousand petals[71]
>>for the light of the lamp I shall hold up the nine-branched candlesticks.
I will observe the aspects of the Three Bodies[72]
>and behold the ten-thousand virtues of the buddhas' deeds.
I will walk among the gemlike stamens of the jeweled trees
>and play by the jade pond of the jasper spring.
I will frolic in the depths of the clouds in the sky
>and have fun below the moon in the land up above.
In the country of peace and joy, there is no anger
>in the village of true joy, there is beatitude.

---

65. An analogy between the difficulty in fishing for a single fish in a vast ocean and the suppression of one's desires.

66. To run the horse of the dharma-mind in order to save errant sentient beings.

67. This world of suffering.

68. The Pure Land.

69. Amitābha and Śākyamuni.

70. Amitābha.

71. Petals of the lotus blossoms in the Pure Land.

72. The dharma body (the enlightened, transcendental body), the reward/enjoyment body (the body that is granted to bodhisattvas for their deeds), and the accommodative body (manifestations that appear to guide sentient beings).

Wandering around the ten direction realms[73]
    I will hear the Perfect Teaching[74] preached.
The birds by the pond will chirp the Three Treasures
    up and down, they fly about here and there.
The winds fan, chanting the Four Virtues[75]
    they blow moving and fluttering.
The parrot stands by the golden beach
    the mandarins ducks play by the jeweled embankment.
The wild geese at the frontier fly over the little green waves
    the cranes on the sandbar dance by the crimson stream.
The birds fly off and keep going
    they whirl and soar, then return to their group.
Hearing all this, the Three Karmas[76] are purified
    seeing this, the Six Roots[77] are cleansed.
Bearing the Buddha Nature upon their jeweled wings
    they chant the dharma sounds off of their precious-stoned beaks.
The golden stream bears deep waters
    in the jade marsh pure ripples arise.
On the betreasured trees there are layers of nets
    upon the golden lotuses there are many spools of thread.
For the sounds, compositions of skilled music
    the harp, the melody flowing naturally.
The *huo* music[78] that praises by the songs and dances
    the great bell, a virtuoso with the correct music.
The superb, amusing tunes are plucked out under the storm
    the wondrous sounds are struck under the moon.
The *xiao* pipes, the flute, the harp, the lyre
    their sounds are clear and pleasing.
The *pipa* lute, the bell, the cymbal
    their resounding is so splendid.

---

73. Places where sentient beings live: east, west, south, north, southeast, southwest, northwest, northeast, above, and below.

74. The teaching of the Buddha.

75. Virtues for the attainment of enlightenment: permanence, peacefulness, selfhood, purity.

76. Action, speech, and thought.

77. The six sensory organs: eyes, ears, nose, tongue, body, and mind.

78. Music of the Shang dynasty, specifically of King Tang's court.

The compositions of the jeweled flute and the golden *zeng* harp,
 the knot-rests of the bejeweled *qin* and *se* harps.
The thoughts of joy grow bigger
 the feelings of pleasure become easier.
During the day and at night I know the blossoming of the lotus
 at dawn and at dusk I realize the withering of flowers.
The lotus platforms of the Nine Grades[79] overlapping
 the flowered seats of the Three Bodies lined up.
Golden ropes lie at the border of the Pure Land
 jeweled nets are hung by the garden fences.
The belvedere made of agate
 the palace tower adorned with lapis lazuli.
Playing in the seven-jeweled palace
 living in the apartments of a thousand alabaster tiles.
The phoenix-shaped roof tiles, arranged like crystal gems
 the mandarin-duck roof tiles, lined up like auspicious stones.
The jeweled lattice windows flow across the golden beams
 the silver foundation stones float the jade supports.
The life of the Buddha is without limit
 its auspicious aspects cannot be fully known.
Its eyes are like the four great oceans
 its head is like five Sumeru mountains.[80]
It is as if the colors of the autumn snow had been collected
 it is something that can be compared to the light of the moon at
 dawn, gathered.
[The Buddha's] auspicious aspects are awe-inspiring
 its Buddha-virtues august.
At its top there is the light from the *uṣṇīṣa* [81]
 within this light are Buddha-manifestations.
Between the eyebrows, there is the aspect of the white hair
 besides these two are the surrounding bodhisattvas.

---

79. In Pure Land thought, there are nine different grades of ōjō as well as nine levels in the Pure Land.

80. A great mountain at the center of the Buddhist universe, surrounded by the four great oceans.

81. The protruding forehead of the Buddha.

I wish to be reborn in that land
    may my wish be granted.
First those who have established karmic connections shall be led
    then those practicing shall be invited.
Poling the boats and rafts on the crossing to the Pure Land
    sent off on the oceans of life and death.
Linch-pinning the carriages and pull-carts of compassion
    crossing the mountains of the roots of suffering.
Pitying the home village of the Six Realms
    visiting the former settlement of the Four Births.[82]
Bowing at the ruins of the Mount Gṛdhrakūṭa[83]
    paying respect at the ancient place of kukkuṭapāda-giri.[84]
At dusk when the soul is sealed into the white coffin
    is the time when the eyes will open on the blue lotus.
The August One of the West[85] leads me
    that he will guide is undoubted.
The teaching of the Middle Path[86] takes pity on me
    the compassion will not betray me.
So I may praise the Buddha Vehicle[87]
    I have taken up the brush to compose this poem."[88]

---

82. The four types of living beings: those born from wombs, those born from eggs, those born from the damp (i.e., insects), and those born out of past karmic deeds (those in hell and those in the *deva* realm).

83. The place where Śākyamuni preached his teachings.

84. The place where Mahākaśyapa, one of the disciples of the Buddha, entered meditation.

85. Amitābha.

86. Buddhist teachings.

87. The vehicle represents the teachings of the Buddha.

88. Tochio, *Tamatsukuri* (Iwanami bunko), pp. 29–164. Whether the quotation mark belongs here or earlier in the poem is open to debate. The first seven lines take the point of view of a third-person author looking at the old woman, but most of the rest of the poem appears to be the old woman's monologue; the last line may again be the voice of a third-person author, declaring the reason for the composition of this poem, or it may still be the voice of the old woman herself.

CHAPTER 4

A. *Shūchūshō*

1. *Aname aname*

> akikaze no   fuku ni tsuketemo   aname aname
> ono towa naraji   susuki idekeri

(Dōmōshō)

According to Kenshō, *aname aname* means "oh, my eyes are in pain, in pain!" (Generally, this poem's meaning, according to *Gōki*: the fifth-rank Middle Captain Ariwara no Narihira took the tonsure because he had wedded the empress [the future Nijō Empress]. After that, in order to [have a chance to] grow his hair [back, he traveled and] reached the province of Mutsu, and he stayed at Yasoshima looking for Ono no Komachi's remains. When he was lodging on this island, all night long there was a voice, saying *"akikaze no / fuku ni tsuketemo / aname aname*, etc.: the autumn wind / every time it blows / oh, my eyes! my eyes!" The next morning he went looking for it, and there was a skull with bracken and fiddleheads in its eye socket. The Middle Captain Narihira wept, and said *"ono towa naraji / susuki idekeri*: it is not Ono / a little field / the pampas grass has come out," and he immediately buried it.)

Dōmōshō says: "This poem is in the collection of poems by Ono no Komachi. In the past, there was a person going through a field. S/he heard a voice reciting this poem, much like the sound of the wind. When s/he stopped and searched for it, listening, there was a skull with pampas grass coming out of its eye sockets. S/he removed and discarded this pampas grass and placed this head in a pure place and went home. That night, there appeared in a dream someone who said, 'I am the person called Ono no Komachi from long ago. I am happy and indebted,' she said. Thus this poem was included in the collection." (I say, the meanings of these two versions are different. *Gōki* says: "Parting Mutsu, [he] stayed at Yasoshima, looking for Komachi's remains." *Dōmō* says: "Traveling through the field, the voice of the wind; a dream oracle sings, 'Ono in a boat.'" In *Gōki*, it is a linked verse: "All through the night there was a voice chanting the first line.") The voice of the wind in the fields is a linked verse. In a later reign, Narihira added the second line. (*Dōmō* says: "One poem was heard in the voice of the wind"; in *Gōki* there is bracken in the skull, in *Dōmō* it says that pampas grass was growing.) *Kokin no mokuroku* says, "Ono no Komachi was a daughter of a district head of Dewa province." For several decades [she] lived in the capital favoring the ways of love. But she returned to her home province to die. Therefore (her remains are in Yasoshima, perhaps?) Ono is perhaps her surname (or her address). In *Kokinshū*, there is a poem by Ono's elder sister:

> toki sugite   kareyuku ono no   asaji nizo
>   ima wa omoi no   taezu moekeru
> Past its season   withering in the little field   the
> short cogongrass;
>   now, the thoughts   burn ceaselessly.[89]

I say, this poem contains the phrase *ono*. It lists her own name. Did this just come about naturally?[90]

B. *Fukuro zōshi*

Ono no Komachi

> akikaze no   uchifuku goto ni   aname aname
>   ono towa iwaji   susuki oikeri
> The autumn wind   every time it blows,   oh, my eyes! my eyes!
>   it's not only in the little field / I will not say it is Ono   that
> pampas grass grows.

In someone's dream, there was a person along a path in the fields who had pampas grass growing out of her eye sockets. She said, "My name is Ono." She composed this poem. When the person awoke from the dream and looked around, there was a skull. From its eye sockets, pampas grass was growing. The person took the skull and brought it over to a quiet place and left it there. From this, the person realized that it was the remains of Ono no Komachi.[91]

---

89. *Kokinshū*, poem no. 790.
90. Kyūsojin, *Nihon kagaku taikei bekkan*, 2: 254–55.
91. Fujioka et al., *Fukuro zōshi kōshō: zatsudan hen*, pp. 432–36.

CHAPTER 5

A. *Kankyo no tomo*, Part II, Story 3

The matter of a deeply resentful woman who became a demon while still alive.

Was it around the middle past—I heard that it occurred in Mino province. It so happened that a not-so-lowly man became engaged in relations with a certain person's daughter in this province. Since the distance was far, there must have been unintended absences; since [she] had not yet been accustomed to the ways of the world, she firmly came to believe that matters had reached a painful end. Even in their rare meetings, he could sense her suspicions, and the man had indeed come to dread her.

Now, the winter grasses withered away completely, and this woman refused to eat anything. It became the new year, but even during the celebrations, nobody paid any heed to the fact that this person was not eating.

As she always put up a screen and pulled up her bedding over herself, nobody was considerate enough to come near her. As she lived like this, one day she took a nearby bucket full of syrup, put her hair up in five sections, and smeared the syrup upon her hair and let it dry so that it resembled horns. Nobody knew this was happening. She then put on a crimson divided skirt, and after nightfall she secretly ran away and disappeared. This was also undetected by those at home. The family then tried to find her, asking, "This person has disappeared. She had lost her mind due to a no-good man; has she thrown herself in the deep waters or a river?" However, this was not the case, so why would there be any such evidence?

The days passed by like this, as did the months and years. The father and mother both died. About thirty years later, in the same province, in the middle of a wide field there was a broken-down [temple] hall; everyone said that a demon lived in it, and that the demon would snatch up young children who herd horses and cows and eat them. Those who looked from afar claimed that the demon was hiding above the ceiling of the hall.

All the people in the village each said to each other: "Since matters are like this, let's set the hall on fire. Afterwards, we can all gather to rebuild the hall. It won't be a sinful crime because we are not setting it on fire out of hostility for the Buddha." Thus saying, they decided on a date; they held on tightly to their bows and arrow holders, and straightened the gaps between their protective clothing, and drew nearer to the hall. They then set fire to it and burned it; after about half of the hall was burned down, something with five horns with a red overskirt wound around its hips—indescribably repulsive—came running down from the ceiling. "Just as we thought!" said the villagers, and each drew his bow and faced the demon. The demon then said, "I would like to speak for a moment. Don't just kill me in haste." The villagers asked, "Who are you?" To which the demon answered, "I am the daughter of such-and-such a person of a certain place. A regrettable feeling arose in my heart, and I did this and that, and I left. I eventually killed the man who left me. After that, I could not return to my former appearance, and I was wary of people's eyes; without anywhere to live, I have been hiding in this hall. As it was like this, the living body is a wretched thing—I could not bear it when I became hungry. Everything was painful; my suffering has been indescribable. At night and during the day, I felt as if the inside of my body was burning up, I was regretful and felt useless without end. What I wish for is that you promise to gather together and carefully copy the Lotus Sutra in a day, offer it, and pray for me. Also, if among you there are those who have wives (and children), you must tell them what I have told you—preach to them that they must never let rise the thoughts that arose in my heart." The demon then wept and flung herself into the flames and died.

It is a repulsive matter, but it is also sadly moving. Indeed, out of impatience in her heart, she was fooled by a single moment's erratic thought into long suffering—this is indeed regrettable and sad. This person's destination in her afterlife is surely not a good place. Did the villagers make offerings and pray for her—I don't remember whether the storyteller told me that much.[92]

---

92. Koizumi et al., *Hōbutsushū, Kankyo no tomo, Hirasan kojin reitaku*, pp. 422–24.

Reference Matter

Bibliography

Abe Akio et al., eds. and annots. *Genji monogatari*, vols. 2, 5. Nihon koten bungaku zenshū, 13. Tokyo: Shōgakkan, 1972, 1975.

Abe Yasurō. "Seizoku no tawamure to shite no geinō." In Moriya Takeshi, ed., *Geinō to chinkon*, pp. 173–218. Taikei bukkyō to Nihonjin, 7. Tokyo: Shunshūsha, 1988.

Akegawa Tadao. "Komachi densetsu no kōzō." *Nihon bungaku* 31, no. 5 (May 1982): 43–52.

Akimoto Kichirō, annot. *Fudoki*. Nihon koten bunka taikei, 2. Tokyo: Iwanami shoten, 1958.

Amano Fumio. "Denkiteki sekai e no keisha—*Soga monogatari, Gikeiki, fu Kōwakamai kyoku*." In Kitagawa Tadahiko, ed., *Gunkimono no keifu*. Kyoto: Sekai shisōsha, 1985.

Amino Yoshihiko. "Asobi tachi no kyozō to jitsuzō." Special issue: *Nihon no rekishi, chūsei I-3, Asobi, kugutsu, shirabyōshi*. *Shūkan Asahi hyakka* (April 1986).

———. *Chūsei no hinin to yūjo*. Tokyo: Akashi shoten, 1994.

———. "Chūsei no tabibito tachi." In Amino Yoshihiko, ed., *Hyōhaku to teichaku—teijū shakai e no michi—*, pp. 153–266. Nihon minzoku bunka taikei, 6. Tokyo: Shōgakkan, 1984.

———. "Kyōkai ryōiki to kokka." In Asao Naohiro et al., eds., *Kyōkai ryōiki to kōtsū*, pp. 325–71. Nihon no shakaishi, 2. Tokyo: Iwanami shoten, 1994.

———. "Mizube no nigiwai: toshi no dekiru ba." Special issue: *Nihon no rekishi, chūsei I-6, Kaimin to henreki suru hitobito*. *Shūkan Asahi hyakka* (May 1986).

———. *Muen, kugai, raku*. Tokyo: Heibonsha, 1987.

———. "Yūjo to hinin / kawaramono." In Miyata Noboru, ed., *Sei to mibun*, pp. 93–128. Taikei bukkyō to Nihonjin, 8. Tokyo: Shunshūsha, 1989.

Amino Yoshihiko et al., eds. *Ama no hashi, chi no hashi*. Ima wa mukashi, mukashi wa ima, 3. Tokyo: Fuku'onkan shoten, 1991.

Araki Ayumi. "Ono no Komachi no kōshoku setsuwa." *Dazaifu kokubun*, no. 7 (Mar. 1988): 18–23.

Asami Kazuhiko. "Komachi henbō." *Seikei kokubun*, no. 9 (Jan. 1976): 12–34.

Asami Kazuhiko, annot. and trans. *Jikkinshō*. Shinpen Nihon koten bungaku zenshū, 51. Tokyo: Shōgakkan, 1997.

Baba Akiko. *Oni no kenkyū*. Tokyo: San'ichi shobō, 1971.

Baba Mitsuko. "Asobi wo sen to ya umareken." *Kokugo tsūshin*, no. 308 (Spring 1982): 11–19.

———. "Hachiman imayō jigentan: *Ryōjin hishō kudenshū* kan dai jū chūyaku nōto kara." *Shōwa gakuin tandai kiyō*, no. 26 (Mar. 1990): 5–18.

———. *Hashiru onna: uta no chūsei kara*. Tokyo: Chikuma shobō, 1992.

———. "'Imayō gatari' no hōhō to hyōgen." *Kokugo to kokubungaku*, special ed. (Nov. 1991): 61–74.

———. *Imayō no kokoro to kotoba—"Ryōjin hishō" no sekai—*. Tokyo: Miyai shoten, 1987.

———. "*Ryōjin hishō* seiritsu kō: Otomae no shi." In Nihon kayō gakkai, ed., *Nihon kayō kenkyū—genzai to tenbō*, pp. 161–76. Osaka: Izumi shoin, 1994.

———. "Uta to setsuwa." In Honda Yoshinori et al., eds., *Setsuwa no kōza, 6, setsuwa to sono shūhen—monogatari/geinō*, pp. 143–63. Tokyo: Benseisha, 1993.

Bell, Catherine. *Ritual Theory, Ritual Practice*. New York: Oxford University Press, 1992.

Bhabha, Homi K. *The Location of Culture*. New York: Routledge, 1994.

Bourdieu, Pierre. *Distinction: A Social Critique of the Judgment of Taste*. Cambridge, Mass.: Harvard University Press, 1984.

Brown, Todd. "'Even Sinners Like Us': Overtures to Warrior Converts in the *Yūgyō shōnin engi e*." Paper presented at the Association for Asian Studies Annual Meeting, Mar. 1998.

Brownstein, Michael. "From Kokugaku to Kokubungaku: Canon-formation in the Meiji period." *Harvard Journal of Asiatic Studies* 47, no. 2 (Dec. 1987): 435–60.

Butler, Judith. *Gender Trouble: Feminism and the Subversion of Identity*. New York: Routledge, 1990.

Cranston, Edwin A. "Shinkei's 1467 *Dokugin hyakuin*." *Harvard Journal of Asiatic Studies* 54, no. 2 (Dec. 1994): 461–507.

Crewe, Jonathan. "Defining Marginality?" *Tulsa Studies in Women's Literature* 10, no. 1 (Spring 1991): 121–30.

Culler, Jonathan. *On Deconstruction: Theory and Criticism After Structuralism*. Ithaca: Cornell University Press, 1982.

Emoto Hiroshi and Watanabe Shōgo, eds. *Shomin bukkyō to koten bungei.* Kyoto: Sekai shisōsha, 1989.

Enchi Fumiko. "Ono no Komachi." In Enchi Fumiko et al., eds., *Karei naru kyūtei saijo,* pp. 112–34. Jinbutsu Nihon no joseishi, 1. Tokyo: Shūeisha, 1977.

Enoki Katsurō. *Nihon bukkyō bungaku to kayō.* Tokyo: Kasama shoin, 1994.

Finnegan, Ruth. *Literacy and Orality: Studies in the Technology of Communication.* Oxford: Basil Blackwell, 1988.

Foucault, Michel. *Language, Counter-memory, Practice: Selected Essays and Interviews.* Trans. Donald F. Bouchard and Sherry Simon; ed. Donald F. Bouchard. Ithaca: Cornell University Press, 1977.

Fujii Sadakazu. "Sotoori-hime no nagare: Komachi wo sakanoboru." *Kokubungaku: kaishaku to kyōzai no kenkyū* 28, no. 9 (July 1983): 115–19.

Fujioka Tadaharu et al., annots. *Fukuro zōshi kōshō: kagaku hen.* Osaka: Izumi shoin, 1983.

———. *Fukuro zōshi kōshō: zatsudan hen.* Osaka: Izumi shoin, 1991.

Fujioka Tadaharu et al., eds. and annots. *Izumi Shikibu nikki, Murasaki Shikibu nikki, Sarashina nikki, Sanuki no Suke no nikki.* Nihon koten bungaku zenshū, 18. Tokyo: Shōgakkan, 1971.

Fukazawa Tōru. *Chūsei shinwa no rentanjutsu: Ōe no Masafusa to sono jidai.* Kyoto: Jinbun shoin, 1994.

Fukuda Akira. *Chūsei katarimono bungei—sono keifu to tenkai—.* Tokyo: Miyai shoten, 1981.

Fukutō Sanae. *Heian chō no haha to ko.* Tokyo: Chūōkōronsha, 1991.

———. *Heian chō no onna to otoko.* Tokyo: Chūōkōronsha, 1995.

———. "Ukareme kara asobi e." In Joseishi sōgō kenkyūkai, eds., *Nihon josei seikatsushi,* 1, *genshi/kodai,* pp. 217–46. Tokyo: Tōkyō daigaku shuppankai, 1990.

Fuss, Diana. *Identification Papers.* New York: Routledge, 1995.

Geddes, John Van Ward. "A Partial Translation and Study of the *Jikkinshō.*" Ph.D. dissertation, Washington University–St. Louis, 1976.

Geinōshi kenkyūkai, eds. *Nihon geinōshi,* 2, *Kodai–chūsei.* Tokyo: Hōsei daigaku shuppankyoku, 1982.

Gomi Fumihiko. "Goshirakawa hō-ō no jitsuzō." In Kodaigaku kyōkai, eds. *Goshirakawa-in—dōranki no ten'nō,* pp. 3–22. Tokyo: Yoshikawa kōbunkan, 1993.

———. *Inseiki shakai no kenkyū.* Tokyo: Yamakawa shuppansha, 1984.

Goodwin, Janet. *Alms and Vagabonds: Buddhist Temples and Popular Patronage in Medieval Japan.* Honolulu: University of Hawaii Press, 1994.

Gorai Shigeru. "Chūsei josei no shūkyōsei to seikatsu." In Joseishi sōgō kenkyūkai, ed., *Nihon joseishi,* 2, *Chūsei,* pp. 103–36. Tokyo: Tōkyō daigaku shuppankai, 1982.

Gotō Norihiko. "Asobi to chōtei, kizoku: chūsei zenki no asobi tachi." Special issue: *Nihon no rekishi, chūsei I-3, Asobi, kugutsu, shirabyūshi. Shūkan asahi hyakka* (Apr. 1986): 4-72-82.

Gunsho ruijū, vol. 4. Tokyo: Keizai zasshisha, 1898.

Haga Yaichi, ed. and annot. *Yōkyoku sōsho*, vol. 3. Tokyo: Hakubunkan, 1915.

Harada Kōzō. *Chūsei setsuwa bungaku no kenkyū*, vol. 1. Tokyo: Ōfūsha, 1982.

Harootunian, H. D. *Things Seen and Unseen: Discourse and Ideology in Tokugawa Nativism*. Chicago: University of Chicago Press, 1988.

Hashimoto Fumio et al., eds. and annots. *Karonshū*. Nihon koten bungaku zenshū, 50. Tokyo: Shōgakkan, 1975.

Homma Yōichi, annot. *Honchō mudaishi zenchūyaku*, vol. 1. Tokyo: Shintensha, 1992.

Hosokawa Ryōichi. *Idatsu no Nihon chūsei—kyōki, tosaku, ma no sekai—*. Tokyo: JICC shuppankyoku, 1993.

———. *Onna no chūsei: Ono no Komachi, Tomoe, sono ta*. Tokyo: Nihon editā sukūru shuppanbu, 1989.

Hyōdō Hiromi. *Ōken to monogatari*. Tokyo: Seikyūsha, 1989.

———. "*Yashirobon no isō.*" *Kokubungaku: kaishaku to kyōzai no kenkyū* 45, no. 5 (Apr. 1995): 76–82.

Ichiko Teiji, ed. and annot. *Heike monogatari*, vol. 2. Kan'yaku: Nihon no koten, 44. Tokyo: Shōgakkan, 1985.

Ichiko Teiji and Ōshima Tatehiko, annots. *Soga monogatari*. Nihon koten bungaku taikei, 88. Tokyo: Iwanami shoten, 1966.

Ikeda Shinobu. "Kassen-e no naka no joseizō—'sei' wo shirusareta karada—." In Itō Seiko and Kōno Nobuko, eds., *Onna to otoko no jikū—Nihon joseishi saikō, 2, Onna to otoko no tanjō—kodai kara chūsei e*, pp. 166–76. Tokyo: Fujiwara shoten, 1996.

Imahori Taitsu. *Jingi shinkō no tenkai to bukkyō*. Tokyo: Yoshikawa kōbunkan, 1990.

Imazeki Toshiko. "*Irogonomi" no keifu—onna tachi no yukue*. Tokyo: Sekai shisōsha, 1996.

Inoue Mitsusada and Ōsone Shōsuke, annots. *Ōjōden, Hokke genki*. Nihon shisō taikei, 7. Tokyo: Iwanami shoten, 1974.

Inui Katsumi et al., eds. *Nihon denki densetsu daijiten*. Tokyo: Kadokawa shoten, 1986.

Inukai Kiyoshi et al., annots. *Heian shikashū*. Shin Nihon koten bungaku taikei, 28. Tokyo: Iwanami shoten, 1994.

Ishida Jōji et al., annots. *Genji monogatari*, vol. 3. Shinchō Nihon koten shūsei, 18. Tokyo: Shinchōsha, 1978.

Ishida Mizumaro. *Nyobon—hijiri no sei*. Tokyo: Chikuma shobō, 1995.

Ishida Mizumaro, annot. *Ōjō yōshū*, vol. 1. Tokyo: Iwanami shoten, 1992.

Ishihara Shōhei. "Kagakusho ni miru Komachi: aname no susuki wo chūshin ni." *Kokubungaku: kaishaku to kanshō* 60, no. 8 (Aug. 1995): 39–45.

————. "Uji no denshō." In Akiyama Ken et al., eds., *Kōza: "Genji monogatari" no sekai*, 8: 14–32. Tokyo: Yūhikaku, 1983.

Ishizaka Taeko. "Ōchō no 'hashi'—sono kūkansei—." *Bungei kenkyū*, no. 123 (Jan. 1990): 23–32.

Itō Masayoshi, annot. *Yōkyokushū*, vol. 1. Shinchō Nihon koten shūsei, 57. Tokyo: Shinchōsha, 1983.

Itō Takahiro. "Imayō no ba ni okeru shutai no mondai: *Ryōjin hishō kudenshū* kan jū shoshū no sayō wo tegakari to shite." *Ryōjin: kenkyū to shiryō*, no. 10 (Dec. 1992): 18–23.

Iwano Masao, ed. *Kokuyaku issaikyō: shosōbu*, vol. 3. Tokyo: Daitō shuppansha, 1939.

Izumi Motohiro, ed. and annot. *Jikkinshō: honbun to sakuin*. Tokyo: Kasama shoin, 1982.

Izumoji Osamu. *Setsuwashū no sekai*. Tokyo: Iwanami shoten, 1988.

Izumoji Osamu, annot. *Sanbō-e*. Tōyō bunko, 513. Tokyo: Heibonsha, 1990.

Joseishi sōgō kenkyūkai, ed. *Nihon josei seikatsushi, 1, Genshi, kodai*. Tokyo: Tōkyō daigaku shuppankai, 1990.

————. *Nihon josei shi, 1, Genshi, kodai*. Tokyo: Tōkyō daigaku shuppankai, 1982.

————. *Nihon josei shi, 2, Chūsei*. Tokyo: Tōkyō daigaku shuppankai, 1982.

Kakimura Shigematsu, annot. *Honchō monzui chūshaku*, vol. 1. Kyoto: Naigai shuppan, 1922.

Kamioka Yūji. *Waka setsuwa no kenkyū—chūko hen*. Tokyo: Kasama shoin, 1986.

Kanda Hideo et al., eds. and annots. *Hōjōki, Tsurezuregusa, Shōbōgen zōsui monki, Tannishō*. Nihon koten bungaku zenshū, 27. Tokyo: Shōgakkan, 1971.

Kaneda Motohiko. "Komachi to Ono shi." *Kokubungaku: kaishaku to kyōzai no kenkyū* 28, no. 9 (July 1982): 113–15.

Katagiri Yōichi. *Tensai sakka no kyozō to jitsuzō—Ariwara no Narihira, Ono no Komachi*. Nihon no sakka, 5. Tokyo: Shintensha, 1991.

————. *Ono no Komachi tsuiseki: "Komachishū" ni yoru Komachi setsuwa no kenkyū*. Tokyo: Kasama shoin, 1975. 2d ed., 1993.

————. "Saijo wo meguru jitsuzō to kyozō." *Kokubungaku: kaishaku to kanshō* 60, no. 8 (Aug. 1995): 10–18.

Katagiri Yōichi et al., eds. and annots. *Taketori monogatari, Ise monogatari, Yamato monogatari, Heichū monogatari*. Shinpen Nihon koten bungaku zenshū, 12. Tokyo: Shōgakkan, 1994.

Katano Tatsurō and Matsuno Yōichi, annots. *Senzai wakashū*. Shin Nihon koten bungaku taikei, 10. Tokyo: Iwanami shoten, 1993.

Kawaguchi Hisao. "Kusō zu." *Kokubungaku: kaishaku to kanshō* 47, no. 11 (Oct. 1982): 125–28.

Kawaguchi Hisao and Shida Nobuyoshi, eds. *Wakan rōeishū, Ryōjin hishō*. Nihon koten bungaku taikei, 73. Tokyo: Iwanami shoten, 1965.

Kawamata Kei'ichi, annot. *Shiryō taisei: Chōshūki*, 1. Tokyo: Naigai shoseki, 1934.

Kawamura Zenji, ed. and annot. *Jikkinshō zenchūyaku*. Shintensha chūyaku sensho, 6. Tokyo: Shintensha, 1994.

Keene, Donald. *Anthology of Japanese Literature*. New York: Grove Press, 1955.

Kido Saizō, annot. *Tsurezuregusa*. Shinchō Nihon koten shūsei, 10. Tokyo: Shinchōsha, 1977.

Kifune Shigeaki, annot. *Gosen wakashū zenshaku*. Tokyo: Kasama shoin, 1988.

Kim, Yung-Hee [*see also* Kwon, Yung-hee Kim]. *Songs to Make the Dust Dance: The "Ryojin Hisho" of Twelfth-Century Japan*. Berkeley: University of California Press, 1994.

Kishi Shōzō, ed. and annot. *Shintōshū*. Tōyō bunko, 94. Tokyo: Heibonsha, 1967.

———. *Zen'yaku: Azuma kagami*, vol. 3. Tokyo: Shinjinbutsu ōraisha, 1977.

Kitagawa Tadahiko. *Gunki monogatari kō*. Miyai sensho, 18. Tokyo: Miyai shoten, 1989.

Kobayashi Chishō, ed. and annot. *Uji shūi monogatari*. Nihon koten bungaku zenshū, 28. Tokyo: Shōgakkan, 1973.

Kobayashi Shigemi. *Ono no Komachi kō: ōchō no bungaku to denshō kōzō*, vol. 2. Tokyo: Ōfūsha, 1981.

Kobayashi Yasuharu, annot. *Kojidan*, vols. 1–2. Tokyo: Gendai shichōsha, 1981.

Kobayashi Yoshinori et al., annots. *Ryōjin hishō, Kanginshū, Kyōgen kayō*. Shin Nihon koten bungaku taikei, 56. Tokyo: Iwanami shoten, 1993.

Koizumi Hiroshi et al., annots. *Hōbutsushū, Kankyo no tomo, Hirasan kojin reitaku*. Shin Nihon koten bungaku taikei, 40. Tokyo: Iwanami shoten, 1993.

Kojima Noriyuki et al., eds. and annots. *Man'yōshū*, vol. 5. Kan'yaku Nihon no koten, 6. Tokyo: Shōgakkan, 1986.

Kojitsu sōsho henshūbu, ed. *Shintei zōho kojitsu sōsho*, vol. 23. Tokyo: Meiji tosho shuppan and Yoshikawa kōbundō, 1953.

Kokumin tosho kabushiki kaisha, ed. *Kōchū kokka taikei*, vol. 23. Tokyo: Kokumin tosho, 1930.

Komachiya Teruhiko, annot. *Shūi wakashū*. Shin Nihon koten bungaku taikei, 7. Tokyo: Iwanami shoten, 1990.

Komatsu Kazuhiko. *Ijinron—minzoku shakai no shinsei*. Tokyo: Seidosha, 1985.

———. "Yōkai: yamanba wo megutte." In Gorai Shigeru et al., eds., *Kami kannen to minzoku*, pp. 330–55. Kōza: Nihon no minzoku shūkyō, 3. Tokyo: Kōbundō, 1979.

Kondō Yoshihiro. *Nihon no oni—Nihon bunka tankyū no shikaku—*. Tokyo: Ōfūsha, 1975.

Konishi Jin'ichi. *A History of Japanese Literature*, vol. 2. trans. Aileen Gatten; ed. Earl Miner. Princeton: Princeton University Press, 1986.

———. "*Ryōjin hishō*" *kō*. Tokyo: Sanseidō, 1941.

Koyama Hiroshi et al., eds. and annots. *Yōkyokushū*, vol. 1. Nihon koten bungaku zenshū, 33. Tokyo: Shōgakkan, 1973.

―――. *Yōkyokushū*, vol. 2. Kan'yaku: Nihon no koten, 47. Tokyo: Shōgakkan, 1988.

Kubota Jun. "Gaikotsu no hanashi: *Senjūshō* no niwa wo jiku to shite." *Bungaku* 2, no. 1 (Winter 1991): 95–106.

Kubota Jun and Hirata Yoshinobu, annots. *Goshūi wakashū*. Shin Nihon koten bungaku taikei, 8. Tokyo: Iwanami shoten, 1994.

Kudō Shigenori. *Heianchō no kekkon seido to bungaku*. Tokyo: Kazama shobō, 1994.

Kufukihara Rei. "Tawabure uta no jidai: Heian kōki waka no kadai." *Kokugo to kokubungaku* 63, no. 7 (July 1986): 43–57.

Kumagai Tadaharu. "Ono no Komachi no shinjitsu." *Kokubungaku kenkyū*, no. 47 (June 1972): 24–32.

Kurihara Hiromu. *Takamura Itsue no kon'in joseishizō no kenkyū*. Tokyo: Kōka shoten, 1994.

Kuwabara Hiroshi. *Chūsei monogatari no kisoteki kenkyū: shiryō to shiteki kōsatsu*. Tokyo: Kazama shobō, 1969.

Kuwabara Hiroshi, annot. *Mumyō zōshi*. Shinchō Nihon koten shūsei, 7. Tokyo: Shinchōsha, 1976.

Kwon, Yung-Hee Kim [*see also* Kim, Yung-hee]. "The Emperor's Songs: Go-Shirakawa and *Ryōjin Hishō Kudenshū*," *Monumenta Nipponica* 41, no. 3 (Autumn 1986): 261–98.

―――. "The Female Entertainment Tradition in Medieval Japan: The Case of the Asobi." In Sue-Ellen Case, ed., *Performing Feminisms: Feminist Critical Theory and Theatre*, 316–27. Baltimore: Johns Hopkins University Press, 1990.

Kyōto daigaku, Bungakubu, Kokugogaku kokubungaku kenkyūjo, ed. *Shohon shūsei Wamyō ruijushō (honbun hen)*. Kyoto: Rinsen shoten, 1968.

Kyūsojin Hitaku. "Kofudoki itsubun 'uji no hashihime' sono ta ni tsuite." *Kokugakuin zasshi* 42, no. 12 (Dec. 1936): 29–33.

Kyūsojin Hitaku, ed. *Nihon kagaku taikei bekkan*, vols. 1–3, 5. Tokyo: Kazama shobō, 1959, 1958, 1964, 1981.

Liu, Xinru. *Ancient India and Ancient China: Trade and Religious Exchanges A.D. 1–600*. Delhi: Oxford University Press, 1988.

Mabuchi Kazuo et al., eds. and annots. *Konjaku monogatari shū*, vols. 2, 4. Nihon koten bungaku zenshū, 24.Tokyo: Shōgakkan, 1972, 1976.

Maeda ikutokukai sonkyōkaku bunko, ed. *Gō shidai*, vol. 3. Sonkyōkaku zenbon ei'in shūsei, 12. Tokyo: Yagi shoten, 1997.

Maeda Yoshiko. *Ono no Komachi*. Tokyo: Sanseidō, 1943.

Marra, Michele. "The Buddhist Mythmaking of Defilement: Sacred Courtesans in Medieval Japan." *Journal of Asian Studies* 52, no. 1 (Feb. 1993): 49–65.

————. *Representations of Power: The Literary Politics of Medieval Japan.* Honolulu: University of Hawaii Press, 1993.

Matsui Kenji. "Ono no Komachi dokuro eika kō." *Shōwa gakuin tanki daigaku kiyō,* no. 25 (1988): 10–20.

Matsumura Hiroji, annot. *Eiga monogatari zenchūshaku,* vols. 6–7. Nihon koten hyō-shaku/zenchūshaku sensho. Tokyo: Kadokawa shoten, 1976, 1978.

————. *Ōkagami.* Iwanami bunko. Tokyo: Iwanami shoten, 1964.

McCullough, Helen. *Brocade by Night: "Kokin wakashū" and the Court Style in Japanese Classical Poetry.* Stanford: Stanford University Press, 1985.

McCullough, William H., and Helen Craig McCullough. *A Tale of Flowering Fortunes: Annals of Japanese Aristocratic Life in the Heian Period.* Stanford: Stanford University Press, 1980.

Miki Sumito, annot. *Hōjōki/Hosshinshū.* Shinchō Nihon koten shūsei, 5. Tokyo: Shinchōsha, 1976.

Mima Shigetoshi. "Kūya shonin rui no kōtei oyobi kundoku to kōtei ni kansuru shiken." *Nanto bukkyō,* no. 42 (Dec. 1979): 88–121.

Minamoto Yoshiharu. "Komachi 'aname' setsuwa no keisei ni tsuite." In Hamaguchi Hiroaki kyōju taishoku kinen kokubungaku ronshū kankōkai, ed., *Hamaguchi Hiroaki kyōju taishoku kinen: kokubungaku ronshū,* pp. 79–91. Osaka: Izumi shoin, 1990.

Minegishi Sumio, ed. *Kazoku to josei.* Chūsei wo kangaeru. Tokyo: Yoshikawa kō-bunkan, 1992.

Minemura Fumito, ed. and annot. *Shin kokin wakashū.* Nihon koten bungaku zenshū, 26. Tokyo: Shōgakkan, 1974.

Miyoshi Teiji. *Ono no Komachi kōkyū.* Tokyo: Shintensha, 1992.

Moi, Toril. *Sexual/Textual Politics: Feminist Literary Theory.* New York, Methuen, 1985.

Morisue Yoshiaki. "*Ryōjin hishō* no warabeuta." In "Monthly Report Attachment" to Kawaguchi Hisao and Shida Nobuyoshi, eds., *Wakan rōeishū / Ryōjin hishō.* Nihon koten bungaku taikei, 73. Tokyo: Iwanami shoten, 1965.

Moriya Takeshi, ed. *Geinō to chinkon/kanraku to kyūzai no dainamizumu.* Taikei bukkyō to Nihonjin, 7. Tokyo: Shunshūsha, 1988.

Morohashi Tetsuji. *Dai kanwa jiten,* vol. 1. Tokyo: Taishūkan shoten, 1989 [1955].

Mosume Takami, annot. *Shinchū kogaku sōsho,* vol. 6. Tokyo: Kobunko kankōkai, 1927.

Motoki Yasuo. "Goshirakawa-in to heishi." In Kodai gakkyōkai, ed., *Goshirakawa-in: dōranki no tennō,* pp. 61–83. Tokyo: Yoshikawa kōbunkan, 1993.

Murai Yasuhiko. "*Konjaku monogatari:* kage no bubun e no shōsha—kai'itan no kataru mono." *Kokubungaku: kaishaku to kyōzai no kenkyū* 29, no. 9 (July 1984): 71–74.

Murofushi Shinsuke. "Uta monogatari ni okeru uta no imi." *Kokubungaku: kaishaku to kyōzai no kenkyū* 37, no. 4 (Apr. 1992): 44–49.

Nagata Mizu. "Bukkyō ni miru boseikan: bukkyō wa boseiku wo dō toita ka." In Kagiya Akiko et al., eds., *Bosei wo tou*, 1: 259–86. Kyoto: Jinbun shoin, 1981.

Nagazumi Yasuaki and Shimada Isao, annots. *Kokon chomonjū*. Nihon koten bungaku taikei, 84. Tokyo: Iwanami shoten, 1966.

Nakajima Tomoe. "Uji no sekai—Hashihime no maki—." In Imai Takuya et al., eds. *Genji monogatari kōza, 4, Kyō to Uji no monogatari / monogatari sakka no sekai*, pp. 34–47. Tokyo: Benseisha, 1992.

Nakamura Hajime. *Bukkyōgo daijiten*. Tokyo: Tōkyō shoseki, 1981.

Nakamura Tanio. "*Kusō shi emaki* no seiritsu." In Komatsu Shigemi, ed., *Gaki zōshi, Jigoku zōshi, Yamai zōshi, Kusō shi emaki*, pp. 165–70. Nihon emaki taisei, 7. Tokyo: Chūōkōronsha, 1977.

Nakamura Yasuo, "*Fukuro zōshi* zatsudanbu ni tsuite no kokoromiteki kaisetsu." In Fujioka Tadaharu et al., eds., and annots., *Fukuro zōshi kōshō: zatsudan hen*, 498–512. Osaka: Izumi shoin, 1991.

Nakayama Tarō. *Baishō sanzen-nen shi*. Tokyo: Shun'yōdō, 1927.

Nakazumi Yasuaki and Shimada Isao, annots. *Kokon chomonjū*. Nihon koten bungaku taikei, 84. Tokyo: Iwanami shoten, 1966.

Namihira Emiko. *Kegare*. Tokyo: Tōkyōdō shuppan, 1985.

Nei Kiyoshi. "Hashi to kanjin hijiri." *Indogaku bukkyōgaku kenkyū* 39, no. 1 (Dec. 1990): 272–75.

Nihon koten bungaku daijiten henshū iinkai, eds. *Nihon koten bungaku daijiten*, vols. 1–6. Tokyo: Iwanami shoten, 1983-85.

Nishigaki Harutsugu. "Hashi, kyōkai, hashiuranai." *Nihongaku*, no. 9 (June 1987): 134–40.

Nishiguchi Junko. *Onna no chikara: kodai no josei to bukkyō*. Tokyo: Heibonsha, 1987.

Niunoya Tetsuichi. "Chūsei teki geinō no kankyō." In Amino Yoshihiko et al., eds., *Chūsei no sairei—chūō kara chihō e—*, pp. 9–50. Taikei Nihon rekishi to geinō, 4. Tokyo: Heibonsha, 1991.

Nomura Sei'ichi, annot. *Izumi Shikibu nikki, Izumi Shikibu shū*. Shinchō nihon koten shūsei, 42. Tokyo: Shinchōsha, 1981.

Ogawa Hisako. "Toshiyori to imayō." *Kokugo to kokubungaku* 59, no. 6 (June 1982): 13–25.

Ogihara Asao, ed. and annot. *Kojiki*. Kan'yaku: Nihon no koten, 1. Tokyo: Shōgakkan, 1983.

Ōgoshi Aiko and Minamoto Junko. *Kaitai suru bukkyō: sono sekushuaritī kan to shizen kan*. Tokyo: Daitō shuppansha, 1994.

Ōgoshi Aiko, Minamoto Junko, and Yamashita Akiko. *Seisabetsu suru bukkyō*. Kyoto: Hōzōkan, 1990.

Ohara Hitoshi. *Bunjin kizoku no keifu.* Tokyo: Yoshikawa kōbunkan, 1987.

Okami Masao and Akamatsu Toshihide, annots. *Gukanshō.* Nihon koten bungaku taikei, 86. Tokyo: Iwanami shoten, 1967.

Ong, Walter J. *Orality and Literacy: The Technologizing of the Word.* London and New York: Routledge, 1982.

Ono Yukiyasu. "Ryōjin hishō hōmon no uta no shinkō to hyōgen: imayō reigendan kara imayō ōjōron e." *Sōdai kokubungaku kenkyū,* no. 100 (Mar. 1990): 58–68.

Origuchi hakase kinen kodai kenkyūjo, ed. *Origuchi Shinobu zenshū / nōto hen,* vol. 13. Tokyo: Chūōkōronsha, 1970.

Ōshima Tatehiko, ed. and annot. *Uji shūi monogatari.* Shinchō Nihon koten shūsei, 71. Tokyo: Shinchōsha, 1985.

Ōsone Shōsuke et al., annot. *Honchō monzui.* Shin Nihon koten bungaku taikei, 27. Tokyo: Iwanami shoten, 1992.

Ōsone Shōsuke et al., eds. *Man'yō/kayō.* Kenkyū shiryō Nihon koten bungaku, 5. Tokyo: Meiji shoin, 1985.

Ōta Junzō. "Chūsei no minshū kyūzai no shosō—hashi kanjin, hinin shikō, tsuzuri hōshi." In Minshūshi kenkyūkai, ed., *Minshū seikatsu to shinkō, shisō,* pp. 62–90. Tokyo: Yūzankaku, 1985.

Ōtsuka Hideko. "Komachi no yume, Ōō no yume." In Wakan hikaku bungakukai, ed., *Kokinshū to kanbungaku,* pp. 165–86. Wakan hikaku bungaku sōsho, 11. Tokyo: Kyūko shoin, 1992.

Ōwa Iwao. *Yūjo to tennō.* Tokyo: Hakusuisha, 1993.

Oyamada Ryōzō. *Hashi.* Mono to ningen no bunka, 66. Tokyo: Hōsei daigaku shuppankyoku, 1991.

Ozawa Masao and Matsuda Shigeho, eds. and annots. *Kokin wakashū.* Shinpen Nihon koten bungaku zenshū, 11. Tokyo: Shōgakkan, 1994.

Pandey, Rajyashree. "Women, Sexuality, and Enlightenment: *Kankyo no tomo.*" *Monumenta Nipponica* 50, no. 3 (Fall 1995): 325–56.

Quan Tangshi, vol. 4. Beijing: Zhonghua shuju, 1985.

Saeki Junko. *Yūjo no bunkashi.* Chūōkōron shinsho, 853. Tokyo: Chūōkōronsha, 1987.

Saeki Tsunemaro, annot. *Shinkō gunsho ruijū,* vol. 13. Tokyo: Naigai shoseki, 1929.

Sakamoto Tarō et al., annots. *Nihon shoki,* vol. 1. Nihon koten bungaku taikei, 67. Tokyo: Iwanami shoten, 1967.

Sakamoto Yukio and Iwamoto Yutaka, annots. and trans. *Hokkekyō,* vol. 1. Tokyo: Iwanami shoten, 1962.

Sangren, P. Steven. *History and Magical Power in a Chinese Community.* Stanford: Stanford University Press, 1987.

Sasaki Nobutsuna, ed. *Nihon kagaku taikei,* vols. 1–3. Tokyo: Kazama shobō, 1971, 1956, 1963.

Sasamoto Shōji. *Tsuji no sekai—rekishi minzokugaku teki kōsatsu.* Tokyo: Meicho shuppan, 1991.

Satō Kenzō and Haruta Noboru, eds. *Yashirobon Heike monogatari,* vol. 2. Tokyo: Ōfūsha, 1973.

Scott, Joan W. "Experience." In Judith Butler and Joan W. Scott, eds., *Feminists Theorize the Political,* pp. 22–40. New York: Routledge, 1992.

Sekine Yoshiko and Furuya Takako, annots. *Sanboku kikashū: shūchūhen,* vol. 2. Tokyo: Kazama shobō, 1999.

Shigematsu Akihisa, annot. and ed. *Shin sarugakuki / Unshū shōsoku.* Tokyo: Gendai shichōsha, 1982.

Shimada Ryōji. *Heian zenki shikashū no kenkyū.* Tokyo: Ōfūsha, 1968.

Shimizu Masumi. "*Ryōjin hishō kudenshū* kan jū e no renkan: Fujiwara no Asakata, Fujiwara no Sadasuke wo chūshin ni." *Ryokkō shirin,* no. 15 (Mar. 1991): 28–43.

Shimozaki Yū. "*Ryōjin hishō* ni miru nyonin ōjō (jōbutsu) to Goshirakawain no shinkōshin ni tsuite." *Gunma kenritsu joshi daigaku kokubungaku kenkyū,* no. 11 (Mar. 1991): 29–36.

Shinma Shin'ichi and Shida Nobuyoshi. *Kayō,* vol. 2. Kanshō Nihon koten bungaku, 15. Tokyo: Kadokawa shoten, 1977.

Shinma Shin'ichi and Tonomura Natsuko, eds. and annots. *Ryōjin hishō.* Kan'yaku: Nihon no koten, 34. Tokyo: Shōgakkan, 1988.

Shinpen kokka taikan henshū iinkai, ed. *Shinpen kokka taikan,* 2, *Shisenshū hen/kashū.* Tokyo: Kadokawa shoten, 1984.

Smits, Ivo. "Reading the New Ballads: Late Heian *kanshi* Poets and Bo Juyi." In *Wasser-Spuren: Festschrift für Wolfram Naumann zum 65. Geburtstag.* Weisbaden: Otto Harrassowitz, 1997, pp. 169–84.

Sōgō bukkyō daijiten henshū iinkai, ed. *Sōgō bukkyō daijiten,* vol. 1. Kyoto: Hōzōkan, 1987.

Sōgō joseishi kenkyūkai, ed. *Nihon josei no rekishi: bunka to shisō.* Tokyo: Kadokawa shoten, 1993.

———. *Nihon josei no rekishi: sei, ai, kazoku.* Tokyo: Kadokawa shoten, 1992.

Spivak, Gayatri Chakravorty. "Can the Subaltern Speak?" In Cary Nelson and Lawrence Grossberg, eds., *Marxism and the Interpretation of Culture,* pp. 271–313. Urbana and Chicago: University of Illinois Press, 1988.

———. *In Other Worlds: Essays in Cultural Politics.* New York: Methuen, 1987.

———. *Outside in the Teaching Machine.* New York: Routledge, 1993.

———. "Theory in the Margin: Coetzee's *Foe* Reading Defoe's *Crusoe/Roxana.*" In Jonathan Arac and Barbara Johnson, eds., *Consequences of Theory,* pp. 154–80. Baltimore: Johns Hopkins University Press, 1991.

Stein, Michael. *Japans Kurtisanen: eine Kulturgeschichte der japanischen Meisterinnen der Unterhaltungskunst und Erotik aus zwölf Jahrhunderten.* Munich: Iudicium, 1997.

Street, Brian V. *Literacy in Theory and Practice.* Cambridge, Eng., and New York: Cambridge University Press, 1984.

Strong, Sarah M. "The Making of a Femme Fatale: Ono no Komachi in the Early Medieval Commentaries." *Monumenta Nipponica* 49, no. 4 (Winter 1994): 391–412.

Sugano Fumi. "Goshirakawain no imayō." In Amino Yoshihiko et al., eds., *Chūsei no sairei—chūō kara chihō e—,* pp. 51–73. Taikei Nihon rekishi to geinō, 4. Tokyo: Heibonsha, 1991.

————. "Ryōjin hishō zenshi: onmyōdō so to keizō wo chūshin ni." In Nihon kayō gakkai, ed., *Nihon kayō kenkyū—genzai to tenbō,* pp. 193–204. Osaka: Izumi shoin, 1994.

Suzuka Chiyono. "Yūjo gensō." In Itō Seiko and Kōno Nobuko, eds., *Onna to otoko no jikū—Nihon joseishi saikō, 2, Onna to otoko no tanjō—kodai kara chūsei e,* pp. 66–91. Tokyo: Fujiwara shoten, 1996.

Tabata Yasuko. *Nihon chūsei no josei.* Tokyo: Yoshikawa kōbunkan, 1987.

Taira Masayuki. *Nihon chūsei no shakai to bukkyō.* Tokyo: Hanawa shobō, 1992.

Takagawa Tomohaya. "Asobibe denshō kō." *Waseda daigaku daigakuin bungaku kenkyūkai kiyō: bessatsu/bungaku, geijutsugaku hen* 15 (1988): 1–11.

Takagi Yutaka. *Heian jidai hokke bukkyōshi kenkyū.* Kyoto: Heirakuji shoten, 1973.

Takahashi Kazuhiko, annot. *Mumyōshō.* Tokyo: Ōfūsha, 1975.

Takahashi Tōru. *Irogonomi no bungaku to ōken: "Genji monogatari" no sekai e.* Tokyo: Shintensha, 1990.

Takamure Itsue. *Nihon kon'in shi.* Tokyo: Ibundō, 1963.

Takenishi Hiroko. "*Kokinshū,* Narihira, Komachi, ōchō shūkasen." *Kokubungaku: kaishaku to kyōzai no kenkyū* 28, no. 9 (July 1983): 60–63.

Takeoke Masao, annot. *Kokin wakashū zenchūshaku,* vol. 2. Tokyo: Yūbun shoin, 1976.

Takikawa Masajirō. *Ukareme, asobi, kugutsume—Eguchi, Kanzaki no yūri.* Tokyo: Ibundō, 1965.

————. *Yūjo no rekishi.* Tokyo: Ibundō, 1965.

Tanaka Kimiharu. *Komachi shigure.* Tokyo: Kasama shoin, 1984.

Tanaka Takako. *Akujo ron.* Tokyo: Kinokuniya shoten, 1992.

————. "Chūsei no josei to bungaku—Mumyō zōshi wo chūshin ni." In Wakita Haruko and S. B. Hanley, eds., *Jendā no Nihonshi, 2, Shutai to hyōgen, shigoto to seikatsu,* pp. 83–110. Tokyo: Tōkyō daigaku shuppankai, 1995.

Tanaka Yutaka and Akase Shingo, annots. *Shin kokin wakashū.* Shin Nihon koten bungaku taikei, 11. Tokyo: Iwanami shoten, 1992.

Tanaki Keiko. "Komachi dokuro densetsu 'aname aname' kō." *Kokubungaku kenkyū,* no. 45 (Sept. 1971): 10–17.

Teiser, Stephen. "T'ang Buddhist Encyclopedias: An Introduction to *Fa-yüan chu-lin* and *Chu-ching yao-chi.*" *T'ang Studies* 3 (1988): 109–28.

Tochigi Yoshitada, et al., annots. *Hōgen monogatari, Heiji monogatari, Jōkyūki*. Shin Nihon koten bungaku taikei, 43. Tokyo: Iwanami shoten, 1992.

Tochio Takeshi. *"Tamatsukuri Komachishi sōsuisho" no kenkyū*, vols. 1–2. Kyoto: Rinsen shoten, 1990.

———. *"Tamatsukuri Komachishi sōsuisho* shūshi no ki." *Seijō kokubungaku*, no. 8 (Mar. 1992): 1–9.

Tochio Takeshi, annot. *Tamatsukuri Komachishi sōsuisho*. Iwanami bunko. Tokyo: Iwanami shoten, 1994.

———. *"Tamatsukuri Komachishi sōsuisho."* In *Iwanami kōza: Mujō*, pp. 29–52. Nihon bungaku to bukkyō, 4. Tokyo: Iwanami shoten, 1994.

Tokue Gensei. "Setsuwa kara mita takai." In Kokubungaku kenkyū shiryōkan, ed., *Bungaku ni okeru "mukōgawa,"* pp. 67–92. Kokubungaku kenkyū shiryōkan kyōdō kenkyū hōkoku, 4. Tokyo: Meiji shoin, 1985.

Tōkyō kokuritsu hakubutsukan, ed. *Tokubetsuten: emaki*. Tokyo: Tōkyō kokuritsu hakubutsukan, 1974.

Tonomura, Hitomi. "Black Hair and Red Trousers: Gendering the Flesh in Medieval Japan." *American Historical Review* 99, no. 1 (Feb. 1994): 129–54.

Toyonaga Satomi. "Chūsei ni okeru asobi no chōja ni tsuite." In Yasuda Motohisa sensei tainin kinen ronshū kankō iinkai, ed., *Chūsei Nihon no shosō*, 2: 403–29. Tokyo: Yoshikawa kōbunkan, 1989.

Toyoshima Shūkichi, annot. *Gunsho ruijū, 9, bunpitsubu/shōsokubu*. Tokyo: Zoku gunsho ruijū kanseikai, 1928.

Trinh T. Min-ha. *Woman, Native, Other: Writing Postcoloniality and Feminism*. Bloomington: Indiana University Press, 1989.

Tsing, Anna Lowenhaupt. "From the Margins." *Cultural Anthropology (Journal of the Society for Cultural Anthropology)* 9 no. 3 (Aug. 1994): 279–97.

———. *In the Realm of the Diamond Queen: Marginality in an Out-of-the-Way Place*. Princeton: Princeton University Press, 1993.

Tsunoda Bun'ei. "Ono no Komachi no mibun." *Kokubungaku: kaishaku to kyōzai no kenkyū* 28, no. 9 (July 1983): 47–53.

Uchida Sennosuke. *Hakushi monjū*. Chūgoku koten shinsho. Tokyo: Meitoku shuppansha, 1968.

Ueki Gaku. *Tamatsukuri Komachi to Ono no Komachi*. Tokyo: Shinjinbutsu ōraisha, 1978.

Vollmer, Klaus. *Professionen und ihre "Wege" im mittelalterlichen Japan: eine Einführung in ihre Sozialgeschichte und literarische Repräsentation am Beispiel des Tōhoku'in shokunin utaawase*. Hamburg: OAG, 1995.

Wakashi kenkyūkai, ed. *Shikashū taisei*, 1, *Chūko*, vol. 1. Tokyo: Meiji shoin, 1973.

Wakita Haruko. "Bosei sonchō shisō to zaigyōkan: chūsei no bungei wo chūshin ni." In Kagiya Akiko et al., eds., *Bosei wo tou*, 1: 172–203. Kyoto: Jinbun shoin, 1985.

————. *Nihon chūsei joseishi no kenkyū—seibetsu yakuwari buntan to bosei, kasei, seiai.* Tokyo: Tōkyō daigaku shuppankai, 1992.

Watanabe Hideo. "Ono no Komachi: ai no jigoku—*Tamatsukuri Komachishi sō-suisho.*" *Kokubungaku: kaishaku to kyōzai no kenkyū* 28, no. 9 (July 1983): 80–84.

Watanabe Kunio and Kondō Yoshihiro, eds. *Shintōshū/Kawanobon.* Tokyo: Kadokawa shoten, 1962.

Watanabe Shōgo. *"Ryōjin hishō" no fūzoku to bungei.* Tokyo: Miyai shoten, 1979.

Watanabe Shōkō and Miyasaka Yūsho, annots. *Sangō shi'iki, Seireishū.* Nihon koten bungaku taikei, 71. Tokyo: Iwanami Shoten, 1965.

Xie Tiao. *Xie Xuancheng ji.* Sibu beiyao. Shanghai: Zhonghua shuju, 1927–36.

Yamada Naomi. "Kyōkai no bungakushi—jibutsu kigen kō (7)—." *Kokubungaku nōto,* no. 24 (Mar. 1987): 1–23.

Yamada Shōzen. "Goshirakawa wa naze teihen no imayō ni tandeki shita ka." *Kokubungaku: kaishaku to kyōzai no kenkyū* 26 no. 8 (June 1981): 32–37.

Yamada Yōji. "Kagakusho to setsuwa." In Honda Yoshinori et al., eds. *Setsuwa no kōza,* 3, *Setsuwa no ba—shōdō, chūshaku,* pp. 150–75. Tokyo: Benseisha, 1993.

Yamada Yoshio. *Sanbō-e ryakuchū.* Tokyo: Hōbunkan, 1951.

Yamada Yoshio et al., annots. *Konjaku monogatarishū,* vols. 3–4. Nihon koten bungaku taikei, 24. Tokyo: Iwanami shoten, 1961, 1962.

Yamagishi Tokuhei et al., annots. *Kodai seiji shakai shisō.* Nihon shisō taikei, 8. Tokyo: Iwanami shoten, 1979.

Yamaguchi Hiroshi. *Keien no shijin: Ono no Komachi.* Tokyo: Sanseidō, 1979.

Yamaguchi Masao. *Bunka jinruigaku no shikaku.* Tokyo: Iwanami shoten, 1986.

————. *Bunka to ryōgisei.* Tokyo: Iwanami shoten, 1975.

————. *Chi no enkinhō.* Tokyo: Iwanami shoten, 1978.

————. *Tennōsei no bunka jinruigaku.* Tokyo: Rippū shobō, 1989.

Yamamoto Kizō et al. "Ryōjin hishō kudenshū chūkai." *Esukisu,* no. 90 (June 1990): 18–41.

Yamamoto Kōji. *Kegare to ōharae.* Tokyo: Heibonsha, 1992.

Yamamoto Ritatsu, annot. *Murasaki Shikibu nikki, Murasaki Shikibu shū.* Shinchō Nihon koten shūsei, 35. Tokyo: Shinchōsha, 1980.

Yamashita Hiroaki. *Katari to shite no "Heike monogatari."* Tokyo: Iwanami shoten, 1994.

Yamashita Hiroaki, annot. *Taiheiki,* vol. 2. Shinchō Nihon koten shūsei, 38. Tokyo: Shinchōsha, 1980.

Yamauchi Junzō et al., eds. *Tamatsukuri Komachi sōsuisho.* Tokyo: Kasama shoin, 1981.

Yanagita Kunio. *Teihon Yanagita Kunio shū,* vols. 5, 8, 26. Tokyo: Chikuma shobō, 1962, 1962, 1964.

Yanase Kazuo, annot. *Kōchū: Kamo no Chōmei zenshū.* Tokyo: Kazama shobō, 1956.

Yasuda Motohisa. *Goshirakawa jōkō.* Tokyo: Yoshikawa kōbunkan, 1986.

Yasuda Takako et al., annots. *Senjūshō,* vols. 1–2. Tokyo: Gendai shisōsha, 1985, 1987.

Yokoi Kiyoshi. *Chūsei minshū no seikatsu bunka.* Tokyo: Tōkyō daigaku shuppankai, 1975.

Yokota Yukiya. *Ono no Komachi denki kenkyū.* Tokyo: Kazama shobō, 1974.

Yokoyama Shigeru and Matsumoto Takanobu, eds. *Muromachi jidai monogatari taisei,* vol. 10. Tokyo: Kadokawa shoten, 1982.

Yoshida Kazuhiko. "Ryūnyo no jōbutsu." In Ōsumi Kazuhiko and Nishiguchi Junko, eds., *Sukui to oshie,* pp. 45–91. Shirīzu josei to bukkyō, 2. Tokyo: Heibonsha, 1989.

Yoshikai Naoto. "*Hashihime monogatari* no shiteki kōsatsu—*Genji monogatari* haikeiron I—." *Kokugakuin daigaku daigakuin kiyō bungaku kenkyūkai* 13 (1981): 105–34.

———. "*Shūi Hashihime monogatari.*" *Kokusho itsubun kenkyū,* no. 9 (Aug. 1982): 63–70.

Yoshizawa Yoshinori, ed. *Mikan kokubun chūshaku taikei,* vol. 4. Tokyo: Teikoku kyōikukai shuppanbu, 1935.

Zoku gunsho ruijū kanseikai, ed. *Gunsho kaidai,* vol. 5. Tokyo: Zoku gunsho ruijū kanseikai, 1965.

———. *Zoku gunsho ruijū,* vol. 19. pt. I, vol. 32, pt. II. Tokyo: Zoku gunsho ruijū kanseikai, 1912, 1927.

Index

Harvard East Asian Monographs
(* out-of-print)

Harvard East Asian Monographs

Harvard East Asian Monographs

Harvard East Asian Monographs

Harvard East Asian Monographs

Harvard East Asian Monographs

Harvard East Asian Monographs

Harvard East Asian Monographs